PRECARIOUS POWER

PRECARIOUS POWER

Compliance and discontent under Ramaphosa's ANC

SUSAN BOOYSEN

WITS UNIVERSITY PRESS

Published in South Africa by:
Wits University Press
1 Jan Smuts Avenue
Johannesburg 2001

www.witspress.co.za

First published 2021

http://dx.doi.org.10.18772/12021026451

978-1-77614-645-1 (Paperback)
978-1-77614-649-9 (Hardback)
978-1-77614-646-8 (Web PDF)
978-1-77614-647-5 (EPUB)

Project manager: Inga Norenius
Copyeditors: Monica Seeber and Lee Smith
Proofreader: Inga Norenius
Indexer: Margie Ramsay
Cover design: Hothouse
Typeset in 10 point Minion Pro

CONTENTS

TABLES AND FIGURES

recarious Power is about how South African politics revolves around a powerful but contradictory main character, the African National Congress (ANC), in the time of Cyril Ramaphosa.

It delves into politics in a way that helps us to understand the unspoken texts, the often near-imperceptible rules. It leads us to see how 'the system' of ANC dominance flounders yet survives. This story of South African politics pieces together and reinterprets the trends we think we have seen and know – but we don't always see them for what they are. My study connects the dots and draws the lines. It reveals the rules and laws of an ANC intermingled (if not fused) with South African politics. It is a bottom-up case study of how a mammoth but meandering former monolith created more layers of politics while the people forged alternative politics rather than trade their ANC for another party. It is a politics that rewrites the textbooks.

The process of writing this book was like a rollercoaster of political despair and hope, and the story remains incomplete. It started with a coincidental meeting at a Sophiatown jazz club when my publisher Veronica Klipp and I reflected on ANC politics. Jacob Zuma's fall was gathering momentum, a mere few months after I had completed *Dominance and Decline* and five years after I had set out the fundamentals in *The ANC and the Regeneration of Political Power*. The story was continuing, the plot gaining character and the finale uncertain. I *had* to continue analysing the saga. The narrative of the immediate events kept on changing – dramatic scenes moved from the Nasrec cliff-hanger to the recall and continuous fall of Zuma; Ramaphoria as the new panacea; elections that were ambiguous at best; the disillusionment and reality checks that followed, aggravated by the complex Covid-19 moment while the curse of corruption throttled Ramaphosa's 'new' ANC. But the otherworld of South African politics, of ANC and of popular creation, continued opening in the wings, and the ANC lived and lives to see another political day.

The more the narrative ran on, the more the trends cohered and painted a curious picture of 'the system' in which the ANC ruled. Whether I investigated the institutions of the state, public policy-making, election practice or people's protests, the trends were there in a system with strength that depended not simply on the veracity of its institutions and formal processes but also on indulgence in and tolerance of supplementary processes, alternative layers, complementary institutions. It was a parallel politics and, above all, a suspension of popular disbelief that the former liberation movement could be fatally flawed and faltering.

My research took five years of intense observation, collection of details, mapping of patterns, reinterpretation of political reality – ANC conferences and briefings, speeches, ANC statements, policy documents, government records, court and commission proceedings and investigative reports and writing. I observed; monitored events; analysed content; did interviews with those prepared to speak without trying to mislead; engaged with communities to hear first-hand how cadres and others related to the ANC; and dissected the reliable public opinion polls to help in seeing the bigger picture. On many of the topics in this book I developed sets of in-depth case studies to build the picture of people and protests, policy, the Presidency, state institutions and party politics. It was a continuous, 360-degree research operation. Then analysis followed.

My analysis is about seeing and synthesising the patterns and trends. What were the commonalities and consistencies, perhaps even the surprising realities, that the mass of research details revealed? The answers – my arguments and interpretations – fill the pages of this book.

The pages of references at the end of each chapter reveal much of my style of analysis, and the character of *Precarious Power*. The sources in many of these notes are not cited as the source of arguments – rather, they illustrate the type of information, provide typical examples or highlight an event that proves an argument. Many points like these, detected and recorded in my personal database of research – which I have been constructing since my research for *The ANC and the Regeneration of Political Power* – inform my inferences and insights. The book is about critical analysis, not 'solutions' … unless the reader is prepared to perceive the solutions through an understanding of the present and its precise dynamics. This understanding of praxis is what I see as the contribution of this book.

There was no boring moment. There would not have been a manuscript had the ANC not provided me with so much, such rich and such vexing information.

My heartfelt thanks go to Wits University Press for the confidence in my scholarship and authorship. This journey of three books on the ANC in ten years would not have been possible had it not been for the core team of Veronica Klipp, Roshan Cader and my astute editor, Monica Seeber.

Susan Booysen
20 October 2020

ACRONYMS AND ABBREVIATIONS

AIC	African Independent Congress
ANC	African National Congress
ANCYL	African National Congress Youth League
ANCWL	African National Congress Women's League
ATM	African Transformation Movement
BLF	Black First Land First
Concourt	Constitutional Court
Cope	Congress of the People
Cosatu	Congress of South African Trade Unions
Covid-19	Coronavirus disease of 2019, caused by the novel coronavirus SARS-CoV2
CR17	Cyril Ramaphosa 2017 ANC presidential campaign
DA	Democratic Alliance
EFF	Economic Freedom Fighters
EISA	Electoral Institute for Sustainable Democracy in Africa
KZN	KwaZulu-Natal
IEC	Electoral Commission (of South Africa)
IFP	Inkatha Freedom Party
IMC	Inter-Ministerial Committee (of Cabinet members)
IMF	International Monetary Fund
MP	Member of Parliament (of South Africa)
NCCC	National Coronavirus Command Council
NDPP	National Director of Public Prosecutions
NEC	National Executive Committee
NGC	National General Council
NNEECC	National Nuclear Energy Executive Coordination Committee
NPA	National Prosecuting Authority
PAC	Pan Africanist Congress
PCAS	Policy Coordination and Advisory Services

PEC	Provincial Executive Committee
PIC	Public Investment Corporation
SABC	South African Broadcasting Corporation
SACP	South African Communist Party
Sanral	South African National Roads Agency Limited
SARB	South African Reserve Bank
SARS	South African Revenue Service
SOE	State-owned Enterprise / Entity
SPPs	Small political parties
SSA	State Security Agency
VAP	Voting-age population
VBS	Venda Building Society

The ANC and Precarious Power

DISCORD AS THE ANC HOVERS IN POWER

It was no longer the near-mythological liberation party, nor had its days in government bestowed unadulterated glory. Yet, the African National Congress (ANC) remained in power, and generally politically dominant. Its electoral supremacy was dented yet ongoing, evident in the way ANC politics were often substituted for national politics. Its discourses and ideas frequently set the parameters of national debate. The culture and practice of post-liberation struggle party politics, seasoned by 25 years and more in government in South Africa, had bequeathed a lingering form of political dominance to the ANC. No opposition party was in place or rising to challenge it for power.

The times of the coronavirus exposed deep layers of ANC weaknesses and failures, state ruptures and opposition party inability to capitalise on them. The ANC had control of the instruments of state power, yet was unstable and depended on a delicate balance of forces and agencies that operated challenges and protests, and offered support and endorsement in return. The ANC's historical legitimacy, and its continued assurances that it was organisationally united and had firm intentions to improve policy and governance, had helped citizens to continue suspending their disbelief in the ANC as a viable political force and to continue granting sequential second chances.

The ANC's slippages in power showed on various fronts. The organisation was riven and at the mercy of shifting balances of factions. As deeper and cross-cutting crises like Covid-19 descended on the ANC, prior organisational battles persisted and shaped the base on which new politics took root and grew. Its command of the state was uncertain, and its electoral support, while not in inexorable decline, was volatile. Its dominance did not extend into the media, economy, civil society, intellectual and policy debates. The Covid-19 times brought reprieves, resets and enclaves of amnesia to prior ANC let-downs. The ANC won some accolades but those did not rebuild former exaltation. As Covid-19 sapped already sparse public resources, the ANC's state power declined – and yet there was a clamour of contests to own it. Its power was refracted and dispersed among old and new factions, grassroots and state institutions of various ANC-based assemblages. There were few certainties amid many questions as to the exact locus of power.

A loose network of opposition, diverse and largely uncoordinated, operated in the policy and governance space, subsuming the power that the ANC shed, or gathering tools to engage with the ANC. At the elite politics and business levels, there were structured, in-state opportunities for influence and forms of deliberative democracy. The grassroots and the unorganised and often lawless citizenry often devised de facto policy, frequently making use of protest action or self-governance in defiance of state power. Some of their actions were hostile to the ANC government, but in many instances they formed a symbiotic relationship. New, parallel 'rules' of state operation were commonplace in state and government and were accentuated in the time of the Covid-19 pandemic. State institutions operated analogously to the formal ANC-controlled state apparatus and pursued own agendas or projects to undermine the prevailing opposing faction and claim institutions for themselves.

Much of policy and governance in the time of the presidency of Cyril Ramaphosa was determined in this way. The ANC was in command and was fairly unchallenged in retaining its party political dominance nationally. The authority of its instruments of state power was still accepted – in the final instance and despite wide-ranging popular protests and resistance – and no general uprising was threatening. Yet, the many permutations under the surfaces of electoral majority and final-instance authority *revealed a world of politics that supplemented conventional expectations of multiparty democracy.*

The transmutations included shadow institutions, parallel operations, the informalisation and de-institutionalisation of engagement, lawlessness both harmless and destructive, impunity and the appropriation of voids left by soft law and government failures.

In this book I dissect these dynamics across the four pillars of ANC power: the ANC organisationally, in elections, in relation to the people and in state and governance. In some respects, the ANC was dominant despite the extensive contests and its diminished power. It remained *the* societal focus among political parties; its elections and internal contests absorbed national attention; its internal policy debates regularly became *the* national discourse. Yet, in most respects the ANC's control and capacity were dented beyond the hope of restoration to former glory, presumed or real. Problems prevailed organisationally: in elections, in leadership, in government and in the ANC-controlled state. The problems that the ANC experienced, as movement and as government, were cumulative and a downward spiral in which events and developments often mutually reinforced one another. Its relations with its own members and with the people of South Africa were in ebb and flow, informed by hope and often driven by desperation. In crucial national and provincial elections, its outright majorities were often by the barest of margins. As political party, it was no longer deemed to be a saviour. Its ostensibly heroic past was questioned; at best, it was seen as preferable to the party political alternatives. It suffered a growing disbelief as to whether any of its leaders had sufficient integrity to lead South Africa into a better future – the belief had dissipated that it was only a question of time before policy delivery would come to the hitherto forgotten or neglected citizens. The ANC government oversaw the national finances but was unable to counter deficits and stop the drain of public funds in ways that could guarantee sustainability. Problems of economic growth, unemployment and budget shortfalls were endemic, even before the crisis of the coronavirus, and recovery would take far longer than the Ramaphosa presidential term. Trust in multiparty democracy and the institutions of the state was dwindling.

Alternative, community-grown politics, ranging from protest to de facto policy-making by popular action, were common. The ANC tolerated and condoned: as long as it did not act punitively against citizens who broke the law for socio-economic survival, it retained assurance that voters would probably not attach themselves to opposition parties. Across the board, the formal processes of state power persisted at the same time that the informal, alternative and supplementary varieties flourished.

POLITICAL LAND WHERE THE ANC IS DOMINANT

These dynamics amounted to a political Neverland where the ANC prevailed, not for its inherent strengths but because the opposition was weaker. The ANC's party political dominance relied on holding out the hope that a new and better ANC was rising. This forever-next-new ANC, exemplary and true to the ideals of the movement's nearly mythological struggle past, still promised to bring economic emancipation and seal political freedoms.[1] The ANC, by the time of my analysis, was not only living by legitimation in terms of struggle credentials (with emphasis on the exiled armed component far more than on the internal mass uprising) but was feeding off its own organisational truth: that it possessed an indefatigable ability for self-correction.

Voters and citizens continued to hold out hope that the time of self-destruction was not upon the ANC. In the ANC's view, it had retained the will and the ability to give effect to its 1912 foundational ideas and democratic South Africa's 1994 founding ideals – even if, 25 years later, they were questioned increasingly. One of the ingredients of the ANC's self-renewal formula was its cyclical populist calls when its presidents rotated – new entrants came together with renewed hope. New cohorts of deployee cadres carried forward the mobilisation to ring in changes and to refurbish policy debates, and the tranches of conference resolutions created auras of new ideas, vigour and commitment.

On the ground, there were few signs that the reassurances and rituals were work-ing for the ANC fully and in ways that would still secure deep legitimacy besides helping the ANC to extract itself from quagmires. The practices did work in creat-ing space for the ANC to roll over assurances that it was attending to policy imple-mentation and was in the process of cleaning up government.

The decay at the heart of the ANC was amply revealed in the first two decades of the twenty-first century and in the ANC's own organisational reports presented to conferences.[2] At its 2017 conference, for example, the ANC passed resolutions on anti-corruption, part of the repertoire for organisational renewal. Outright ethical condemnation and resolve to bring in consequences for this form of lawlessness were overshadowed by the 'protection of the ANC brand':

> The ANC need[s] to decisively attend and act to issues of corruption, ill-dis-cipline, and misconduct across ANC membership … this needs to be consid-ered a vehicle to improve [the ANC's] electoral support base and strengthen the development of BRAND ANC.[3]

Investigations proceeded around – not *in*, because that would have been called 'purging' – the ANC to try stopping the impunity with which corruption had been committed, and to extract accountability. Superficially, there was a new era of accountability, but not one that could be practised unapologetically and be pursued with uncompromised organisational backing. This was clear, again, when in the spring of 2020 Ramaphosa took on ANC members in an open letter, challenging them to implement ANC conference resolutions:

> As the NEC has determined, we now need to draw a line in the sand. We need
> to act urgently, we need to be decisive and we need to demonstrate a clear
> political will. The time has come for the ANC to be unflinching in restoring
> the values, ethics and standing of our organisation. Our deeds must, always,
> match our words … Let us together make this a turning point in the fight in
> corruption. Let us together restore the integrity of our movement and earn
> the trust that the people of South Africa have placed in us.[4]

A strong ANC National Executive Committee (NEC) statement tried to link specif-
ics to matters of principle.[5] Under scrutiny, however, the pillars of anti-corruption
action in the statement crumbled – policies and guidelines to direct anti-corruption
action still had to be developed, the ANC's Integrity Commission still lacked capacity and authority, and investigations remained to be done or completed. Investigations and events like the arrest of the secretary-general changed the political culture
nevertheless; it meant that the ANC's transgressions and excesses in dealing with
state power went on public display – and public accountability was demanded. The
details of the malaise sat uncomfortably with the traditions of struggle nobility and
heroic liberation deeds, and were exacerbated by justice seen to be taking time, and
compromised politicians remaining in place – often because there was no one clean
enough to be taking action without being exposed themselves.

The ANC showed awareness: arguably, a sense of guilt that on governance and
public service it had delivered insufficiently to the citizens, and particularly its own
followers, as measured against its own aspirations and political undertakings. The
time of Covid-19 brought an inadvertent benefit to the ANC: framed in tragedy,
it nevertheless gave the ANC government the chance to claim a blank slate and
restart. New policies would be introduced, and the governance failures and disap-
pointments of even the recent past would be blanked out. This gave the grassroots
a level of leverage over the ANC in government. Poor and marginalised citizens,
around whom much of society and politics revolved, were guaranteed sympathetic
treatment by the ANC government when they ignored the law. After all, the ANC
itself was setting the standard of governance beyond the formal agreed rules and
practices: corrupt and compromised ways of policy-making, implementation and
securing benefits for individuals or the party had been commonplace, as had the
adoption of policies and making of laws that remained in states of pre-implemen-
tation or flawed realisation.

Popular politics in this context, instead of finding traction in some opposition
party, established a mildly challenging and generally symbiotic inside track of direct
political engagement with the ANC. It aligned with the growing culture of party

political de-alignment, as evidenced in Election 2019. Alternative ways of political participation flourished as a form of protest that was a de facto agreement with the ANC to work directly for government deliveries instead of endorsing opposition parties. It was valid as a general rule of engagement; there were many cases (especially evident at the local level) where voters did switch allegiance away from the ANC, albeit not on a scale that matched their dissatisfaction. Protest diversified. On occasion, it also assumed anarchic and anti-systemic, or anomic, forms. Protest was, in essence (and underlying the antagonistic motions of community protests), largely interdependent on the ANC in government, and displayed cooperation between government and the protesting community.

The protests only rarely amounted to outright political rebellion against the ANC as predominant governing party but were aimed at socio-economic living-condition targets. Many of those who had moved away from the ANC party politically, or who had become more politically anomic, remained willing to re-engage with the state and the governing party when it was to their advantage.

A parallel system of supplementary government, albeit never all-encompassing, thus took hold over a wide front. It was a dispersed system of government, of policy delivery through citizen 'self-help' to social benefits such as free water and electricity beyond the basic free allowances, unpunished looting of foreigner-owned businesses and big business delivery trucks, or land occupation in new informal settlements. Government tolerated or condoned many of these bottom-up actions. Desperate socio-economic conditions (and, in some cases, opportunism) triggered by government inaction and neglect encouraged citizens to use the formal channels of political engagement (including voting) and then to act along these alternative avenues. Citizens simultaneously (and mostly) tolerated the pretence that budgets were forthcoming and that the state and its functionaries had the capacity to deliver effective and clean government. It amounted, in many respects, to parallel tiers of government alongside the formal system.

ASSERTIONS ABOUT THE ANC AND POLITICAL POWER

A set of assertions concerning the state of the ANC – in particular the nature of political power in and around it – is substantiated by the research offered in this book. The arguments run a circle: from the point of ANC electoral dominance that had weakened but persisted to the approximate closing of the circle. The ANC operated to maintain power partly in a de-institutionalised political world, on the basis of supplementary forms of legitimacy and in symbiosis with community politics.

The focus is on how informal, supplementary and parallel processes of politics – both in government and in communities at the grassroots – shadowed, complemented and undermined the formal side of government and politics but, in the process, helped to maintain the ANC in power. The processes ran in tandem, and the blending formula varied over time, and from one event or development to the next. My analysis makes the call for full recognition of both the standard and constitutionally mandated and the informal, sometimes 'dark', side of politics. Both are indispensable parts of South Africa's political praxis.

The ANC had indisputable power, but it was of a precarious and porous form. The ANC was in control; it had the monopoly on instruments of coercion and its final authority was accepted in matters of governance – and yet this control was tenuous in many places, and ineffectual. In these voids, in the time of Ramaphosa's ANC, party, government and people were weaving new threads of political operation to fill the openings. Democracy was characterised by the formal, as much as the de facto, the parallel and the informal. South Africa had become host to a hybrid political system, accommodating the coexistence of institutional multiparty democracy and informal or populist 'street politics'. Such ground-level politics was reflected at a high level in the ANC in state and government: many alternative and shadow operations, driven by informal sets of rules that constituted the operational principles, were as notable as the formal, legal and constitutional. This complex of political practices was central to explaining ongoing albeit dented ANC power.

In the period covered by this book, there were far fewer claims by the ANC to the venerated status which I described in a previous work. Regeneration and ANC survival in power are explained in that book with reference to concrete details of configuration, deflection and inadvertent fortune that are evident in unfolding developments in South African politics.[6]

This volume's interactive assertions about the unfolding dynamics of ANC power illuminate the organisation's contemporary repertoire – metamorphosed, mutated and amended over time – of organisational and governmental survival. The 11 assertions cover the ANC organisationally, the ANC in elections, the ANC and the people, including protest, and the ANC in state, policy and governance.

1. Porous electoral standing, despite stemming the decline

Elections were one of the stages on which ANC survival unfolded. The ANC's electoral standing had been in decline generally, and then its support line strengthened at national level in 2019. It was a fragile improvement, however, in light of the lower voter turnout, an ambiguous ANC mandate and the splintering of the opposition. The majority was boosted artificially through the electorate's acceptance that President Cyril Ramaphosa represented a reinvigorated, clean and united ANC; its crafted message to the electorate was that of an inclusive, doggedly anti-corruption post-Nasrec ANC with the deputy secretary-general, Jessie Duarte, spreading the gospel, insisting that the ANC's 2017 conference had given a clear mandate – it 'did not elect one side over the other; it elected a joint leadership'.[7] The name of the ANC electoral game was to deflect attention, to expose other parties as the enemy; they had to be targeted and diminished.[8] The ANC's war rooms were in full flight. Strategists diverted attention away from internal problems to focus, on the one side, on 'Cyril the redeemer of the united party' and, on the other, the opposition's problems of inclusivity, racialism and racism.

The national result offered the ANC a reprieve from the expectation, after the 2016 local elections setback, that come Election 2019 it might lose its outright national majority. The post-election party coalitions in major metropolitan municipalities demonstrated the governance chaos that might accompany situations where the ANC fell short of outright majorities. Had the ANC slipped below the outright level nationally in 2019, it might have entered into a governing coalition with the Economic Freedom Fighters (EFF). The ANC's 58 per cent national result was sufficient, however, to keep it electorally dominant. A buffer zone of close to 40 percentage points also continued between the ANC and its nearest rival, the Democratic Alliance (DA). A further gap of close to 10 percentage points differentiated the DA from the EFF, the fastest growing of the political parties – but not growing fast enough at the time to imply catching up with the ANC.

2. ANC weakened by corruption, the 'unity accord' and shifting factionalism

The slim CR17-Nasrec victory in December 2017 was the bridge into the ANC's outright election victory 18 months later. Ramaphosa's Nasrec campaign hinged on provincial trump cards that had remained uncertain right into the conference; it brought a dual-factional set of leaders that would only gradually and partially mutate as the Ramaphosa term advanced. Ramaphosa's victory at presidential level was recognised, even though there were threats of undoing the entire conference result,[9] and ongoing allusions to the extent that delegates might have been paid for their votes.[10] Zuma-ists, who later loosely coalesced around ANC secretary-general Ace Magashule, were conflicted: they wanted to reap the benefits of 'Ramaphoria', win Election 2019 and regain local ANC support in 2021, but many refused to end the battle against Ramaphosa and his associates. At stake was the Zuma-ist way of running the state, associated with state corruption and capture. Practices of corruption had been well-established in ANC government by the time Zuma came to office,[11] and questions continued arising from the contradiction between Ramaphosa's presumed campaign for clean government and his failure to act except through running for top office and issuing appeals to ANC members and leaders. The excesses and brazenness of Zuma's variations on the theme of corruption came to epitomise much of the state and haunt the ANC.

The ANC's 2019 counterfoil was that Ramaphosa would be the antithesis to corruption and the capture of public institutions once he was in power. Trust in leadership was variable. Ramaphosa's popular 2019–2020 approval scores, based on credible public opinion polls, continued to hover in the late 50s and 60s, even as Covid cynicism took hold. But among Zuma-ists and associates, and with the help of social media bot-networks, Ramaphosa was depicted as a sell-out and accomplice of apartheid security police,[12] then as the corrupt recipient and money-laundering dispenser of funding from 'white monopoly capital' who lied to Parliament,[13] and finally as the president who was too weak to lead. The mutations of ANC factions evolved as the ANC moved towards its 2022 elective conference. Many Zuma-ists had moved on to be converted Ramaphosa-ists, and Ramaphosa-ists were split between those who wanted one or two Ramaphosa terms (driven in part by those hoping to position a woman successor and those not seeing a worthy successor in the ANC women's ranks).

3. The ANC's uber-task of unity: Splitting prohibited

The ANC was fragile organisationally, home to discordant yet interdependent and shifting factions. The fact that it had moved at times close to the 50 per cent electoral support level meant another split-off – such as that of the Congress of the People (Cope) in 2008 or the EFF in 2012, or minor splits like that of the United Democratic Movement in 1997 – would endanger ongoing ANC dominance.

Even if they were constituted on mutually exclusive terms, the ANC factions had to find ways to coexist – notwithstanding their (real or invented) policy contests, battles for party positions, public differences of opinion and mutual sabotage. The ANC was effectively an acrimonious alliance of factions, held together by silences over moral lapses. The binary Ramaphosa-Zuma factional contest was one of the most destructive internally. At the time, Ramaphosa had to work with the Zuma faction, ensuring its consent to vexed decisions on removing corrupt cadres from influential positions in the state and government. Ramaphosa had to slalom between cleaning up and fielding charges of purging the Zuma faction. A tweet by the Zuma-ist NEC member, Tony Yengeni, about the North West process of premier removal was a variant of such charges:

> Wholesale purging of those who did not support you at conference is divisive and has a destabilizing effect on the ANC! If anybody has done wrong the law must take its course ... removing leaders through violent protests, burning of govt buildings is a very dangerous thing to do.[14]

Subsequent factional variants intensified rather than weakened the earlier lines of division. The battle line between Ramaphosa and Zuma-ists remained, even if Magashule appropriated the space opened by, for example, the public protector's assault. Magashule used it to try to diminish and distract Ramaphosa, but in the course of the Ramaphosa term slow action and inaction against corruption took its own toll. Several of the factional warfare strategies were aimed at imploding the broad-based Ramaphosa alliance and opening up political space away from Ramaphosa without putting in place a specific alternative. The choices ranged from the deputy president D.D. Mabuza to the ANC treasurer-general Paul Mashatile, to the ANC Women's League's (then) new protégé Lindiwe Sisulu, to the 2017 deputy presidential candidate and cabinet member Zweli Mkhize, who had chosen not to contest the ANC deputy presidency in 2017.

4. Party-state fusion, the backbone of ANC power

Organisationally, the ANC was weakened, but it was fused with the South African state to such an extent that its power was elevated. State resources and positions were used to build ANC, and ANC leadership, legitimacy. The ANC was entrenched in the state and possibly no opposition party would, in the foreseeable future, be able to overturn this, even if it were to win more electoral support than the ANC. Post-Polokwane, the Zuma faction was able to replace the Mbeki-ists in state deployment, but the Ramaphosa-unity round of attempted rotation proceeded with difficulty and delay. Change was slow, especially in the strategic state institutions. As Ramaphosa's term proceeded and many of his own deployees also turned out to be corrupt, the gap between the factions (and Ramaphosa's power to re-legitimate the ANC) grew smaller.

5. Opposition rerouted away from opposition parties and into direct action

Opposition to the ANC was only occasionally and provisionally driven into the ranks of opposition political parties. Instead, it often found its way into a supplementary layer of political engagement manifested, particularly, in popular protest.

The contemporary ANC was responsive to popular demand as it readily acknowledged that it had not done justice to rightful citizen needs and expectations. Popular protest against government flourished in the years of Zuma power-holding, and continued afterwards. It constituted a regularised stream of supplementary political engagement; at times it became the predominant stream. It related to exasperation with government delivery and socio-economic transformation, coupled with inadequate policies. From the Zuma epoch onwards, protest was focused concertedly on the lapses in ANC governance and on ANC leadership responsibility.

The ANC reaped benefits from the infrequent channelling of dissent and dissatisfaction with government into electoral politics. Street politics did not challenge the ANC for power except when it came to demands on issues like the faltering system of municipal governance, the collapse of local services and municipal ward councillor responsibility. Protests by interest communities (in some cases manifested nationally) coexisted with service delivery protests. Community action included labour action, taxi association protests, e-toll protests, anti-femicide and gender violence protests, and mobilisation to counter the presence of foreign citizens in the communities and passive resistance in defying impracticable coronavirus lockdown measures. Service delivery protests, ranging from problems with water and sanitation to security, anti-gangsterism and xenophobic looting unrest were usually community-anchored. Other community-centred protests and unrest focused on housing and, in particular, the availability of land for new urban settlements. Two specific xenophobic indicators were the truck burnings (protesting against the employment of foreign citizens as truck drivers) and looting of businesses owned by foreigners (mostly in shanty and downtown areas). School-burning protests were organised in Limpopo province by factional-ethnic community leaders who resented municipal re-demarcation that would destabilise their patronage networks. Many of these protests channelled dissent away from party political expression as participants found outlets for anger without targeting the ANC government.

6. Protest objectives are largely socio-economic, and citizens act to 'take' services

Protest was directed generally at deficits in policy, services and the realisation of socio-economic rights, and went hand in hand with protest that was not directed into the formal political system and parties. The grassroots exercised 'self-make, self-help' policy to deliver and broaden socio-economic rights.

Poverty protests grew (and were exacerbated by the economic fallout and escalation of unemployment related to Covid-19), also lending themselves to abuse by criminals. Citizens often took the option of 'self-help' – loot for subsistence (especially from foreigners, but also from small-scale private sector, localised businesses, storage warehouses or any truck carrying consumable or usable goods). Another option was for them to occupy land (they were usually rebuffed, but gained bridgeheads for the next round of government delivery of plots or houses), or tap into electricity and water without payment (apart from a fee to a local facilitator), or disregard municipal by-laws and erect backyard or pavement dwellings (an activity that was elevated when Covid regulations constrained demolitions and evictions), or generate income through crime or shack-farming.

7. Protests are handled in soft-law style[15]

Soft-law treatment of protest and community dissent entailed that there were minimal consequences for protesters doing damage to infrastructure or foreigner property, illegal invasions, arson and looting. There would often be multiple arrests, followed by a handful of court appearances, which then tapered off to the point where there might be a conviction or three, but mostly not. Strict law enforcement to prosecute on poverty crimes (as well as crimes assumed to be driven by deprivation and suffering) would focus more attention on the ANC's underperformance and shared liability.

The ANC government generally wanted to steer clear of antagonising citizens and voters through action in areas in which it had, in the first place, failed to deliver to acceptable standards. Such governance 'populism' resulted from government's inability to run an efficient, well-functioning state, or to pursue policies beyond promulgation into realisation. The ANC government was aware that its own policies and provision of services and infrastructure had not worked as intended and realised that the problem of poverty crimes was, to a significant extent, due to the failure of the state. These failures were also accentuated in Covid times. Protests were limited at first, owing to higher security force deployment and citizen fear, but soon resurfaced and reached new record frequencies paired with minimal consequences. In many cases, failures were linked to policies that had not been implemented or had been implemented insufficiently and corruptly.

8. ANC government leads by operating through malleable rules and law in state and government

Laws, policies and public service guides were often disregarded by government officials, politicians and citizens alike. Politicians and bureaucrat-politicians, irrespective of which president was in charge of party and state, became laws unto themselves; a huge degree of lawlessness permeated much of political society and society at large. The ANC and its government frequently did not play by the formal rules of state and government either. In a minimalist sense, the ANC and citizens played the same game: that of operating sometimes in lawless mode, making up convenient rules along the way, and using words (policies, pronouncements) that were not matched by action.

For credibility and legitimation, the ANC relied extensively on progressive, grass-roots, pro-poor, antiracism, anti-apartheid-colonial legacy policy narratives. Its policies were presented to provide the proof of political goodwill and transformational intent. Its policy monitoring and evaluation operations in government recorded its successes – beyond the Covid peaks it was the 'ideology' of (another) new beginning that helped the ANC blank out the lapses of the first 25 years of democracy.

The ANC government used but supplemented the formal structures, policies and rules. The alternate, supplementary rules in the time of this study, however, were often out of control, as evidenced in corruption, and in politicians taking private gain from many of the core state institutions and their lucrative projects. Similarly, the 2020 national budget statement proceeded on the basis of core funding from argued savings in the public sector salary budget, which could not be assured and had not been negotiated. In the subsequent austerity budget of mid-2020, hundreds of billions were shifted from core social functions like education and health to feed the Covid-related stimulus packages. In general, and on multiple governance fronts, ideals were posited through policy proclamations, ranging from land reform to economic growth to measures to compensate for Covid-19 hardship, which could not be realised – but presented by the government as being on track.

9. Courts and commissions help the weakened ANC to reassert lawful state and government operations

Lawless operations in state and government (through corruption, capture and conscious maladministration and mismanagement), combined with a weakened ANC organisationally, meant that the Ramaphosa ANC required help from the courts and commissions to take decisions. The Constitutional Court, along with the High Courts and multiple commissions of inquiry increasingly stepped in to help pull politicians back into line, in both party political and state matters. In Covid time, the courts helped to maintain legality and constitutionality in government operations. Even the threat of legal action against government helped to maintain accountability to Parliament and ensure that executive power would not be subsumed by the National Coronavirus Command Council.

The court processes had helped Ramaphosa to circumvent some of the accusations of purging opposing factions, but the bigger-issue commissions and court cases, including the Zondo Commission of Inquiry and legal proceedings to bring Zuma to account on corruption charges, were necessarily longer-term projects. There were also intermediary processes and new structures to follow up as the work of the commissions unfolded. While the courts and commissions were playing a role, political obstacles to the implementation of their work were not disappearing.

10. ANC reinventing itself through leadership rotation and claiming new associated policy directions

The ANC fine-tuned its repertoire of letting periodic top-leadership change signal that the organisation was reinventing and purifying itself or radicalising its policies to better serve the people. The ANC has always been a hotbed of factional contest over how radical and how revolutionary its policies ought to be – followed by intense introspection on what had caused the less radical, mainstream turns that its radical intent had assumed on multiple occasions. Still, opponents attempted the ongoing delegitimation of the Ramaphosa project, using radical economic transformation as a weapon of choice.

Citizens, voters and ANC supporters had been ever-ready to embrace serially this message that the new ANC, the presumably radicalised ANC, or new dawn ANC, had seen the light – or needed another term to fulfil its promises. When Thabo Mbeki took the mantle from Nelson Mandela, it was assumed briefly that delivery of the economic transformation part of South Africa's liberation would follow. Zuma claimed power from Mbeki promising radical policy and reconnection with the people. The Zuma regime instead deviated from the professed ideals. Late in his term, the Zuma faction tried to claim the mantle of radical economic transformation[16] and policed the Ramaphosa government for implementation. This thrust metamorphosed into the project to try and limit Ramaphosa to one term. Ramaphosa's ANC stressed that radical economic transformation as mantle for capture and corruption was the project to prevent state and government from emerging as the cleaned-up servant of the people and the greater ANC.

Ancillary action characterised the Covid times, as suggested by the Ramaphosa refrain of 'forging a new economy in a new global reality'. The ANC, along with other governments internationally, claimed a new start. This time around, new leadership was not required to gain a pardon for unfulfilled past promises and policies. The post-Covid economic reality was harsh and had political implications, but it blurred issues of accountability and liability.

11. Weakened state, constrained social wage prospects and legitimation through radical policy positioning

The state had been weakened institutionally, procedurally and in its ability to mobilise resources. The national budget was unable to extend the social wage into, for example, national health insurance, and was ravaged further by coronavirus economics; the expansive state and state-owned enterprises employment programmes had become unsustainable; despite employment generation initiatives, unemployment rates kept on rising and were exacerbated by the devastation wreaked by the pandemic. The albatross of corrupted, drained state-owned enterprises was harming the state, which was insufficiently capacitated and could not spend itself into a better future. In terms of health services, education and basic services, it often failed the people. Widespread state corruption meant that public institutions and their resource bases were compromised, diverted from concerted attention to developmental and socio-economic needs.

These state institutional apparatuses were used to service the needs of the political-economic elite and for generating employment, in equal measure to looking after the public interest. State operations became infested with ANC-captured business. As some layers were cleaned up, others emerged. The ANC's clean-government reformists could often not entrust state institutions with core work. The weight of investigation, prosecution and law enforcement overwhelmed many of the state institutions.

These 11 intersecting assertions guide the analysis in *Precarious Power*. They show how politics was in a melting pot of gradual political de-alignment from the ANC, how populism became an adjunct medium of expression for both people and government, and how a decapacitated state worked to prolong the myth that the liberation movement monolith was on track to bring 'revolutionary change'.

CONCEPTUAL INTERPRETATIONS GUIDING THE ASSERTIONS

The set of assertions may be interpreted further as a collection of generalisations (in italics below) about the phenomena associated with the ANC's continuous hold on political power in South Africa, despite problems and lapses.

There was a substantial extent of *de-institutionalisation and informalisation* of politics in the symbiotic relationships between the ANC, the ANC-controlled state and the people. There was quite routinely a strong populist dimension to the engagements, which was well tolerated by state, government and party.

Parallel streams of public operations became institutionalised top-down from the government side as well. On the state prosecutorial and watchdog sides, the National Prosecuting Authority and the Public Protector periodically became institutions that operated on state capture-based mandates. Lack of effective law enforcement by the South African Police Service enabled high levels of crime and lawlessness. Such top-down populism allowed for parallel and shadow operations by state agencies. In some instances, the formal state institutions, for example in security and intelligence, were so compromised that formal parallel institutions had to be created to execute essential state functions.

There were high levels of ongoing ANC *dominance of South African politics*. The ANC conducted self-legitimation routinely, using the history of apartheid–colonialism, the struggle and the ANC's position in the struggle, and public policies. The ANC had succeeded in positioning and keeping itself at the centre. ANC struggles and discourses were South Africa's battles, assuming equal importance.

The centrality of the ANC in political life, and its direct and populist relations with communities, meant there were limited prospects for the natural evolution of party politics. An inward-feeding politics was manifest in the ANC, an acrimoniously constituted organisation – yet it could not dare split; there were substantial pressures on it to stay as one. There was little chance therefore of new party political opposition evolving naturally through splits and major party political reconfiguration and realignment. The local level coalition chaos of 2016–2020 also reinforced the reality that governing coalitions were unlikely to be a conduit to political realignment. Pressures were directed internally in the ANC, and internal disruption, peace-making and compromise consumed energy which could have been expended on governance.

Laws, policies and rules were simply all-around rough guides for doing politics. When communities broke laws in executing their protests, they found an ANC government that was also in an ambiguous relationship with the law and the formal benchmarks of its rule. It was a government that was committed to rights, to policies and to projects, but fell short of its own goals, and rationalised the shortcomings of its own leaders who had deviated (but who had not been called to order in good time and with effect, despite extensive knowledge within and beyond the ANC). There was broad agreement that the letter of the law, and formally agreed rules of engagement, were not the only ways to do politics. This was evident, too, in the corruption manifested in government – senior (and other) politicians and bureaucrats were operating a shadow state with its own 'laws'.

Protests were mostly not a challenge to national government or its right to govern. In case of protests, the broader consensual frame still prevailed: it was not about challenging the legitimacy and right to rule by national government. Rather, protests were overwhelmingly by citizens trying to barter for a better life, for delivery of more rights and services in conditions of economic austerity. An increasingly weak state was asked to do more for the population. Depending on how this dimension would evolve, the relatively consensual nature of protest was still robust but not immune to future change.

It is these dualistic political practices, in multiple applications across the ANC and the government, that came to characterise the power of the ANC in the period of this analysis. The ANC was in power and, party politically, relatively unchallenged, while its base was fragile and decaying further. The Covid-19 ravages that graphically re-exposed desperate societal injustice and inequality slotted into the pre-existing framework. It was a time of growing populism,[17] of a variant that helped sustain ANC command, for the time being.

CONCLUSION: THE TALE OF THE ANC'S PRECARIOUS SURVIVAL AND DOMINANCE

Precarious Power is the third part to my trilogy of books on the changing role of the ANC in South African politics. The set of analyses started with *The ANC and the Regeneration of Political Power* (2011). It set a baseline of analytical approach, while taking stock of the ANC living through the transition from Thabo Mbeki to Jacob Zuma. *Dominance and Decline: The ANC in the Time of Zuma* (2015) followed. The analysis ended at the point when intra-ANC counter-mobilisation against Zuma was gaining momentum. *Precarious Power* details how and in what form the ANC continued to persist, how the ANC continued regenerating itself in changing political, political-cultural and Covid-related economic conditions, when its legitimacy and credibility were faltering although it was not being eclipsed electorally. It remained uncertain whether the ANC would sustain the reprieve the voters afforded it in Election 2019. Voters and citizens granted the ANC time and space to show that it had not been reduced to the political wrecking act of the Zuma era. Political events, as the research for the current manuscript was concluding, suggested that the ANC was not 'self-correcting' in ways that would sustain the reprieve. Simultaneously, socially–politically–economically the global, and South African, political reality was set to change through the Covid-19 pandemic and its unfolding aftermath. The book's analysis identifies the ground rules and configurations on which that new world, and new South African politics, would be constructed.

The book centres on the question: How did compliance and discontent in and around the ANC materialise, and how was it managed in the time of Cyril

Ramaphosa? Translated into party-political and organisational terms, the secondary layers of questions can be stated as: What happens when voters become disenchanted with the variant of multiparty liberal democracy in which the liberation party's dominance meant that to alternate political parties in government was not part of the deal? The analysis hypothesises that in light of the ANC's ongoing although dented legitimacy, and inability to address poverty and inequality in definitive ways, there was a movement towards channelling dissent from the ANC and its rule into informalised politics. Such politics came through variations on populism, civil society activism that engaged with the ANC directly (or indirectly through courts), and through popular 'self-help' to policy where the governing party faltered. From the ANC's side there was the 'great pretend' that it was managing state, public policy and public budgets to ensure delivery on the liberation ideals. This was possible only as long as opposition parties faltered and did not surmount the ANC logic that they were extensions and variations of apartheid, colonialism and neoliberalism.

Precarious Power dissects a make-or-break period in the life of the ANC. The research and analysis take a macro view on how it is that the ANC retained dominance and stayed in charge, despite lapses. Using grounded theory, the book extends the literature on South African politics and the ANC in the time of 25-plus years of democracy. It draws on the observation and experience of politics, and on the rich primary literature on the ANC in the time of corruption and misrule.[18] My fieldwork and analysis gained from these insights, but my own work pursued a concerted focus on researching the ANC in party, government and state, in relation to the people in particular. It assessed the ways in which ANC political power was being realised.

This book relates the tale of how the ANC had at one point become reduced to a two-parties-in-one party; how this shaped its near-collapse to minority status (yet survival) at the time of Election 2019; how the old dominant factions metamorphosed and were reconfigured into new factions attuned to evolving leadership dynamics and adept at creating an aura of anti-corruption action amid ongoing institutionalised corruption; and how the ANC prevailed in a political world of growing protest, consensual lawlessness, parallel government structures and populist practices.

To shed light on the metamorphosis of the ANC itself, its survival and ability to adapt despite decline and much disgrace, the rest of this book explores the ANC's organisational mutations; its presidential politics disappointing and alternatives floundering; its variable benchmarks of electoral predominance; its compromised state operations that reconfigure and rehabilitate its operations only to the point of not alienating dissenting ANC formations; its policy operations and choices that leave room for popular uptake; and its relating to populist protest tendencies that convert discontent into muted forms of compliance.

NOTES

1   The different worlds of the ANC are illustrated, inter alia, in works by Thula Simpson, 2016, *Umkhonto we Sizwe: The ANC's Armed Struggle*, Johannesburg: Penguin Books, depicting the world of struggle for liberation, and Rushil Ranchod, 2013, *A Kind of Magic: The Political Marketing of the ANC*, Johannesburg: Jacana, which shows how the myth-making complements the authentic struggle narratives.

2   *ANC Organisational Report*, 2012, 2017, as presented to the ANC elective conferences at Mangaung, 2012, and Nasrec, 2017.

3   ANC 54th National Conference Report and Resolutions, December 2017, p. 58.

4   Cyril Ramaphosa, 23 August 2020, Open Letter to the ANC, https://ewn.co.za/2020/08/23/read-the-full-letter-ramaphosa-sent-to-the-anc-on-corruption, accessed 23 August 2020.

5   ANC NEC, 31 August 2020, Media statement delivered by President Cyril Ramaphosa.

6   See Susan Booysen, 2015, *Dominance and Decline: The ANC in the Time of Zuma*, Johannesburg: Wits University Press, Chapter 1. My 2011 book, *The ANC and the Regeneration of Political Power*, Johannesburg: Wits University Press, sets out the principles of the process of regeneration.

7   Jessie Duarte, 23 May 2018, ANC media briefing, Luthuli House, Johannesburg.

8   See, for example, James-Brent Styan and Paul Vecchiatto, 2019, *The Bosasa Billions: How the ANC Sold its Soul for Braaipacks, Booze and Bags of Cash*, Pretoria: LAPA Publishers, p. 25. Such war rooms became a standard feature of ANC election campaigns, where teams of workers fine-tuned and disseminated ANC campaign messages in line with pollster interpretations of public opinion polls.

9   In January 2018 there was an effort to nullify the entire top-six election results, but it was scrapped from the roll, probably after ANC negotiations and conciliation or compromise. There were murmurs of challenging the entire Nasrec election result. ANC deputy secretary-general Duarte asked that the matter be struck off the roll with costs against Vincent Myeni, who claimed to be chairperson of a branch in Ward 32 in the Msunduzi ANC subregion, a claim that was disputed by Luthuli House; https://www.news24.com/SouthAfrica/News/bid-to-set-aside-anc-top-6-removed-from-court-roll-20180130, accessed 3 March 2018. Myeni argued that there had been insufficient time to file a responding affidavit.

10   Tokyo Sexwale, 'Money swayed the outcome of 2017 NASREC conference', *Briefly*, 28 February 2020, https://briefly.co.za/55427-tokyo-sexwale-money-swayed-outcome-2017-nasrec-conference.html, accessed 1 March 2020; Open Letter by Jacob Zuma to President Cyril Ramaphosa, 28 August 2020, https://www.polity.org.za/article/open-letter-by-jacob-zuma-to-president-cyril-ramaphosa-2020-08-28, accessed 5 September 2020.

11   The first meeting of the ANC's National General Council, in 1999 in Port Elizabeth, lamented the new reality in ANC ranks of cadres who join the ANC for the sake of financial benefits and deployment.

12   This was at the hand of the leader of the Congress of the People (Cope) in Parliament. In 2008, Cope had been the great hope that the ANC's monopoly on power would be coming to an end.

13   See, for example, Tom Head, 'EFF credit Jacob Zuma for "removing white monopoly capital" in South Africa', *The South African*, 11 July 2019, https://www.thesouthafrican.com/news/eff-praise-jacob-zuma-white-monopoly-capital/, accessed 11 July 2019.

14   Tony Yengeni, 2018, https://twitter.com/tyengeni1954/status/994084428577198081, accessed 1 March 2020.

15   Stéphanie Lagoutte, Thomas Gammeltoft-Hansen and John Cerone, 2016, *Tracing the Roles of Soft Law in Human Rights*, Oxford: Oxford University Press, elaborates on these terms.

16   See, for example, Tom Head, op. cit.

17   Roger Eatwell and Matthew Goodwin, 2018, *National Populism: The Revolt against Liberal Democracy*, London: Pelican, offer interpretations of populism that articulate with the current analysis.

18   The following authors and projects have assisted greatly in shedding light on the world of corruption and capture in the time of Zuma: Adriaan Basson and Pieter du Toit, 2017, *Enemy of the People: How Jacob Zuma Stole South Africa and How the People Fought Back*, Johannesburg: Jonathan Ball; Adriaan Basson, 2019, *Blessed by Bosasa: Inside Gavin Watson's State Capture Cult*, Johannesburg: Jonathan Ball; Jacques Pauw, 2017, *The President's Keepers: Those Keeping Zuma in Power and out of Prison*, Cape Town: NB Publishers/Tafelberg; Pieter-Louis Myburgh, 2019, *Gangster State: Unravelling Ace Magashule's Web of Capture*, Cape Town: Penguin Books; James-Brent Styan and Paul Vecchiatto, 2019, op. cit.; Rajesh Sundaram, 2018, *Indentured: Behind the Scenes at Gupta TV*, Johannesburg: Jacana; Mandy Wiener, 2018, *Ministry of Crime: An Underworld Explored*, Cape Town: Pan Macmillan; Crispian Olver, 2017, *How to Steal a City: The Battle for Nelson Mandela Bay*, Cape Town: Jonathan Ball; Johann van Loggerenberg with Adrian Lackey, 2017, *Rogue: The Inside Story of SARS's Elite Crime Busting Unit*, Johannesburg: Jonathan Ball; Hennie van Vuuren, 2017, *Apartheid Guns and Money: A Tale of Profit*, Johannesburg: Jacana.

2

Shootouts Under the Cloak of ANC Unity

MULTIPLE CENTRES HOLDING

The state of the ANC organisationally was epitomised by the unceasing debates over whether the 'centre is holding'. The emblematic ANC centre had been 'holding' at the time of transition from Jacob Zuma to Cyril Ramaphosa, provided it was accepted that there were – in essence but metamorphosing continuously over time – competing centres locked in combat and which dared not separate because that might collapse the solidity of the organisation. The two main centres persisted, but mutated beyond the Nasrec moment and were partially suspended amid Covid-19 political uncertainty.[1] Zuma's power base continued contracting and was adopted by Ace Magashule and the radical economic transformation group; the Ramaphosa centre consolidated somewhat but sought clarity as to its champion from 2022 onwards. The choices included Ramaphosa for a second term, or D.D. Mabuza, Paul Mashatile, Lindiwe Sisulu or Zweli Mkhize as the heir to the Ramaphosa centre. Ramaphosa, once a determined one-termer, considered running for a second.[2] It was possible, too, that Ramaphosa could gain an extended first term, should the impact of Covid-19 on party schedules, an amendment of South Africa's electoral system and the ANC's wish for elimination of the gap between ANC and national elections bring alignment in a timeframe beyond 2024.

The ANC's in-essence dual centre was rooted in the ambiguous Ramaphosa victory at Nasrec 2017 and the subsequent ongoing inter-factional acrimony that was reminiscent of Zuma-ists versus Mbeki-ists post-Polokwane. The two main factions were each strong enough to hope for control of the organisation overall – and to keep the losing faction in the ANC fold. The ANC could not survive another Cope-like split, and ANC political power had become thoroughly fused with state power; unscrambling along factional lines had become unfathomable. It was affected at the time by the ANC's pending 2019 national election campaign requiring *one voice* for outright victory – and only an anti-corruption and counter-capture voice would suffice. The centre held, too, as the protracted stalemate between the two main factions (more clean and less clean) defeated the achievement of a definitively cleaned-up state and party.

Two-centre ANC politics had been the norm since at least the early days of Thabo Mbeki's rule.[3] The intensity of the battle grew over time, to the extent that an ANC top official designated ANC meetings as 'shootouts'.[4] Despite the elections unity talk and enforced Covid unity to save the ANC from blame for losses of life and livelihood, the competing centres persevered beyond the small Prague spring of the 2019 election campaign and the Covid crisis. The battling centres – the original main factions, plus several derivatives that morphed and flourished over time – permeated and debilitated ANC government, limited the abilities of the party in government and raised questions about the electoral sustainability of the ANC's project of political domination in perpetuity. The main Ramaphosa faction appealed to the electorate over the heads of the semi-defeated Zuma faction. Ramaphosa himself appealed to the general public and ANC membership over the heads of the ANC leadership, as in his August 2020 open letter to ANC members. This type of unity brought Zuma-ists, too, into power, handing them lifelines, on the coat-tails of *Thuma Mina*.[5] A truce on corruption became the operational principle of the Ramaphosa government: moderate questions and investigations, determined words on always more definitive action, and assurance that the ANC remained the home for all. This truce, however, was also the arena for the next round of the battle: a recognition that the Ramaphosa-ists were paralysed while the Magashule faction held trump cards of counter-accusations and control over the ANC head office.

The ANC relied emphatically on this unity which required regular denial of the contest for factional control and demanded that the ANC finely balance issuing convincing public commitments on eradicating corruption with evidence of steps against members and leaders. This chapter dissects the building blocks of the ANC's jagged transition from Jacob Zuma to Cyril Ramaphosa as imperfect metaphors for corruption in the party and the state, and the clean-up of those institutions. The transition to and designation of a new organisational identity was precarious. There was ambiguity about the extent of organisational change, about the viability of it and over the leadership's prevarication between embodying a new ANC or being so thoroughly compromised (despite being in the Ramaphosa camp) that the 'new

ANC' was set to flounder. The presumed reality of the change from Zuma's ethos to Ramaphosa's was sufficient for a while to redeem the ANC in the eyes of the electorate. Then, Covid-related corruption set in, much of the public goodwill dissipated and the Ramaphosa regime had to prove itself anew.

This chapter tracks the tale of ANC organisational survival from the time of the contest for Nasrec, through the removal of Zuma from power, the preliminary 'new dawn' transition up to Election 2019, and the incessant political contest – in trying economic conditions – up to the point of the early run-up to the ANC's next round of internal elections. It is the story of the severe antecedents to the Ramaphosa era, emanating from the time of unadulterated state capture and endemic corruption, and the struggles to turn the ANC and the ANC-controlled state and government away from the decline epitomised by (but not invented in) the Zuma years. It traces the saga using the ANC organisationally as point of reference while the remaining three pillars of ANC power – the state, the people and the electoral verdicts – slip in and out of the timeline.

NASREC FULCRUM, FIGHTBACK AND FUTURE: THE STATE OF THE ORGANISATION

The Ramaphosa-ists marginally won the ANC national elections at Nasrec, and the battle was just beginning. The marginal faction victory at this ANC national elective conference of December 2017 at the Nasrec convention centre on the outskirts of Johannesburg was at the centre of the ANC's attempted organisational metamorphosis into an entity that could survive electorally. The era of Zuma's incriminatory rule, paired with the Ramaphosa camp's years of self-compromising complicity, plus recognition by the ANC that it was governing itself into a minority electoral status, wrought the transition. Former president Jacob Zuma had pulled together a powerful 'empire', covering party and state, in the preceding 12 years. His influence was diffused across influential and strategic state institutions. Without control over the ANC, the Zuma kingdom risked losing important footholds of patronage and influence. Nasrec was not simply about winning the ANC high office, for victory was the key to the continuous accessibility of extended benefits to the Zuma-ist circle.

The Ramaphosa camp's Nasrec feat was remarkable, slight majorities and sharing places on the winning slate with the Zuma camp notwithstanding. To forestall recounts, Ramaphosa settled for a 'unity mandate', the instrument to protect the result from legal challenge. Contests at this level could possibly have reversed the prevailing 'designer' results – a mixed slate reminiscent of carefully constructed compromise, rather than the result of a robust internal ANC election. Ramaphosa argued to his followers at Nasrec:

… we must try … to protect the integrity of this conference. We mustn't allow this conference to degenerate into controversy and legal suits that will nullify the result that we've come up with … [N]otwithstanding the fact that it may not be what we all wanted [it] gives us a beach-head to be able to start the process of reinstilling the values of our movement … hoping that people will embrace that … I have no doubt that the majority of our members want an ANC that subscribes to the values set in our constitution, the values that our founding fathers and mothers of our movement [believed in].[6]

The Ramaphosa ANC presidential campaign had required around R400 million.[7] The expenditure details had become public because of the ongoing onslaught on Ramaphosa, and high-level surveillance by political opponents was part of it. An ANC-Ramaphosa campaigner observed: 'ANC leadership contests are highly funded – these have become [like] American campaigns. It was the same at Polokwane, Mangaung …'[8]

Beyond the Nasrec results announcement, Ramaphosa appeased the 'Nasrec losers' and pledged to be the president for all factions.[9] The divided ANC had to be shored up, with the help of a divided National Executive Committee (NEC). The balance of power in the NEC was marginally in Ramaphosa's favour and it accelerated the exorcism of Zuma from the presidency. It also averted immediate Zuma-ist counter-mobilisation from his KwaZulu-Natal base. It was a gradual process, along a jagged curve. Over time, NEC outcomes confirmed that inter-factional compromise and calculated silences over corrupt or complicit colleagues had become routine practice. Amidst waves of further evidence of corruption, albeit by now cross-factional, Ramaphosa declared in late 2020 that unity in the ANC is paramount.

The longer-term price to pay by the Zuma-ists was that of a gradually decaying fightback. The ongoing battle was often low-key, but sufficient to ensure that the Ramaphosa ANC remained restrained and threatened. It included that the clean-up-ANC had to defend its actions against unrelenting accusations of purges against Zuma-ists when those actions were directed against the tainted ones in the Zuma camp. There had to be wise management of the multiplicity of little Stalingrads each time legal processes followed against implicated Zuma-ists.[10] It also meant that whatever unsavoury content there was on Ramaphosa-ists would be aired.[11] The objective was to show that action against Zuma was about plots and purges, not principle, and that Nkosazana Dlamini-Zuma would have been the 'rightful president'.[12] Pursuing Ramaphosa through the courts of law was par for the course. State institutions, the Public Protector and State Security Agency added to the fightback, pinning down Ramaphosa and his strategic associates whenever possible.

The Ramaphosa camp meanwhile extended its reach, metamorphosing gradually. It benefited from inroads into ANC provincial structures. KwaZulu-Natal, for example, divided at the time of Nasrec, became a conquered bastion that then reconstituted itself with a view to successful provincial results at the next ANC elective conference. As Zuma's operational space shrank, his support base contracted and fractioned, but it did not disappear. New factional alliances arose in provinces such as Gauteng and Mpumalanga, as cadres realigned themselves for the next round of contests. Early on at the national level, the ANC's NEC backed Ramaphosa-ists in core decisions such as insisting on Zuma's resignation as president of South Africa. After crucial 2020 NEC meetings, Ramaphosa won the chance to address the public by direct media broadcast and media briefings, rather than waiting for Magashule's Luthuli House ANC to filter and spin NEC resolutions. Ramaphosa had to tiptoe around the NEC, yet by late 2020 he was in a seemingly well-ensconced truce with a large majority in the NEC.[13]

Ramaphosa exercised presidential powers, made new high-level and strategic appointments and backed legal processes to create the openings for renewal. He had to pay respects to ANC public policy decisions and create economic trust and confidence in a country veering in and out of political crises, while remaining stuck in economic crisis. He had to counter charges that he had lied to Parliament about his campaign funding; that he was prejudiced in backing action to remove the public protector; and that he was not condoning resolutions on land reform, the Reserve Bank or the creation of a state bank. It was a drawn-out battle for the control of the ANC when the president did not have the benefit of an economy that was growing, creating opportunities and a sense of national well-being.

The state of ANC alliances

The ANC, at the end of the Zuma decade and amid the ongoing Zuma-Ramaphosa transition, was weakened structurally. Its Tripartite Alliance was strained, not for the first time but in particularly challenging ways. The Alliance partner, the South African Communist Party (SACP), was weak as a flagbearer for a left voice and frequently consumed by the accessing of government positions. Its help in achieving the 2017 presidential transition[14] did not translate into building the post-Zuma period of governance renewal. The Congress of South African Trade Unions (Cosatu) had split a few years before, buckling under the pressures of having been critical of Zuma, and its membership had been declining – in the last months of Zuma rule, it realigned with the Ramaphosa-ists. The ANC was torn between employee or worker interests (especially in the civil service) and restructuring a bloated and expensive civil service in times of economic austerity and Covid.[15] The ANC veterans attempted to move beyond their particular differences; the pro-Zuma Military Veterans Association and those critical of Zuma's actions and leadership (the uMkhonto weSizwe National Council) held a unity conference in 2020 and stressed that their collective agenda superseded efforts to divide the mother body. ANC Elders had filled the void, becoming an internal lobby group and an occasional voice of reason. The Youth League (ANCYL) and Women's League (ANCWL) tried to gain post-Zuma identities, but the Zuma years had extracted a toll. In a renewed post Dlamini-Zuma quest for centrality, the ANCWL dabbled with the possibility of the 2017 ANC deputy presidential candidate, Lindiwe Sisulu (unsuccessful at the time), as its future power project.[16] The ANCYL was unable to peacefully build credible structures,[17] as seen through the multiple casualties and the ongoing failures in the ANC task team's efforts to rebuild the ANCYL. They found it difficult to get a legitimately elected leadership to assume and maintain control without high-level political interference.

The ANC could not count on an obliging civil society base. A strong civil society coalition had assisted the ANC to loosen Zuma's hold on state power. Non-governmental organisations (NGOs) continued winning cases that helped to hold the ANC and government to account and to bring the state capture practitioners in government and business to heel. NGOs helped the ANC in cases when the ANC itself was too weak to extract accountability – for example, to challenge the veracity of the Seriti Commission, to halt the unaffordable nuclear power deal, to thwart unfair legislation generally, or to help bring Zuma to trial (on occasion with the help of opposition parties). In the Covid era, civil society, along with opposition parties and others, helped to keep the ANC government accountable and political power centred in constitutionally mandated institutions.

Civil society protest was widespread and became more anarchic; in many respects, crime was out of control. Lawlessness ruled in domains where the security and judicial apparatuses were unable to assert authority. It was also a structured lawlessness – protesting communities operated in the knowledge that the ANC would 'go softly' in law enforcement because it did not wish to risk alienation. There was a discrepancy between this de facto policy and words such as those of D.D. Mabuza when, as deputy president, he declared that lawlessness and land grabs were the 'antithesis of what we stand for as constitutional state'.[18]

ANC membership contraction and expansion mirroring trouble at the top

Membership figures shed instant light on the health of an organisation. The ANC's membership showed far-reaching declines in the period after 2012,[19] when massive mobilisation was effected, first in the run-up to the 2012 ANC centenary celebration and followed by select growth in the months thereafter: Zuma-ists bolstered pro-Zuma provinces to swell delegate numbers available to vote for Zuma at the Mangaung elective conference. The 2012 centenary figures were in all probability inflated (besides conference years quite routinely being the time of ANC membership boosts): 2017 showed mild resuscitation. In late 2020 when Magashule was threatened, and challenged the ANC to let the branches speak, membership had just surged to 1.4 million.

Table 2.1 highlights the extent of changing provincial power blocs of ANC membership. Mpumalanga rose through the ANC provincial ranks on the basis of a sharp increase in membership figures and became a 2017 kingmaker. It followed the time of the massive growth in KwaZulu-Natal ANC membership figures in 2011–2012, when Zuma needed numbers to defend his ANC presidency come December 2012. The province's figures signalled to the then challenger for the ANC presidency, Kgalema Motlanthe, that his challenge would be futile.

By the time of the ANC National General Council (NGC) meeting of 2015, the party's membership figures were declining steeply in relation to the antecedent elective conference of Mangaung. The ANC's 2017 organisational report showed improvement on 2015, yet numbers remained far below the centenary mark. Branch mobilisation and membership recruitment determine the outcome of elective conferences, and high levels of exclusion, purchasing of memberships and attempted political exclusion of opponents at branch level were rife in the run-up to Nasrec 2017.[20] In 2020, in preparation for the NGC that was postponed to May 2021 due to Covid, the ANC launched its online membership system that allowed electronic membership renewal and was said to speed up the delivery of membership cards while discouraging gate-keeping. December 2020's membership of 1.4 million remained to be certified as free of manipulation by Luthuli House, for purposes of influencing conference decisions.

NASREC REPRIEVE AND ENTRAPMENT IN RAMAPHOSA'S UNITY ACCORD

The full story of the Ramaphosa victory 'in unity' at Nasrec continues to unfold. Deception; conceit; double agendas and dual-factional promises; brown-envelope politics; head counts that did not add up; and reports of manufactured deals that substituted for results ruled dissections of the ANC's December 2017 Nasrec national elective conference.[21] The results in Table 2.2 prompted the ANC into a precarious internal factional coalition, at first bi-factional, later with various sub-factions and adjunct factions emerging. The ANC had hoped for a Polokwane-style outcome (clear-cut outright factional victory), even if there were reminders of the Mangaung-style result (a three-quarter, manufactured pre-conference factional victory). Nasrec delivered a

Table 2.1: ANC membership figures, 2007–2017

Province	2007 Polokwane 52nd national conference	%	3rd National General Council	%	2012 Mangaung 53rd national conference	%	4th National General Council	%	2017 Nasrec 54th national conference	%
Eastern Cape	153 164	24.7	161 161	21.5	187 585	15.4	124 050	16.1	140 696	14.2
Free State	61 310	9.9	41 627	5.6	121 074	9.9	51 088	6.6	91 910	9.3
Gauteng	59 909	9.6	70 305	9.4	134 909	11.1	87 759	11.4	99 245	10.0
KwaZulu-Natal	102 742	16.6	192 618	25.7	331 820	27.2	158 199	20.6	181 860	18.4
Limpopo	67 632	10.9	101 971	13.6	161 868	13.3	84 413	11.0	130 347	13.2
Mpumalanga	54 913	8.8	46 405	6.2	132 729	10.9	96 799	12.6	158 598	16.0
North West	47 535	7.7	57 911	7.7	75 145	6.2	78 922	10.3	119 830	12.1
Northern Cape	37 262	6.0	37 122	5.0	36 428	3.0	38 680	5.0	38 791	3.9
Western Cape	36 497	5.9	40 427	5.4	38 499	3.2	49 960	6.5	28 459	2.9
Total	620 964	100	749 547	100	1 220 057	100	769 870	100	989 736	100

Notes: The figures differ occasionally from previous numbers released by the ANC. Differences are minor and the ANC explains them in terms of the exact date of the release, and changes that arise in the process of auditing membership figures. The 5th National General Council was postponed because of Covid-19. Due to rounding, column totals deviate minimally from 100.

Source: ANC Organisational Reports, 2007–2017, plus own calculations

Table 2.2: Branch delegate allocations per province at ANC elective conferences

Province	Change in province's proportion of overall number of delegates 2007 to 2017			Provincial delegates				
	% 2007	% 2017 (calculated on figure a)	Change percentage point on figure (column a)	Polokwane 2007	Mangaung 2012	Nasrec 2017 Expected (a)****	Nasrec 2017 Registered (b)	Nasrec 2017 Valid votes cast (c)
Eastern Cape	24.7	13.7	−11	906	676	648	636	632
Free State	9.9	8.7	−1.2	363	324	409	355	349
Gauteng	9.6	10.7	+1.1	354	500	508	491	491
KwaZulu-Natal	16.5	18.4	+1.9	608	974	870	840	804
Limpopo	10.9	13.6	+2.7	400	574	643	553	567
Mpumalanga	8.8	15.6	+6.8	325	467	736	722	708
North West	7.6	11.4	+3.8	280	234	538	511	446
Northern Cape	6.0	4.2	−1.8	220	176	197	193	193
Western Cape	6.0	3.9	−2.1	219	178	182	146	136
Total branch delegates***				3 675*	4 103**	4 731	4 447	4 326

Notes: * Ongoing changes in branch credentials resulted in an adjusted 3 983 ballots being issued on Polokwane voting day. ** To illustrate the proportionate role of the provincial delegates: 91.2% of the delegates were from the provinces and branches; the ANC Women's, Youth and Veterans' Leagues each had a further 60 in 2017 (45 in 2012) voting delegates, the NEC 86 (82 in 2012), and the provincial executive committees a total of 243 in 2017, 189 of which were permitted (180 in 2012). This constituted in 2012 an additional 397 delegates (8.8% of the total in 2012 and 505 or 10.7% in 2017). The 2012 total included the Free State vote (324 delegates) that was eventually disallowed. *** The numbers of non-branch delegates (from leagues and leadership structures) remained the same in 2007 and 2012, but rose in 2017. **** Figures (column a) as announced by the ANC, October 2017; subsequent figures accounted for disqualifications (column b); valid votes that were cast and counted (column c).

Sources: ANC media briefings, update on preparations for the ANC 52nd National Conference, 11 October 2007; for the ANC's 53rd National Conference, 6 October 2012; ANC secretary-general statement, 6 October 2017; own calculations

presidential winner but also a bi-slate victory board without definitive margins, which came to haunt the ANC, even if the Ramaphosa victory had brought organisational reprieve and electoral success. The battle of Nasrec continued far beyond the moment of the conference, nationally and in the provinces.

Headcounts of delegates at mass factional caucus meetings two days before the vote raised expectations of either a sizeable Ramaphosa victory or an anticipated Zuma-ist victory but the dual-factional ANC leadership result ended such hopes.[22] This outcome came to constitute the next generation of ANC mythology: that the delegates had chosen 'unity', following the D.D. Mabuza–Paul Mashatile tactical move, and the leadership had to follow. The accommodation of the corrupt and the captured, and the implementation of battle-proxy policy positions became the manifestation of this higher voice of wisdom.

The ANC reeled as it worked through the dual-factional result. There was a real possibility that challenges would plunge the ANC into a morass of mutual intolerance. Recounts and court challenges of both the result and delegate statuses, for example, would deepen rather than resolve the victory fault-lines. Scrutiny of the two camps' slate lists (they were banned officially but were the voting booth accessory of voting delegates)[23] revealed that there was the closest of margins between the two camps on the NEC, and the alternation of winners from one top-six position to the next (see Table 2.3). 'Unity' could not have been better served.

The ANC decided to sanctify the 'unity' message: it was ordained as the singular direction that the conference, as the highest decision-making body, had dictated. Its origins were found in the accord between the ANC deputy president candidate on the Zuma-ist slate, D.D. Mabuza (Mpumalanga province), and Paul Mashatile (Gauteng province) on the Cyril Ramaphosa slate shortly before the conference. They would mobilise their constituencies to support each other for the respective ANC positions of deputy president and treasurer-general; they also envisaged this as a cooperative pact for the next national elective conference. Mabuza told his supporters (despite his then association with the Zuma slate and the Premier League[24]) to vote with their consciences. The province had already made a statement by nominating for the top position not just the slate candidates but also a third candidate, 'unity'. Mabuza's 'conscience vote' deprived the Dlamini-Zuma bloc of critical numbers. Mabuza thus aligned himself and his followers with Ramaphosa:

> Cyril's instinct was to stay away from dealing with [businessman Robert Gumede and his associate, Mpumalanga's D.D. Mabuza] … But one of [Ramaphosa's] supporters told him to get real if he really wanted the presidency. He could not have won it without Mabuza … that was the bitter truth.[25]

Table 2.3: Polokwane, Mangaung, Nasrec election results for the top-six officials, 2007, 2012, 2017

Position	2007		2012		2017	
	Zuma slate	Mbeki slate	Zuma slate	Motlanthe slate	Ramaphosa slate	Dlamini-Zuma slate
President	Jacob Zuma 2 329 (62%)	Thabo Mbeki 1 505 (38%)	Jacob Zuma 2 983 (75%)	Kgalema Motlanthe 991 (25%)	Cyril Ramaphosa 2 440 (52%)	Nkosazana Dlamini-Zuma 2 261 (48%)
Deputy president	Kgalema Motlanthe 2 346 (62%)	Nkosazana Dlamini-Zuma 1 444 (38%)	Cyril Ramaphosa 3 018 (76%)	Mathews Phosa / Tokyo Sexwale 470 / 463 (12 / 12%)	Lindiwe Sisulu 2 159 (46%)	David Mabuza 2 538 (54%)
National chairperson	Baleka Mbete 2 326 (61%)	Joel Netshitenzhe 1 475 (39%)	Baleka Mbete 3 010 (76%)	Thandi Modise 939 (24%)	Gwede Mantashe 2 418 (52%)	Nathi Mthethwa 2 269 (48%)
Secretary-general (SG)	Gwede Mantashe 2 378 (62%)	Mosiuoa Lekota 1 432 (38%)	Gwede Mantashe 3 058 (77%)	Fikile Mbalula 901 (23%)	Senzo Mchunu 2 336 (49.8%)	Ace Magashule 2 360 (50.3%)
Deputy SG	Thandi Modise 2 304 (61%)	Thoko Didiza 1 455 (39%)	Jessie Duarte	Unopposed	Zingiswa Losi 2 213 (47%)	Jessie Duarte 2 474 (53%)
Treasurer-general	Mathews Phosa 2 328 (63%)	Phumzile Mlambo-Ngcuka 1 374 (37%)	Zweli Mkhize 2 988 (76%)	Paul Mashatile 961 (24%)	Paul Mashatile 2 517 (54%)	Maite Nkoana-Mashabane 2 178 (46%)

Notes: In 2017 there were disputes around 'missing votes' (votes not adding up to total number of voting delegates) followed by threats of recounts and of court action. The 'missing votes' were accounted for in the ANC 54th National Conference Report and Resolutions, 2017, pp. 4–8.

Percentages reflect proportion of the valid vote (figures are rounded).

Sources: Polokwane, Mangaung and Nasrec conference announcements, 18 December 2007; 19 December 2012; 19 December 2017; own calculations

Mabuza's reward was the deputy presidencies of the ANC and South Africa.

In Mabuza's words, what 'prevailed [at the Nasrec conference] was "unity". That means branch delegates heard my voice, heard my story that said it looked like this person is making sense … Because if we did not go the way we went, probably we will be talking about the ANC limping today.'[26] In his Nasrec closing speech, Ramaphosa elevated the slate-mix result to the next level of unity: 'You as delegates you decided you want a united leadership.'[27]

Simultaneously, the Premier League's Ace Magashule became the ANC secretary-general, the second most powerful position in the ANC, one that had previously been held by the likes of Cyril Ramaphosa, Kgalema Motlanthe and Gwede Mantashe. Mabuza, now on the Ramaphosa side and ensconced as the deputy president, leveraged his chances to one day succeeding Ramaphosa. This weakened the presumably clean (or cleaner) Ramaphosa ANC. Mabuza had previously been implicated in siphoning money from schools and other public services in Mpumalanga to 'buy loyalty and amass enormous power'.[28] Magashule was, by all available evidence, complicit at a high level in the Gupta-linked money-laundering Estina dairy project and was linked to mass enrichment through the asbestos roof scam.[29] In 2020 he was also arrested and faced corruption charges related to the Free State asbestos roofing project. Magashule was now responsible for Luthuli House functions ranging from branch organisation and membership oversight to preparation for ANC conferences and communicating ANC revolutionary rhetoric, when Covid halted political activity. After the first wave of Covid the ANC announced a membership increase of around 42 per cent, under Magashule's guiding hand. Magashule was potentially as dangerous to Ramaphosa as Zuma had been to Thabo Mbeki.[30]

Top-leadership ascension 'logic'

The top-six leadership acquisition and ascension dynamics realised at the time of Nasrec helped to envision possible futures. All ANC presidents since the early 1990s had risen through the ranks of the top six (see Table 2.4). This was evident most of all in the case of Jacob Zuma, whose rise had been relentless. When the time came for Thabo Mbeki to exit after having served two terms (it was possible to get a third ANC presidential term, but not desirable, as the ANC had proclaimed), Zuma was the only alternative. Mbeki had managed, prior to Polokwane, to get an ANC constitutional amendment that left open the option for an ANC president to gain a third term, but grassroots mobilisation in ANC structures created the unstoppable momentum that helped push Zuma past Mbeki. Once Zuma was in the presidency, presidential challengers like Motlanthe in 2012 stood little chance – even if Zuma had become tainted.

Table 2.4: The rise of presidents through ANC ranks, 1991–2017

Position	1991	1994	1997	2002	2007	2012	2017
President	Nelson Mandela	Nelson Mandela	**Thabo Mbeki**	**Thabo Mbeki**	**Jacob Zuma**	**Jacob Zuma**	**Cyril Ramaphosa**
Deputy president	Walter Sisulu	**Thabo Mbeki**	**Jacob Zuma**	**Jacob Zuma**	Kgalema Motlanthe	**Cyril Ramaphosa**	David Mabuza
National chairperson	Oliver Tambo	**Jacob Zuma**	Mosiuoa Lekota	Mosiuoa Lekota	Baleka Mbete	Baleka Mbete	Gwede Mantashe
Secretary-general (SG)	**Cyril Ramaphosa**	**Cyril Ramaphosa**	Kgalema Motlanthe	Kgalema Motlanthe	Gwede Mantashe	Gwede Mantashe	Ace Magashule
Deputy SG	**Jacob Zuma**	Cheryl Carolus	Thenjiwe Mtintso	Sankie Mthembi-Mahanyele	Thandi Modise	Jessie Duarte	Jessie Duarte
Treasurer-general	Thomas Nkobi	Makhenkesi Stofile	Menzi Msimang	Menzi Msimang	Mathews Phosa	Zweli Mkhize	Paul Mashatile

Notes: Bold: the rise of eventual ANC presidents.

Source: www.anc.org.za, various windows, accessed 2000–2020

In the early post-Nasrec days there was more flexibility, but it was not guaranteed. D.D. Mabuza had entered into the deputy presidency. That, and the fact that Ramaphosa depended on him for stability, contributed stature to his otherwise adverse profile. The full details of the Mabuza-Mashatile alliance added complexity to future contests. There was a possibility of Mashatile's challenging Mabuza for the presidency at the next elective conference, at the time still planned for 2022. Ace Magashule was the most likely heir apparent on the still-persisting Zuma slate. Lindiwe Sisulu lost the deputy presidency to Mabuza, but resuscitated her aspirations with a view to challenging again for the second highest ANC position come the next conference, despite not having emerged through the top-six ranks. KwaZulu-Natal's Zweli Mkhize (treasurer-general from 2012 to 2017) had decided not to contest for the ANC deputy presidency in 2017, but his province had bigger plans for the next contest, provided this candidate could escape the corruption axe that was falling over multiple ANC leaders. By late 2020 there was a growing possibility that Ramaphosa would contest a second term rather than make room for a president who would not help the ANC into general electoral victory.

A sidebar dynamic to ANC internal elections was gender and the ANCWL's advocacy of a woman for president. The gender ticket had failed on two previous occasions – when Nkosazana Dlamini-Zuma contested on the Mbeki-Polokwane ticket for the deputy presidency, and again in 2017, when on the Zuma ticket she opposed Ramaphosa for the presidency. The ANC and ANCWL had long professed to 'readiness for a woman president', and Ramaphosa had at one stage added his voice. Yet it was uncertain whether Sisulu would muster the strategic-mindedness and political presence to counter the rise of the men.

Neither Sisulu nor any of the prior women candidates for the ANC presidency had risen through the leadership ranks systematically. The only other ANC top leaders on the grid (see Table 2.4) who were continuously active in the top ANC leadership stakes were Gwede Mantashe, Jessie Duarte and Ace Magashule. Both Mantashe and Magashule had been accumulating malfeasance baggage and Duarte was not in the league of top political leadership.

UNITY AND THE LONG REVENGE OF THE ZUMA RECALL

The ANC Nasrec results kept reverberating through the organisation. That former president Jacob Zuma's proxy candidate, Dr Nkosazana Dlamini-Zuma,[31] had not won the Nasrec ANC elections, and that Zuma himself was then forced out of national presidential power 15 months before the end of term, propelled the ANC onto a new – but compromised and contested – track.

Zuma was extracted from the South African presidency – largely consensually (except when, finally, the NEC *instructed* him to resign) through extended, protracted deliberation. Zuma-ists at the time wanted to retain their remaining power and recover power lost. The Zuma faction had not been prepared for the Nasrec loss; the 'new and united' ANC had to live with the revenge for Zuma's exit. The road of post-partum recovery was as long as the road to get Zuma out of power.

Zuma's recall came when projects of extreme capture and corruption were still in mid-air. Although Zuma had bargained on a Dlamini-Zuma Nasrec victory, he was also attempting to rush through the disputed Russian nuclear deal and he embraced the campaign for fee-free higher education the day before Nasrec voting started. He was not ready to relinquish either state power or his accumulated benefits. He also needed his head of state position to help in guaranteeing state resources for multiple defences in courts of law. The chances were slim, however, of Zuma's hanging onto power. In the preceding two years, civil society mobilisation against his transgressions and abuse of public resources (evident in the corruption-driven arms deal, the Nkandla scandal and his connections into the Gupta capture empire) had altered the political landscape.[32] Civil society asserted itself in ANC organisational decision-making.

ANC veterans, a minority group of ANC members of Parliament (MPs) and a handful of NEC members built on the 2017 civil society blocs. Some initiated motions of no confidence in Zuma at the NEC. In August 2017, a parliamentary motion of no confidence in Zuma was defeated, but a notable number of ANC MPs sided with opposition parties against Zuma. Opposition parties mobilised against Zuma consistently – and Zuma came ever closer to the tipping point of being toppled through parliamentary motions of no confidence.

The Nasrec result unleashed national euphoria. The public were ready to reward the ANC.[33] There was a belief that a new party had been incarnated. Zuma appeared weak and corrupt for his now notorious Stalingrad strategy.[34] The goodwill towards the ANC would go to waste if Zuma had been left to see out his state-presidential term.

In one of the most telling turning points in ANC history, the NEC stuck together in the weeks of January to February 2018, rising above factionalism to 'turn on Zuma', putting ANC interest first. Zuma continued to play the card of 'no legal judgments against me', and 'no one tells me what I did wrong'. The court of public opinion, as recorded at the time in authoritative public opinion polls,[35] including the ANC's own internal polls, offered this clarity: they related the tale of a president who had brought his party into disrepute to the point of staring into the likely loss of an outright majority in the pending 2019 election.

Table 2.5: Process of removing a president from power: The case of Jacob Zuma, December 2017 to February 2018

19 December 2017	Announcement that Zuma protégé-proxy Nkosazana-Dlamini Zuma lost to Cyril Ramaphosa in the ANC presidential election, Nasrec.
7 January 2018	Zuma and Ramaphosa meet in KwaZulu-Natal, starting a process of 'continuous engagement'.
7 January 2018	ANC's top-six leaders brief Zulu king Goodwill Zwelithini and Xhosa king Zwelonke Sigcawu about their plans to ask Zuma to resign.
9 January 2018	Zuma appoints a commission of inquiry into state capture the day before the ANC NEC gathering in East London.
10 January 2018	NEC meeting focuses on ANC January 8 statement; Zuma escapes a potentially bruising debate in the first meeting of the new NEC; after months of resistance by Zuma against complying with former public protector Thuli Madonsela's instruction to institute a commission of inquiry into state capture, Zuma makes the announcement after getting the instruction from Ramaphosa.
13 January 2018	Ramaphosa delivers annual January 8 ANC statement, East London
19 January 2018	ANC NEC raises motion to recall Zuma – proposed by David Masondo, supported by Bheki Cele; Ramaphosa in his political report tells the meeting that he is working well with the head of state and is 'managing the transition'.
22 January 2018	ANC lekgotla, after which ANC SG says ANC officials will continuously engage Zuma both on his stepping down and on coordination between Luthuli House and government; he adds: 'We have not arrived at a decision that Zuma must go or must not go'; NEC gives Zuma the ultimatum to resign or face motion of no confidence in Parliament.
4 February 2018	ANC top six meet with Zuma in an unsuccessful bid to persuade him to resign; Zuma tells the meeting 'the people still love me'.
5 February 2018	The top six have an evening meeting with the ANC's National Working Committee; talks continue until late; in Johannesburg, Zuma supporters lead a 'Hands off Zuma' demonstration to Luthuli House and clash with a group of opposing ANC supporters.
6 February 2018	ANC confirms that a planned NEC meeting is cancelled after a 'fruitful and constructive discussion' between Zuma and Ramaphosa, Cape Town; Magashule says they want the opportunity to continue their talks; they meet after Parliament's presiding officers postpone the State of the Nation address that had been scheduled for 8 February; speaker Baleka Mbete says Parliament has 'looked realistically at developments … and [came] to the conclusion that there is little likelihood of an uneventful joint sitting of Parliament'.
7 February 2018	President Jacob Zuma, deputy president Cyril Ramaphosa, with ministers and deputies, attend Cabinet and Zuma chairs committee meetings in Cape Town; a planned NEC meeting is postponed – it would have discussed Zuma's fate as head of state.

8 February 2018	State of the Nation address, originally scheduled for this day, is postponed (decision taken on 6 February).
12 February 2018	ANC orders Zuma to step down as head of state without giving an exact date or timeline, argues his continued presence could 'erode the renewed hope and confidence among South Africans'; NEC is divided on the details; Zuma asks for a period of three to six months to prepare for and execute his exit; nine-hour marathon NEC meeting is held.
12 February 2018	Ramaphosa leads a late-night NEC delegation (including Magashule) to Zuma who is at the official presidential residence, Mahlamba Ndlopfu.
13 February 2018	ANC NEC resolves to recall Zuma, giving him 48 hours to resign or be recalled; in a meeting with Ramaphosa and Magashule, Zuma refuses to resign; ANC NEC calls a media briefing at Luthuli House.
14 February 2018	ANC announces its MPs will vote with opposition parties in support of a motion of no confidence against Zuma and that the speaker of Parliament had agreed to bring forward the motion from 22 to 15 February.
14 February 2018	A defiant Zuma speaks out in an interview with the SABC, saying he has done nothing wrong and has not been told the reasons for his recall; without such information he is not willing to leave the Union Buildings; he warns that his recall will plunge South Africa into crisis; he says he is being victimised.
14 February 2018	Zuma resigns in a live television broadcast to the nation – after a rambling television interview, in which he gave no clarity on his exact chosen option.
15 February 2018	Ramaphosa is elected unopposed as president of South Africa by the National Assembly.
16 February 2018	Ramaphosa delivers his first State of the Nation address, emphasising the theme of *Thuma Mina*.
22 February 2018	A scheduled no-confidence motion in Parliament proposed by the EFF no longer takes place (if it had been conducted and passed, Zuma plus his whole Cabinet would have had to resign).

Source: Author's monitoring, December 2017–February 2018, through observation and media reportage

The cut was neither pleasant nor clean. Zuma's exit from state-presidential power was not in the categories of the graceful retirement of Nelson Mandela, the angry but accepting greater-statesman act of Thabo Mbeki, or the dignified and limited-period caretaker repertoire of Kgalema Motlanthe. Zuma played the victim and wronged former president. He continued attending NEC meetings (a reticent figure, side-by-side with a handful of his former cabinet deployees); he put in rebellious court appearances and addressed shrinking squads of supporters. His legal representatives argued innocence and victimisation. When he appeared at the Zondo Commission, he feigned lack of recollection in between maligning former colleagues, invented plots and slandered former colleagues on Twitter, followed by 'illness and medical treatment'. Throughout, he (and associates) threatened to spill the beans on yet unspoken matters concerning the ANC and former colleagues.

The Zuma revenge unfolded gradually, carried forward by the seeming heir apparent of the Zuma-ists, ANC secretary-general Ace Magashule. The action included plots, manipulated election candidate lists, policy interpretations at variance with general NEC understandings, appointments of Zuma-ists to senior parliamentary positions, heightened scrutiny of implementation under Ramaphosa's watch of Nasrec policy positions, and preparing branches for future warfare. Revenge on Ramaphosa blended with the ANC's unity-seeking mission, to try and move the organisation away from the uncomfortable Nasrec balance of power. The tightrope act became the new character of the ANC.

Anti-Ramaphosa revolt by stealth in Luthuli House

Magashule's alternative interpretations of ANC messages, and his dissemination of those messages, using his base of secretary-general of the ANC, in command of Luthuli House, harmed Ramaphosa's authority. Similarly, Ramaphosa's inability/ unwillingness to ensure that fellow cabinet members toe a consistent and persuasive Covid-fighting line that did not contradict him, harmed his public image and his authority in the ANC. In the early post-Nasrec period Magashule had amassed Zuma-ists around him at Luthuli House, including the discredited cut from public positions, former Gupta employees and leading figures in anti-Ramaphosa proxy parties.[36] In the interregnum between Nasrec and the sixth administration, the Ramaphosa-ists had been well represented at Luthuli House, but then stepped into government to claim their high-office rewards for having backed Ramaphosa. The Zuma-ists included former ministers Nomvula Mokonyane (implicated but in denial of the Bosasa scandal), Malusi Gigaba (resigned from Cabinet after revelations of Gupta deals), Carl Niehaus (openly associated with ANC dissident parties in addition to being associated with Zuma, and offering his opinions regularly at public events), deputy secretary-general Jessie Duarte, a long-time Zuma loyalist,[37] and several others who had come from the Gupta-linked media establishment of ANN7 television and The New Age newspaper.

These persons were in command of the ANC organisational apparatus that prepared for future high-level ANC meetings. The Nasrec curse was catching up with the ANC: it had to maintain unity between factions while the factions were either at war, or were deceptively at peace.

Zebra stripes in the provinces

The ANC's cross-faction unity approach, in some cases mixed with tentative rea-lignment, found sustenance in post-Nasrec provincial conferences, at least up to the point of these conferences being halted pending the passing of Covid-19. Following through on the Mpumalanga 'unity' tactic, the ANC's mid-2018 provincial elective conferences adopted the inter-factional zebra approach, alternating candidates of the two factions on party lists and in deployment to party positions. The new 'unity ANC' was enabled through the de facto confirmation that provinces like KwaZulu-Natal (at least at top-leadership level) had increasingly been backing Ramaphosa for Election 2019, despite having opposed him at Nasrec.

In some respects, the Gauteng provincial conference resembled the December 2017 Nasrec elections. It was also one of the first illustrations of how the shifting lines of ANC combat were fostering new internal groupings or factions, accepting Nasrec and repositioning for the future. This became the 'zebra ANC'. Some of the new Provincial Executive Committee (PEC) members were CR17 people (those who had campaigned for a Ramaphosa win at Nasrec 2017); others were Ramapho-sa-ist, but wanted to oust the David Makhura contingent. Staunch Zuma-ists were among the ANC Youth Leaguers who emerged in the province, including those who had accused the media of harbouring an agenda against the ANC following reportage on Zuma's wrongdoings. The Gauteng ANC's election results saw its ide-als of organisational reinvention clash with governance skeletons, and these were dealt with piecemeal. Among the elected ones were Qedani Mahlangu of Life Esidi-meni infamy, Jacob Khawe of the failed mayorship of Emfuleni, and Brian Hlongwa under whose watch Gauteng health was burdened by fraud and corruption.

The Gauteng examples were a drop in the ocean of ANC leaders and govern-ment figures across municipalities, provinces and national government whose ongoing employment testified to factional accommodation as a stepping stone to ANC peace, but not the answer to governance problems. Zuma and his cap-ture exploits epitomised the ANC government's problems, but difficulties went deeper, and also spanned factions. The problems were so rampant that the ANC ran the risk of destroying itself should it try to cleanse itself and its governance act entirely. This was evidenced too in the reinstatement of high-level ANC Limpopo figures who were implicated in the VBS bank scandal, the Ramaphosa camp's indictment when its own were caught in profiteering from Covid funds, and the contested redeployment of former eThekwini mayor Zandile Gumede to the KwaZulu-Natal legislature. Ramaphosa's 'new dawn' became, at best, a long-term transitional period. It was going to be slow to break through economically while kingpins of looting were evading justice endlessly and where ANC election candidates would be the products of compromise and organisational inclusivity, rather than binding scrutiny.

The zebra ANC was embedded in ANC electoral candidate lists and worked to ready itself for Election 2019 and local elections 2021, and to legitimise its factional compromises. It handled the question of unity and 'which ANC is speaking' by playing the notion of 'one organisation, many voices'. Notable were Ramaphosa's words of 'we need a mixed leadership; a leadership that has different perspectives, different approaches, voices to be brought together to enrich the processes of the ANC', and that the ANC needed to convey 'one message told with many voices'.[38]

Dark dawn of list conferences, candidates and new compromises

The ANC's list processes in preparing for the 2019 elections, conducted at its branch and provincial structures, validated the Ramaphosa ANC's *character of compromise*. They built on past practice – but factional inclusivity prevailed far more than in the transition from Mbeki to Zuma. The nominations revealed how the remaking was progressing, amounting to an agglomeration of mixed signals. Personal ambition, some individual commitment to build a post capture-corruption ANC, and mutating factional warfare were the building blocks. The battle lines were being redrawn for control over the next generation of patronage-dispersing institutions.

The nomination processes unfolded from 2018 to early 2019, more slowly than anticipated because of the complexities of balancing factional interests and circumventing rules to try and outmanoeuvre the opposing faction.[39] An ANC guiding document had given the branches and provinces the processes and criteria for the nomination and selection of provincial and parliamentary candidates: at both levels, 10 per cent of the voting delegates were to come from the leagues, the Alliance and other ANC structures. The extended ANC NEC assumed the role of final national list conference, along with provincial list conferences that centred on the PECs.[40]

There were fragile ANC provincial truces, with the two sides to the Nasrec divide reminding Ramaphosa of the unity accord – the holders of the Nasrec majority would not overinterpret their modest victory. Zebra-mixed provincially elected slates emerged, for example, in Gauteng, Limpopo and, to some extent, in KwaZulu-Natal where there had been a unity election of the provincial chairperson. Gauteng first veered in a uni-factional direction, until delegates corrected it by voting in non-Ramaphosa-ist candidates as well.

The delegitimation of court action to counter the results of the provincial elective conferences of 2017 and 2018 was another unity-oriented trend in the major provincial centres. It followed only after the pre-Nasrec conference spate of lawsuits, which had been driven and funded by the respective presidential campaigns. In this corrective phase, cross-factional legal action to challenge the processes of gate-keeping, fake membership, concocted branch meeting records (and multiple variations of these manoeuvres) were labelled increasingly as 'counter-revolutionary'.[41]

The North West was an illustration of counter-factional corrective action in the top leadership intervention to stop spiralling court cases. The former Zuma-ist chairperson-premier, Supra Mahumapelo, and associates, fought through court cases for reinstatement in ANC positions; they won and when the ANC appealed they settled on an NEC instruction for a negotiated compromise. In the Eastern Cape, one group remained set on getting the dismissal of the extraordinary 2017 Eastern Cape provincial conference, designated the 'festival of chairs', which elected Oscar Mabuyane as chair and helped to seal the province for the CR17 camp.[42] They called for an interim structure to rerun the 2017 elective conference, a step that would have had knock-on implications for the legality of the Nasrec conference. ANC deputy president Mabuza's pronouncement that the Mabuyane executive committee was legitimate and recognised by the NEC did not appease the opposing camp, who continued arguing for nullification of the violent provincial conference. The ANC NEC intervened and, in North-West style, ordered the opposing factions to cooperate.

Mpumalanga continued in a state of limbo until, according to the Economic Freedom Fighters (EFF), on the instruction of Mabuza after Election 2019 the new premier, Refilwe Mtsweni, announced her zebra cabinet that accommodated experience and tolerated poor previous performances by provincial heavyweights – but also delivered gender balance and representation of both factions. The Western Cape had a peace-keeping ANC relic, Ebrahim Rasool, for the electoral face of the ANC campaign, while other former, contentious (and corruption-implicated) leaders were recycled onto a compromise-driven, inclusive task team that tried unsuccessfully to resurrect the ANC in the province.

The Msholozi[43] backlash at the time appeared to be contained (albeit not eliminated) in the formation of the post-election provincial governments. The space created through the ANC nomination processes, through factional inclusion in provincial governments, through tolerance where charges of corruption had not been formalised, and through biding time, delivered opportunities to extend and consolidate political careers, and were helping to close spaces for Zuma-ist subversion of the mainstream ANC processes.

As Covid-19 took hold, many ANC organisational operations froze in time, for much of 2020. The Mpumalanga provincial conference, scheduled for April 2020, was postponed indefinitely. Across the country, ANC branch general meetings had started materialising in preparation for the then planned NGC meeting, sub-sequently postponed to May 2021.[44] Covid-19 pushed the events into temporary political hibernation. Much of the post-Covid ANC contests and compromises would be determined by how Ramaphosa was to emerge from both the pandemic's economic devastation and the scandal of the political elite's looting of Covid relief funds: relatively unscathed and as an asset for the ANC, or as damaged goods and a good sacrifice for the ANC to make.

Remaking the ANC for national elections 2019 onward

The remaking of the ANC circa 2019, with the specific purpose of winning a national election by outright majority, in trying circumstances that resembled a hostile takeover for about half of the leadership, holds lessons for ANC modus operandi in years to come. A divided ANC entered into the 2019 elections while it was veering close to the 50 per cent cliff. It had to persuade voters not only that it was a *united* party-movement, where good people were in charge, and that Rama-phosa's one year in power was only the beginning of the big clean-up of party and government – but also that this ANC still embodied a liberation struggle ethos.

The ANC pursued a strong narrative of unity in its purported quest to counter corruption and power abuse. The reality was one of thinly constructed unity, forged by necessity to win the pending election, while factional dissent was suppressed. Plots and subversive public statements from the Zuma faction persisted. The Zuma-ist 'Maharani plot' against Ramaphosa, entailing legal measures to undo the Nasrec ANC election outcomes, featured in 2018.[45] Ramaphosa waited for the Cosatu 13th national congress platform to respond, warning the main protagonist, Magashule:

> Our people want to see a united ANC; we have to focus on renewal and unity. Even those comrades who did not love one another, it is time to unite now … We cannot go to those [2019] elections with a divided leadership … Any attempt to divide the ANC will be counter-revolutionary. Let us move forward as a united army.[46]

Ramaphosa asserted his authority on the NEC, invoking the mantra of unity. At the memorial lecture for Winnie Madikizela-Mandela, following a vital ANC NEC meeting, Ramaphosa reprimanded the plotters: '[Madikizela-Mandela] understood that unity was vital and necessary if the ANC was to remain at the forefront of the liberation struggle.' He stressed that unity was central to the then just-completed NEC deliberations:

> I can assure you … [t]he discussion that has raged the whole day has been about how we can forge unity and how we can make sure that whatever may be areas of difference can disappear so that we unite the ANC. I can assure you, we are finding each other.[47]

The unity baton was handed to secretary-general Magashule when he led the post-NEC media briefing. The deliberations epitomised the ANC's crisis of unity. Magashule led the discussion, along with ANC spokesperson, Pule Mabe (who oversaw 'the junior official' who presumably had issued a statement second-guessing the mandate of the Reserve Bank). Magashule repeated that the ANC was 'focused on unity', but evaded the issue of actions to achieve unity: 'This is the time to plot against poverty, this is the time to plot against unemployment, this is the time to plot against inequalities.' He added: 'We're working together and united. We're not focused on rumours.'[48]

The fightback was muted, with a view to getting through Election 2019. The process of constructing election messages, besides composing ANC candidate lists (also for post-election deployment), complicated the peace. Magashule's position as secretary-general assured him of influence over the lists. There were complaints that Magashule had interfered and changed the sequences and the inclusions and exclusions of his opponents, in particular in his Free State power base. Both the list process and post-election determination of parliamentary committee chairpersons confirmed that the struggle for control of the ANC was metamorphosing, but not dissipating.

Post-election factional mauling

With a sound 2019 electoral victory secured, the ANC internal war was ratcheted up again. By then the factions had been partly reconstituted, and the anti-Ramaphosa grouping was intent on destroying Ramaphosa and his associates. An NEC meeting of late July 2018 was an early epicentre. Talk of recalling Ramaphosa at the next NGC featured on the sidelines. A year later, in a 2019 NEC meeting, Ramaphosa dared the plotters to try and recall him.[49] Come 2020, Ramaphosa assumed responsibility personally to address the nation and the media on NEC outcomes, rather than see Luthuli House manipulating messages. Ramaphosa, his inner circle and their efforts to address national economic crises and stay on the right side of the public protector while implementing Nasrec policy resolutions, were the targets.

The public protector, Busisiwe Mkhwebane, had become a 'principal agent' in the attack. The SACP's Solly Mapaila described Mkhwebane as a 'hired gun of the fightback agenda', asserting that her office was used by rogue elements within the intelligence community.[50] Her findings that Ramaphosa had 'deliberately misled' Parliament in his response regarding a R500 000 Bosasa donation, and that he had breached the Executive Ethics Code in not declaring donations to his CR17 campaign, were intended as ammunition – but backfired when the High Court in Pretoria set aside the report largely because of material errors in law committed by the protector. She then sought the Constitutional Court's permission to appeal the ruling. Some attack fronts against Ramaphosa also came from KwaZulu-Natal where, for example, the axed (for corruption) former mayor of eThekwini, Zandile Gumede, threatened that she and her supporters would not be dictated to by the KwaZulu-Natal PEC and provincial chair, Sihle Zikalala, as to whether they might raise leader recall issues at NGC meetings.

ANC factional divisions would become more complex as the contingent of implicated yet not charged or convicted senior ANC leaders grew. The net of anti-corruption spread and then started contracting. However, the net bulged as growing numbers of Ramaphosa-ists were included, and the ANC was paralysed in the grip between action and inaction. The follow-up game in town was 'destroy Ramaphosa', or neutralise him by showing him as duplicitous and baggage-ridden, just like Zuma, or as ideologically more compromised than his adversaries. The public protector and the EFF were some of the main attackers.[51] The battle was a reminder that unity, in itself essential to sustain the ANC, was also a self-defeating ANC project.

POST-ZUMA REARGUARD STRATEGY DEFINING THE ANC COMPROMISE[52]

Several strands of unity-disunity permeated the ANC as it worked to solidify its new identity. While using this volatile formula, the ANC had been making peace with itself as the inclusive organisation that was obligated to root out corruption in ways that would satisfy the electorate, and yet remain the home of 'the tainted ones'. The positive side was notwithstanding the compromise that entailed going softly on the corruption-tainted ones who had been on the Zuma side but had warmed to Ramaphosa power. This reconfigured type of unity was forged at national and provincial levels, in developments around electoral preparations, and throughout the 2019–2024 sixth democratic administration.

Buy-in into this imperfect formula remained far from flawless. The cases of Jacob Zuma, Ace Magashule and a range of associates who had come to epitomise the fightback side of the ANC, sketch the transition to the imperfect-formula ANC.

Zuma's court appearances, such as that of mid-2018, give the contours of the battle as it unfolded in the fightback phase.

'What has changed?' was the question as Jacob Zuma made his way towards yet another court appearance in the Durban High Court in mid-2018. Vigils and prayers to support his court appearances played out each time he appeared, at least until the ANC, towards late 2018, started putting brakes on the serial embarrass-ments that unfolded for the ANC at each appearance. There was a fascination with Zuma in the dock. As the pressures on Zuma mounted, important developments materialised. First, the circle of mobilisation around Zuma (mostly beyond the ANC but also in provincial ANC enclaves and a few minor national structures) suggested there was a Zuma force. Second, Zuma's own words and arguments accu-mulated. Jointly, they highlighted trial defence arguments and Zuma's short- to medium-term political strategy.

Zuma's rearguard fightback actions grew, up to a point, amid occasional signals of setbacks and forced strategic changes. There was talk (or threats) of a new polit-ical party, the African Transformation Congress with extra-ANC origins (therefore not a split). The ANC in KwaZulu-Natal appeared not to be in this loop. How-ever, intra-ANC, Supra Mahumapelo and Mosebenzi Zwane were on a reported North West, Free State and KwaZulu-Natal crusade, mobilising ANC branches to ask Luthuli House for a special NGC meeting, and they were feeding on Zuma's motivational pearls of subterfuge and subversion.

The name 'Zuma' at this time was synonymous with manipulative, calculated strategy. Zuma was a wounded man, increasingly cornered. His list of options had shrunk since he had lost his proxy Nasrec war, the net of Ramaphosa-driven state clean-up appeared to be rolling out, and Zuma's own legal trials inched closer, court appeal by court appeal. Examples of shrinkage from 2018 to 2020 included the unfolding work of commissions of inquiry, including the Zondo Commission, the High Court's setting aside the Seriti Commission's arms deal report,[53] Zuma's tap of state funding for legal defence being turned off tentatively,[54] the Supreme Court of Appeal rejecting Zuma's application to appeal a High Court decision that he should stand trial for corruption, and a trial date finally being set. Yet, even the trial date was being challenged by Zuma's legal team – Zuma was not going to submit to trials and commission hearings.

As part of his tactics, Zuma repeatedly feigned innocence, ignorance and, later, failing memory, poor health and preoccupation with other court cases – even sim-plicity of character. He knew about minimising paper trails and inverting pointed fingers. He seamlessly combined declarations of undying love for the ANC with drawing the dagger to deal with the 'traitors of Ramaphosa' or 'enemy' agents (for some of his former cabinet members and struggle associates). Zuma's strategy included a calculated pulling-down of the pillars of ANC and government under Ramaphosa, as was evident in pronouncements at the Zondo Commission of Inquiry. There were refrains of 'I am innocent', 'I have never committed a crime', 'Zuma is not corrupt' and 'I have done nothing wrong'. Zuma executed his martyr act, presented prospects of going behind bars as nothing, because 'I have done time', with reference to Robben Island. He contrasted the events of the day with his struggle time in prison: '... at that time I didn't commit any crime, I was fighting for my freedom. I spent ten years, six months [in jail] without any problem.'[55]

Zuma tried to pull down South Africa's vulnerable investigative authorities, largely before gradual change in their Ramaphosa-era leadership started taking effect, musing at the initial clean-up setbacks (initial investigations were botched by the public protector, possibly deliberately) on the matter of Estina dairy and Gupta money flows: 'They investigated until they became tired because they couldn't find anything.' The Zuma logic continued, without specifying exact targets, suggesting racist operators, using 'they': 'They never expected anyone to build such a house in Nkandla and they concluded that I stole the money ... They investigated but they never found the money that they accused me of stealing.'[56] There was no place in the Zuma strategy to recognise avoidance of court appearances through unrelenting legal processes, efforts to refute and discredit public protector reports and the close to R40 million of public funds used, up to that point, to keep himself out of exacting court appearances.

At the heart of the Zuma strategy were his attempts to delegitimise the judiciary, as was heard at the Zondo Commission of 2019: 'I'm not talking bad about judges, but we all know that sometimes it happens that they convict someone who hasn't done anything, but another court could come to a different conclusion.'[57]

Zuma attempted basic politics and conceptual tricks on state capture: 'The state consists of three organs, Parliament, the judiciary and the executive. If you tell the country that there's state capture in South Africa, you mean those three organs are captured. That's wrong.' He hinted that his defence tactics would include 'meetings with and introductions to the Guptas – yes'; 'evidence and paper trails – no'. In his words, 'I've heard that there was a certain family [the Guptas] which spoke to a few people including ministers. You can't just say that by speaking to those people the state has been captured.' One of Zuma's religious leader backers tried to ignite a flame of revolutionary nostalgia: 'We are telling you to be strong as there are comrades who are targeted instead of white people who stole our land.' The disciple added that 'the things that Baba Zuma has done that have advanced and improved the life of a black child ... have to be continued'.[58]

These arguments were present, too, in the narratives of often-discredited activists who mobilised in Zuma's name and then became a political party. Zuma would not be the face of any ANC-opposing party, because he would forfeit the status of representing the ANC. In Zuma's own words, people who thought he would leave the ANC one day to start another party 'have no idea who I am'.[59] The party in question, the African Transformation Congress that became the African Transformation Movement (ATM), took off with involvement of the former government spokesperson under Zuma, Mzwanele (Jimmy) Manyi. He was accused of having hijacked the party (he denied it). The ANC balked on several occasions at investigating the links between the Magashule front in the ANC, the ATM and also Hlaudi Motsoeneng's African Content Movement. There was a seamless movement of staff between these parties, the former ANN7 Gupta television service, and Magashule's office at Luthuli House.[60] The MKMVA brought a further variation on the theme, becoming an 'internal opposition party' when it threatened the ANC with violence should Zuma be arrested for walking out of the Zondo Commission, or led anti-foreigner protests in eThekwini.

SHIFTING BALANCES OF POWER IN THE WAR ON RAMAPHOSA'S ANC

The factional war for the heart and soul of the ANC came to centre on the contest between Ramaphosa and Zuma, and what they represented. Zuma was fading, through both lack of sustained controversy about his 'persecution' and revised public priorities in the wake of Covid. The older ANC factional forces were hibernating and mutating, but remained on standby for resuscitation. Ideological battle lines were nurtured to serve the personalised-factional lines of division. Deep intellectual reflection on the ANC in relation to the arguably continuously unfolding revolution had faded and had been replaced by contemplation on how to survive blame for the economic fallout of the Covid pandemic, construct the next ANC electoral majority and circumvent coalition government. These considerations, in turn, were often superseded by positioning in relation to the political kingpins.

Zuma's network of malfeasance, conducted frequently in the name of radical policy and socio-economic justice, was omnipresent but it had declined in scope as Zuma slipped into the political margins. He was never brought to explain how and why, under his presidential watch, more radical changes had not been effected: first in Polokwane he had been elected on the promise and fleeting belief that the ANC was reconnecting with the people and that it was set to drive far-reaching change;

next, his re-election at Mangaung had promised that his second term would be the arena for radical change.

A collective comprising in the main Magashule and Duarte, a set of former Zuma kingpins in Cabinet and state-owned enterprises, the public protector, figures in a few proxy parties, and a small band of rogue politicians, including fraudster Carl Niehaus, stepped in to continue the Zuma assault on Ramaphosa. Attacks were concentrated and destructive. The weapons used revealed much about the contemporary character of the ANC organisationally: adoption of so-called radical economic transformation policies for mainly factional ends; agitation over Ramaphosa's alleged reluctance to implement conference resolutions; allegations in conjunction with public protector Mkhwebane that Ramaphosa had corrupt relations with 'white monopoly capital', had lied to Parliament on Bosasa, and wanted to privatise state-owned enterprises and diversify energy production to benefit a small band of his associates.

Ramaphosa's image of warrior against corruption and the embodiment of a new dawn was the main prize. Ramaphosa was victorious in important 2020 court cases,[61] and benefited from the Covid inter-factional truce. Yet, the assault was amplified through the afflicted economy that depended on confidence and trust in political leaders – the exact item that hinged on Ramaphosa's being shown as ethical and honest in governance. The more doubts were sown, the louder became the calls for Ramaphosa to be more decisive or forceful in his low-key leadership style[62] – even before the onset of Covid, and far more in subsequent times.

In conjunction with questions about the ethics of the leader of the new dawn, the absence of vigorous upfront leadership by Ramaphosa triggered despondency. The fight for control of the ANC was so potent – amid the enforced unity – that there was even conjecture that xenophobic riots had been instigated to embarrass Ramaphosa.[63] On the ANC front he was in a continuous battle of tactical positioning and outmanoeuvring. His strategy according to associates was to push for compacts, 'negotiate to death' – until all warring ANC parties could no longer hold out. Ramaphosa's State of the Nation addresses[64] revealed much about the balance of power in the ANC. It showed in 2019, for example, that Ramaphosa was mild in his assertion of power over counter-forces; 2020 confirmed that there were few new ideas and initiatives to pull the country from its by then Covid-exacerbated quagmire – preoccupation with power contests had been paralysing. There were multiple initiatives to radicalise public policy under the cover of Covid, but the only success was when the social security net was widened to help veil the long-existing inequalities[65] and deprivation that were brutally spotlighted through the Covid experience. It was still uncertain whether the Covid-19 crisis would also help to unify the ANC. The Ramaphosa-ists had taken power and assumed (alternatively, propagated convincingly) that the government had the policy blueprint in its National Development Plan.[66] Conference policy resolutions then forced them to move further, and faltering budgets due to additional demands amid shrinking tax collection and recurrent recessions and crises worked towards equalising the Ramaphosa and Zuma regimes.

Ramaphosa appeared confident that he had the backing of the NEC while he persevered and fed off ongoing high (with some variation) levels of public opinion poll endorsements. Ramaphosa remained the ANC saviour – there was no leader yet with a comparable measure of public trust and endorsement, who could step in to lead the ANC. Even amid mounting criticisms of Ramaphosa in Covid context, vacillating and deferring to cabinet colleagues when it was imperative for him to lead from the front, an online Ipsos poll rated him 7.34 out of 10 for handling his job during the Covid-19 outbreak.[67]

CONCLUSION: ANC LEGEND TROUBLED, TRANSITIONING

The notion of the 'nine wasted years' of Jacob Zuma's rule became synonymous with the ANC's living out two dictums that defined the organisation: 'the centre holds' and 'democratic centralism'. With the ousting of Jacob Zuma from ANC and government power, Cyril Ramaphosa's 'new dawn' ANC scrambled to put distance between themselves and Zuma. The Tripartite Alliance tried to reconstitute itself. The SACP did its utmost to never refer again to the fact that it (and its general secretary, Dr Blade Nzimande, in particular) had led the campaign to replace Thabo Mbeki with Jacob Zuma. Cosatu realigned and went silent on having split for the sake of allegiance to Zuma. In 2014, Ramaphosa, in the early days of his deputy presidency of the ANC, and in response to the public protector's report on Nkandla, argued:

> We are saying that the integrity of the president remains intact and that this president has the ability and know-how to lead our government and South Africa going forward ... [t]here was no corruption, nothing to do with Nkandla was unlawful. The 'fire pool' is not even as big as an Olympic swimming pool.[68]

The Zuma period, however, was an *ANC period*. It was the ANC as it existed that put Zuma at the helm – and facilitated, tolerated and condoned his exercise of power. The silences of those who were close to Zuma, who shared responsibility but pardoned Zuma and his circle in the name of the ANC self-correcting, came to haunt the ANC in time.

In name, slogans and calls to mobilisation, the Ramaphosa (but with Zuma-ism indelible) ANC was organisationally remarkably similar to the ANC that had entered state power a quarter of a century earlier. It carried legitimacy and a pop-ular, majoritarian mandate that was unmatched by other parties. To a lesser extent than in 1994, but still powerful in defining the organisation, it believed at some level that it was the bearer of a revolutionary future, and it let its leaders propagate the belief that it was steering South Africa towards revolutionary change. Below this surface, however, was an organisation marked by power that was tenuous: its electoral majority carefully constructed and manoeuvred; its project of schooling political cadres unable to take off; and its Integrity Commission without impact and emasculated by subjection to NEC override. Specific constituencies were mobilised to help deliver continuous dominance.

The people of South Africa were enlisted to help the ANC restore its image as the party of the people that could still deliver a better future. The process of support, however, had become more transactional. The state was still the ANC's platform for the leveraging of support and dispensing of goodwill. The ANC and national presidencies were fused, and so were state and party – and citizens had become more distrustful of both. The Zuma decade had changed the ANC and government incontrovertibly, and the people observed and experienced the unsavoury process. Full recovery was not possible, yet the ANC was surviving. The new and at best ten-uous ANC hold on state power did not offer much room for comfort. The ANC had changed, but so had society, political culture, the state and party politics in general.

NOTES

1   The work of Francoise Boucek, 2009, 'Rethinking factionalism: Typologies, intra-party dynamics and three faces of factionalism', *Party Politics*, 15 (4), 455–485, captures much of the nature of factionalism as conceptualised in this chapter.

2   Details confirmed in an interview with a CR17 campaign organiser and ongoing adviser, 22 February 2020, Johannesburg.

3   'Two centres' are more than the centres emanating from the lack of alignment between ANC elections and national elections: in this chapter the phrase denotes longer-term manifestations that compete for ownership of the ANC far beyond the roughly 18 months between ANC and general elections.

4   Gwede Mantashe, December 2017, *ANC Organisational Report*, presented to the ANC's elective conference at Nasrec. This has become a literal truth as well: from 2011 to 2019, more than 90 ANC members were assassinated, of whom roughly 80 were from KwaZulu-Natal, in intra-ANC wars for access to and control over lucrative state-busi-ness contracts. See https://www.nytimes.com/2018/09/30/world/africa/south-africa-anc-killings.html, accessed 1 March 2020.

5   Cyril Ramaphosa's inspirational call of 'Send me', in the State of the Nation address, Parliament of South Africa, 16 February 2018, https://www.gov.za/state-nation-address, accessed 17 February 2018; Qaanitah Hunter, 2019, *Balance of Power: Ramaphosa and the Future of South Africa*, Cape Town: NB Publishers, writes that speechwriter Wonderboy Peters had penned the phrase in preparation for a speech that would originally have been delivered by former president Zuma.

6   Cyril Ramaphosa, by video broadcast from within an ANC Ramaphosa faction briefing at Nasrec, 20 December 2018, leaked to eNCA by 6 pm on this date.

7   Ferial Haffajee, 'How Ramaphosa's campaign spent R400-million – and why it matters', *Daily Maverick*, 26 August 2019, https://www.dailymaverick.co.za/article/2019-08-26-how-ramaphosas-campaign-spent-r400-million-and-why-it-matters/, accessed 15 February 2020.

8   See Haffajee, 26 August 2019, op. cit. These expenses pertained to just one of the two major camps. The overall inclusive Nasrec campaign costs are likely to have been close to R1 billion.

9   Not winning the ANC presidency equated with being losers, even if a mixed slate had been voted into the top six and the NEC.

10   With reference to Zuma's associates emulating Zuma's Stalingrad strategy, also using every possible legal recourse and avenue to seek legal review and appeals of judgments that do not go their way; see also Genevieve Quintal, 'Zuma resumes Stalingrad bid to fend off prosecution', *Business Day*, 9 April 2018.

11   For example, details of the Ramaphosa campaign funds became known through illegally intercepted selected emails that were then leaked to the media to attempt the smear of improper personal conduct.

12   See Twitter campaigns from the Gupta-ist Heller–Mngxitama stable, for example https://twitter.com/hashtag/cr17leaks?lang=hr, https://blackopinion.co.za/2019/08/17/beware-of-preemptive-leaks/, accessed 1 February 2020.

13   The ANC's NEC of late August 2020 agreed on steps to counter corruption, including broad guidelines for members reporting to the Integrity Commission, or stepping aside from public duties and ANC positions should they be accused, charged or convicted. There was comfort for perpetrators, however, in the fact that, by December 2020, many of these guidelines and policies for organisational action still needed to be developed, and Integrity Commission powers still had to be firmed up.

14   Both Alliance partners by 2017 were trying to make good on their 2007 roles in leading the campaign to have Zuma instated as ANC president; see Susan Booysen, 2011, *The ANC and the Regeneration of Political Power*, Johannesburg: Wits University Press.

15   These tensions came to a head in the 2020 austerity budget that had relied on civil service salary sacrifices to limit the national budget rate of borrowing and national indebtedness.

16   ANCWL president, Bathabile Dlamini, was appeased with high-level state deployment in Sisulu's department, despite a damning track record and being cut from Ramaphosa's cabinets. Scandals in Sisulu's Department of Water Affairs about dividing up the spoils of Covid-related community assistance dented her image.

17   One of the incidents was the shooting-killing of a Congress of South African Students ANCYL member at Hammanskraal after demanding that the regional leadership resigns (November 2019).

18   D.D. Mabuza, addressing the National Council of Provinces, Parliament of South Africa, 3 March 2020.

19   For select details up to 2015, see Anthony Butler, 2015, 'The politics of numbers: National membership growth, and subnational power competition in the ANC', *Transformation*, 87, 13–31.

20   Such purchases were confirmed in revelations about items on which some of the CR17 campaign millions were spent. See Ferial Haffajee, 26 August 2019, op. cit.

21   In 2006 former Western Cape ANC premier Ebrahim Rasool's government was accused of paying two *Cape Argus* journalists, Joseph Aranes and Ashley Smith, for favourable coverage. Western Cape High Court justice Bennie Griesel released the internal ANC report to Independent Newspapers in 2012. See *Mail & Guardian*, 6 February 2012, 'Rasool's "brown envelope" report released', https://mg.co.za/article/2012-02-06-rasools-brown-envelope-report-released, accessed 1 March 2012.

22   Supra Mahumapelo, 16 December 2017, interview with Susan Booysen on sidelines of the Nasrec plenary opening session, Nasrec, Johannesburg.

23   Delegates from both camps had shared their respective lists with the author.

24   The Premier League was a group of ANC provincial chairpersons who supported Jacob Zuma from the North West, the Free State and Mpumalanga. This alliance weakened and mutated when some adopted the 'ANC unity ticket' as new line of contest.

25   Crystal Orderson, 'Ramaphosa: Destiny delivered, compromises made', *The Africa Report*, 25 March 2019, https://www.theafricareport.com/10564/ramaphosa-destiny-delivered-compromises-made/, accessed 26 March 2019.

26   As quoted in Zimasa Matiwane, 'Without Nasrec "unity slate" ANC would be limping, says David Mabuza', *Business Day*, 9 January 2019, https://www.businesslive.co.za/bd/politics/2019-01-09-without-nasrec-unity-slate-anc-would-be-limping-says-david-mabuza/, accessed 3 August 2019.

27   See Eric Naki, 'Ramaphosa calls for ANC unity and end to corruption', *The Citizen*, 21 December 2017.

28   Norimitsu Onishi and Selam Gebrekidan, 'South Africa vows to end corruption: Are its new leaders part of the problem?' *The New York Times*, 4 August 2018, https://www.nytimes.com/2018/08/04/world/africa/south-africa-anc-david-mabuza.html, accessed 4 April 2019. Works by Rehana Rossouw, 2020, *Predator Politics: Mabuza, Fred Daniel and the Great Land Scam*, Johannesburg: Jacana Media; and Sizwe Sama Yende, 2018, *Eerie Assignment: A Journalist's Nightmare in Mpumalanga*, Cape Town: Lesedi House Publishers, offer insights into Mabuza's politics.

29   See Jeanette Chabalala, '"Magashule should be behind bars", Dukwana tells state capture inquiry', *News24*, 28 August 2019, https://www.news24.com/SouthAfrica/News/magashule-should-be-behind-bars-dukwana-tells-state-capture-inquiry-20190828, accessed 11 September 2019. Leaked emails, banking records and other documents, referred to as the Igo Files in the book *Gangster State*, revealed that Magashule appeared to have had a direct financial interest in the huge contract. Before he was gunned down in Sandton in 2017, businessman Igo Mpambani and his wife, Michelle, reaped the benefits of a contentious R255 million asbestos audit project in the Free State. Leaked emails and documents link then Free State premier and subsequent ANC secretary-general, Magashule, to some of the proceeds of this deal; see Pieter-Louis Myburgh, 2019, *Gangster State: Unravelling Ace Magashule's Web of Capture*, Johannesburg: Penguin Random House South Africa.

30   Zuma was elected as Mbeki's deputy in the ANC in 1997 and became deputy president of South Africa in 1999. Claims of arms deal corruption mounted and Mbeki fired Zuma in 2005. The process snowballed, Zuma was elected ANC president in 2007, Mbeki recalled in 2008, and Zuma installed as national president in 2009. On back-

ground dynamics, see Prince Mashele and Mzukisi Qobo, 2016, *The Fall of the ANC: What Next?* Johannesburg: Picador Africa.

31 Nkosazana Dlamini-Zuma, a high-level ANC and government member in her own right, was groomed politically by former husband, Jacob Zuma, for the ANC presidential position. This was done with the extensive use of South African state resources, which were used to get her elected as chairperson of the African Union, to orchestrate her anointment by the ANCWL, and to gain her deployment to Parliament at a time that was optimal for campaigning.

32 #GuptaLeaks.com, #Guptaleaks, A collaborative investigation into state capture, see https://www.gupta-leaks.com/, accessed 2 March 2019.

33 The South African rand strengthened, and a pro-investment economic mood was encouraged.

34 The Seriti Commission of Inquiry into the arms deal had exonerated Zuma, and others. Yet the commission report was nullified in August 2019. See, for example, Greg Nicolson, 'Reversing the whitewash: Seriti Commission inquiry slammed in court', *Daily Maverick*, 12 June 2019, https://www.dailymaverick.co.za/article/2019-06-12-reversing-the-whitewash-seriti-commission-inquiry-slammed-in-court/, accessed 12 June 2019.

35 See, for example, TNS media statement, 5 April 2017, Kantar-TNS omnibus survey on Zuma's standing as president of South Africa, Johannesburg.

36 See also Juniour Khumalo, 'Tables turn as Magashule faces suit', *City Press*, 22 March 2020. The string of threats of legal suits appeared to confirm that Magashule was behind the African Transformation Movement's 2019 electoral challenge to the ANC (denied by Magashule, who nevertheless withdrew a lawsuit that he had instituted to refute the claims).

37 Duarte's son-in-law, Ian Whitley, was appointed as chief of staff for Des van Rooyen, the 2015 three-day minister of finance; she was also implicated in the state capture scandal when it was alleged that she had offered deputy finance minister, Nhanhla Nene, the role of finance minister in collaboration with the Guptas. See, for example, https://www.biznews.com/undictated/2017/12/19/tracking-anc-top-six-since-1994, accessed 2 April 2019.

38 Cyril Ramaphosa, 'Ramaphosa congratulates new ANC Limpopo leadership', *SABC News*, 24 June 2018, http://www.sabcnews.com/sabcnews/ramaphosa-congratulates-new-anc-limpopo-leaders/, accessed 25 June 2018.

39 See ANC, 2018, 'ANC candidate selection process 2019 elections', Luthuli House, Johannesburg.

40 The ANC list's quota matrix was: gender (50%), youth (35 or younger, 20%), skills (33%) and continuity of representation (40–50%). Prospective nominees also had to fulfil criteria such as 'no history of ill-discipline or corruption, no history of involvement in fostering divisions and conflict, no other breaches of the ANC's code of conduct'. Removal from the list of aspirants required 80 per cent support from list conference delegates. With the NEC itself divided and operating in truce conditions, this level constituted a guarantee of enforced consensus.

41 An example of sustained gate-keeping to eliminate anti-Zuma ANC branch representatives came from the ANC Gaby Shapiro branch, Cape Town. The branch delegate was told at Mangaung that he was not a member in good standing, despite being a member of the provincial legislature at the time. In the run-up to Nasrec the ANC regional office instructed that the branch be split in two, which would have pushed both into the below-100 member category – the minimum number of members for a branch to be in

good standing and entitled to send a voting delegate to conference. The tactic was over-ruled. Upon arrival at Nasrec the Gaby Shapiro delegate was told his membership was 'in dispute'. His vote for Ramaphosa was kept aside, and only in the end was it accepted into the final tally. Personal communication by a branch member, January 2020.

42 See Lizeka Tandwa, 'It was a "festival of chairs" – Ramaphosa on violent ANC elective conference', *News24*, 1 October 2017, https://www.news24.com/SouthAfrica/News/it-was-a-festival-of-chairs-ramaphosa-on-violent-anc-elective-conference-20171001, accessed 2 November 2018.

43 Msholozi is Jacob Zuma's clan name.

44 Ace Magashule, 7 July 2020, interview with Newzroom, https://www.youtube.com/watch?v=-hQlLEBNWZ8, accessed 8 July 2020.

45 Qaanitah Hunter and Jeff Wicks, 'Exposed: Zuma plot to oust Cyril', *Sunday Times*, 8 September 2018, https://www.pressreader.com/, accessed 2 May 2019.

46 See eNCA, 17 September 2018, 'Ramaphosa addresses Cosatu congress', https://www.enca.com/news/watch-ramaphosa-addresses-cosatu-congress, accessed 2 April 2019.

47 Cyril Ramaphosa, 30 September 2018, Winnie Madikizela-Mandela memorial lecture, City Hall, Johannesburg.

48 ANC media briefing, 1 October 2018, Luthuli House, Johannesburg.

49 Sibongakonke Shoba and Qaanitah Hunter, 'I dare you!', *Sunday Times*, 28 July 2019. The occurrences at the NEC were confirmed to the author in an interview with a presidential associate, 2 August 2019, Johannesburg.

50 Solly Mapaila, as quoted in Sheldon Morais, 'ANC parliamentary caucus' position on Mkhwebane was not on NEC meeting's agenda – Jessie Duarte', *News24*, 30 July 2019, https://www.news24.com/SouthAfrica/News/anc-parliamentary-caucus-position-on-mkhwebane-was-not-on-nec-meetings-agenda-jessie-duarte-20190730, accessed 2 August 2019.

51 In mid-2020 the public protector lost her Pretoria High Court battle to find Ramaphosa in breach of section 94(2)(b) of the Constitution, the Executive Members' Ethics Act and the Executive Ethics Code. The EFF filed for leave to appeal.

52 Earlier versions of selected parts of this section were published in my article 'The not-so-merry Zuma go-round', *Daily Maverick*, 6 June 2018, https://www.dailymaverick.co.za/opinionista/2018-06-06-the-not-so-merry-zuma-go-round/, accessed 6 June 2018.

53 Andrew Feinstein, Paul Holden and Hennie van Vuuren, 'Decision to set aside Seriti Commission findings will have a profound impact', *Daily Maverick*, 21 August 2019, https://www.dailymaverick.co.za/article/2019-08-21-decision-to-set-aside-seriti-commission-findings-will-have-a-profound-impact/, accessed 13 September 2019. See also, Arms Procurement Commission (Seriti Commission), Final Report, December 2015.

54 See Karyn Maughan, 'Desperate Jacob Zuma to appeal against R16m cost order', *Business Day*, 14 August 2019, https://www.businesslive.co.za/bd/national/2019-08-14-desperate-jacob-zuma-to-appeal-against-r16m-cost-order/, accessed 20 August 2019. Zuma was petitioning the Supreme Court of Appeal for the right to challenge a ruling that he was not lawfully entitled to state sponsorship of his legal costs. He was liable for legal fees estimated between R15 million and R32 million.

55 See also the Covid-times virtual platform 'Zooming with the Zumas', in which Zuma converses with his son Duduzane, https://www.youtube.com/watch?v=RE4uBWFupYo, accessed 21 July 2020.

56 For these quotes, see *News24*, 31 May 2018, "'I've never committed any crime" – Zuma', https://www.dailysun.co.za/News/National/ive-never-committed-any-crime-zuma-20180531-2?mobile=true, accessed 2 June 2018.

57 Susan Booysen, 6 June 2018, 'The not-so-merry Zuma go-round', https://www.wits.ac.za/news/sources/wsg-news/2018/the-not-so-merry-zuma-go-round.html, accessed 2 April 2020.

58 Ibid.

59 See Paddy Harper and Dineo Bendile, 'JZ's apostles to launch new party', *Mail & Guardian*, 1 June 2018, https://mg.co.za/article/2018-06-01-00-jzs-apostles-to-launch-new-party/, accessed 3 June 2018.

60 Interview with a journalist who is familiar with these personalities, 2 July 2019, Johannesburg. One of the original African Transformation Congress leaders, Buyisile Ngqulwana from the messianic churches, claimed that Magashule was behind the formation of the ATM. Magashule denied this.

61 The Gauteng High Court in Pretoria in March 2020 set aside the public protector report into Ramaphosa which had found that he had misled Parliament deliberately about a donation to his CR17 Nasrec campaign.

62 David Everatt, 'South Africans are trying to decode Ramaphosa (and getting it wrong)', *The Conversation*, 11 January 2018, https://theconversation.com/south-africans-are-trying-to-decode-ramaphosa-and-getting-it-wrong-89886, accessed 2 March 2019.

63 See Lester Kiewit, 'Justice cluster details crime busting plan, insists unrest is not xenophobic', *Mail & Guardian*, 10 September 2019, https://mg.co.za/article/2019-09-10-government-details-anti-crime-plan, accessed 11 September 2019.

64 See also Susan Booysen, 'Endgame is far from over', *Daily Maverick*, 6 February 2019.

65 Inequality had not lessened since 2008, and by 2018 was higher than in 1995, with a consumption Gini coefficient of 0.63; see World Bank, 2018, *An Incomplete Transition: Overcoming the Legacy of Exclusion in South Africa*, South Africa Systematic Country Diagnostic, Cape Town: UCT Press, p. 23.

66 The plan dated fast, without achieving its target or being accurate in its forecasts; by 2020 it was being updated: National Planning Commission, 2020, *A Review of the National Development Plan*, Pretoria.

67 The online poll was representative of South Africans 18 years and older who have access to the internet at home or on a smart phone (about two-thirds of South Africa's adult population); details by WhatsApp from Marí Harris, Ipsos, 21 July 2020. The poll was done before the revelations of widespread Covid corruption.

68 Cyril Ramaphosa, 24 March and 17 March 2014, respectively; https://www.politicsweb.co.za/opinion/the-anc-in-its-own-words-50-quotes, accessed 29 August 2019.

3

Boosted Election Victory, Porous Power

RESTARTING THE ELECTIONS GAME

National elections were the ANC instrument for obtaining majoritarian endorsements and asserting dominance over other political parties, irrespective of its own
organisational fragilities. As the ANC kept on sliding in the national electoral
stakes, then made a tentative but precarious recovery in 2019 and started viewing
the next round of its own internal and then national and provincial elections, a
major set of new uncertainties entered. Covid-19 brought the possibility of delays
in electoral schedules and affected political parties in their internal electoral and
campaign processes, and in their viability. This indicated the need for a longer lead
and recovery time.

A Constitutional Court judgment of mid-2020 added complications.[1] It declared
the Electoral Act No. 73 of 1998 unconstitutional in its requirement for a citizen to
be a member of a political party in order to hold national or provincial office. The
court ordered that the electoral system be amended to accommodate participation
of independent candidates in national and provincial elections. The Electoral Commission (IEC) was given two years to effect the arrangements, which may entail
minor tweaking rather than a major overhaul.[2]

The political and economic uncertainties that came with Covid-19 meant that
political parties developed a new appetite for consolidating and possibly postponing
elections. The ANC NEC 'considered the desirability' of synchronising national–
provincial elections with local elections, weighing in at one stage with possible post-
ponement of local elections.[3] The Economic Freedom Fighters (EFF) joined the

call. In times of financial austerity, the parties argued, it made sense to cut costs and focus energy on recovering from Covid. The complexities of the required constitutional change to effect a possible rescheduling were immense.

The ANC's desire to align its internal elections better with the national elections also clouded specificities of future elections. The ANC wanted to eliminate the interval between its internal and the national elections – the time lapse of roughly 18 months had become a toxic gap. A culture had taken hold, through the cases of former presidents Thabo Mbeki in 2008 and Jacob Zuma in 2018, to recall the ousted, possibly discredited ANC president from national office. Closing this gap was on the cards for the ANC, and Covid-19 assisted. The ANC's internal meetings, ranging from branch meetings to the mid-term National General Council, had all been affected and were postponed. This had effected a de facto elimination of the gap: it would offer the ANC the chance to bring its elective conference right to the doorstep of future national elections.

FRAGILE VICTORIES AND PRECARIOUS ANC POWER

Gap politics had played out ferociously in the preceding ANC transitions from internal to national elections. Voter sentiment in pre-Nasrec times revealed to the then Zuma-supportive ANC party structures that the party's days of outright majorities were limited unless it shed Zuma. The ANC's Nasrec follow-through and Ramaphosa's ascendancy into state power helped to convert positive pro-Ramaphosa citizen sentiment into ANC votes in Election 2019. Opposition party supporters rewarded the ANC for extracting itself from Jacob Zuma's pincer grip; they helped to defend Ramaphosa against his enemies in ANC ranks. These acts disrupted fragile balances of power within the main opposition, the Democratic Alliance (DA), and contributed to post-election opposition meltdown. The Ramaphosa-led ANC was proof that the ANC would be as strong as the opposition was weak – and in many instances it was easier for the ANC to keep the opposition weak than let the ANC be strong in its own right.

The ANC won Election 2019 by a margin of eight percentage points above an outright majority, and with a 37 percentage-point lead over the second-placed DA. It was the first time since the national election of 2004 that the ANC had recorded an upward movement in its overall percentage. It arrested the trend of inexorable decline. Its national result was three percentage points up on the modest base of its 2016 local election results, besides the Gauteng ANC having retained the province – against expectations – by a marginal majority. By 2019, the ANC needed every single vote in this core province.[4] Electorally, at the national level, it retained the status of a dominant party, by far overshadowing opposition party performances.

Several caveats nevertheless rendered the victory precarious. Cyril Ramaphosa rescued the ANC by buying it time, and yet inside the ANC, and at several political sites around the ANC, Ramaphosa was maligned and undermined. The ANC pulled off the major 'unity' ruse in Election 2019 yet remained divided. Much of the precarity of ANC power was not in its losing to an opposition party, but in the danger of its slipping below the *outright* majority level and finding itself in the coalition zone. Further precarity was about the ANC state and government faltering on many fronts, being unable to deliver further significant transformation and keeping voters' economic hopes alive – a factor with proven status as precursor of electoral support. In the details of the victory, there were haunting questions about its sustainability, how the ANC had secured its dominance, and the meaning it had for multiparty democracy. The questions were amplified in the Covid interregnum. The ANC government took the lead in combating Covid but also accumulated blame for failures, especially in the economy. Popular endorsements of the president remained strong, yet conversion into electoral support a few years down the line was uncertain, especially when cadres' profiteering from Covid funds was added to the mix. This tranche of cadre-led public sector corruption spanned the factions and undermined public trust that Ramaphosa could be the ethical saviour of the party.

In the multiparty context, the overall electoral verdict of 2019 was an endorsement of status quo politics – even if the electorate had been expressing profound discontent with political parties, elections and the public institutions that depended on elections. The number of participants declined, but South Africans still voted for and continued endorsing the party political options and, broadly, their policy options. Despite immense inequality and socio-economic injustice, well over 80 per cent of the participating electorate voted for parties of the political and economic centre. A key to this was arguably the ANC's unorthodoxy of playing populism, of the party itself operating between the formal rules and keeping itself positioned as the continuously renewing party, reinventing itself (in narrative), again, in 2019 as the ethical and caring party of the people working tirelessly to bring liberation. Simultaneously, the numbers constituting the popular endorsement were shrinking and cast doubt on the sustainability of the ANC's 2019 majority into future elections, unless opposition parties fared even worse.

The ANC's 2019 result revealed that the pillars of the ANC victory were fragile and probably reversible. The outcome was built on a disproportionately low level of registration by new and young voters (higher youth registration and participation would have favoured the EFF), a lower turnout (many voters disengaged or de-aligned), a diffusion of votes to insignificant micro political parties, vote-lending to Ramaphosa by opposition party supporters, an anti-Ramaphosa faction in the ANC that was opportunistically quiet in the course of the campaign but ready to pounce again post-election, and the reality of citizens having lower levels of trust in the public institutions.[5] The EFF, with the third biggest party results (and the party that showed the biggest growth even while being affected adversely by low registration in its core youth constituency), was also a party that ambiguously threatened violence as supplementary action to electoral politics. Beyond the party political endorsements, as a regular feature of South African politics multiple communities continued to complement voting with protest. There was growing evidence, too, of protests being used to obstruct voting.

Despite ringing endorsements and the successful 2019 elections, much of political activity had either moved beyond electoral participation, or elections had become hollowed out. For many, it was superficial, a national carnival, without expectations that much would come of the manifestos and their promises – except, this time around, that it was also a celebration of liberation from Zuma-ists, an expectation not entirely realistic. Dissent, disappointment and disillusionment with the ANC often moved into withdrawal from voting and diversion into minor parties, trends that helped minimise ANC damage in this game of electoral majorities. The election helped construct sustained ANC dominance, albeit of a precarious type.

The carnival character was amplified through developments in the ANC and its campaign. Ramaphosa and his CR17-ers, along with the then-under-control and quiet Zuma-ist camp (which had to slip into the background in order to enable the Ramaphosa-ists to win the election for the ANC), had convinced ANC supporters and the bulk of the active electorate that was still favourably disposed to finding reasons to vote for the ANC that it had retained the capacity to self-correct. As the election proceedings, results and aftermath showed, the scarred ANC remained the voters' predominant choice. The ANC's fight was not against any of the opposition parties in particular but, rather, to retain an outright majority, against sacrificing the credibility of public institutions in its care, and struggling against citizens and voters absconding from the electoral process, or searching for more effective ways to participate and influence future politics. These trends seemed likely to recur in future elections.

RUN-UP TO ELECTION 2019: FACTIONS, FISSURES AND ESTIMATED ELECTORAL FUTURES

It seemed entirely possible that the ANC dynamics defining Election 2019 would play out as variations to a theme in the election planned for 2024, subject to the shifting ground of post-Covid schedules and uneven damage to established parties. In 2017, in the early run-up to Election 2019, before reliable public opinion polls stabilised and indicated that the voters were standing by an arguably transformed ANC, there were strong arguments that South Africa nationally and in select provinces was destined to become the site of continuous, unstable minority and coalition governments[6] formed especially with now-exorcised former ANC members who had relocated to the EFF. Another possibility was that the DA might scoop up angry splinter groups of disaffected ANC supporters and then help the ANC to build majorities.

Ramaphosa, inhibited by his narrow Nasrec victory, his unity accord and the baggage of the Zuma epoch, had a difficult dual task in Election 2019. He had to balance taking the ANC forward to a more secure, guaranteed future through national electoral victory with simultaneously keeping the ANC factions united. 'Retaining ANC unity' was a task in the line of a higher, ordained mission to serve the hallowed former liberation movement with its reputation of 'self-correcting'.[7] It was also dictated by practical necessity. Holding the ANC factions together was synonymous with stopping a further split, even if it meant prevarication on policy, governance and ANC ethics. Another major party split, in the mode of the United Democratic Movement (UDM), Congress of the People (Cope) and the EFF, would guarantee ANC slippage below the level of outright majority. 'Ramaphoria' – then palpable rather than ephemeral – entered to facilitate this task by contributing the belief that Ramaphosa would be more ethical and efficient than his predecessor. Ramaphosa's approval ratings (see Figure 3.1) were relatively stable, declining slightly after the original wave of Ramaphoria but stabilising again above 60 per cent on national approvals. For the ANC, Ramaphosa's entrance meant that at last the party had a leader whose ratings exceeded the ANC's. In the late 2017 ratings, the last of Zuma as president, a substantial gap existed between Zuma's continuously declining and dismal public endorsements and the ANC's moderated but still high electoral support – Zuma's approval ratings were less than half of those of the ANC.[8] Voter rejection of Zuma was further demonstrated in the Citizen Surveys poll that asked ANC supporters how his ongoing, post-resignation role in the ANC election campaign would influence their vote – 53 per cent of potential ANC voters responded that they would be less likely to vote for the ANC.[9] Ramaphosa's popular base was confirmed in the finding that 65 per cent of ANC supporters preferred Ramaphosa to Zuma as leader of the ANC. ANC performance in elections would be improved (see Figure 3.2) if there was a leader with higher endorsements than the party. After the election period, citizens also appeared to be looking beyond the post-election accusations of impropriety by Ramaphosa's centring on campaign donations and truthfulness in responding on these issues in Parliament.[10]

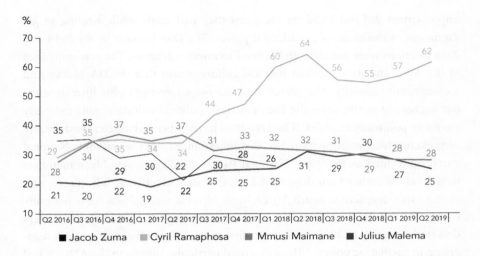

Figure 3.1: Ramaphoria and support for other party political leaders, 2016–2019

Note: Citizen Surveys, 2019, based on the quarterly survey in a representative sample of 3 900 South Africans; the margin of error was 1.5%.

Source: https://www.dailymaverick.co.za/article/2019-09-05-eff-violence-up-but-popularity-ratings-way-down/, accessed 2 May 2019

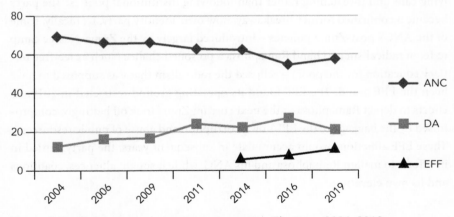

Figure 3.2: Support gap between main parties, Elections 2004–2019

Source: IEC, www.elections.org.za, multiple windows, accessed 5 July 2019

The ANC's 2019 electoral fortunes were enhanced by the weaknesses of the opposition parties. Deficits in opposition party performances were both self-induced and actively facilitated by the ANC, which realised that it could only be as strong as the opposition parties were weak. Hence, the DA's retreat and EFF's modest improvement did not build on the gains they had made while helping to get Zuma out of positions of presidential power. The DA's inroads in the 2014 and 2016 elections were tentative and limited to minor advances. The predominance of the ANC and its associated political culture meant that the DA had to find a compromise identity. The presence of the old-white-right plus liberals without anchorage in the changing South African political culture meant the party would be politically exposed. It had retained its old liberal character (and, largely unspoken, white racial/racist-nationalist inheritance from the erstwhile National Party, reinvented as the 'New' National Party). Its diverse new black members were 'visitors' rather than drivers of a focused new identity. A full quarter of a century into democratic South Africa, being 'diverse' still did not come naturally to the DA, and many in its core constituencies among white and coloured voters deserted the party in 2019, for reasons that ranged from objection to weak leadership to vacillating policy.[11] The EFF posed particular threats to the ANC. It had a sustained footing among the rising group of youthful, frequently unemployed and angry parts of the electorate (a potential voting bloc that could increasingly pose dangers to the ANC post-Covid, insofar as they were interested in voting). It brought many (but not all, by far) of these youths into the system. Simultaneously, the EFF played the electoral game conditionally by mastering populist rallying calls and threatening rather than following institutional politics. The party became a confirmed former breakaway, now own-identity party. Ironically, some of the ANC's post-Zuma policies – introduced largely by the Zuma-Nasrec camp to feign radicalism and hand Ramaphosa a poisoned chalice (such as fee-free tertiary education for the poor) – eclipsed the radicalism that was supposed to have been the EFF brand. The EFF found its operating ground restricted in 2019. Its efforts to depict Ramaphosa as the next corrupt Zuma took off haltingly, compromised by the baggage of the EFF's own corruption and abuse of public resources.[12] These EFF afflictions would accumulate in subsequent years: the party battled in its efforts to malign Ramaphosa and his ANC, while it sought alliances, coalitions and its own elevation.

ANC CAMPAIGN, 'STAY ON MESSAGE!'

In the run-up to Election 2019 the ANC was in a weak state. Much depended on its ability to persuade the electorate that Ramaphosa rather than Zuma was in charge, even if Ramaphosa by now was the ANC's and the national president. Ramaphosa's ANC had to convince the electorate that the process of state clean-up of corruption and capture was on track and that a next ANC government would stabilise, and then grow, the economy. With post-election and Covid-context hindsight, this metamorphosed into 'persuading the electorate that the Ramaphosa-ists are not also substantially compromised, tainted, complicit and unable to act to the extent of becoming indistinguishable from Zuma-ists, for most practical purposes'.[13]

The ANC was well aware (judging by a report delivered to central ANC structures a year before the 2019 election) that it had alienated much of the electorate and would need to campaign determinedly to retain its outright majority. The hard-hitting report highlighted:

> 'For the first time in the history of our democracy the ANC faces the possibility of receiving less than 50% of the votes in national elections. Through our own weaknesses and negative tendencies we have squandered the goodwill we enjoyed from voters in the past 24 years. We now face the possibility of losing majority support in most large cities and in much of the economic heartland of South Africa.'
>
> 'If we want to make a significant impact on voter mood we need to use the next 15 months to demonstrate political will, concrete actions, and capacity to deal with these issues. This includes concrete and drastic action (not just statements) against corruption, especially among our leaders, and [to] strengthen the capacity of the state to investigate and prosecute offenders. We also have to provide clear action and proof that we are prioritising job creation and economic development and that our efforts are bearing fruit.'[14]

The lingering presence of Jacob Zuma blocked the ANC campaign repeatedly. The ANC was never fully in charge of its own campaign. The commissions of inquiry had a relentless albeit slow dynamic – as the campaign progressed, revelations of malfeasance (affecting mostly the Zuma-ists, but also Ramaphosa's ANC) and evidence of politicians beholden to the interests of corrupt business, unfolded across the Zondo, Mokgoro, Nugent and other commissions of inquiry. Simultaneously, before the 2019 election and even more harshly thereafter, the public utility company, Eskom, faltered; South African Airways imploded and international ratings companies continued to downgrade the country. The commissions were only scratching the surface and the problems of state-owned enterprises accumulated. The voters who still nurtured ANC loyalty had no choice but to suspend their disbelief, aided by the knowledge that there were no assurances the opposition parties would fare better.

ANC CAMPAIGN MESSAGES: GETTING HELP FIGHTING FOR CHANGE

The ANC tried to let its campaign messages and slogans project a thread that connected its 2019 campaign to preceding, victorious ones. It had to show in 2019 that
it remained *the same* liberation movement-party, and that the current ANC was as
determined as its predecessors to serve South Africans and bring transformation
and service delivery. It conceptualised this as the ANC's ongoing revolution. The
ANC campaign slogans from 1994 to 2019 wove this thread, showing consistency
if not repetition:

- A better life for all. Now is the time (1994)
- Together fighting for change (1999)
- A people's contract to create work and fight poverty (2004)
- Working together we can do more (2009)
- Together we move South Africa forward (2014)
- Let's grow South Africa together (2019).

Voters were asked to believe that there was *one* ANC that was contesting, *one*
policy direction to vote for,[15] and that this party in the next term would be making
more substantive progress than before in transforming the country socio-econom-
ically and removing corrupt cadres. The message veiled volumes of information
about dissidence and factional fightback, proxy policy battles and determination
in parts of the ANC to bring down Ramaphosa. Part of the ANC campaign was in
the open – for example, triumphant Ramaphosa campaigning in Zuma heartland,
KwaZulu-Natal.[16] The ongoing factional contest played out in many of the ANC
branches where the battle was to transfer (or subvert) factional loyalties into the
next set of representatives for provincial legislatures and Parliament. There were
serial contraindications to 'ANC unity' as well. Voters were mindful, for example,
of the September 2018 Maharani plot orchestrated by ANC secretary-general Ace
Magashule, and the ANC candidate list controversy when Magashule reportedly
manipulated the list to favour Zuma-ists. The ANC made a fair display of unity at
its campaign launch. The mass rally was a politically civil occasion: no humiliation
of President Cyril Ramaphosa, despite pro-Zuma chanting. Imposed discipline in
Zuma heartland helped to manage tensions – but there was neither fervour nor
excitement. This was a parade of the tactically constructed, post-Zuma ANC that
came without heart, but was sufficient to persuade the voters of renewal.

Opposition parties had ammunition on the continuously vulnerable Ramaphosa.
He had had a role, albeit indirect and not unambiguously attributable, in the 2012
Marikana massacre; he had received controversial and suspected-to-be-corrupt

funding, including from the implicated-in-corruption Bosasa (African Global Investments, subsequently liquidated) to fund his Nasrec internal ANC election campaign (and was alleged to have lied to Parliament about the Bosasa donation and his knowledge generally of who his donors were); he was complicit in Zuma's 'nine wasted years'; he was accused, probably unfairly, of having sold out Mass Democratic Movement comrades in the popular resistance of the 1980s, and in being a billionaire, regularly placed in the categories of 'big capital' and associated with 'white monopoly capital'. Reliance on this single leader rendered the ANC precariously vulnerable.

Then, there was the knowledge derived from several high-level surveys that voter trust in the state institutions run by the ANC had been declining. After the election it was confirmed that fewer than one-third of the voters who had voted for it had actually *felt close* to the ANC and that a majority of the voting electorate did not believe at the time of the election that South Africa *was heading in the right direction*.[17] They also did not have hope that *the economy was about to create a better future*, a recognised indicator of sustained voting for governing parties. Their *trust in the ANC* was also below 40 per cent. Ironically, the ANC won an outright majority while in a state of internal ambiguity and extensive external doubt about the party-movement.

The ANC's self-projection as the continuous personification of the struggle for liberation was, again in 2019, the most treasured of its campaign tools. It portrayed itself as *the authentic struggle party*. There were frequent reminders of the work of the heroes of the struggle, the physical and psychological brutality of apartheid, and how the struggle to defeat the legacies of apartheid was helping to explain the deficit in transformation that persisted to the time of Election 2019. It would not make sense, the argument went, to thrust aside the liberator.

OPPOSITION PARTY CAMPAIGNS FAILING TO CAPITALISE ON ANC WEAKNESSES

The contests over the character and ownership of the ANC made an impact on opposition parties. The electorate's attention remained on the ANC, which had, in many respects, been running against itself. Many ANC supporters chose abstention over the multipartyist option of a vote for some opposition party; many opposition party supporters acted similarly.

As the DA embraced liberalism but attempted to transform into a more socially conscious party with appeal to larger numbers of previously-ANC voters, it became more fragile, more susceptible to internal disputes and fractioning and was experienced as divided and indecisive. The EFF, with problems of its own, was the 'big' (at a four percentage point gains level) 2019 winner. It established sound footholds in coastal provinces (for example, in KwaZulu-Natal) where it had previously had a negligible presence.[18] The opposition parties, however, did not come to constitute externalised threats to Ramaphosa's ANC. The main threats remained within.

When the ANC catapulted into Ramaphoria, the opposition parties could no longer equate the ANC with Zuma, and lost the Zuma bait, the low-hanging fruit that had discredited the ANC. From late 2018 on, they started reclaiming some footholds, latching onto the major ANC fault-line of vacillation between Zuma past, Ramaphosa present and ambiguous future. The ongoing, vocal presence of discredited people in the ANC top structures, repeated actions and reports of planned revenge on Ramaphosa, the slow turning of the wheels of justice through the commissions of inquiry, and public outrage at Covid-related corruption offered platforms for opposition parties that remained poorly utilised. The trends towards de-institutionalisation and de-alignment in party and electoral politics resonated with the directions of the political parties themselves, and all of the main parties in Election 2019 used populist rhetoric, appearing to mobilise those who had lost (or had never had) trust in the avenues of liberal multiparty democracy.[19] Based on a study of the parties' policy stances, it has been argued that all main parties displayed this rhetoric, yet it was defeated by people still refusing to vote – the DA lost rather than gained votes through its populist rhetoric.[20]

SHIFTING POLITICAL CULTURE AND CHANGING TEXTURE OF DEMOCRACY

Nowhere were the changes in the texture of belief in democracy more tangible than in Election 2019. South African political culture had been changing, conditioned by popular experiences that ranged from enduring exposure to corrupt and self-serving politicians, to paper tiger policies, to widespread state institutional failures that were frequently due to corruption and incompetence – and protracted lack of political will to acknowledge and address these problems. Evidence of the changes in political culture was all around. Cynicism, discontent and at best a poorly substantiated belief that Election 2019 'would help make things better' had replaced starry-eyed trust in leaders and political parties, the multiparty system and competitive elections. The ANC had prevailed as government nevertheless. The UN World Happiness Report revealed that South Africa came in at 107 on the list of 156 countries surveyed.[21]

The public narratives on voter (dis)engagement with Election 2019 often centred on apathy, lack of interest or even laziness (of voters). These symptoms were part of a complex process of the de-institutionalisation of political dissent and de-alignment from political parties. Disengagement from the ANC was often in the form of politically emotive dissent – that was not channelled pro rata into opposition political parties. Some transfer occurred, but much of it moved instead into a political Neverland that also constituted a broader band of ANC diffuse hegemony – in the sense of these voters feeling alienated from the ANC but not transferring identification and loyalty elsewhere.

UNFOLDING DE-ALIGNMENT FROM PARTY POLITICS

Despite his formal departure, Zuma reoccurred continuously in ANC politics, either personally or through his disciples and de facto successors and heirs. The former president was still revered by loyalists, tolerated and elevated by others – and in the process gave voters little reason to suspend their questioning of the extent to which Ramaphosa really represented a new ANC with values that replaced those of the Zuma era.

For many, non-participation in elections was in response to disillusionment with the politics of parties and government or due to a decline in trust in political parties.[22] An Ipsos poll at the time found that around 40 per cent of the respondents in this nationally representative study (including those who endorsed the ANC as their party of choice) were sceptical about their chosen parties' abilities and character. In a follow-up survey, 37 per cent of the registered voters in the poll series said that none of the political parties represented the views of the respondent (while a meagre 45 per cent felt some political party *did* represent that respondent's view).[23] Such orientations were corroborated through a Citizen Surveys poll, which found that 70 per cent of citizens did not believe political parties could solve the problems of South Africa.[24] In a Gauteng study, similarly, about a third of the middle class attributed their intended electoral abstention to scepticism of political parties that fail to represent citizen interests.[25] In addition, in Gauteng about half of the 2019 voters identified themselves as floating voters (undecided as to which party to vote for), while two-thirds indicated their cynicism, and 60 per cent of the poor were disengaging. A high proportion of even those who had voted in 2019 – close to 30 per cent – had decided either in the month prior to the election (19 per cent) or on voting day (10 per cent) which party would get their vote.[26]

There is an accumulating volume of data that corroborates the unfolding process of voter de-alignment, including from many other polling organisations and scholarly projects. Afrobarometer data confirm the loss of trust in the ANC among the electorate in general, which had reached 38 per cent in 2018, down from 62 per cent in 2006.[27] Ipsos analyses focused on the trust levels of party supporters in their own parties (percentages were obviously higher than those of the electorate in general in any specific party): from November 2017 to April 2019, among its own supporters, the ANC had gained resurrected internal trust levels; they matched those of the main opposition parties, showing that in the early days of Ramaphosa the ANC had corrected its declines and was retaining its own support base.[28]

Citizens did not believe that voting was necessarily helpful to gain better representation, realised rights and accountability. When Ipsos counterposed protest and voting, 40 per cent agreed that 'protest is the only way to get service delivery' – and another 42 per cent said it was 'not the only way'. The results affirmed the findings of more than a decade earlier, when survey respondents first registered their dual repertoire of believing in both protest and voting, rather than choosing between the two.[29] Although the repertoire persisted, the configuration of the interface between the two had been changing – while many voters still embraced voting, their belief in it had declined.

RAMAPHOSA THE ANC ELECTORAL SAVIOUR WITH SUSPECT WINGS

Election 2019 illustrated the extent to which party political engagement and choice in the ANC at the time had come to centre on individual party leadership, and in particular on Cyril Ramaphosa. Even in the post-Ramaphoria days, such as Covid times when Ramaphosa was criticised and popular trust in him declined, other ANC leaders did not rise to surpass him. ANC internal research of late 2016 had suggested that in an election with Zuma or a Zuma associate as the top candidate, the ANC would fail to get an outright majority (and this weighed heavily on the minds of delegates to the Nasrec elective conference).[30]

An Ipsos Mobile Pulse poll in May 2018, still at the height of Ramaphoria, confirmed high-level positive evaluations of Ramaphosa's performance in government and in relation to the ANC in government.[31] Of registered voters, 76 per cent said they approved of the job that Ramaphosa was doing as president of South Africa, while 79 per cent approved of the job he was doing in handling the economy.[32] With regard to the ANC polling result of the May 2018 period, it was reported that citizens' levels of confidence and trust in government were both on the rise.[33] With public opinion behind him, Ramaphosa helped elevate the ANC from polling below 50 per cent under the leadership of Zuma or a Zuma proxy, to presidential approval ratings of well over 60 per cent and party polling of around 60 per cent. In pre-Nasrec public polling, it was shown that Ramaphosa, at 47 per cent support in the fourth quarter of 2017, was 18 percentage points stronger than the Zuma-associated rival, Nkosazana Dlamini-Zuma.[34]

The ANC campaign head for 2019, Fikile Mbalula, reflected on how Ramaphosa had resuscitated trust in the ANC: '[Ramaphosa] became a game changer with the Nasrec conference of the ANC. If things did not change for the better, who knows? We would have dropped to 40 per cent …'[35] Besides confirming the ANC's findings, the sentiment aligned with a 2017 Ipsos survey that had found that only 18 per cent of adults had wanted Zuma to see out his presidential term, and that his approval rating had fallen to 2.8 out of 10, compared with the 6.7 and 8.7 for presidential predecessors Thabo Mbeki and Nelson Mandela respectively.[36] This testified to the damage Zuma was inflicting. It affected party organisers and ANC branches, and Nasrec conference delegates swung sufficiently to enable Ramaphosa's ascendance. Irrespective of whether they liked and believed in Ramaphosa, or whether they were corruption-free or intended turning their backs on public sector corrupt practices, delegates realised that there would not be outright ANC political control over the state beyond Election 2019 without putting Ramaphosa in power.[37]

FRAGILE ANC SURVIVAL PLAYING OUT IN THE DETAILS OF ELECTION 2019

Modest and declining participation in national and provincial elections combined cumulatively with declining levels of ANC support (and insubstantial advances of opposition parties) to present a changing picture of the South African electorate and electoral politics. Lower levels of registration to vote and lower turnout rates revealed details of declining participation (Table 3.1).

The results of Election 2019 also backed notions of the de-institutionalisation of politics and elections. As voters decided on how to engage with multipartyism in Election 2019, a spectrum of participation–non-participation actions was evident. All options were practised – and they revealed much of the changing character of South Africa's multiparty democracy:

- Apathy, in its pure form or as political statement, conscious refusal to register as voter;
- Registration as voter, followed by either voting or abstention from voting;

Table 3.1: National turnout in South African elections, 1994–2019

Variable	1994	1999	2004	2009	2014	2019
Estimated SA population (range)	38.6–40.6m	41.3–44.8m	42.8–47.8m	49.1–50.1m	54.0–55.0m	55.9–58.6m
Estimated voting age population (VAP; ranges) (2)	22.5–23.1m	25.3–26.2m	27.9–30.2m	30.2–33.1m	31.4–36.5m	37.4–39.8m
Total number of votes cast	19.9m	16.2m	15.9m	17.9m	18.7m	17.7m
Total number of valid votes cast	19.5m	16.0m	15.6m	17.7m	18.4m	17.4m
Number of registered voters	No registration	18.17m	20.68m	23.18m	25.39m	26.78m
Voter turnout (%)		89.3	76.7	77.3	73.5	66.0
Spoilt votes (%)		1.55	1.48	1.31	1.29	1.33
Turnout of VAP (%)	86	71.8	57.8	59.8	57.1	49.3
ANC vote as proportion of total valid votes (%)	62.6	66.4	69.7	65.9	62.2	57.5
ANC vote as proportion of registered voters (%)	53.8	46.9	39.6	38.8	35.00	28.0
ANC vote as proportion of VAP (%)	54.4	41.9	36.0	35.1	31.3	25.2

Sources: Author's calculations, also informed by Bruce Bartlett, 27 May 2019, 'South Africa's voter turnout: A mathematician runs the numbers', https://theconversation.com/south-africas-voter-turnout-a-mathematician-runs-the-numbers-117199, accessed 12 June 2019; Jonas, 2019; Booysen, 2015; IEC, 2019, https://www.elections.org.za/NPEDashboard/app/dashboard.html, accessed 3 August 2019; Collette Schulz-Herzenberg, 2014, *Voter participation in the South African election*, Institute for Security Studies, Policy Brief No. 61; StatsSA, 2018, Mid-year population estimates 2018. Statistical Release P0302, http://www.statssa.gov.za/publications/P0302/P03022018.pdf, accessed 14 June 2019; GroundUp, 2019, https://www.groundup.org.za/article/first-time-most-adults-didnt-vote/; IDEA, https://www.idea.int/data-tools/country-view/310/40, accessed 3 June 2019 and 2 March 2020

- Voting on only one of the ballots, even if entitled to do both, or voting on both ballots;[38]
- Voting for the same party on both ballots, or splitting the vote, voting for different parties on the national and provincial ballots;[39]
- Deliberately spoiling one or both of the national and provincial ballots; and
- Community protest in conjunction with voting, or protest action as substitute for voting.

REGISTRATION AND VARIABLE CITIZEN UPTAKE OF ELECTION 2019[40]

Large numbers of South African voters chose to withdraw from electoral participation, or simply not to become involved by not registering in the first place. This was true for young, under-30 voters, but also extended to a broader age range. The gap between eligible and registered voters had been hovering at around 6 to 8 million from 1999 (when registration became a requirement for voting) to 2014.[41] In Election 2019 it rose to 10 million. The 2019 voter registration level of about 72 per cent was far lower than the 80 per cent attained in 2014. The IEC said that a total of 9.8 million eligible voters did not register to vote and that 6 million of these voters were under the age of 30. In the 2016 municipal elections, of the 11.9 million 18- to 29-year-olds eligible to vote, only 6.3 million (53 per cent) had been registered.

The lowest registration ever across the general population was also reflected among youth. Among the eligible youth – those aged from 18 to 29 years – there was a 47 per cent drop in the registration of 18- and 19-year-olds in comparison with the 2014 national elections, and a 9 per cent drop over the same period in the 20–29 age group.[42] Some of this was attributable to the lack of interest and apathy that generally characterise youth in their engagement with elections; for the rest, factors specific to South African politics and the spirit of the time came into play. Voter apathy among the youth had been growing since the early days of democracy. The statistics generated by the Parliamentary Monitoring Group confirmed that overall there were 6 million young people between 18 and 29 years of age who had not voted in Election 2019. There was a sense among the youth that politics can be done better using alternative channels, including protest and campaigns through social media, or direct action.

Disengagement had been growing over time. A comparison of the 2014 and 2019 registration figures highlighted the extent of the drop (Table 3.2). The born-frees commonly lacked interest in registering for Election 2019, despite many attempts

Table 3.2: Declining voter registration by gender and age group, Elections 2014–2019

Age groups – ages in years	18–19	20–29	30–39	40–49	50–59	60–69	70–79	80+
2014 – Total number of registered voters: 25.39m								
Female	289 408	2 327 288	2 361 236	2 086 363	1 729 369	1 048 480	536 401	217 735
Male	244 657	1 823 625	1 912 716	1 623 711	1 295 653	759 782	308 710	89 446
2019 – Total number of registered voters: 26.78m								
Gender								
Female	194 310	2 884 191	3 532 579	2 873 555	2 352 758	1 573 858	829 506	465 712
Male	155 646	2 434 588	3 147 158	2 594 868	1 865 228	1 152 765	498 486	180 965
Age								
% Registered	1.3	19.8	25.0	20.5	15.8	10.2	5.0	2.4
% of VAP	5.1	27.3	25.1	17.0	12.2	7.9	3.8	1.5

Sources: www.elections.org.za/content/elections/election-reports, various windows, accessed 11 July 2019

to mobilise them.[43] There was a stern message for the ANC: that it was no longer a liberation movement that the youth felt it needed to reward and bolster, through electoral participation, as recognition for its contribution to liberation. For the EFF there were comparable indications: that its core constituency, the young, was largely unavailable to bolster the party's performance.

Turnout and confirmed citizen uptake of Election 2019

The voting age population increased from the estimates of 22.9 million in 1994 to approximately 38.7 million in 2019.[44] The total number of registered voters showed an associated (although not proportionate) increase, rising by about 35 per cent from 18.2 million in 1999 (there was no voter registration in 1994) to 26.8 million in 2019. Despite these increases, the total number of votes cast declined by 1 million in 2019 compared with 2014 – on national totals, 983 155 fewer voters voted in 2019.

Turnout in Election 2019 was noticeably lower than in previous national-level elections. It declined from 73.5 per cent in 2014 to 66.0 (65.99) per cent in 2019, a drop of 7.49 percentage points (Table 3.1). (Turnout in the two local elections of 2011 and 2016 was 57.6 per cent and 58.0 per cent respectively – lower turnout in local elections is commonplace.) In the course of the preceding two decades, national-level participation thus dropped from 89 to 66 per cent and in some provinces these declines were even more pronounced. Simultaneously, from 2014 to 2019 the number of votes cast declined by 1 million – from 18.7 to 17.7 million, despite the rise overall in the number of registered voters. For the first time since 1994, slightly more than half the adult voting age population did not go out and vote.[45] This trend of voters losing interest in participating, or deciding to abstain in protest against unsatisfactory politics, is best illustrated through the drop from the estimated 86 per cent in 1994 to 49 per cent in 2019 of voter turnout as a proportion of the estimated voting age population. Based on these population estimates, only about one-quarter of citizens eligible to vote had endorsed the ANC in Election 2019 (Table 3.1).

Lower turnout was realised differentially across the nine provinces, ranging from 56 to 68 per cent. Gauteng, the province with the highest number of voters, also had the highest provincial turnout. (It was the province with the closest contest.) KwaZulu-Natal, the province with the second highest number of registered voters, had the third highest turnout, just behind the Western Cape. The hierarchy of 2019 provincial turnout was, from highest to lowest: Gauteng, Western Cape, KwaZulu-Natal, Northern Cape, Mpumalanga, Free State, Eastern Cape, North West and Limpopo (Table 3.3).

Table 3.3:   South Africa's national and provincial voter turnout in elections, 1999–2019

Province	2019 number of registered voters	2019 number of voters who voted	Turnout percentages, 1999–2019				
			1999	2004	2009	2014	2019
Gauteng	6 381 220	4 357 348	89.2	74.2	75.6	73.0	68.2
Western Cape	3 128 567	2 073 728	85.9	71.3	75.5	72.8	66.2
KwaZulu-Natal	5 524 666	3 654 701	87.4	72.8	78.8	76.0	66.1
Northern Cape	626 471	401 663	88.2	74.7	74.0	71.3	64.1
Mpumalanga	1 951 776	1 233 544	90.1	78.3	77.6	72.9	63.2
Free State	1 462 508	897 185	90.4	77.8	75.6	71.0	61.3
Eastern Cape	3 363 161	2 001 262	89.9	79.3	74.9	68.3	59.5
North West	1 702 728	970 669	86.9	75.6	70.1	66.3	57.0
Limpopo	2 608 460	1 470 230	91.1	74.8	67.1	60.7	56.3
National	26.8m	17.7m	89.3	76.7	77.3	73.5	66.0

Source: IEC, 27 May 2019, cited in https://africacheck.org/reports/quick-read-south-africas-2019-election-in-numbers/, accessed 17 June 2019

The total number of voters registered and the ANC's 2019 totals connect in important ways. In 2019, the ANC received its *lowest number of votes* across all six of the national elections since 1994, despite the estimated size of the voting age population having grown by roughly 13 million in the 25-year period. The votes the ANC received in the six elections were 12 237 655 (1994); 10 601 330 (1999); 10 880 915 (2004); 11 650 748 (2009); 11 436 921 (2014); and 10 026 475 (2019). It was, nevertheless, worse proportionately for opposition parties.[46] Whereas the ANC shed 1.4 million votes from 2014 to 2019, the DA, on a far smaller base, lost 480 000.[47]

GroundUp confirmed the likely link between anger at governing parties and non-participation, summarising '[t]he inevitable disappointment of ruling parties – and we use the plural because not only the ANC rules at provincial and local level – failing to fulfil their promises plus the massive corruption of the Zuma administration have probably contributed to low participation'.[48]

Spoilt and split ballots as expression of discontent

Fewer ballots were spoilt in Election 2019 than in 2014; hence spoilt ballots had a relatively minor impact and were unlikely to be a major indicator of voter discontent. However, if one adds spoilt ballot papers to non-registration and abstention, the overall chunk suggests deliberate refusal by a significant number of South African voters to participate in the electoral system and/or to exercise a party political choice. It was notable, though, that across the provinces there were higher levels of spoilage at national than provincial levels. There was no evidence of disproportionate spoilage coming from specific provinces.

The ANC is no newcomer to benefiting from tactical voting in the form of split ballots. The details in Table 3.4 show how the ANC had, in previous elections, received more votes on the national than the provincial ballots. In Election 2019, this became more pronounced. Larger differences occurred in national versus provincial tallies for the three main opposition parties, indicating decisions by significant numbers of opposition voters to support the national leadership of the ANC.

The ANC's national edge (number of votes more for the ANC at national than at provincial level, in a particular province) was an indicator of this phenomenon.[49] In Gauteng, the ANC had a huge edge in 2019, ascending since 2014. The number was also remarkable because of the ANC's national vote count that was roughly 1 million lower than in 2014. In other provinces, the ANC edge dropped to small and even marginal across the two elections (Table 3.5): opposition party voters' 2019 endorsements of the ANC at national level were substantial, even if only

136 605 votes more than five years previously. Both the two main opposition parties (and especially the DA) forfeited a portion of national-level votes in favour of the ANC, probably in aid of 'saving Ramaphosa' (from his intra-ANC opponents). It was only a part of the gap that could be attributed to out-of-province-of-registration voting. The EFF had started in 2014 with a relatively strong standing in terms of getting more votes nationally than provincially. The DA could only muster more votes nationally than provincially in North West.

Table 3.4: National 'vote edge' of the ANC, DA and EFF, 2014–2019

ANC			
Province	2014 ANC edge Votes more (+) or fewer (−) at national than provincial level	2019 ANC edge Votes more (+) or fewer (−) at national than provincial level	Gain (+) or reduction (−) in ANC edge, 2014 to 2019
Gauteng	+203 448	+245 726	+42 278
KwaZulu-Natal	+55 786	+75 042	+19 256
Western Cape	+39 555	+70 493	+30 938
Limpopo	+53 557	+66 791	+13 234
Mpumalanga	+46 233	+60 167	+14 558
North West	+30 314	+42 446	+12 132
Eastern Cape	+58 993	+42 318	−16 675
Free State	+12 406	+29 445	+17 039
Northern Cape	+6 487	+10 956	+4 469
DA			
Province	2014 DA edge Votes more (+) or fewer (−) at national than provincial level	2019 DA edge Votes more (+) or fewer (−) at national than provincial level	Gain (+) or reduction (−) in DA edge, 2014 to 2019
Gauteng	−39 139	−72 860	−33 721
KwaZulu-Natal	+28 031	+20 118	−7 913
Western Cape	−18 221	−33 582	−15 361
Limpopo	+5 838	+2 706	−3 132
Mpumalanga	+168	−2 865	−3 033
North West	+3 381	+5 679	+2 298
Eastern Cape	+2 734	−7 238	−9 972
Free State	+3 300	−2 244	−5 544
Northern Cape	+966	−1 221	−2 187

continued

	EFF		
Province	2014 EFF edge Votes more (+) or fewer (−) at national than provincial level	2019 EFF edge Votes more (+) or fewer (−) at national than provincial level	Gain (+) or reduction (−) in EFF edge, 2014 to 2019
Gauteng	+19 756	−21 642	−41 398
KwaZulu-Natal	+5 561	+14 471	+8 910
Western Cape	+5 518	+5 353	−165
Limpopo	−494	−11 049	−10 555
Mpumalanga	+1 614	−9 147	−10 761
North West	−2 615	−8 103	−5 488
Eastern Cape	+9 007	+1 078	−7 929
Free State	−1 115	−6 199	−5 084
Northern Cape	+1 132	+1 352	+220

Note: 'Vote edge' designates the number of votes more (+) or fewer (−) at national than provincial level. The figures in the 2nd and 3rd columns are derived by subtracting the provincial vote per province from the national vote per province, first for 2014 and then for 2019. '+' in the 2nd and 3rd columns indicates that the party's national vote was bigger than its provincial vote, and '−' indicates the national vote was smaller than the provincial.

Source: Author's calculations, using IEC data at www.elections.org.za, accessed 16 June 2019

Small, new and proxy parties as vehicle of discontent

The huge number of small and new, unproven parties contesting Election 2019 constituted one of the alternatives to abstention.[50] There were 76 parties contesting nationally *and* in one or more of the provincial elections. Besides the 48 parties on the national ballot (19 in 1994; Table 3.5), a further 28 competed only in one or more of the nine provincial elections. Eight out of 14 parties that won representation in the National Assembly in 2019 (seven in 1994) can be classified as small political parties (SPPs): the UDM, National Freedom Party, African Independent Congress, Cope, African Transformation Movement (ATM) and Good won two seats each, and the Pan Africanist Congress (PAC) and Al-Jama-ah one seat each. The ten 'biggest' SPPs that failed to win seats had a total of approximately 102 000 votes between them. The spectacle of the SPPs was attributable to discontent with mainstream party politics.

Threats and questions in 2019 about which ANC faction constitutes the *real ANC* thrived amid small breakaway political parties regarded as pro-Zuma.[51] These parties facilitated the loosening up of the ANC voting bloc, offering opportunities to punish the ANC without delivering it out to the main opposition parties. Their

Table 3.5: Number of political parties participating, Elections 1994–2019

Number of parties participating – national		
National ballot	Participating	Winning seats
1994	19	7
1999	16	12
2004	21	12
2009	26	13
2014	29	13
2019	48	14

Number of participating parties – provincial				
Provincial ballots	2009 Participating	2014 Participating	2019 Participating	2019 Winning seats
Western Cape	22	26	34	7
Gauteng	20	22	36	6
Limpopo	18	20	34	4
Eastern Cape	17	18	26	6
KwaZulu-Natal	17	18	31	7
Free State	14	17	28	4
Mpumalanga	15	16	28	4
Northern Cape	13	16	21	4
North West	16	16	29	4

Source: IEC, 27 May 2019, cited in https://africacheck.org/reports/quick-read-south-africas-2019-election-in-numbers, accessed 12 June 2020

principal movers hinted at having Zuma's endorsement. Both Zuma and Magashule denied this, claiming that their loyalty was to the ANC. Magashule nevertheless withdrew his defamation charges against the person who had claimed he was instrumental in forming the ATM.[52] Besides the ATM, high-profile parties among the proxy SPPs were Hlaudi Motsoeneng's African Content Movement and Black First Land First (BLF). The BLF positioned itself as the embodiment of radical-ism that encompassed black consciousness (and had a persistent Zupta-bot pres-ence before and after the election; it remained by Zuma's side steadfastly in his trial period post-election).[53] Its positioning was concordant with the Bell-Pottinger narratives.[54]

The deluge of parties was a symptom of an era of low trust and voters' views on a lack of efficacy of party politics, along with the abuse of party politics to damage the reformist ANC of Ramaphosa. Confirmed post-election party political trends were set to deepen distrust: the ANC was returning to its status quo ante of internal fractioning and disagreement; the DA continued soul-searching and its post-mor-tems after the election triggered leader resignations, split-offs and losses of coalition metros; and the EFF confirmed that election engagement was a platform for power overreach and disruption. Although distrust of political parties and questioning of the usefulness of elections did not add up to immediate and outright electoral boy-cotts, there was a significant decline in participation and belief that elections truly matter, illustrated on an international Afrobarometer scale.[55] South Africans were prepared in declining but still substantial numbers to continue voting, *but elec-tions would be supplemented with other forms of action* ranging from direct action (including protest) to between-election withdrawal from politics.

ANC IN ELECTION 2019: VOTERS MISLED OR APPEASED?

The ANC received 11 436 921 votes in 2014 and 10 026 475 in 2019; its vote count declined by 1 410 446. The decline pulled the ANC down by five percentage points compared with 2014's national result (Table 3.6) but was still a three percentage point improvement on the ANC's nationally projected local election result of 2016 (Table 3.7).[56] Thus, the ANC had possibly turned a corner or, at least, had averted the seemingly precipitous decline that had been indicated. The 2019 result was porous, nevertheless. Multiple factors rendered the ANC majority ambiguous and subject to reversals.

Lower registration and turnout meant that if voters who had used these types of withdrawal from electoral politics instead of voting for an opposition party

Table 3.6:   Comparative trends across six national elections, 1994–2019

Party	1994		1999		2004		2009		2014		2019	
	% support	Number of votes	% support	Number of votes	% support	Number of votes	% support	Number of votes	% support	Number of votes	% support	Number of votes
ANC	62.65	12.2m	66.35	10.6m	69.69	10.9m	65.90	11.6m	62.15	11.4m	57.50	10.02m
NP (NNP)	20.39	3.9m	6.87	1.1m	1.65	257k						
DA (DP)	1.73	338k	9.56	1.5m	12.37	1.9m	16.66	2.9m	22.23	4.1m	20.77	3.62m
IFP	10.54	2.1m	8.58	1.4m	6.97	1.1m	4.55	804k	2.40	441k	3.38	588k
Cope							7.42	1.3m	0.67	123k	0.27	47k
EFF									6.35	1.2k	10.79	1.88m
ID					1.73	269k	0.92	162k				
UDM			3.42	546k	2.28	355k	0.85	149k	1.0	184k	0.45	78k
ACDP	0.45	88k	1.43	228k	1.60	250k	0.81	142k	0.57	104k	0.84	146k
FF+					0.89	139k	0.83	146k	0.90	165k	2.38	414k

Source: IEC, www.elections.org.za, multiple windows, accessed 5 July 2019

Table 3.7: Party support across 11 national and local elections, 1994–2019 (percentages)

Parties with national representation	1994 National	1995/6 Local	1999 National	2000 Local (2)	2004 National	2006 Local (3)	2009 National	2011 Local (4)	2014 National	2016 Local (4)	2019 National
ANC	62.6	58.0	66.4	59.4	69.7	67.7	65.9	62.9	62.2	54.5	57.50
DA (1)	22.1	21.5	17.0	22.1	12.4	13.9	16.7	24.1	22.2	27.0	20.77
EFF									6.4	8.3	10.79
IFP	10.5	8.7	8.6	9.1	7.0	8.4	4.6	3.6	2.4	4.3	3.38
NFP								2.4	1.6	0.02	0.35
UDM			3.4	2.6	2.3	1.98	0.9	0.6	1.0	0.6	0.45
FF+ (5)	2.2	2.7	0.8	0.1	1.0	1.0	0.8	0.4	0.9	0.8	2.38
Cope							7.4	2.2	0.7	0.5	0.27
ACDP	1.2	1.4	0.8	0.4	1.6	1.2	0.8	0.6	0.6	0.4	0.84
AIC									0.5	1.0	0.28
ID					1.7	1.4	0.9				
Agang SA									0.3	0.02	0.08
PAC	1.3	0.7	1.2	1.2	0.7	1.2	0.3	0.4	0.2	0.2	0.19
MF		0.4	0.3	0.3	0.4	0.3	0.3	0.4	0.1	0.04	0.07
Azapo			0.2	0.3	0.3	0.3	0.2	0.2	0.1	0.07	0.07
UCDP			0.8	1.0	0.8	0.8	0.4	0.2	0.1	0.07	
Al Jama-Ah							0.15	0.04	0.14	0.1	0.18
ATM											0.44
Good											0.40

Notes: (1) In some instances the IEC website combines the support for the DP and NP/NNP; the current table does not dissect it. Hence, in the first few columns DA+NP/NNP=DA. (2) Stated by the IEC website to be the percentage for the proportional representation (PR) component of the local vote. (3) Stated by the IEC website to be the percentage for the 'Party overall'. (4) Percentages on the PR ballot. (5) FF+CP.

Sources: Booysen, 2015; IEC, 2019, https://www.elections.org.za/NPEDashboard/app/dashboard.html, accessed 3 August 2019

decided to return to the electoral process, their votes could be used against the ANC. Vote-splitting to the advantage of the ANC nationally was a tactic specific to the circumstances around the relationship between Ramaphosa and the ANC. This trend could very well have continued into the future to sabotage ANC support.

Many of the voters who had continued voting ANC possibly did so in response to the ANC's campaign message of *being one, united party* – and of *its leader being in charge firmly of the party*. Should the ANC in the period 2019–2024 fall short on these fronts, voters would be most likely to feel betrayed and punish the ANC in a next election. Early signals were mixed: post-election, the ANC's factional warfare ruled again, moving beyond the truce of the campaign period, and there were signals of factional realignment that obfuscated the preceding binary arrangements. In addition, there was rampant, embarrassing public sector corruption, involving ANC representatives, functionaries and figureheads, when large sums of funds were released for the fight against the coronavirus. The ANC under Ramaphosa was far from corruption-free.[57]

CONCLUSION: SUPPLEMENTATION AND RELEGATION OF ELECTIONS

The ANC as a party was a far cry from the struggle-authentic movement living on in the pages of memoirs on revolutionary struggle against the oppressive ancien régime. The footprints of that order ran deep; it should have been seamless for the ANC to connect its outstanding democratic-order tasks to struggle authenticity. Yet, its own transgressions and deficiencies made it difficult to absolve the ANC from complicity in the democratic deficits. Voters noticed.

The Ramaphosa effect lifted the ANC election results but this was likely to be erratic, at best. ANC campaigning in 2019 convinced many wavering supporters that the ANC was unified and that the Ramaphosa clean-up would be flowing and effective. The post-election period, running into the time of Covid, by contrast, revealed a Ramaphosa regime that had to tread between factional and labour traps and landmines, obstructions planted by enemies of clean-up. Commissions of inquiry took time while the country leaked confidence in the political and state orders. Ramaphosa was presented as an upright, scrupulous leader who would turn the ANC around again – and contrary evidence was likely to alienate voters. The process to break Ramaphosa down or expose his own 'skeletons' was not going to cease.

As cynicism about elections and supplementation of the ballot mounted, the contrasts with the democracy of 1994 stood out. The euphoria of liberation had subsided, if not dissipated entirely. The great hope that Election 1994 would ring in the ultimate new dawn in the form of tangible equality, and widespread, profound socio-economic emancipation[58] made way for a 'new dawn' that depended on the mirage of 'the good ANC faction' winning the battle for control. A less pleasant face of the governing party had been dominant for a considerable time, and this left an imprint on party politics and elections. In mid-2018, around 52 per cent of ANC supporters had agreed that the future of their party was uncertain and little change was likely owing to 'leadership issues'. Only one in five felt certain about the future of the party.[59]

Election 2019 confirmed that the ANC was in continuous national-level decline, recorded through the porosity of the victory rather than simply the percentages of the results. It was a weak victory, even if the ANC's edge over other political parties bestowed continued dominance. In *majoritarian electoral game theory*, the ANC was far from collapse or from surrendering power. Because of the porous base, however, the ANC entered an intermediate zone between undisputed dominance and reconfiguration, which was filled with contradictory and often disagreeable symptoms.[60] Many of the signals were highlighted in the 2019 election season. Multiparty democracy ruled, but citizens and voters were redefining it and moving their political energies into supplementary or alternative politics. Others voted ANC but redefined their votes as entrance tickets into a world of state benefits and explained it as normal in a society of poverty in which the state stands central.

Enthusiasm for electoral participation goes hand in hand with the character of the political parties, the entry points into multiparty democracy and elections. The aftermath of Election 2019 saw rampant turmoil in the DA, questions about ethics and belief in democracy in the EFF, and the ANC's factional war setting down even more roots. The opposition political party that would damage the ANC lethally at the polls did not exist yet – while the ANC no longer had 'one centre' that could hold. In many respects, the ANC was shrinking but consolidating its power.

There were cumulative signals that multiparty democracy and elections were growing pale – and substitutes or supplementations that fell into place were potentially taking the country to disruption at worst, or new spaces of creative additions to multiparty democracy at best. The overall quality of multiparty democracy was assessed best in the context of ANC party political dominance, in light also of liberation movement legitimacy. The ANC had entered the multiparty democratic system of 1994 (agreed through the interim and final constitutions of 1993 and 1996) with a substantial advantage over other contestants. In the period since, it worked unabated through action and political information (or marketing) to uphold its dominance.[61] It also had the benefit of state power. Of particular advantage was its ability to fuse state and party power. The ANC became an 'unusual' party political contestant. The electorate remained extraordinarily willing to not punish it electorally for abusing public trust and state resources.

The ANC became the recipient of second chances, as was evident in Election 2019 and the post-Covid tabula rasa: a party whose previous failures were overwhelmed by a new and bigger crisis that was not of its own making. The public generally, and the electorate specifically, were willing to spur the ANC on, in large numbers and beyond the ANC support base, to remain in outright government power and to 'do better' next time around. They were willing to put the deliberations of multiple commissions of inquiry into corruption and capture into virtual abeyance, to take these deliberations as evidence of commitment on the part of the ANC to correct past weaknesses, or just to appreciate that the ANC was pretending to be addressing corruption. They accepted, against many odds at the time, that the 'new dawn' flagbearers had the abilities and reputations to turn the page for the ANC. If not, the voters would be ready to turn their backs to an even greater extent on electoral politics and embark on supplementary tracks of political participation.

NOTES

1   *New Nation Movement NPC and Others v President of the Republic of South Africa and Others* (CCT110/19) [2020] ZACC 11, 11 June 2020, http://www.saflii.org/za/cases/ZACC/2020/11.html, accessed 14 June 2020. NGOs, in main the little-known New Nation Movement and the Organisation Undoing Tax Abuse (Outa), brought the action, starting in September 2018 with an application to the Western Cape High Court. The court dismissed the application and in 2019 they approached the Constitutional Court, which ruled in their favour in 2020.

2   Glen Mashinini, 6 August 2020, Electoral Commission of South Africa, webinar on different electoral systems for National Party Liaison Committee members, said: '… we must caution against some misperception that the judgment of the Court will necessarily result in fundamental changes to the electoral system'.

3   Officially the ANC pronounced minimally, and the media filled in some gaps. See *BusinessTech*, 11 June 2020, 'ANC wants to make changes to South Africa's elections – what you need to know', https://businesstech.co.za/news/government/406689/anc-wants-to-make-changes-to-south-africas-elections-what-you-need-to-know/, accessed 7 July 2020. Author's telephonic interview with an electoral official, 2 August 2020.

4   Nomvula Mokonyane said to protesters in the campaign: 'People can threaten us and say they won't vote but the ANC doesn't need their dirty votes', 25 November 2013, https://www.politicsweb.co.za/opinion/the-anc-in-its-own-words-50-quotes, accessed 2 January 2019.

5   Details are explained by Mikhael Moosa, April 2019, 'Small improvements, not yet a "new dawn": South Africans still see high levels of corruption', Afrobarometer Dispatch No. 292.

6   This scenario was envisaged by Leon Schreiber, 2018, *Coalition Country: South Africa after the ANC*, Cape Town: Tafelberg.

7   The frequent former allusions to this higher order of party (see Susan Booysen, 2015, *Dominance and Decline: The ANC in the Time of Zuma*, Johannesburg: Wits University Press) had subsided but not disappeared entirely.

8   See, for example, David Everatt, 'New survey data shows Zuma cost the ANC dearly in the 2016 election', *The Conversation*, 7 April 2017; and TNS media statement, 2017, Kantar-TNS Omnibus Survey on Zuma's standing as president of South Africa, 5 April.

9   This survey was conducted in January 2019 and used a nationally representative sample of 1 900. See *The Citizen*, 20 March 2019, based on a Citizen Surveys media release.

10 The Pretoria High Court in mid-2020 dismissed the allegations of impropriety based on questions of law and public protector incompetence (evidenced in her associated report), but general questions of funding of party and leadership campaigns remained. Ramaphosa pointed out that the ANC had not yet developed guidelines governing fundraising for internal campaigns.

11 Alexandra Leisegang, 2018, From 'White Liberal' to 'Rainbow Nation' and Beyond: The Dynamics of Party Adaptation in a Racialised Environment, PhD thesis, University of the Witwatersrand, Johannesburg. See also Ryan Coetzee, Tony Leon and Michiel le Roux, 21 October 2019, *A Review of the Democratic Alliance: Final Report*, https://www.politicsweb.co.za/documents/what-is-wrong-with-the-da-and-how-to-fix-it, accessed 4 March 2020.

12 With reference to, for example, Julius Malema's On Point consultancy business (the subject of a public protector report), the EFF and Floyd Shivambu benefiting from the VBS banking scandal, and deals while they were heading the transport department in Herman Mashaba's DA-led coalition in the Johannesburg council.

13 There were still voices in the ANC who tried to steer the ANC onto the high road; see Joel Netshitenzhe, 2020, 'Impact of balance of forces on the cause of social transformation', *Umrabulo*, Issue 49, https://www.ortamboschool.org.za/2020/06/30/impact-of-balance-of-forces-on-the-cause-of-social-transformation-by-joel-netshitenzhe/, accessed 2 July 2020.

14 Quotations from Sibongakonke Shoba, 'Alarm in ANC over possible 2019 disaster', *Sunday Times*, 13 May 2018, from an ANC report presented by top officials to its March 2018 elections workshop in Boksburg. The ANC did not dispute this media report.

15 At a NEC meeting of October 2018, Ramaphosa chided ANC leaders to stick to one script, and not to contradict one another on policy issues such as those concerning the status of the South African Reserve Bank. Ramaphosa argued that unity would increase the ANC's prospects in Election 2019. This trend was illustrated by Qaanitah Hunter, 'Stick to the script, Cyril chides leaders', *Sunday Times*, 30 September 2018.

16 Paddy Harper, 'Ramaphosa passes KZN test', *Mail & Guardian*, 11 January 2019, highlights some of the inroads Ramaphosa made.

17 These trends are from the Afrobarometer data series, 2005–2018, http://afrobarometer.org/online-data-analysis, accessed 20 May 2019.

18 EFF leader Marshall Dlamini was credited with quadrupling EFF support in KwaZulu-Natal in 2019, taking the party provincially from 70 000 to 350 000 votes, or from two to eight seats in the provincial legislature.

19   Michael O'Donovan, 9 July 2019, 'The voter turnout on May 8, 2019: The loyal, the optimistic, the apathetic and angry', *EISA Post-Election Review*, Johannesburg; David Everatt, 8 July 2019, 'Trouble in the centre and the strengthening of the left and the right', *EISA Post-Election Review*, Johannesburg.

20   See O'Donovan, 9 July 2019, op. cit.

21   *City Press*, 24 March 2019, 'How happy are South Africans? Not very, says World Happiness Report', https://city-press.news24.com/Voices/how-happy-are-south-africans-not-very-says-world-happiness-report-20190324, accessed 2 February 2020, reported on these trends.

22   See the account by Tshidi Madia, 'Confessions of a "floating voter"', *News24*, 3 May 2019, https://www.news24.com/Elections/Voices/confessions-of-a-floating-voter-20190502, accessed 1 June 2019.

23   Marí Harris, April 2019, The People's Agenda, Ipsos SA, PowerPoint presentation.

24   Eric Naki, 'Cyril's popularity has dropped, according to new survey', *The Citizen*, 4 October 2018, https://citizen.co.za/news/south-africa/2017956/cyrils-popularity-has-dropped-according-to-new-survey/, accessed 4 October 2018, reporting on the Ipsos survey.

25   David Everatt, 'Who will South Africa's black middle class vote for?' *The Conversation*, 4 May 2019, https://businesstech.co.za/news/government/314340/who-will-south-africas-black-middle-class-vote-for/, accessed 13 June 2019, reporting on the Citizen Surveys findings.

26   As found by the Human Sciences Research Council (HSRC), 15 May 2019, National Results, Report for the Electoral Commission of South Africa (IEC), p. 3.

27   See Afrobarometer data series, 2005–2018, http://afrobarometer.org/online-data-analysis, accessed 20 May 2019.

28   See Harris for Ipsos SA, April 2019, op. cit.

29   Susan Booysen, 2007, 'With the ballot and the brick ... The politics of service delivery in South Africa', *Progress in Development Studies*, 7 (1), 21–32.

30   Susan Booysen, 2018, 'The African National Congress and its transfer of power from Zuma to Ramaphosa: The intraparty-multiparty nexus', *Transformation*, 98, 1–26.

31   Poll findings reported in Rapule Tabane, 'Cyril's first 100 days: So much has happened, while so much has remained the same', *City Press*, 27 May 2018, p. 4; and Aphiwe de Klerk, 'Soaring approval numbers as Ramaphoria grips citizens', *Sunday Times*, 27 May 2018.

32   These approval ratings were comparable to those achieved by Nelson Mandela towards the 1999 end of his term as South African president.

33   Cyril Ramaphosa, interview, SABC-TV3, 9pm bulletin, 27 April 2018.

34   See South African Citizens Survey Core Report, Quarter One, January–March 2019, citizensurveys.net › wp-content › uploads › 2020/06, accessed 6 October 2020.

35   Chisom Jenniffer Okoyo, 'With a Cabinet cut, Ramaphosa could launch a real "new dawn"', *The Citizen*, 11 May 2019, https://citizen.co.za/news/south-africa/elections/2129309/with-a-cabinet-cut-ramaphosa-could-launch-a-real-new-dawn/, accessed 20 June 2019, reporting on the utterances. Magashule hit back, trying to detract from Ramaphosa's role in the 2019 victory: 'People are electing the ANC. It is not about any individual ... Is comrade Mbalula saying that I was not going to be part of the campaign if the leader was somebody else?'

36   Marí Harris, interview on South African Broadcasting Corporation (SABC), 3 August 2017.

37   Author interviews with two high-level ANC delegates to the Nasrec conference, 5 and 18 February 2018, Johannesburg.

38 When voters voted out-of-province, they were not entitled to cast a provincial ballot.
39 Vote-splitting was notable in Gauteng and the Western Cape in that many voters divide their votes between the ANC nationally and the DA provincially.
40 Parts of this section rely on the report I edited for Mistra in 2019, *Voting Trends 25 Years into Democracy: Analysis of South Africa's 2019 Election*, Johannesburg.
41 For a detailed explanation of the concept, see Collette Schulz-Herzenberg and Roger Southall (eds), 2019, *Election 2019: Change and Stability in South Africa's Democracy*, Johannesburg: Jacana, pp. x–xi.
42 Parliamentary Monitoring Group, 3 April 2019, 'Parliament not told about 47% drop in registered 18 & 19 yr olds for elections', https://pmg.org.za/blog/2019elections, accessed 26 May 2019.
43 See Nancy Hakizimana and Grant Masterson, 22 May 2019, '2019 elections: Where did the youth vote go?' EISA Elections Resource Center, *Weekly Review of South Africa's 2019 Election Period*, Issue 7.
44 The voting age population (VAP) is a bigger group than the voting eligible population (VEP) – eligible to vote but not necessarily registered. VAP includes, for example, non-citizens or foreigners residing in the country, or those prohibited by the Constitution and law from voting. The last two figures are the upper points of the ranges within which these estimates generally fall. There is usually much correspondence between voting age population and eligible population.
45 For a definitive analysis, see Tom Lodge, 1995, 'The South African general election, April 1994: Results, analysis and implications', *African Affairs*, 94 (377), 471–500.
46 In 1994 the then National Party got more votes than the DA did in 2019, as pointed out by GroundUp, 13 May 2019, 'Groundview: For the first time most adults didn't vote', https://www.groundup.org.za/article/first-time-most-adults-didnt-vote/, accessed 26 May 2019.
47 The DA lost disproportionately from the white voter constituency, and substantially in the coloured constituency in 2019. For full details, see Coetzee et al., 2019, op. cit.
48 GroundUp, 13 May 2019, op. cit.
49 The specific data concerns the political parties' provincial and national vote totals, plus the associated vote proportions; data extraction and calculation are available on request.
50 They were often interest organisations, or proxy parties playing in on internal ANC fault-lines, and small protest 'movements', rather than fully fledged political parties.
51 See Susan Booysen, 8 July 2019, 'The proliferation of parties and limited voter choice in the 2019 elections', The South African 2019 National and Provincial Elections: A Post-Election Review, EISA, Johannesburg.
52 See, for example, Ace Magashule, as quoted in 'Fightback? What fightback?' *Sunday Times*, 8 September 2019. In 2020 Magashule withdrew charges he had brought against an African Transformation Congress/ATM leader who had referred to the links between Magashule and the ATM.
53 See Govan Whittles, 'BLF wants the ANC's pro-Zuma votes for 2019', *Mail & Guardian*, 18 May 2018.
54 See Superlinear, for example, 13 December 2018, http://www.superlinear.co.za/quantifying-the-spread-of-eff-ret-disinformation, accessed 1 May 2019.
55 See, for example, South African Social Attitudes Survey, http://www.hsrc.ac.za/en/research-data/view/9092, accessed 29 June 2019.
56 For further details, see Ulf Engel, 2016, 'Zupta's next nightmare: The South African local government elections of 3 August 2016', *Africa Spectrum*, 51 (2), 103–115.

57　Ramaphosa announced a special initiative of nine state institutions to investigate, prosecute and reclaim proceeds of Covid corruption; address by president of South Africa, SABC3, 23 July 2020.

58　See Martin Murray, 1994, *The Revolution Deferred*, London: Verso; Abebe Zegeye and Julia Maxted, 2002, *Our Dream Deferred: The Poor in South Africa*, Pretoria: SAHO and Unisa Press.

59　Poll findings reported by Iavan Pijoos, 'More than half of South Africans say ANC's future is uncertain, poll shows', *News24*, 18 August 2018, https://www.news24.com/SouthAfrica/News/more-than-half-of-south-africans-say-ancs-future-is-uncertain-poll-shows-20180818, accessed 2 February 2019.

60　For this analogy, see Antonio Gramsci, 1971, 'Wave of materialism, and crisis of authority', in Quintin Hoare and Geoffrey N. Smith (eds and trans.), *Selections from the Prison Notebooks*, London: Lawrence and Wishart, pp. 275–276.

61　See Rushil Ranchod, 2013, *A Kind of Magic: The Political Marketing of the ANC*, Johannesburg: Jacana, which places this phenomenon in broader context.

4

Presidency of Hope, Shadows and Strategic Allusion

HOPE FUSING WITH COMPOUND SHADOWS OF THE PAST

The lesson from the presidency of Cyril Ramaphosa was that hope for new beginnings depended on the intensity and persistence of shadows of the past and the incumbent's skill to keep alive people's trust that the presidency embodied hope. Ramaphosa's presidency brought in many of the antitheses to the dispensation of his predecessor, Jacob Zuma. Yet, the experiences of the Zuma years, anchored in the ANC's pre-Zuma times, haunted Ramaphosa. Zuma had left the presidential positions, but in legacy and institutional culture the disruptive bequests lingered, and Ramaphosa's presidency carried the burden.

A frequently weak and malfunctioning state apparatus and a notorious inability to give effect to well-meaning policies further muddled Ramaphosa's presidency. When Covid-19 struck, the Ramaphosa presidency shone briefly. As the nation reeled, Ramaphosa was seen to lead, but then critical consciousness returned when the ravages of lockdown were manifested and the Ramaphosa team misstepped. The crisis laid bare a presidency that struggled to assert leadership from the front, a porous presidency steeped in consultative approaches. The advice to the president was haphazard – and he was unable to assert the compassionate but determined leadership that was demanded. He let the National Coronavirus Command Council (NCCC) displace the constitutionally mandated, accountable institutions of top government, until resurgent legal action brought reconsideration. His weakness in Cabinet resulted in ministers contradicting him, promulgating Covid regulations and secu-rity force practices that detracted from his credibility. Ramaphosa tried to rein in corruption in the scramble for anti-Covid tenders by issuing stern letters to his ANC comrades and working to sway the NEC into acting unambiguously and persuasively against all public sector perpetrators of corruption, but the clamber for tenders epit-omised ANC avarice in government and the greed contrasted with destitution on the ground. Such inconsistencies dealt a severe blow to the Ramaphosa presidency.[1]

Ramaphosa became the custodian of the introduction of the district develop-ment model of government – in typical ANC governance fashion bringing in sup-plementary institutions when formal-constitutional ones failed, such as in the case of local government.[2] It acknowledged the inability of top government, and the presidency, to control rogue local governments, coastline to coastline, that could not manage public resources. In the period of combating the devastation wreaked by Covid, when the government tried to let infrastructure development drive recovery, concentration of power in this new sphere of local government spoke of the weakness of the Ramaphosa presidency. Lines of accountability circumvented the constitutionally mandated processes in the name of reconstruction.

The Ramaphosa presidency came at a time when society had started applying higher demands for transparency and state clean-up action. Ramaphosa's victory in the ANC was leveraged by public support and by the hope of the ANC support base that he would deliver an alternative to the Zuma years. He won Election 2019 for the ANC on the basis of such a mandate. Never before in the ANC's years of rule had the president been so directly accountable to the public. His task was to steer the ANC out of operational and delivery crises, before, during and after Covid, in conditions complicated by continuous failures in state apparatuses and the econ-omy. Even when he was under attack by opponents in the ANC, they depended on him to ensure ongoing public trust. Ramaphosa's public ratings declined sharply but still remained relatively high as faltering amid Covid mounted. Legal challenges to the government's Covid interventions accumulated, and the fault-lines of economic failures were evident. Yet the ANC relied on Ramaphosa. The National Working Committee declared that it supported the 'inclusive and decisive leadership that President Ramaphosa continues to provide'.[3]

Layers of cynicism

The Zuma years had inserted layers of cynicism between the political leaders and the people and had destroyed much of the preceding liberation movement-related gen-eral trust.[4] While organisational weakening was being exacerbated by deep structural fault-lines in the economy, the public and the party were looking for a president who could bring redemption. Cyril Ramaphosa was the best they could find – far from flawless and conceivably fated to disappoint, but there was no alternative.

Ramaphosa's rise into the presidency of the country in the early days of 2018 completed a circle of strategy and planning that had started at the time of his unscripted entrance in 2012 as deputy president of the ANC. He had won the ANC deputy presidency controversially under the discredited Zuma leadership. The ANC nominated Ramaphosa in 2012 when Kgalema Motlanthe, contesting for the ANC presidency against Zuma, refused to become part of a unity ticket and Ramaphosa was the Zuma faction's substitute, unwanted but useful for the time being.

With these foundations as a point of departure, Chapter 4 focuses on the dual ANC and state presidencies of Cyril Ramaphosa, always struggling to transcend the long shadow of Zuma but carried forward by popular trust and expectations. Much of ANC politics had become *leadership politics*. Intensifying contests for the internal groupings' control over levers of state power were omnipresent. In a vicious circle, these preoccupations in ANC ranks leveraged poor governance, compromising levels of delivery and worsening popular disillusionment. The attention in the rest of the chapter is predominantly on Ramaphosa's occupancy of the *presidency of South Africa*, to the extent that it can be differentiated from that of the ANC. The chapter focuses on Ramaphosa's settling into political power and occupying the presidency of South Africa on the canvass of an extended fightback, in which foes planned relentlessly for the future beyond him. It considers simultaneously how the moment of Covid rupture froze ANC politics in time, for a while, but brought in new uncertainties.

THE CURIOUS CASE OF THE PRESIDENCY AND THE NCCC FAUX PAS

South Africa's Covid moment illustrated the uncertainties and effects of faltering in party and state, affecting the credibility of the executive of South African government, and in particular the presidency of South Africa. Ramaphosa lost credibility for centralising the NCCC over Cabinet at the onset of the Covid crisis. His own presidency was seen not as virtuously consultative (in usual Ramaphosa mode), but as uncertain of its own abilities and as deferring to an unconstitutional body. He underestimated the demands for direct accountability and ongoing transparency, and overestimated the reach of popular and civil society trust in his presidential position.

Early in the crisis, on 15 March 2020, he announced the establishment of the NCCC (referred to initially as the National Command Council), to 'coordinate all aspects of our extraordinary emergency response' to the Covid crisis.[5] Next, he backtracked serially to emphasise that the NCCC merely recommended actions and policies to Cabinet. Lawyers questioned the NCCC's legality, and multiple civil society organisations confronted the ANC government in court on specific regulations. At one stage, in June 2020, Nkosazana Dlamini-Zuma, minister responsible for implementation under the Disaster Management Act, shared with the National Council of Provinces that there had been 116 Covid-related court cases against the state (84 resolved at the time; many of the remainder were proceeding through the High Courts, Supreme Court of Appeal and Constitutional Court). In explaining the NCCC to opposition MP questions, Ramaphosa said the NCCC was established in March 2020 at a cabinet meeting as a committee of Cabinet.

Ramaphosa's early Covid speeches asserted NCCC authority, amid hard lockdown and severe restrictions on citizen rights, enforced by all security forces, including the defence force. In his national addresses to the nation the president said that the NCCC 'has decided to enforce a nationwide lockdown' (24 March 2020). Then, he announced that 'after careful consideration of the available evidence', the NCCC had 'decided to extend the lockdown' (9 April 2020). A few days later he announced that the NCCC 'determined the national coronavirus alert level' (23 April 2020). At first, the president had stressed that the NCCC (with 19 or 20 cabinet members serving on it) took binding decisions; next, he explained that the NCCC approved draft regulations which go to Cabinet for ratification.[6] If such draft regulations amount to decision-making, they would be invalid because the NCCC does not have a constitutional standing.[7] Suspicion mounted, too, because the NCCC was supported by the National Joint Operational and Intelligence Structure (NatJoints), hinting of security force influence. To counter this reaction, the presidency foregrounded the NCCC's advisory role and expanded the NCCC to include all cabinet members.

The NCCC was in full flight while Parliament was in recess, until civil society and opposition parties sensed the emergence of a shadow government. It was seen to be eclipsing Cabinet and Parliament. Lawyers were concerned that the power of the NCCC went against the constitutional bodies of government and undermined Parliament's oversight over the executive.

THE DUAL PRESIDENCIES AND THEIR CONFLICTING DEMANDS

Being the president of South Africa and president of the ANC were two conflicting deployments. Ramaphosa's emphasis on new beginnings and renewed commitment to public service moved from his New Deal in CR17 campaign time, and *Thuma*

Mina upon becoming president of South Africa, to a contradictory season of hope for renewal, countered by growing doubts about his abilities.[8] The ANC reaped the benefits of mass popular endorsement in Election 2019. The early Ramaphosa times brought an exaggerated hope that his dual presidency would be sufficiently force-ful to override adverse, on occasion paralysing, effects of the ANC's organisational problems. There were hopes, too, that Ramaphosa might change the groundswell of protest especially against local government failures, an economy that had become deeply flawed and faltering strategic state institutions.

Ramaphosa's fire-fighting tasks on the two presidential fronts were daunting. He had to win over an affirming working majority in the continuously evolving factionally divided leadership structures of the ANC, while being threatened with ANC National General Council retribution in the form of a premature recall from the ANC presidency.[9] While under sustained attack by old and regrouping segments of the ANC he was to spearhead a government turnaround, dodging a line-up of agents from opposing ANC factions who were fused into state institutions and were willing to use their positions to trip up the Ramaphosa promises. Some of the out-breaks were triggered by opposition parties, the Democratic Alliance (DA) in Par-liament playing its opposition role and asking the public protector to investigate CR17's campaign funding. The Economic Freedom Fighters (EFF) aligned at cru-cial times with the public protector to try and neutralise Ramaphosa and his lieu-tenants, including public enterprises minister, Pravin Gordhan. Micro 'parties', such as Black First Land First (Gupta-Zuma-aligned) and its bot task force, together with elements in the State Security Agency (SSA) and others, enflamed narratives. They tried to keep Ramaphosa under constant pressure and show him as compromised and duplicitous on state capture, persecuting Zuma for offences less than his own.

Ramaphosa had to deliver by showing that he could clean up government and run it efficiently. With the help of courts and commissions, Ramaphosa effected change at institutions like the National Prosecuting Authority, the South African Revenue Service (SARS) and, tentatively, at state-owned enterprises. Below that top level, however, practices of corruption and capture persevered and discredited Ramaphosa's pledges to bring in consequences for malfeasance.

Ramaphosa's politically predominant set of tasks was to steer government policy towards alignment with the ANC policy positions that were adopted controversially in the heat of the Nasrec contest. It was for him to convert ANC government policy into economic realities that would grow the economy and bring South Africa closer to elusive (and worsening)[10] economic freedoms. Ramaphosa was expected to use his mandate to get the economy to grow and create jobs, and to reduce the size and expenditures of a government and civil service that had become notorious for being overly remunerated (to the point of draining the fiscus) and, commonly, ineffective sheltered employment. He had to restructure overstaffed and non-functional, often corrupt state-owned enterprises that were also unaccountable and reckless in handling public resources – this complicated by the need to attain more efficient public management without touching unionised public sector workers. His tasks multiplied and were drawn further into the realm of the impossible when Covid-related economic meltdown struck. Covid nevertheless was a 'reprieve' for Ramaphosa and his government: their previous failures were dwarfed as the new Covid explanation for hardship and state dysfunctionality fell into place.

Ramaphosa's presidency of South Africa proceeded, before and after the advent of Covid, amid multifarious attacks and constraints. The mammoth presidency and the president's executive deployees had to help redeem the politically afflicted president, sheltered in many ways in the time of Covid but subject to a new wave of assaults in the aftermath. In the Mbeki presidency the ANC had become an increasingly limp attachment to the state. Mbeki was punished for relying on his deployees in the state to manage the ANC on policy and governance. The Zuma-ists reversed the relationship of state over party, reinstating the ANC. Few had imagined the extent to which this U-turn would reshape the ANC. It was the ANC's Luthuli House and Zuma's hold on ANC power that towered over the president's private office in the Union Buildings west wing.[11] The primacy of Luthuli House became the life of Ramaphosa.

STRONGMEN, DENSIFYING PLOTS AND POPULAR APPEAL

The Ramaphosa presidency gained considerable traction and protection from the large numbers of citizens willing it on to surmount those in the governing party who tried to undermine and subvert him. Ramaphosa's public endorsements at the time of Election 2019 were higher than both those of the ANC and of any other ANC leader, and his popular supremacy over other ANC leaders continued through the time of Covid.[12] Ramaphosa's public endorsements were higher than the proportion of South Africans that voted for the ANC; many non-ANC members also endorsed him. It helped legitimise his actions when on policy he adhered to ANC prescripts but had to merge ANC policy into government action.

Mbeki, Zuma and Ramaphosa had all been afflicted by the politics of 'plots' and 'conspiracies'. It was a revolving wheel, as presidents tried to control who might succeed them and plotters became presidents. Ramaphosa, unlike his two predecessors, was not, himself, the one to cry wolf.[13] In the Mbeki days, Ramaphosa was one of three persons accused of plotting to oust Mbeki. Then, and in the Zuma days, the accusations related to routine politics of campaigns to rotate leadership, or to hang onto power directly or through proxies. By the time Ramaphosa entered the presidency, plotting was a standard ingredient of ANC internal politics. Ramaphosa conducted his presidency amid 'plotting actions' that Mbeki would never have tolerated silently. Mbeki's cries of 'plot happening!' illustrate the lack of differentiation in the ANC between relatively ordinary organisational politics and 'conspiracies' in the sense of state security being affected or regime change attempted. Mbeki conflated the two in order to discredit contestation. In mid-2001, the then minister of safety and security, Steve Tshwete, acting for Mbeki, announced that Mathews Phosa (Mpumalanga premier, 1994 to 1999), Tokyo Sexwale (1994 premier of Gauteng) and Cyril Ramaphosa (who at the time was on a business track) were being investigated for a plot to oust Mbeki.[14] The charge followed ANC members having circulated pamphlets advocating 'one president, one term' while Mbeki was readying himself for a second (which he would win). Zuma manoeuvred himself into the plotting line-up and, despite not having been mentioned in the first place, assured South Africa that he was not aspiring to Mbeki's job either.[15]

Mbeki continued equating state security with intra-party contestation. In 2005–2006, he accused so-called progressive forces in the ANC of plotting against him in Zuma's name, citing pro-Zuma demonstrations and media columns as evidence.[16] Next, Mbeki associates revealed the 'top secret' Special Browse Mole Consolidated Report, alleging a plot by Zuma, his left allies and former Umkhonto we Sizwe leaders. They had 'conspired' with then president José Eduardo dos Santos of Angola and former Libyan leader Muammar Gaddafi to overthrow Mbeki, their deeds comprising covert funding of the Zuma campaign. The document argued that Zuma's 'presidential ambitions are fuelled and sustained by a conspiracy playing out both inside South Africa and on the African continental stage'.[17] Next, the tables turned on Mbeki, and the Zuma camp called out a Mbeki plot to prevent Zuma from rising into the ANC presidency (allegedly by discrediting Zuma through legal charges). Zuma continued levelling these accusations well into the Ramaphosa term, and as the legal and prosecutorial nets were tightening around him.

Zuma often portrayed himself as the victim of political conspiracy.[18] He saw conspiracy in simple criticism – the corruption charges against him were inspired by the West, he argued.[19] His ANC and Tripartite Alliance partners took the cue: Gwede Mantashe accused 'foreign forces' of attempting to use the strike by the Association of Mineworkers and Construction Union to 'destabilise' the South African economy, and 'enemies' of the Congress of South African Trade Unions (Cosatu) of taking advantage of its internal battles to try to destroy the labour union (the battle was about Cosatu's loss of independence to the ANC, at the height of Zuma's incumbency). Blade Nzimande denoted Nkandla as 'white people's lies' and accused the media of an anti-Zuma 'liberal offensive'. Journalists critical of Zuma were a '[paid] mouthpiece of factionalists' in the ANC.[20]

Zuma continued on this track, trying to turn charges accumulating against him to work against Ramaphosa. Zuma had suffered a series of setbacks: his proxy presidential candidate, Nkosazana Dlamini-Zuma, was not elected at Nasrec and he was ousted from the presidency; his state funding for legal defence was curtailed; his proxies in state power were being constrained increasingly; and his final-ditch attempts to avoid his day in court and at the Zondo Commission were on the verge of failure. Zuma used his appropriated epithet as apostle of radical economic transformation to argue that the plot that brought these misfortunes on him came from Ramaphosa's links to capital and, in particular, from white monopoly capital.[21] The pre-2018 anti-Zuma project to cut short Zuma's term as South African president had gained traction when Zuma installed minion proxy ministers of finance, and markets reacted. Zuma-ists construed this as capital conspiring with the Ramaphosa camp and found corroboration in the public protector's revelations that the CR17 campaign had benefited from huge capital contributions. In Zuma's post-presidential trajectory in the High Court in Pietermaritzburg, when he applied for a permanent stay of prosecution, his legal counsel argued that the arms deal corruption charges were part of a political plot, driven by a sinister and divisive agenda from within the ANC. At the Zondo Commission Zuma maintained that there were enemies in the ANC, agents for the old apartheid regime, who were behind the allegations against him.

The public protector, Busisiwe Mkhwebane, and several proxy political parties, augmented the Zuma-ist serial plot arguments, either to have Ramaphosa removed from power or to sow suspicion about his integrity and willingness to adhere to left-leaning ANC policies. In her report on the flows of Ramaphosa's CR17 campaign funding (subsequently dismissed by the High Court in Pretoria owing to material errors in law and lack of jurisdiction in relation to the campaign), Mkhwebane flagged the role of white monopoly capital as the major Ramaphosa funder, alleging that Ramaphosa was beholden and set on delegitimising the rightful Zuma-ist crusade against the white monopoly capital-captured Ramaphosa-ists. The ultimate delegitimation of legal action against Zuma then followed in a further layer as a conspiracy by the illegitimate capitalist-beholden Ramaphosa regime to bring charges of corruption and capture against Zuma and his associates.

In 2018 there was a twist in this world of plotting, which concerned an intra-ANC plot by Zuma-ists to use legal challenges to the Nasrec result (the marginal and possibly contestable 179 majority in the Nasrec presidential outcome in particular). The plot centred on the Maharani-Umhlanga meetings of September 2018 where such legal actions were discussed. Zuma, by now, had less access to the state apparatuses necessary to keep him safe, even though there were still loyal moles and flanks in the often-corrupted and captured state security apparatuses and other strategic institutions. And at the Zuma court appearances the supporter ranks were no longer swelling. Zuma was increasingly isolated in the media stakes – the Gupta-linked *The New Age/Africa Voice* and ANN7 were no longer available to spread the Zuma news.

A successful legal case against the Nasrec delegate statuses, and hence the conference's voting outcomes, with a court-ordered rerun of the conference, was possible, if the ANC could afford it. Had it materialised, it could also have destabilised the ANC's 2019 election campaign. In the post-election period, given that the ANC had won a mandate for renewal and state clean-up, it would, in effect, have dismissed the mandate that the electorate had given the ANC.

It is remarkable that Zuma featured in all of the plots, across the presidencies. There were alleged plots to prevent him from political ascendance, then allegations spearheaded by former crime intelligence head, Richard Mdluli, of attempts to remove Zuma from power. The ascending plot lines[22] show how the earlier plots and alleged plots changed – from bringing leadership change to an organisation to endangering the electoral fortunes of the governing party and threatening an entire regime.

Ramaphosa continued to govern, managing the plot culture via state institutions and a platoon of agents and campaigners. He let legal and inquisitorial processes unfold. In the 2020 phase of the contest, a plot equivalent arose when the *Sunday Independent* newspaper penned a series of revelations about Ramaphosa 'plotting' to remove certain cabinet members.[23] Always based on unnamed sources, the reports identified those incumbents whom Ramaphosa relied on (or did not wish to alienate) as the targets of the 'pending' reshuffles. In the world of plots the articles could have been a conspiracy to weaken Ramaphosa's strategic alliances, on which his running for a second term would rely.

RAMAPHOSA'S LONG GAME OR WEAK GAME?

In its first, pre-Covid 2020 phase, Ramaphosa faced the task of turning government around. In the post-Covid time, this task would escalate exponentially. State-owned enterprises across the phases had to be re-engineered, and state departments liberated from political and economic corruption – in Ramaphosa's own circle as well.

Many corrupted ones had been endearing themselves to Ramaphosa to gain political protection and continuous benefits. The intra-ANC opposition that Ramaphosa faced was illustrated by ANC secretary-general Magashule's denying that Ramaphosa's clean-up task had broad popular support, telling an ANC gathering that ANC stalwarts like Nelson Mandela and Oliver Tambo were the last icons of the party. '[Ramaphosa is] not that popular, we last saw a popular leader in the time of Mandela …'[24]

Ramaphosa had to develop his leadership style amid relentless internal political impairment, the economically dismal (and worsening) conditions, and a range of unfolding socio-ethical crises. Governance issues – managing xenophobia, femicide and child killings, and correcting poverty and inequality in relation to Black Lives Matter – were accompanied by the public sector remuneration crisis, ratings agency downgrading, public health sector problems and, specifically, recovering from the Covid-19 disaster. Ramaphosa was required to lead South Africa out of these conditions while the public protector and other detractors were working to destabilise the presidency and discredit the judiciary which had become a crucial spoke in the wheel of the Ramaphosa modus operandi for dealing with some intractable problems.

Ramaphosa's presidential game was argued to be 'the long game' – presumably strategic, calculated and wise.[25] This was offered as justification for Ramaphosa's often not leading the ANC from the front but, rather, letting judicial commissions of inquiry, the High Courts and Constitutional Court, cabinet clusters, parliamentary committees and a range of other institutional actors play out their respective hands. This was a way of conducting government while slaloming around obstacles; but on the other hand, his style created the images of exasperating caution, reluctance to lead or simply being unequal to the task.[26] Even in the time of Covid-19, with its manifest need for a strong president to lead from the front, Ramaphosa was forefronting his consultative and team approaches. His style of not leading from the front was complemented by a reputation for 'resolving' problems and demobilising opponents by pegging them down in endless deliberations, negotiations and consultations.[27] Ramaphosa acknowledged this as his style – and gave himself credit for it, especially for its contrast with dictatorship:

> I build consensus. Some people would like me to be a dictator, and it is not in my make-up to be a dictator … I have built and led a number of organisations without being a dictator, working very well with people and making them feel worthwhile and worthy to work in an organisation, and respecting the ability not to give in to shouting and screaming at people, and so on. That is my style.[28]

Ramaphosa was seen to be spinning out problems, preferably non-antagonistically, in anticipation of the matter at hand losing urgency or being eclipsed. This was more difficult in the time of Covid-19 when, as president, he was called on regularly to address the nation in direct public broadcasts. In the public protector's anti-Ramaphosa offensive generally, the president relied on the judiciary, as well as the ANC parliamentary caucus (which remained factionally unstable), whereas the fightback forces went for the jugular of the judiciary by alleging political capture.[29]

In the realm of ordinary party and government politics, pressures mounted as opposition parties alleged that Ramaphosa spent more energy on ANC politics than on matters of state and government.[30] Before the bigger Covid crisis surpassed routine politics, Ramaphosa appeared at times paralysed by the legal net that the EFF, public protector and Magashule were trying to tighten around him. It was time-consuming to rely on the judiciary to bring turnaround and accountability, a core part of his strategy, given the ANC internal dictates of 'unity' and 'no purges'.

Ramaphosa's manifest weakness of leadership was evident in his entrapment in ANC disunity. Appeasement and spinning problems out were the lifeblood of much of his governance: he was forced to be more accommodating of Zuma-ists, for example, when he was accused of selective action in confronting Magashule for the Maharani plot but tolerating Ramaphosa-ist Thabang Makwetla for confessing to a bribe. In the period of the Bosasa money controversies, including payment to the Ramaphosa campaign, Ramaphosa himself did not pronounce on whether his campaign's acceptance of the funds from Bosasa might have been in exchange for anticipated favours should he become president. The ANC accepted Ramaphosa's explanation about his Bosasa deal,[31] but the mood was one of popular doubt in Ramaphosa's abilities to overcome the afflictions of the ANC, even if there were occasional glimpses of a president taking charge.[32]

Ramaphosa was affected, too, by his historical enlistment into the Zuma order of things through becoming the Zuma Mangaung running mate. In the years that followed, Ramaphosa never openly opposed Zuma. He served quietly as deputy president, aware that he could be fired for resistance against Zuma – and this would undermine his presidential ambition.[33] His critical colours only appeared when Zuma fired the then finance minister, Pravin Gordhan. Gordhan was recalled from an international investment roadshow before he was fired and replaced with the Gupta associate, Malusi Gigaba, in March 2017.[34] Ramaphosa remarked:

> Here was another occasion when another report, which I believe was false, was being used to remove Pravin Gordhan. The decision I then had to make

was whether to keep quiet about something I truly believed was truly incorrect. But then I broke ranks and spoke out. It was a difficult decision.[35]

Zuma was believed to have made the decision based on information gained from an intelligence report which claimed that Gordhan was part of a covert operation working against the country's interests. Ramaphosa said the report's allegations reminded him of his own pain when he once stood accused of trying to overthrow president Mbeki.[36]

Ramaphosa was also weak in his inability as president to bring the economy under control, first to get more than decimal-point growth in the economy, next to avoid recession, and then to deliver the country out of the severe coronavirus-related decline. Throughout, he had to attempt to restore governance at the state-owned enterprises, and get job creation going. In the early days of his presidency it had been expected that he would deliver on these exact functions. Instead, budgets were 'balanced' through deficits, international borrowing, quantitative easing by the South African Reserve Bank, limiting growth of the public sector wage bill, de facto raids on public sector pensions via the Public Investment Corporation and select state-owned enterprise freezes. Change was slow and tentative; the Ramaphosa government wavered to restructure major state-owned enterprises while organised labour regrouped and resisted. It did, nevertheless, keep the ANC government looking out for its deployees, on a mass scale, preventing the loss of an important voting bloc – as South Africa slipped deeper into national debt, even before the Covid crisis.[37]

Ramaphosa perfected water-treading. This was largely interpreted as part of a weakness in personal style, indecision – or the bankruptcy of the ANC and government on the policy-governance front. The Ramaphosa presidency became synonymous with crisis of governance,[38] while Ramaphosa played his 'longer' game and remained standing. The times of the coronavirus were also kind to Ramaphosa's ANC. Joblessness combined with job losses and major reversals in business, manufacturing and the service industry to cast the economy in restart mode. Ramaphosa's ANC could in a way erase the slate of previous failures, and become the benefactor spreading goodwill and widening the security net, while it reorganised state organisations to centralise the district development model. Major post-Covid funds would flow into these structures, and the ANC was positioned at the centre of post-Covid reconstruction. The ANC was possibly winning the next national election in the course of the Covid crisis, under Ramaphosa's leadership. That would be subject to whether Covid looting and corruption by well-placed ANC insiders (with possible benefits accruing to the ANC itself, in terms of the formula spelled out by Nomvula Mokonyane at the Zondo Commission)[39] could be pulled back definitively. However, this type of evidence was accumulating – ANC fundraising was meshed with corporate and individual corruption. At the Zondo Commission, evidence indicated that Johannesburg Mayor Geoff Makhubo solicited donations to the ANC in exchange for state contracts. The Free State asbestos contract showed similar trends, as did the contracts between Prasa and Swifambo, the company responsible for maldesigned locomotives. ANC fundraising was compromised and so was the organisation.

THE GHOST OF CORRUPTION INFILTRATING THE RAMAPHOSA PRESIDENCIES

Given Ramaphosa's muted style, it was often difficult to know whether the prevailing expressions in presidential politics simply epitomised his imprint, or whether the political ghost of former president Zuma was hovering, afflicting the Ramaphosa presidency.

If indeed Ramaphosa would win lasting strength from his government's management of corona devastation, it would have been the first sign of the Zuma-Ramaphosa transition becoming definitive, albeit compromised by malfeasance across faction lines. Up to this point it had been an inconclusive presidential transition. Both 'smallanyana' and major matters of malfeasance were rife in ANC and government ranks. It was within the power of many of its aggrieved powerful leaders to bring the ANC down, using information about past and persistent skeletons. Havoc would be unleashed, for example, should rogue politician Zuma publicly reveal sensitive information about party finances and personal corruption in ANC ranks. Dozens of previous leaders had continued regarding the ANC as bigger than the interests of any of its constituent leaders. Zuma was different. He felt so wronged by Ramaphosa's ANC that he serially threatened that he could and would break the rule of silence including (at the Zondo Commission) doing so together with associates such as the former 'spy boss' Arthur Fraser.[40] Others had already confirmed to Zondo that it was normal for the ANC to award state tenders and require quid pro quo paybacks from the recipients.

The Ramaphosa ANC was itself an alliance of the truly corruption-free and the almost-clean but bearing minor skeletons; the skeleton-ridden converts from the Zuma camp who crossed in pursuit of political protection; the utterly suspect ones who were politically powerful and mostly untouchable; and many shades in-between. The words of Bathabile Dlamini of the Women's League, 'all of us in the NEC have our smallanyana skeletons',[41] were one of the few public acknowledgements of this pervasively tainted character, until Mokonyane testified at the Zondo Commission.

While these ANC relationships with business started to become more public, Zuma's threats to expose more permutations loomed over Ramaphosa. Zuma's background in ANC intelligence and his roles in government at various levels over many years supplied him with many accomplices and loyalists – in the state and the security services in particular. In November 2016, for example, Zuma claimed to have full knowledge of who was stealing from the public purse. In his own administrations he often appointed flawed and corruption-prone cadres to important positions; in June 2018, he once again threatened to go public on who in the ANC did what, as he did again in mid-2019 at the Zondo Commission. The threat hollowed out when, at the Zondo Commission, Zuma named as 'spies' his former cabinet ministers Ngoako Ramatlhodi and Siphiwe Nyanda. Both denied it and commenced legal action; he later added Derek Hanekom as a 'known enemy agent'.[42] Hanekom took legal action for defamation and won his case. Zuma appealed but lost without the appeal being heard: the Supreme Court of Appeal stated there was no reasonable prospect of success.[43] Zuma continued the string of threats and allegations, including that agents planted in the ANC by the apartheid regime were still working against him.[44]

The general ANC tone of strong words against corruption (in ANC and state ranks), but inability to follow through and get action and reform, was a notable characteristic of the Ramaphosa presidency.[45] The words included the ANC's 54th conference resolutions that a member 'accused of or reported to be involved in corrupt practices accounts to the Integrity Committee immediately or faces [disciplinary committee] processes', and that the ANC would 'summarily suspend people who fail to give an acceptable explanation, or to voluntarily step down while they face disciplinary, investigative or prosecutorial processes'.[46] These words were reaffirmed in ANC National Executive Committee statements of August and December 2020, but the policies and guidelines to undergird the words remained work in progress. There were repeated undertakings to give the Integrity Commission more power and resources and yet it remained a subjugated sub-organ of the National Executive Committee.

Clean-up was almost invariably paired with accusations that the actions constituted factional purging or, with an additional twist, pre-emptive action to forestall investigations into the parties initiating them.[47] In the SSA, for example, there was talk of senior agents threatening to topple Ramaphosa at the 2020 (subsequently postponed to 2021) National General Council, should his government proceed with the restructuring and clean-up of the intelligence services.[48]

RAMAPHOSA PRESIDENCY THROUGH THE LENS OF THE CABINETS

The Ramaphosa presidency tried to adapt the prior rules of deployment to Cabinet. It had to consolidate its power in the aftermath of the contested Nasrec result and Zuma's forced resignation as president of South Africa. Ramaphosa spoke the language of unity while ensuring that the 'Gupta ministers' were removed, at least from Cabinet. He avoided alienating those with constituencies of note even when implicated in wrongdoing or suboptimal performance.

Rules included the ANC election list's tolerant criterion that charges of corruption did not stick unless formalised through court judgments. Other rules were that loyalties and key roles in bringing Ramaphosa into power would be rewarded, while gender, youth, provincial power bases and Tripartite Alliance associations had to be cross-cutting factors in the mix. There also had to be rewards for powerful ones in the ancien régime who were prepared to switch allegiance to Ramaphosa. The rules included pragmatism, allowing tainted persons to remain in power – evidence came with the Ramaphosa Cabinet reshuffle when he took power from Zuma.[49] He appointed a half-new Cabinet, and made further changes after the 2019 election, including bringing back in some of the fallen Zuma cabinet members. There were a handful of minor Cabinet changes when ministers resigned (under force) or died. Several of the Zuma-ists who had missed out on Cabinet status under Ramaphosa were confirmed nevertheless as chairpersons of the parliamentary committees.[50] The strategy was to keep them in the ANC unity loop even if Ramaphosa's clean-up image and promises to voters suffered in the process. 'Factional unity' was Ramaphosa's game – and the ghost of Zuma was the constant companion in cabinet appointments.

The appointments testified to the depth of the Ramaphosa compromise (Table 4.1). In the ranks of the redeemed were ones discredited through questionable Zuma governance projects, such as Tina Joemat-Pettersson (of nuclear policy infamy) who moved into the Portfolio Committee on Police; Faith Muthambi (failed communications minister) into the Portfolio Committee on Cooperative Governance and Traditional Affairs; Bongani Bongo into the Portfolio Committee on Home Affairs (previously on the Justice and Correctional Services Portfolio Committee);[51] and Mosebenzi Zwane (Zuma capture implementer) into the Portfolio Committee on Transport. Supra Mahumapelo, former North West premier, chaired the Portfolio Committee on Tourism.[52] Bongo also served as state security minister in October 2017 when Zuma had to replace Mahlobo, whom he moved into Energy to try and pull through South Africa's disputed nuclear build programme.[53] The Ramaphosa appointments raised questions of veracity and being fit for purpose, given the multitude of ANC cadre considerations that superseded guarantees that the jobs of sound governance would be done.

Between May 2009 and October 2017, Zuma had made close to 130 changes to the national executive in 12 major and minor Cabinet reshuffles: around 64 changes to ministerial positions and over 60 changes to deputy ministerial positions. The average Cabinet lifespan under Zuma was around eight months. Ramaphosa's term brought more stability, although it was dogged by rumours of *pending changes*, many public criticisms of incumbents misfiring, and Ramaphosa's solving problems by moving tasks to supplementary bodies.

Zuma's reshuffles in strategically important portfolios were to see through his projects of, for example, manipulating the Treasury or undermining the efficiency of SARS; getting the nuclear deal with Russia confirmed; and positioning sympathetic ministers in public enterprises so that he, the Guptas and associated people could benefit. Several of his deployments to the departments of Finance, Public Enterprises, Energy and Mineral Resources were cases in point. In Zuma's penultimate Cabinet change, March 2017, he changed ten ministers and ten deputy ministers. In the twelfth of his Cabinet reshuffles, that of October 2017 (a relatively modest set of changes and the last before he was ousted), the Department of Energy got its second leadership change in seven months, David Mahlobo replacing Mmamoloko Kubayi.[54] In the government's nuclear build programme the Department of Environmental Affairs had granted permission to construct a new nuclear plant – yet in May of that year the Western Cape High Court had set aside all nuclear deals South Africa had concluded with countries such as Russia, South Korea and the United States, a decision Kubayi did not challenge. At the end of Zuma's term, the ministers plus deputy ministers totalled 72: 35 ministers and 37 deputy ministers. Of these, only seven ministers were in the same positions that they had occupied in 2009.

As a result of Zuma's manipulation of Cabinet appointments, deep suspicion took hold in the executive. Post-Zuma, this was also fostered by the anti-Ramaphosa fightback champions. The knock-on effect was that deployments of Ramaphosa-ists or CR17 campaigners to public positions would be publicised or scandalised. Two cases in point were the independent power producers and state procurement of pharmaceuticals. In early 2019, the EFF scandalised the fact that Ramaphosa and then minister of energy, Jeff Radebe, had personal interests in independent power producers through their family links to billionaire Patrice Motsepe,[55] whose African Rainbow Energy and Power was invested in independent power producer projects. Radebe gave assurances of the integrity of the independent power producer bidding process: the 'tender process and the awarding of contracts are fair, open and transparent and the security around the evaluation process mitigates the risks of

Table 4.1:   Ramaphosa's Cabinet reshuffles and other executive changes

Date	General action	Select moves
	First Ramaphosa Cabinet	
26 February 2018	Ten Zuma ministers are fired, others are moved to new portfolios; new ANC deputy president David Mabuza becomes deputy president of South Africa. Fired in this round: Fikile Mbalula, Faith Muthambi, Des van Rooyen, Mosebenzi Zwane, Lynne Brown, Bongani Bongo, Hlengiwe Mkhize, Nkosinathi Nhleko, David Mahlobo and Joe Maswanganyi.	Nkosazana Dlamini-Zuma becomes minister in the Presidency, tasked with performance management and evaluation; Nhlanhla Nene (fired in 2015) is reinstated as minister of finance. Nomvula Mokonyane moves to communications, Jeff Radebe to energy, Naledi Pandor to higher education; Malusi Gigaba is removed from finance and returned to home affairs, Lindiwe Sisulu assigned to international relations. Bathabile Dlamini heads portfolio of women in the Presidency; Derek Hanekom (fired by Zuma) returns to tourism; Zweli Mkhize gets cooperative governance and traditional affairs; Siyabonga Cwele, formerly of telecommunications, intelligence, moves to home affairs.
9 October 2018	Former Reserve Bank governor Tito Mboweni appointed as finance minister, in the place of Nhlanhla Nene who resigns following discrepant statements regarding meetings with Guptas.	In Nene's testimony at the Zondo Commission it emerged that he had lied about meeting the Gupta family; Ramaphosa accepts his resignation after 'due consideration of the circumstances' and 'in the interests of good governance'.
22 November 2018	Malusi Gigaba resigns just before Ramaphosa acts against him following recommendations by the public protector. Siyabonga Cwele, moved from telecommunications, replaces him. Nomvula Mokonyane survives despite being implicated in Zondo Commission evidence.	Public protector finds that Gigaba had lied in court, violating the Executive Members' Ethics Act regarding Fireblade aviation issue. Supreme Court of Appeal and Constitutional Court uphold earlier finding that Gigaba had lied to the High Court. Mokonyane (previously minister of communications) becomes minister of environmental affairs to replace deceased Edna Molewa. Stella Ndabeni-Abrahams appointed to head a new communications ministry (merging with telecommunications).

continued

Date	General action	Select moves
	Second Ramaphosa Cabinet	
29 May 2019	The number of Cabinet members is reduced from 36 to 28 through amalgamation of portfolios. It is a gender-equal Cabinet. Twelve ministers do not return to Cabinet (many get alternative deployment, including special envoys to the president or ambassadorial) – Jeff Radebe, Nomvula Mokonyane, Bathabile Dlamini, Gugile Nkwinti, Nomaindia Mfeketo, Derek Hanekom. Those who exit are Dipuo Letsatsi-Duba, Rob Davies, Siyabonga Cwele, Susan Shibangu, Michael Masutha, Senzeni Zokwana, Mildred Oliphant and Thokozile Xasa.	Major retentions include Mabuza as deputy president, Mboweni in finance, Gordhan in public enterprises; Naledi Pandor moves to international relations. Young people occupy several positions, including Ronald Lamola in justice. Specific expertise or experience-related appointments include Thoko Didiza in land, Lindiwe Sisulu in human settlements, Dlamini-Zuma in cooperative governance and traditional affairs.

Source: Author's Turning Points Monitoring Project (The Changing Dynamics of South African Politics), 2005–2020, drawing on personal observation and media reportage, 2017–2020

corruption and interference'.[56] Similar suspicions were sowed when it emerged that the pharmaceutical giant Aspen had donated to the CR17 campaign. It was construed as having bought influence, notwithstanding that Aspen had played a long-time major role in the provision of drugs in South Africa, including antiretrovirals during the Zuma presidency.[57]

THE PRESIDENT, BOSASA 'WEAKEST LINK' AND PUBLIC PROTECTOR

Ramaphosa was a vulnerable president in that those trying to weaken or oust him moderated their use of direct party political operations (after the exposure and possible defeat of the Maharani plot) and turned instead on Ramaphosa and his links to money. This aligned well with the Bell Pottinger-Gupta thrust of 'white monopoly capital' and even just 'big capital' and its association with economic injustice and inequity. One of the lines of attack was the funding that Ramaphosa had received for his CR17 Nasrec election campaign.[58] The funds were not obtained illicitly, yet his opponents used arguments of beholdenness to capital generally, and white monopoly capital specifically, to discredit him.[59] The public protector problematised that Ramaphosa had not declared the campaign donations in terms of the Executive Ethics Code, an argument that was later dismissed by the Supreme Court of Appeal.

Internal de facto ANC rules on fundraising for its campaigns had not been broken. The raising of substantial funds for internal contests had been in place at least since the time of the ANC's 52nd national elective conference at Polokwane. In a prior case brought in Parliament against the former DA leader, Mmusi Maimane, on his funding for the DA leadership race of 2015, the institution cleared him of wrongdoing and indicated that Ramaphosa would be cleared, as he was in due course.[60]

The Ramaphosa-Bosasa link of weakness started with a parliamentary question by the DA in early November 2018. The DA enquired about a R500 000 Bosasa donation to Ramaphosa's businessman son. Ramaphosa provided inaccurate information, perhaps lied.[61] He then corrected his own answer to Parliament, explaining that he had *not known* who had been contributing financially to his campaign. The DA requested the public protector to investigate and she found adversely; she went further by investigating, obtaining and publishing details of Ramaphosa's 2017 campaign funding. When Ramaphosa attempted to restrain her use of some of the information, her office leaked the details to the media. She was intent on showing that Ramaphosa had misled Parliament. In the public narrative, the donations were less about the money that was disbursed than about the new public awareness of the possibilities of state capture, and the narrative police's keenness to use it against Ramaphosa. The revelations, at roughly the same time that Zuma-ists had probably raided around R20 million for their internal campaign purposes from the SSA, hardly mustered an outcry: there were matching reports about Zuma-ists raiding moneys for Nasrec delegate-buying purposes from the police's secret slush fund.[62]

The spotlight fell instead on the incumbents and Ramaphosa. Given the 2018 record of two cabinet members (Nhlanhla Nene and Malusi Gigaba) falling on their swords because of having been less than honest in Parliament, the public protector was to construct the perfect trap. Journalists from the Independent group tried to get additional traction to the suspicion against Ramaphosa by bringing in North West's Mahumapelo. He forged a white monopoly capital link, arguing that through his business associates Ramaphosa had influenced 'the direction of the revolution' and had used this money 'to divide the organisation'.[63]

Ramaphosa's Achilles heel was that the public protector was targeting him and Gordhan on issues on which their own innocence *needed to be established* and could not be assumed. Yet, a full bench of the Gauteng High Court in Pretoria set aside the public protector's report on Ramaphosa's deliberately misleading

Parliament. The court found that she did not have jurisdiction to investigate the funding of the CR17 campaign, and that her findings included material errors in law. Ramaphosa thus let high-level legal processes unfold and Parliament establish procedurally and in fairness how it ought to act on accumulating adverse High Court, Supreme Court and Constitutional Court findings against the public protector.

PRESIDENTIAL TURNOVER AND THE REGENERATION OF HOPE

Scandals concerning public funds and probity had formed the backdrop of the presidencies of South Africa, from at least the time of Thabo Mbeki (see Figure 4.1). The ANC persisted in government nevertheless, and popular mobilisation against the party brought neither a general uprising in protest against severe lapses in governance, nor direct and immediately tangible electoral change. The ANC's defence comprised not just a level of ongoing organisational legitimacy, but also the ANC serially working to create the image of organisational and leadership change and renewal. In relation to the presidencies, the bulk of the problems were to be blamed (with varying degrees of validity) first on Mbeki when Zuma took over, and then on Zuma when Ramaphosa assumed power. Leap-frogging was in effect too. Nelson Mandela had also been blamed in the immediate aftermath of the 1993 settlement – and subsequently in the ongoing efforts to understand the compromises of 1993–1994 – for deficits in the democratic experience. Against many odds, the ANC continued embodying hope that presidential renewal would ring in organisational improvement and would eclipse the need to change the governing party. Invariably, the motivation for a second term was more time, so that the first-term promises would be realised. In the case of Mbeki, it was supposed to be the time of adding economic to political liberation, and in Zuma's second term the 'radical' was supposed to have been added to policy. Little came of it – and that baton was handed to Ramaphosa.

Ramaphosa's assumption of the presidencies of the ANC and South Africa brought breathing space again, after the Zuma ravages. Ramaphosa, at the time, embodied new hope that ANC presidential rotation would substitute for party rotation. Additions to the list of scandals and disgraces that damaged the ANC's reputation, and which the new president had to counter, included the VBS banking saga, the still-to-be-told-in-full story of political killings (only touched on by the Moerane Commission), the network of corruption in procurement and contracting that spanned local governments, corruption around Covid-related

Figure 4.1: Timeline of major ANC scandals, 1996–2020

1996
Sarafina II
Health department gives playwright Mbongeni Ngema an irregular R12m contract for a musical on AIDS awareness (it failed)

1997
Motheo housing
A friend of housing minister Sankie Mthembi-Mahanyele's is irregularly awarded a R190m low-cost housing construction contract

1999–2010
Arms deal
Procurement project for Strategic Defence Acquisition of R30bn to purchase of military hardware

2005
Oilgate I
Sandile Majali's Imvume Management wins a R15m oil condensate contract from PetroSA; transfers R11m to the ANC

2006
Travelgate
14 ANC (and 1 DA) MPs spend R36m on illegal or fraudulent travel claims; plead guilty and pay back the money

2006
Chancellor House
Investment company Chancellor House exposed as ANC front; its business partner Hitachi wins Eskom contracts while Valli Moosa is Eskom chair and ANC fundraiser; therewith started major boiler design problems at SA's new mega power stations

2006–2019
Bosasa
Suspect deals between facilities management company, owned by the ANC-aligned Watson family, and the ANC emerge and evidence accumulates at Zondo Commission

2007–2010
Agliotti and Selebi
Former national police commissioner Jackie Selebi is convicted on charges of corruption for bribes received from underworld operator Glen Agliotti

2007
Alex mafia
Gauteng ANC leaders apportion provincial government contracts to their own companies and those of family members

2007–2017
World Cup Mbombela
Several whistle-blowers on tender corruption related to building the Mbombela Stadium for the 2010 FIFA World Cup are killed; fingers point to cadres

▶ 2009–2010
Nkandla
R240m state spending on the private residence of Jacob Zuma in rural KwaZulu-Natal

2010
Police headquarter lease
National police commissioner Bheki Cele signs a lease for new police headquarters on a building owned by Zuma-aligned Roux Shabangu at R500m, not using prescribed tender processes

2010–2019
Gupta-ist state capture
Evidence accumulates of Gupta hold over Zuma; e.g. attempted hijacking of mining license for Sishen mine; also in Eskom, Transnet, Denel and several provincial government operations

2010–2019
Amigos case
Gaston Savoi sells overpriced water purification systems to Northern Cape (R112m) and KwaZulu-Natal (R144m) governments

2012
Vrede Dairy
The dairy farm was a shell through which Gupta money was sent to India – while the R250m dairy project's stated goal was to empower black farmers; several Free State ANC leaders implicated

2012–2015
Prasa
Orders 115 trains from Swifambo and manufacturer Vossloh España on a R3.5bn contract; the trains do not fit the SA rail system

2012–2019
Transnet
R39bn contract for procurement of 1 064 locomotives goes wrong as prices are inflated on a post-negotiation rapid delivery deal; R17bn lost including on kickbacks to Gupta network

2014–2019
SARS
SARS decimated when Tom Moyane becomes commissioner; SARS is captured to facilitate deals inter alia for the Gupta network

2015
Social grants
Concourt rules that Sassa's contract with N1 Cash Paymaster Services is unlawful; minister of social development, Bathabile Dlamini, repeatedly fails to correct the system

▶ 2015
Asbestos roofs
Free State human settlements department awards to Blackhead Consulting/Diamond Hill JV an irregular R230m contract to identify asbestos roofed houses; only R21.3m was used for the audit

2015–2020
Oilgate II
Strategic Fuel Fund with approval from energy minister, Tina Joemat-Pettersson, signs away state ownership of SA's strategic oil reserves, selling it for R300m, far below market value

2015–2020
Eskom
Evidence grows about corruption of supply agreements for coal, and top Eskom officials forcing the sale of Optimum Coal Holdings to the Guptas; Eskom and the SIU attempt recovering billions

2016
Highlands Water
Lesotho Highlands Water Project delayed by water affairs and sanitation minister, Nomvula Mokonyane, bringing in LTE Consulting at an inflated price; speculation about R2.6bn donation to ANC

2016–2017
ANC killing fields
Spates of killings in ANC ranks, especially at local level and often in KwaZulu-Natal, for access to local state positions and resources, contracts, and prevention of whistle-blowing

2018
VBS Bank
VBS defrauded of R2bn; senior leaders of both ANC and EFF implicated

2020
eThekwini Solid Waste
Former mayor, Zandile Gumede, and 16 others charged for corruption in the waste tender amounting to R430m

2020
Water tankers
Thami ka Plaatjie, chief adviser of water affairs minister, Lindiwe Sisulu, captured on tape strategising with subordinates to enrich themselves from the department's contracts for water distribution

2020
Covid procurement
Widespread corruption and nepotism as politically connected entrepreneurs enter PPE business ventures to procure for the state; inflating prices, under-delivering, abusing comrade status to loot public funds

Source: Author's Turning Points Monitoring Project (The Changing Dynamics of South African Politics), 2005–2020, drawing on personal observation and media reportage

procurement – and, overall, the uber-scandal of limited consequences in most of these scandals.

In some of the scandals, the ANC gained organisationally; in other cases, it was individuals, including some at high level. There was often a fine line between the deals that came to be categorised as corruption and efforts to correct the skewed class-race structure that followed from the decades of apartheid and centuries of colonial distortion.[64] Over many years, a multitude of business deals were endorsed by Shell House-Luthuli House.[65] Many could still come back to haunt the president and the party at any moment of weakness in 'the centre' that had to work to keep it all together.

The Ramaphosa presidency worked for the ANC in that the heightened popular cynicism was matched by Ramaphosa's endorsements of and trust in commissions of inquiry and judicial processes, when the judiciary still enjoyed high levels of authority and legitimacy (despite some efforts to undo that). The endorsements were complicated by Ramaphosa himself having been maligned by the combined force of the public protector and legal and intelligence agents in, or working with, her office.[66] Courts dismissed the charges, but on principles of flawed investigations and lack of public protector jurisdiction, rather than vindicating Ramaphosa. The anti-Ramaphosa network was joined by ANC fightback-faction forces (albeit metamorphosing; the faction contracted as Ramaphosa consolidated his power, then was invigorated as suspicions against him flared up in 2020) and opposition parties like the EFF. These developments notwithstanding (plus the fact that Ramaphosa's delivery on jobs, economy, investment and state-owned enterprises was full of holes), his popularity ratings remained at their mid-2019 levels – and surpassed those of other politicians by far.[67]

VAST PRESIDENTIAL BUREAUCRACY AND THE WAR OF POSITION

The split character of the ANC amid the transition from Zuma to Ramaphosa, and the permutations in deciding whether Ramaphosa would be second-term material, revealed how scheming to retain power distracted from the core business of government. The Zuma-ists first latched onto the weakness of Ramaphosa's margin of victory and then worked to refute his claims to superiority in public ethics, the inquisition relating to his truthfulness in answering questions in Parliament about Bosasa money, the magnitude and methods of money received from big-pocketed donors who helped him win at Nasrec and remain in power thereafter, and his ability to surmount his own flank's dipping into public funds intended to fight Covid-19.

The contests affected state institutions. Ramaphosa had to handle cleaning up government, stopping the bleeding from state coffers, getting the economy to work before and after Covid and realising outstanding deliverables that had been lingering since the time of liberation. At the point of 25 years plus into democracy, citizens were pegging hopes on Ramaphosa, and he had to shape and control state institutions to drive delivery and reconstruction. He replicated and expanded the vast presidential bureaucracies of his predecessors – to help assert control and achieve progress.

Ramaphosa relied on a huge, personalised infrastructure of advisers and support staff (see Table 4.2), plus supplementary structures such as advisory panels and task teams, including specially designated inter-ministerial task teams and the NCCC (see Table 4.3). These structures could act more rapidly and with more focus than line departments, entities that often suffered from incompetence and political agendas. When Ramaphosa assumed the presidency, he invented some new structures, and adopted and restaffed some of those already existing. Many of these structures operated continuously throughout the period of his presidency.

ANC structures, such as its parliamentary caucus, the National Executive Committee and National Working Committee, had been shown to reconstitute loyalties when presidential power was changing – when Mbeki lost Polokwane but remained president of South Africa, and when the Zuma edifice started cracking. Both Mbeki and Zuma had imagined that they had the guaranteed support of these politically aligned ANC institutions, but things had changed. By the time of Ramaphosa's presidencies, the possibilities of these institutions turning on their political principals, and tumbling state institutions in knock-on effects, had become ingrained. Across the state, in pre-Ramaphosa days, government departments had split loyalties. When Zuma took over in 2007, multiple government departments remained loyal to the Mbeki order, although the introduction of new cabinet members helped convert the departments to the Zuma order. They became aligned with Zuma until, from late 2015 onwards, the tide turned again. Then MPs reconsidered, and many senior ANC personalities saw the point of aiding Ramaphosa's rise. Ramaphosa inherited a Pandora's box of rising and declining loyalties – breakthroughs and setbacks alternated and often detracted from core state business.

Ramaphosa was pulled into contests, among others with the ANC secretary-general and Zuma-ists, the public protector and her aligned forces. Many of the state institutions were enrolled into the battles, besides SARS, the Presidency, High Courts and the Constitutional Court, the Public Protector, the Financial Intelligence Centre, the Information Regulator, and the speaker of Parliament. Within

Table 4.2: Ramaphosa's co-optive, consultative, supplementary leadership structures and events: Select initiatives

Date	Structure appointed, event convened	Core functions	Select appointments
2018 general	Two colloquia convened by finance minister Tito Mboweni: an investment conference; a jobs summit; projects such as the Public Private Growth Initiative	Discussions on ways to grow the economy	Academics, government officials and private sector experts
April 2018	Appointment of four investment envoys	To raise US$100 billion in new investment over the following five years; one of the initiatives by government to bring economic recovery and growth, and to create jobs and prevent further job losses	Former minister of finance, Trevor Manuel; former deputy minister of finance, Mcebisi Jonas; from business Phumzile Langeni and Jaco Maree
April 2018	Inter-Ministerial Task Team to attend to governance and risks facing the North West province	Cabinet invoked section 100(1) of the Constitution to put effectively the whole provincial administration under administration after Cabinet had put the province's health department under administration two weeks earlier	Including ministers Nkosazana Dlamini-Zuma, Obed Bapela, Ayanda Dlodlo, Mondli Gungubele, Derek Hanekom, Michael Masutha, Zweli Mkhize, Angie Motshega, Blade Nzimande, senior Presidency officials
July 2018	Inter-Ministerial Committee on Land Reform, supported by the Advisory Panel on Land Reform	Coordinating, implementing measures to accelerate redistribution of land, extension of security of tenure, provision of agricultural support and redress of spatial inequality within the land redistribution and agricultural development programme	Chaired by deputy president, with ministers of planning, monitoring and evaluation; rural development and land reform; agriculture, forestry and fisheries; cooperative governance and traditional affairs; finance; human settlements; justice and correctional services; public enterprises; public works Advisory panel: President of the African Farmers Association of South Africa, Vuyokazi Mahlati, Ruth Hall, Wandile Sihlobo, Daniel Kriek
October 2018	Inter-Ministerial Committee on the Investment Conference	Facilitate the first of Ramaphosa's big investment conferences	Including chairperson minister of economic development, Ebrahim Patel, Trudi Makhaya

continued

Date	Structure appointed, event convened	Core functions	Select appointments
October 2018	Inter-ministerial task team enhancing integrated planning, budgeting and implementation of service delivery programmes in 57 municipalities	Include the eight metropolitan municipalities, 43 local municipalities and six priority district municipalities	Task team is supported by a programme management office at the Municipal Infrastructure Support Agent (MISA), drawing on the MISA technical team of professional engineers and planners, as well as professionals from national and provincial sector departments
2018 general	Inter-Ministerial Committee on Political Killings	Deployed to KwaZulu-Natal to deal with political killings – Moerane Commission of Inquiry had linked killings to local power struggles	Members of the security cluster and provincial government
October 2018	Presidential Jobs Summit, culminating in signing of a framework agreement, linked to a presidential jobs committee with a joint technical sub-committee; rapid response teams (RRTs)	Promised the creation of 275 000 additional jobs a year; RRTs to assist businesses in crisis	Experts
December 2018	Eskom sustainability task team	Advise government on actions to resolve Eskom's operational, structural and financial challenges, including issues of viability and turnaround strategy	Anton Eberhard, Tsakani Mthombeni, Grové Steyn, Frans Baleni, Mick Davis, Busisiwe Vilakazi
February 2019	Special Cabinet task team established to deal with the Eskom crisis	Provide president with reports daily on state of the power grid and actions needed	David Mabuza (chair), Pravin Gordhan, Jeff Radebe, Blade Nzimande, Bheki Cele, Dipuo Letsatsi-Duba
February 2019	The Mining Indaba	To test investors' confidence in the new Mining Charter	Chaired by the president

continued

113

Date	Structure appointed, event convened	Core functions	Select appointments
May 2019 approved by Cabinet	Presidential State-Owned Enterprises (SOE) Council	Oversee interventions to strengthen governance, address liquidity challenges, implement turnaround strategies, investigate corruption and take steps	Expertise from outside government, and CEOs of these companies, shareholder ministers, strategic SOEs
September 2019	Presidential Economic Advisory Council	Ensure coherence and consistency in implementing economic policy and equipping government to respond to changing economic circumstances	'Brains trust' of 18 people, including Dani Rodrik, Mzukisi Qobo, Fiona Tregenna, Alan Hirsch, Haroon Bhorat, Liberty Mncube, Thabi Leoka, Mamello Matikinca-Ngwenya
March 2020	National Security Council (NSC)	NSC responsible for approving national security strategy, national intelligence estimate and national intelligence priorities, coordinating the work of security services, law enforcement agencies and relevant organs of state	Ramaphosa chairs, plus deputy president, ministers of defence and military veterans, state security, police, international relations and cooperation, home affairs, finance, justice and correctional services, cooperative governance and traditional affairs
March 2020	National Command Council/National Coronavirus Command Council (NCCC)	Coordinate all aspects of government's response to the emergency, handle effect of coronavirus and decide on mitigating it; deals with the economic effect of coronavirus	Chaired by the president, cabinet members including Inter-Ministerial Committee on Covid-19 and their directors-general, head of the SANDF, national police commissioner, whole body with input from National Joint Operations and Intelligence Structure
August 2020	Inter-Ministerial Committee on Covid-19 Procurement	Coordinate data on all government procurement in Covid-19 pandemic; ensure that all contractual agreements are publicly available; coordinate communication on the anti-corruption measures implemented; develop a plan to address Covid-19 procurement corruption; effect measures to strengthen government capacity to fight corruption; it would not usurp powers of the parliamentary oversight function and law enforcement agencies	Minister of justice, Ronald Lamola (chair), minister in the Presidency Jackson Mthembu, police minister Bheki Cele, finance minister Tito Mboweni, public service and administration minister Senzo Mchunu, cooperative governance and traditional affairs minister Nkosazana Dlamini-Zuma

Source: Author's Turning Points Monitoring Project (The Changing Dynamics of South African Politics), 2005–2020, drawing on personal observation and media reportage, 2017–2020

Table 4.3: Changing the guard of presidential advisers and core staff

Presidencies (1)	Mandela	Mbeki	Zuma	Ramaphosa
Chief of staff/Chief operations officer	Trevor Fowler		Lakela Kaunda; Jessie Duarte	Roshene Singh; Lusanda Mxenge (acting COO)
Director-general	Jakes Gerwel (DG, Cabinet secretary, political adviser)	Frank Chikane	Vusi Mavimbela (until 2010); Dr Cassius Lubisi (2010)	Lusanda Mxenge (acting DG and secretary of Cabinet); Dr Cassius Lubisi (until 2020)
Deputy director-general		Lusanda Mxenge (DDG Cabinet Office); Ken Terry (DDG Strategy and Operations)	Vusi Mona (until 2010, then moved to GCIS, which was part of the Presidency); Bongani Ngqulunga (office of deputy president)	Matsietsi Mokholo (corporate services); Thami Ngwenya (office of deputy president)
Presidential spokesperson	Parks Mankahlana	Parks Mankahlana; Bheki Khumalo; Mukoni Ratshitanga	Vincent Magwenya; also Zizi Kodwa, replaced by Mac Maharaj (private office), Bongani Ngqulunga; Bongani Majola	Khusela Diko; Tyrone Seale
Personal assistant	Zelda la Grange		George Moloisi	Mbali Nkosi; Malebo Sibiya
Chief director communications and research, PCAS	Joel Netshitenzhe (systematic M&E, analysis of communication media, govt overall)	Joel Netshitenzhe	Sifiso Moshoetsi (moved to GCIS when CR enters); Vusi Mona	Tasneem Carrim (policy and research)

continued

Presidencies (1)	Mandela	Mbeki	Zuma	Ramaphosa
Advisors (select)	Ahmed Kathrada (political), Fink Haysom (legal)	Titus Mafolo (political), Moss Ngoasheng (economic – until 2000) Wiseman Nkuhlu (economic), Mojanku Gumbi (legal)	Charles Ngqakula (political), Mandisi Mpahlwa (economic); Sandile Zungu (economic), Bonisiwe Makhene (legal); Michael Hully (legal); Lindiwe Zulu (international)	Steyn Speed (political), Donne Nicol, Nokukhanya Jele, Khulu Mbatha (international), Bejani Chauke, Trudi Makhaya (economic), Charles Nqakula (security), Olive Shisana (health & social)
Investment and Infrastructure Unit				Kgosientso Ramokgopa
GCIS/Policy and Research Services		Joel Netshitenzhe		Busani Ngcaweni; Phumla Williams
Parliamentary counsellor	Ahmed Kathrada		Ayanda Dlodlo; Siphiwe Nyanda; Ebrahim Ebrahim	Gerhard Koornhof

Notes: (1) The table excludes the brief care-taking presidency of Kgalema Motlanthe (2008–2009); there was largely a continuation of the Mbeki appointments. Blank blocks appear because positions in the Presidency evolved over time; multiple names per block in most instances mean there were several persons over time; alternatively, there were differentiated positions.

Select sources: Among others, *Mail & Guardian*, 26 April–3 May 2018, 'Presidency shake-up as JZ cronies leave'; *IOL*, 6 September 2009, 'Who's who in Zuma's office'; *Mail & Guardian*, 12 May 1995, 'The people behind the Mandela machine', https://madiba.mg.co.za/article/1995-05-12-the-people-behind-the-mandela-machine, accessed 24 September 2020; The Presidency, 2019, http://www.thepresidency.gov.za/content/contact-us, accessed 2 October 2019; *Sunday Times*, 15 March 2020, 'All the president's people'

the Presidency, Ramaphosa could not always count on fully supportive structures. Despite gradual attrition, several Zuma-ists remained entrenched, along with remnants of Nkosazana Dlamini-Zuma's sojourn in the presidency as minister of performance management and evaluation.

Much like his predecessors, Ramaphosa relied on contingents of special advisers, envoys and task teams. Trudi Makhaya became Ramaphosa's economic advisor. Ramaphosa appointed former finance minister Trevor Manuel; former deputy finance minister Mcebisi Jonas; executive chairperson of the Afropulse Group Phumzile Langeni; and chairperson of the Liberty Group and former Standard Bank head Jacko Maree as economic envoys. Former cabinet members and key operators who helped Ramaphosa into power, Derek Hanekom and Jeff Radebe, were rewarded with envoy statuses. The presidency had to have the resources to fulfil its massive tasks; it was also a sponge to keep the political backbone of Ramaphosa's ANC power apparatus on board, content and mobilised.

The presidency re-established a policy and research operation, the Policy Analysis and Research Services unit. It was modelled on the Policy Coordination and Advisory System in use under Mbeki and dismantled by Zuma in 2009. The new unit worked to resolve uncertainty over policy directions – and then the Covid-19 curveball hit and undid much of its antecedent planning.[68] Its mandate was policy analysis and coordination across government and working with the forum of directors-general and the Cabinet; coordination of presidential advisory councils and working groups; provision of research support to the president's advisory councils and working groups; and offering research support to the president's advisors and coordination of strategic programmes, such as the National Health Insurance.[69] It was well after the start of the sixth administration – in September 2019 and after he had first envisaged appointing the council in February 2018 – that Ramaphosa announced his Presidential Economic Advisory Council. It comprised a 'brains trust' of 18 South African and international public personalities, largely middle-of-the-road ideologically and mostly economists from academia and other scholarly institutions. The aim of the council, the president said in early 2018, would be to ensure greater coherence and consistency in the implementation of economic policy and to certify that government would be better equipped to respond to changing economic circumstances.[70]

CONCLUSION: UNCERTAINTY AND PRESIDENTIAL 'POPULISM'

Uncertainty became the new normal in the time of Ramaphosa's settling into power and working to turn around the ships of state, of the economy and of the ANC itself.

Flaws abounded – challenges were huge and capacity compromised, even before the onset of exponentially escalated demand related to Covid-19. There were multiple flaws in the president's armour – he was a billionaire businessman coming into politics at a time of delegitimation of 'monopoly capital', he was often more strategy than substance, he played a fabled long game that was the code for being calculated and considered, but often with little short-term results and consequences. The early years of Ramaphosa in power brought changes that would have been absent had he not won the presidency. Yet, given intractable and worsening problems as his term proceeded, the biggest certainty seemed that neither Ramaphosa within the ANC, nor the ANC in inter-party context, was being challenged for power. Many crucial policy directions, state resource mobilisation to address problems, and the effectiveness of state-institutional interventions remained unresolved or undetermined.

At the time when Ramaphosa's predecessors had assumed power, the cross-cutting pressures on the positions of the presidencies of the ANC and the state were still modest. His predecessors had had the benefit of the credibility of the promises they and the ANC could make. By the time Ramaphosa took over, 25 years of democracy had transpired and only parts of the shortfalls could be explained through apartheid-colonialism and ingrained racial capitalism. The cross-pressures between the roles of the two presidencies had become immense. The point of departure for Ramaphosa to retain a balanced state-presidency was to keep control over the ANC's NEC – while the secretary-general of the ANC was pursuing low-key but persistent challenges. Backed by 54th conference resolutions, they were pinning down the president and his policy-makers – until the all-encompassing Covid crisis pulled a veil over routine ANC political contests. When Covid started retreating, the pre-eminent political challenge was to save Ramaphosa's ANC from being pulled down lethally by the new manifestations of public and political sector corruption.

The president, the most powerful person in the country, used forms of populism of his own. Top-down, he supplemented the available institutions in the Presidency – some actions were following in the footsteps of his predecessors; others were his new creations. He worked with multiple, old and new, consultative institutions – boards, councils, envoys, along with personally appointed advisors – to help him conduct essential presidential business. The experience with the NCCC was particularly notable – instead of mobilising Parliament and Cabinet in their full strengths and activating all their powers, Ramaphosa initiated this institution in the culture of supplementary bodies to do problem-solving. He was called to account and had to subsume it into the constitutionally mandated structures. Ramaphosa through public poll ratings that exceeded those of the ANC and other ANC leaders also had notable bottom-up popular power. His was a presidency of power contradictions

– huge uncertainties and constraints that fused with abilities to supplement institutions, largely, and draw on that popular base.

NOTES

1   Although public opinion polls in Covid times could not rely on face-to-face interviews (a measure that helps ensure reliability), polling company Ask Afrika did credible weekly opinion tracking and pinpointed how trust in Ramaphosa took a downward turn from the time that his Cabinet members started contradicting him. A further plunge came when high-level profiteering from anti-Covid contracts burst into the open. See for example *IOL*, 4 August 2020, 'South Africans losing faith in President Cyril Ramaphosa's handling of Covid-19 – report', https://www.iol.co.za/news/politics/south-africans-losing-faith-in-president-cyril-ramaphosas-handling-of-covid-19-report-f4a7bdc7-fffa-491d-ad77-41baa65e63ef, accessed 6 August 2020.

2   For a summary of background details, see Ryan Brothwell, 'New district model to be rolled out across South Africa by 2021', *BusinessTech*, 28 February 2020, https://businesstech.co.za/news/government/378061/new-district-model-to-be-rolled-out-across-south-africa-by-2021/, accessed 18 August 2020.

3   ANC statement on the outcomes of the National Working Committee, 10 June 2020.

4   Afrobarometer, multiple years, time-series surveys, https://www.afrobarometer.org/countries/south-africa-0, accessed 2 April 2020, was one of the authoritative surveys that showed how trust in South Africa's public institutions declined over time.

5   Cyril Ramaphosa, 15 March 2020, President Cyril Ramaphosa: Measures to combat Coronavirus Covid-19 epidemic, https://www.gov.za/speeches/statement-president-cyril-ramaphosa-measures-combat-covid-19-epidemic-15-mar-2020-0000, accessed 20 March 2020.

6   Ramaphosa lost face when he announced a relaxation on the banning of cigarette sales but Dlamini-Zuma reversed the position. Ramaphosa's powers within his own Cabinet came to be questioned.

7   The details are elaborated by Marianne Merten, 'Who is in charge – the NCCC or the Cabinet? Ramaphosa unveils the blurring of democratic practice at the highest level', *Daily Maverick*, 10 June 2020, https://www.dailymaverick.co.za/article/2020-06-10-who-is-in-charge-the-nccc-or-the-cabinet-ramaphosa-unveils-the-blurring-of-democratic-practice-at-the-highest-level, accessed 23 July 2020.

8   Cyril Ramaphosa, 'My New Deal for SA – and 10-point action plan for jobs, growth, transformation', *BizNews*, 14 November 2017, https://www.biznews.com/thought-leaders/2017/11/14/ramaphosa-new-deal-for-sam, accessed 16 November 2017; see also Tinyiko Maluleke, 'The deep roots of Ramaphosa's "Thuma Mina"', *Daily Maverick*, 22 February 2018, https://www.dailymaverick.co.za/article/2018-02-22-op-ed-the-deep-roots-of-ramaphosas-thuma-mina/, accessed 23 March 2018. See also Anthony Butler, 2019, *Cyril Ramaphosa: The Road to Presidential Power*, Johannesburg: Jacana; and Ray Hartley, 2017, *Ramaphosa: The Man Who Would Be King*, Johannesburg: Jonathan Ball.

9   At one stage opponents tried to divide the original Ramaphosa alliance by allegations that he was scheming against those around him who were politically ambitious; see Karabo Ngoepe and Mzilikazi wa Afrika, 'Revealed: The 11 senior ANC officials on

"Ramaphosa's hit list'", *Sunday Independent*, 16 February 2020. Reports that Cabinet reshuffles were imminent persisted.

10 *2019 Index of Economic Freedoms – South Africa*, https://www.heritage.org/index/country/southafrica, accessed 2 September 2019; StatsSA, 14 November 2019, *Inequality Trends in South Africa: A Multidimensional Diagnostic of Inequality*, http://www.statssa.gov.za/?page_id=1854&PPN=Report-03-10-19&SCH=7680, accessed 21 November 2019.

11 See Susan Booysen, 2017, 'Semi-presidentialism and subjugation of Parliament and party in the presidency of South Africa's Jacob Zuma', *Politeia*, 36 (1), 1–22.

12 In early 2020 in the Ipsos Pulse of the People poll, 62 per cent of respondents reckoned Ramaphosa was doing his job well or very well, compared with the 20 per cent of the opposite opinion. This was down from Ramaphosa's 70 per cent endorsement just after he assumed office, but compared well with the 51 per cent endorsement of government, and the 55 per cent approval of the ANC.

13 Qaanitah Hunter and Jeff Wicks, 'Exposed: Zuma plot to oust Cyril', *Sunday Times*, 8 September 2018, https://www.pressreader.com/, accessed 2 May 2019, revealed the details of the 2018 plot against Ramaphosa.

14 Ramaphosa was once considered Mbeki's top rival for the ANC presidency. He retired as secretary-general of the ANC to go into business, subsequent to Mbeki's being preferred as Mandela's successor.

15 Rachel L. Swarns, 'South African leader fights a fraying image', *The New York Times*, 28 April 2001; Zuma denied 'unverified, so-called intelligence reports' that he might stand for the deputy president position.

16 Moshoeshoe Monare, 'They are plotting to topple me, says Mbeki', *The Star*, 29 May 2006, p. 1.

17 See http://www.timeslive.co.za/sundaytimes/article35857.ece, accessed 7 October 2009.

18 See Susan Booysen, 2015, *Dominance and Decline: The ANC in the Time of Zuma*, Johannesburg: Wits University Press.

19 *City Press*, 12 October 2014, 'Zuma: Corruption is a western thing', http://www.citypress.co.za/politics/corruption-western-thing-2/, accessed 14 October 2014; Zuma's 2009 written representations to the NPA.

20 The list of references is too long to repeat in this chapter. As two illustrations, see on Nzimande, Troye Lund, 'Blade Nzimande – cutting edge', *Financial Mail*, 30 July 2012, http://www.financialmail.co.za/fm/2012/07/18/cutting-edge, accessed 1 June 2014; on Mantashe, see SABC-SAFM, news bulletin, 07:00, 9 April 2014, accessed 31 October 2014.

21 The letter that Jacob Zuma issued on 28 August 2020, for example, cast Ramaphosa's anti-corruption action against Zuma as a ploy to draw attention away from Ramaphosa's own 'shame'. The letter articulated with the state capture narratives of Bell Pottinger, a company hired by the Gupta family; see https://www.biznews.com/guptaleaks/2017/12/28/bell-pottinger-anc-mk-anti-white-campaign, accessed 1 March 2018.

22 See, for example, Sarah Evans, 'Mdluli letter shows crime intelligence was involved in party politics, ANC conferences – Hawks detective', *News24*, 20 September 2019, https://www.news24.com/SouthAfrica/News/mdluli-letter-shows-crime-intelligence-was-involved-in-party-politics-anc-conferences-hawks-detective-20190920, accessed 24 September 2020; Corruption Watch, 3 July 2012, 'Richard Mdluli: A comprehensive timeline', https://www.corruptionwatch.org.za/richard-mdluli-a-comprehensive-timeline/, accessed 4 July 2012.

23 For example, Piet Rampedi, 'Cabinet reshuffle to remove "untouchables" like NDZ and Cele could backfire', *Sunday Independent*, 5 July 2020, https://www.iol.co.za/sundayin-

dependent/news/cabinet-reshuffle-to-remove-untouchables-like-ndz-and-cele-could-backfire-50449257, accessed 6 July 2020.

24   See Ngwako Modjadji, 'Ace Magashule: We don't need white votes', *City Press*, 18 March 2019, https://city-press.news24.com/News/ace-magashule-we-dont-need-white-votes-20190318, accessed 26 March 2019.

25   David Everatt, 'South Africans are trying to decode Ramaphosa (and getting it wrong)', *The Conversation*, 11 January 2018, https://theconversation.com/south-africans-are-trying-to-decode-ramaphosa-and-getting-it-wrong-89886, accessed 2 March 2019.

26   Peter Bruce, 'Talk of state risk-taking just part of Cyril's dream factory', *Sunday Times*, 25 August 2019, p. 20; Kaizer Nyatsumba, 'The arrogance and disdain of our leaders are our greatest struggle', *Sunday Times*, 15 September 2019, p. 19; Rapule Tabane, 'Act like it's your last chance', *City Press*, 8 March 2020, p. 11.

27   Interview, CR17 campaigner and informal adviser, 23 February 2010, Johannesburg.

28   Cyril Ramaphosa, 3 March 2020, briefing to the media, Tuynhuys, Cape Town.

29   It was part of the broader phenomenon of lawfare in South Africa, in which political forces in party and government get bogged down and turn to courts for presumably neutral assessments. See also Hugh Corder, 'Judiciary under attack', *The Citizen*, 23 August 2019, p. 8; Earl Coetzee, 'Chief justice calls out accusers', *The Citizen*, 14 September 2019, p. 5.

30   See, for example, David Maynier, 'Reform is killing recovery', *Financial Mail*, 5 October 2018, p. 18.

31   The ANC caucus accepted Ramaphosa's written correction (November 2018) and agreed that he had not 'intentionally and wilfully' misled the National Assembly – and therefore his actions were not unparliamentary.

32   See, for example, *Business Day*, 21 June 2019, 'Is Ramaphosa too weak?' editorial; *Mail & Guardian*, 21 June 2019, 'Ramaphosa, heed Césaire's words and be bold and decisive', news analysis; Natashia Marrian, 'President snaps out of dreamtalk', *Mail & Guardian*, 28 June 2019, p. 17; Tabane, 8 March 2020, op. cit.; Natasha Marrian, 'Finally, Ramaphosa is in charge', *Dispatch Live*, 5 September 2020, https://www.dispatchlive.co.za/news/opinion/2020-09-05-finally-ramaphosa-is-in-charge/, accessed 9 September 2020.

33   Such cases of lack of action to stop the rot were also referred to by Rev. Frank Chikane in evidence to the Zondo Commission, 20 November 2019.

34   Zuma did not reveal the reasons for the decision.

35   eNCA, 4 April 2019, 'Zuma, Gordhan & doing things right: Ramaphosa's most difficult leadership moment', https://ewn.co.za/2019/04/04/zuma-gordhan-and-doing-things-right-ramaphosa-s-most-difficult-leadership-moment, accessed 5 April 2019.

36   See Rachel L. Swarns, 'Three businessmen accused of plot to oust South African president', *The New York Times*, 26 April 2001, https://www.nytimes.com/2001/04/26/world/three-businessmen-accused-of-plot-to-oust-south-african-president.html, accessed 2 May 2017.

37   See Centre for Development and Enterprise (CDE), 28 August 2019, *Running out of Road: South Africa's Public Finances and What Is to be Done*, https://www.cde.org.za/running-out-of-road-sas-public-finances-and-what-is-to-be-done/, accessed 29 August 2019; Imraan Valodia, 'The claim that SA's economy has declined by 51% is a misrepresentation of the facts', *Business Maverick*, 9 September 2020, https://www.dailymaverick.co.za/article/2020-09-09-the-claim-that-sas-economy-has-declined-by-51-is-a-misrepresentation-of-the-facts/, accessed 9 September 2020, affirmed that

Covid had a devastating impact on the economy and the recovery process would be tough.

38 See, for example, Letepe Maisela, 'Advice to president under siege', *Weekend Argus*, 30 June 2019, p. 5, analysing Ramaphosa's widely criticised State of the Nation address.

39 Mokonyane revealed in her evidence at the Zondo Commission, 20 July 2020, that it was normal for companies that win tenders from government to give back to the ANC.

40 Fraser, through Advocate Muzi Sikhakhane, threatened in July 2020 to reveal state secrets about presidents, judges and parliamentarians when he gave evidence at the Zondo Commission.

41 See Bathabile Dlamini, 'Dlamini warns on wrong channels to raise issues within ANC', *SABC Digital News*, YouTube, 19 March 2016, https://www.youtube.com/watch?v=Y-iZ_-gd2Cb8, accessed 20 March 2016.

42 There was bad blood between Zuma and Hanekom: in November 2016, Hanekom had proposed a motion of no confidence in the NEC against Zuma.

43 See Siyabonga Mkhwanazi, 'Zuma appeals Hanekom judgement', *Sunday Independent*, 8 September 2019, p. 9.

44 See the details of Zuma's speech at the memorial service for Gavin Watson, 3 September 2019 – he linked Watson to the so-called plot that apartheid agents and international forces were hatching continuously against him, Zuma.

45 For example, two of the specific criteria to become an ANC candidate for public office were: no criminal record (excluding political acts committed before April 1994), and no history of ill-discipline or corruption (besides no history of involvement in fostering divisions and conflict). Yet, nothing came of the strong words when the ANC compiled its 2019 candidate lists. The strong words of late 2020 again created expectations that, this time around, there would be sustained action.

46 ANC 54th National Conference Report and Resolutions, December 2017, p. 21.

47 See, for example, the case of the head of the Special Investigating Unit (SIU) blaming an anonymous complaint to the public protector on corrupt officials in a fightback campaign; see Graeme Hosken, 'SIU boss blames "sinister, corrupt" officials for PP probe', *Sunday Times*, 4 August 2019, p. 6.

48 Dipuo Letsatsi-Duba, former minister of state security, as cited in Qaanitah Hunter, 'Lawless spies threaten Cyril's state clean up', *Sunday Times*, 10 March 2019, p. 2. In July 2020 the minister confirmed to Parliament that 15 of the top SSA positions were still being filled in acting capacities.

49 The Zuma Cabinet members who did not make it into Ramaphosa's first Cabinet were: public enterprises minister, Lynne Brown; mineral resources minister, Mosebenzi Zwane; cooperative governance and traditional affairs minister, Des van Rooyen; police minister, Fikile Mbalula; energy minister, David Mahlobo; state security minister, Bongani Bongo; public works minister, Nathi Nhleko; public service and administration minister, Faith Muthambi; higher education minister, Hlengiwe Mkhize; and transport minister, Joe Maswanganyi.

50 See Andisiwe Makinana, Qaanitah Hunter and Thabo Makone, 'Cyril foils Ace parly "coup"', *Sunday Times*, 16 June 2019, p. 1. Several of these 'Ace persons' still became chairpersons, although mostly not in the exact positions where Magashule had wanted them to be.

51 In late 2019 Bongo was arrested and charged with bribery for having tried to prevent a parliamentary investigation into Eskom. In 2020, after emergence of the new ANC

resolve to act on corruption, Bongo was first expected to step down as chair of Parliament's Portfolio Committee on Home Affairs and the NEC, and then reverted to the position of: If I have not been convicted, why should I? Later he also faced charges of fraud and corruption linked to his time in the Mpumalanga provincial government.

52 For the full mid-2019 list, see https://www.parliament.gov.za/committee-chairpersons, accessed 10 September 2019.

53 Bongo became a key parliamentary player in directing possible changes to South Africa's electoral system in 2020, until he was placed on leave.

54 Journalists at the time had information that Russian president Vladimir Putin had dictated the appointment of Mahlobo to Zuma with the aim of speeding up and concluding the multibillion-rand nuclear deal between the two countries. See Mzilikazi wa Afrika, Thanduxolo Jika and Sabelo Skiti, 'Putin's hand in Cabinet reshuffle', *Sunday Times*, 22 October 2017, p. 1; see also John Matisonn, 'How Russia eased its way into SA nuclear', *City Press*, 2 February 2020, p. 6, and Alexander Areflev, '"Secret nuclear deal": There was no such thing', *City Press*, 16 February 2020, p. 4.

55 Ramaphosa is married to Dr Tshepo Motsepe and Radebe to Bridgette Motsepe, both of whom are sisters to Patrice.

56 See Lameez Omarjee, 'There is "no opportunity for corruption" at IPP procurement office, says Radebe', *Fin24*, 24 February 2019, https://www.fin24.com/Economy/Eskom/radebe-there-is-no-opportunity-for-corruption-at-ipp-procurement-office-20190224, accessed 27 February 2019.

57 For example, Aspen was among four companies that were jointly awarded a R10 billion tender to provide the Department of Health with antiretroviral medication from 2015 to 2017. See Piet Rampedi, Karabo Ngoepe and Mzilikazi wa Afrika, 'Businessman defends HIP Alliance's donation to CR17 campaign', *IOL*, 4 August 2019, https://www.iol.co.za/news/politics/businessman-defends-hip-alliances-donation-to-cr17-campaign-30297924, accessed 5 August 2019.

58 See Piet Rampedi, Mzilikazi wa Afrika and Karabo Ngoepe, 'How the CR17 campaign funds were channelled', *Sunday Independent*, 11 August 2019, p. 1. These journalists themselves became players in the political game, serving as conduits for information that was feeding the political feuds.

59 Kyle Cowan, 'Inside the CR17 leaks and the conflict between Cyril's men', *News24*, 13 September 2019, https://www.dailysun.co.za/News/inside-the-cr17-leaks-and-the-conflict-between-cyrils-men-20190913, accessed 2 June 2019.

60 *Government Gazette*, No. 21399 Notice No. 41 Regulation 6853, 28 July 2000, Proclamation by the Acting President of the Republic of South Africa No. R. 41, 2000, http://pmg-assets.s3-website-eu-west-1.amazonaws.com/docs/020628execethicscode.htm, accessed 21 October 2018; Gary Pienaar and Ashley Fischhoff, 'Executive ethics reform is urgent as yet another Cabinet minister is in serious breach', *Daily Maverick*, 6 November 2018, https://www.dailymaverick.co.za/article/2018-11-06-executive-ethics-reform-is-urgent-as-yet-another-cabinet-minister-is-in-serious-breach/, accessed 7 November 2018.

61 Ramaphosa disclosed to Parliament in November 2018 that his son had had business dealings with Bosasa and had benefited by R500 000. In correcting his own statement, Ramaphosa said he had provided inaccurate information and that the amount had been paid by Bosasa (renamed by then to African Global Operations) into a trust account to fund his Nasrec election campaign. Ramaphosa said the money was returned to Bosasa.

62 *Report of the High-Level Review Panel on the State Security Agency*, December 2018, released March 2019, https://www.gov.za/documents/high-level-review-panel-state-security-agency-9-mar-2019-0000, accessed 30 September 2020; see also Qaanitah Hunter, 'Zuma "spooked" Cyril's campaign', *Sunday Times*, 10 March 2019, p. 1; Khaya Koko, 'Police funds looted to buy ANC votes – claim', *The Star*, 24 June 2019, p. 1.

63 See Piet Rampedi, Karabo Ngoepe and Mzilikazi wa Afrika, 'ANC must act against CR donors – Supra', *Sunday Independent*, 15 September 2019, p. 1.

64 This broad context is outlined by Mahmood Mamdani, 1996, *Citizen and Subject: Contemporary Africa and the Legacy of Late Colonialism*, Kampala: Fountain Publishers.

65 Interviews with two former ANC employees/officials, about the power of ANC endorsements, their high frequency and the wide range of benefits that accrued to the ANC, Johannesburg, 2 February 2016, 5 May 2009. These were also the times when the formation of Chancellor House, and its multiple deals, for example into the energy sector, created outcries but did not assume the status of major scandals. See also, Qaanitah Hunter, 'Chancellor House assets on the block', *Sunday Times*, 17 December 2017, p. 1.

66 The South African Communist Party's (SACP) Solly Mapaila claimed that Mkhwebane received information on cases from rogue intelligence elements that had a strong influence on her office; see Theto Mahlakoana, 'Still no response from SACP's Mapaila after Public Protector's legal threat', *Eyewitness News*, 28 June 2019, https://ewn.co.za/2019/06/28/still-no-response-from-sacp-s-mapaila-after-public-protector-s-legal-threat, accessed 30 June 2019.

67 See Andile Sicetsha, 'Citizen Surveys: President Ramaphosa is SA's most favourite politician', *The South African*, 10 February 2020, https://www.thesouthafrican.com/news/citizen-surveys-president-ramaphosa-sa-most-favourite-politician/, accessed 10 March 2020.

68 Uncertainties included decisions on mining and oil exploration rules and the distribution of spectrum needed by telecommunications companies, and state-owned companies such as power producer Eskom that had become heavily indebted, inefficient and riven with corruption.

69 Alan Hirsch, 'South Africa has a new presidential advisory unit. Will it improve policy?' *Biznews*, 20 May 2019, https://www.biznews.com/sa-investing/2019/05/20/ramaphosa-advisory-unit-hirsch, accessed 25 May 2019.

70 President Cyril Ramaphosa, 16 February 2018, State of the Nation address, Parliament of South Africa, Cape Town.

5

Courts and Commissions as Crutches Amid Self-Annihilation

THE TIME OF COURTS AND COMMISSIONS STABILISING ANC POLITICS

In the time of ANC turmoil, when intra-party conflict became intractable, courts and commissions helped the movement to find its feet, bringing escape routes when other state institutions were bogged down by politicians' contests for control of strategic state operations. Courts and commissions of inquiry were pushed into a zone of political arbitration. They were involved, in effect, in political decision-making – the political organisations and government institutions were engulfed by factional contest and self-interest and could not resolve their own differences any more.

The judicial interventions intensified over the years, especially as ANC factions became bogged down in power struggles, state institutions became sites of struggle and control over them became the trophy. In many respects, the Cyril Ramaphosa presidency was the time of high reliance on the judiciary to resolve, postpone or veil political problems in the ANC and its government. Commissions of inquiry and courts were the go-to agencies to extract South Africa's political and governance systems from quagmires. In other cases, the problems were criminal in nature: corruption and capture could often not be handled politically. The fightback against clean-up and consequences, combined with suspects hiding behind legal-domain quid pro quo counter-actions led to otherwise straightforward legal procedures becoming political.

Ramaphosa could let the commissions and courts run their processes, reducing the political sting, allowing him to watch from the wings rather than taking more direct positions (firing people, for example) in state clean-up. As a rule, Ramaphosa moved in only when the evidence of wrongdoing was delivered by commissions and courts – after considerable lapses in time. He could then escape inter-factional charges of retribution and purges. The exception came when Ramaphosa himself became entrapped in the legal webs spun by the public protector and opposition parties to try to neutralise him by using much of his own legal procedure-cum-executive-ethics tactics.

This chapter investigates the role that the judiciary, through courts and commissions, played in the Ramaphosa era of precarious political power. In this time of ANC factionalism, when dead-ends were reached and hands were tied owing to cries of 'factional purge', the courts and commissions had to forge progress where the ANC could not help itself. The roles of commissions and courts, however, played out in both directions. There were wins and losses, delays and frustrations, in the efforts to move beyond injustice and malpractice in party and state. As the battles intensified, so too did the efforts to delegitimise and malign the judiciary. Those who worked to delegitimise the courts and commissions were out in force, schooled through experiences in the previous era when judges saved presidents and commissions whitewashed offences.

My narrative positions the political role of the courts and commissions in the context of Constitution and law, and then unpacks the ways in which the courts assisted government to resolve issues of policy and political incumbency. First, it focuses on the courts being called on to help political parties manage themselves – and, most of all, the ANC in times of internecine internal battles. Second, it considers the stand-offs in presidential politics and how the courts facilitated resolution and were confirmed simultaneously as high-level political actors.

THE COURTS, ANC POLITICS AND LAWFARE

South Africa's judiciary found itself drawn into high politics when multiple ANC factions fought for control over the state and its resources, but needed 'neutral' mediators in the ambit of the law to help find resolutions. Through judgments, the judiciary mediated, played arbiter and called both government and the political parties to order. The role of the courts vis-à-vis the political system ranged from the Constitutional Court (Concourt) acting as the protector of the Constitution, to the Supreme Court of Appeal and the High Courts stepping in to give direction or resolve conflict.

The judiciary, the third branch of government, is positioned constitutionally to assume the complex function of directing government where government itself fails. Section 19 of the Constitution deals with the right to make political choices and to participate in the activities of a chosen political party, the right to fair elections for any legislative body and the right to vote. On multiple occasions, the judiciary stepped in where politicians across political parties failed to secure these exact rights. Section 157 of the Constitution sets out the apex role of the Constitutional Court in matters of state and government politics when it says that 'only the Constitutional Court may (a) decide disputes between organs of state in the national or provincial sphere concerning the constitutional status, powers or functions of any of those organs of state; (b) decide on the constitutionality of any parliamentary or provincial Bill ...; (e) decide that Parliament or the President has failed to fulfil a constitutional obligation...'.

Judges are in awkward positions, public law specialist Hugh Corder has argued, when they are called on to rule on politically emotive issues: 'judges function on the political plane, not in a party political sense, but because they exercise public authority'.[1] The judiciary, through courts and commissions of inquiry, had been in politicised cases before entering the war zone of the transgressions of South African presidents and the Ramaphosa-Zuma fallout. Its role was exemplified in the wrangles for political power when Zuma clung to his presidential positions; in the fallout after Zuma's departure from state presidential power; and in Ramaphosa's clean-up. It played a role, too, when Ramaphosa fell victim to the public protector's 2019–2020 crusade against him. The judiciary was equally active in cases of civil society and opposition parties seeking to resolve questions about the authority of state organs and policy matters, including disputes of ANC governance in the time of the coronavirus.

Unfolding executive-judicial interface of government: Benchmark cases

The interface between the political executive and the judiciary reveals how the judiciary was drawn into the eye of political storms. In most cases, the judiciary took on the challenges to help secure administrative justice and truthfulness to the Constitution.[2]

The Constitutional Court's landmark 2016 ruling against Zuma set in motion his removal from power. In February 2018, when Zuma, under duress in the dying moments of his presidency, instituted the Zondo Commission of Inquiry, the ANC in effect turned to the judiciary to help bring in political renewal. Together with the former public protector, Thuli Madonsela, the multiple commissions of inquiry lifted the lid on sordid sides of corrupted government and equally corrupt party political practices, with an impact that shook party politics. The commissions did preparatory work, which then helped to launch prosecutions and court action, followed in due course by political results. Some politicians also floundered upon cross-checks of Zondo Commission evidence against parliamentary utterances or public protector reports.

The judiciary itself did not escape unharmed from the political wars (see Table 5.1), whether on issues of public policy or occupancy of state positions. The courts were also accused of political overreach, although in some cases they referred matters back to the politicians. Landmark rulings covering different presidencies showed the extent to which the third arm of government corrected policy, government and the political parties and politicians underpinning it.

In a ground-breaking policy matter in 2001, the Constitutional Court ruled that the Thabo Mbeki administration's HIV/Aids policy was an infringement of the healthcare rights of HIV-positive pregnant women and their babies. It granted an execution order to compel government to give effect to the ruling and ensure that medication reached the dying. The Concourt showed the substantial role the courts can play in detailed matters of policy.[3]

In 2017, the activity of the Department of Social Development revealed how even the top courts can be disregarded by senior politicians. On constitutional responsibility and the implementation of policy instruments, the department in effect dismissed the Constitution by failing repeatedly to implement the Concourt order to stop the Cash Paymaster Services (the dispensing agency) contract. The system of payment of social grants nearly ground to a halt. Neither Cabinet and the minister concerned, nor Zuma, president at the time, took responsibility. The Concourt ruling stated that '[o]ur constitution ensures ... that government cannot be released from its human rights and rule of law obligation simply because it employs the strategy of delegating its function to another entity'.[4]

One of the complex, high-level cases emerged around the Economic Freedom Fighters (EFF) and the public protector contesting Pravin Gordhan, former South African Revenue Service (SARS) commissioner, then minister of finance and later minister of public enterprises, on two overlapping matters. The first was his overseeing of early retirement on pension and subsequent contractual rehiring of senior staff member Ivan Pillay; and of the so-called SARS rogue unit tasked with the investigation of high-profile tax evasion. The question was whether this unit had been established lawfully and whether it had conducted espionage within legal frameworks. Ramaphosa was involved because of an instruction from the public protector for him to implement remedial action against Gordhan. Action,

Table 5.1: South Africa's High Courts and Constitutional Court directing the politicians and government

Four fields of court action with illustrations			
Policy matters	**Party politics**	**Governance**	**Presidential incumbency**
Concourt, in 2002, instructs government to give effect to ARV health policy.	Various courts rule over cases of Cope internal leadership squabbles.	Majority judgment by justices Sisi Khampepe, Leona Theron, July 2019, finds public protector was dishonest, biased, etc. in Bankorp/ABSA report.	Legal deliberations as to Jacob Zuma's suitability to become president take off around 2005.
Concourt, in 2018, instructs government to assume responsibility for social grant payments.	Ongoing multiple court interventions to rule on PAC matters of leadership and organisation.	The apex court in effect labels Mkhwebane a constitutional delinquent; important because EFF's tactics against Gordhan and Ramaphosa are mostly based on Mkhwebane's findings.	Concourt's Nkandla judgment, March 2016, finds that the president of South Africa had failed to uphold, defend, respect the Constitution; finds that Parliament, by absolving the president from complying with prescribed remedial action, breached its duty to hold the executive to account.
High Court rules, in 2019, that Zwelihle land settlers may remain on occupied land, because the Western Cape provincial government is busy buying the land to accommodate new land claimants.	High Court, in 2012, excludes Free State delegates from ANC Mangaung conference.	Gauteng High Court Pretoria, in August 2019, rules Mkhwebane should pay costs in the case relating to her investigation into the Estina dairy farm scandal. High Court had been waiting for Concourt before deciding on whether it will afford personal costs order.	Concourt in majority judgment rules, in 2017, that National Assembly failed to put in place mechanisms to hold Zuma accountable. EFF, Cope, United Democratic Movement had asked Concourt to compel Parliament to hold the president to account following Nkandla judgment.

continued

Four fields of court action with illustrations			
Policy matters	Party politics	Governance	Presidential incumbency
In 2000, in the Grootboom case, the Concourt held that the state was obliged to take action to meet the needs of those living in extreme conditions of poverty, homelessness or intolerable housing.	Multiple High Court rulings determine the statuses of ANC conferences pre- and post-Nasrec.	Pending review applications of minister of public enterprises Pravin Gordhan and President Cyril Ramaphosa.	Judge Chris Nicholson, in 2008, presides over the corruption case against Zuma; sets aside National Prosecuting Authority's decision to prosecute Zuma for money-laundering, corruption and fraud.
In 2017, Concourt rules that before government evicts residents from their homes, it has the duty to engage meaningfully with them about possible steps that can be taken to alleviate their homelessness.	High Courts rule on North West Provincial Executive Committee and Mahumapelo's continuous status, ruling for reinstatement.	Concourt hears Mkhwebane's urgent attempt to appeal against the High Court ruling in favour of public enterprises minister Pravin Gordhan, decided September 2019, despite Mkhwebane having tried to withdraw her appeal.	A unanimous Supreme Court of Appeal bench, in 2009, dismisses Chris Nicholson obiter regarding earlier Zuma judgment, ruling that Nicholson had not understood the legal function and was wrong to declare the charges against Zuma unlawful.

Source: Author's Turning Points Monitoring Project (The Changing Dynamics of South African Politics), 2005–2020

on a decade-old case in which there had been several legal rulings already, would have removed Gordhan from other state clean-up work – the stakes were high and some of Ramaphosa's right-hand persons in government were being targeted. The national director of public prosecutions withdrew the rogue unit charges in 2020.[5]

The contest was even more cutting in the cases that centred on Ramaphosa directly. The courts were asked to determine, after the public protector had found Ramaphosa in breach of the Executive Ethics Code, whether in 2018 he had lied to Parliament regarding a CR17 campaign donation received from Bosasa. Ramaphosa denied knowledge, but leaked emails suggested he had known of at least some donors.[6] Ramaphosa's lawyers argued that the Code did not require the declaration of donations to internal party campaigns such as CR17. The High

Court in Pretoria was scathing in its 2020 judgment. It found that public pro-tector Busisiwe Mkhwebane had been misguided in her legal approach and had reached an irrational and unlawful conclusion, inter alia because she had not had the jurisdiction to broaden the scope of her investigation to cover the CR17 cam-paign donations.

The Constitutional Court judgment had already cast doubt on her integrity and competence. The courts had to disentangle the cluster of issues, while Parliament went through the motions to impeach the protector, starting with the preparation of rules to remove her from office. Then followed the appointment of a panel to determine whether there was a prima facie case for her removal. Mkhwebane and her legal counsel showed every intent to take the Stalingrad[7] route, inter alia by challenging the legality of the rules.

The set of cases illustrates the range of top-level political interventions that the courts made over time, and the extent to which 'political government' had come to depend on 'judicial government'. There were determinations affecting the positions of the president and close associates, and the rulings went to the heart of power of the ANC government. Similarly, the courts were called on regularly to mediate intra-ANC disputes that determined top-level power.

PARTY POLITICS, ANC STRUCTURES AND CONFERENCE DELEGATIONS RELYING ON THE COURTS

Democratic South Africa has a dense history of aggrieved factions in the ANC (and other political parties) turning to the courts to help resolve contests and stalemates. In most cases, the court interventions helped extract parties from degenerative fac-tional stalemates. In the process, judges have been required frequently to practise judicial activism, resolving disputes through the application of administrative law.[8]

Opposition parties required assistance too. The Congress of the People (Cope), the Pan Africanist Congress (PAC) and the Democratic Alliance (DA) were among the opposition parties that had turned to the courts.[9] Cope's intractable leadership disputes saw the party limping from one court case to the next until eventually court cases precipitated the dissolution of the party. The PAC became a political party governed by the courts. It split on several occasions (into three rival factions, in 2015 and 2019). Battles included the court-imposed leadership alternation, the disbandment of party structures, and plans to initiate a judge-led commission of inquiry to find the source of the factionalism. Patricia de Lille had a destructive split from her host party of six years, the DA. In the run-up to the 2019 elections, this war torched the DA. De Lille finally left to form the inconsequential Good party, and gained herself a Cabinet position. On a few occasions, judges have directed politicians to find the resolutions themselves.

Lawfare determining ANC elective conference mandates

Lawfare in the ANC, with the courts becoming involved in essentially internal party matters, became standardised at least from the time of the organisation's 2012 Mangaung conference. In many of the cases law was weaponised to damage or defeat opponents. For example, court action by aggrieved ANC members challenged the processes of electing the delegates, and 324 Mangaung Free State conference votes were disallowed.[10] They had argued that their fundamental rights to fair participation had been infringed.

In the ANC it was often but not exclusively the Zuma-ist faction that was called to order through court rulings. Courts played a major role in the outcome of the ANC's 54th national elective conference of December 2017. The High Courts assisted the ANC and provincial delegates of various factional hues to take their place at the conference or, alternatively, ensured that the preceding illegitimate and illegal election of conference delegates was nullified and delegates disqualified. Zuma-ist Kebby Maphatsoe accused the courts of interfering in internal matters of the ANC because some of the judgments were only issued on the eve of the conference.[11]

The Free State, North West and KwaZulu-Natal Nasrec delegations were major legal process casualties. The National Executive Committee was obliged to put into effect three court judgments that disqualified a number of delegates from the Free State, KwaZulu-Natal and North West's Bojanala region after the courts found their respective provincial and regional conferences, as well as branch general meetings, to have been improperly constituted. The court interventions illuminated the extent of manipulative construction of conference mandates. The High Court in Bloemfontein nullified the Free State ANC elective conference of 10 December 2017. The application, by ANC members who had boycotted the provincial conference, disputed the outcomes of a range of branch general meetings that fed into the provincial gathering. The High Court ruled that 14 branch meetings had been illegal. The argument to the court was that the province failed to comply with an earlier order to rerun 29 meetings in line with the ANC constitution. In early December, the same High Court had ruled that the provincial conference could not take place until the 29 branch general meetings had been rerun.[12] In the process, the court also barred 14 branches and 27 members of the newly elected Provincial Executive Committee from conference participation.

In North West, some ANC members won their court challenge to have the Bojanala regional conference nullified. They had asked the court to order that 40 branch general meetings be set aside and the regional conference of 24 September 2017 nullified. The North West High Court delivered the judgment that the election in North West's biggest region, Bojanala, Rustenburg, had been invalid.[13] North West's number of delegates declined from 538 to 446 as a result of 35 of the province's branches being disqualified as voting delegates.

The 2015 election of the KwaZulu-Natal Provincial Executive Committee, feeding into the 2017 Nasrec conference, was also declared null and void. The High Court in Pietermaritzburg dissolved the KwaZulu-Natal ANC Provincial Executive Committee, disallowing the 27-member executive from participation in the conference.[14] The judge in the Pietermaritzburg High Court granted the Provincial Executive Committee leave to petition the Supreme Court of Appeal and the Constitutional Court, but ruled that the Committee would remain dissolved, as per a previous judgment, until the appeal was filed. The province's delegate number dropped from 870 to 804.

The KwaZulu-Natal and Free State provincial executive committees, the Bojanala regional executive and several branches cited in the court cases were all strongholds of the Zuma faction and its presidential candidate, Nkosazana Dlamini-Zuma. Each of the two committees carried 27 votes. It was announced at the conference that 410 delegates would no longer be voting delegates. The total number of voting delegates dropped from 5 186 to 4 776.

Post-Nasrec lawfare and political-judicial compromises

Post-Nasrec ANC lawfare continued across the provinces, and also expressed the changing factional dynamics. Litigation continued at first to settle pre-Nasrec factional scores, but the 2015–2017 battles faded as new lines of division solidified with a view to future succession strategies. National Executive Committee-driven dispute resolution mechanisms negotiated across several provinces in terms of the ANC's new unity-inclusion formula linked to the Ramaphosa side attempting to defuse Nasrec factional fallout, and working to make Ramaphosa the unity president of all factions. The cases of KwaZulu-Natal and North West revealed the changing ANC dynamics as Ramaphosa's position became relatively consolidated and Zuma's increasingly marginalised (and no clear, strong, Zuma-faction successor emerged).

The ANC in KwaZulu-Natal exemplified how political unity solutions gradually replaced the compulsion to litigate. The KwaZulu-Natal Provincial Executive Committee was disbanded after the High Court in Pietermaritzburg ruled that the results of the province's November 2015 elective conference had been unlawful. In

June 2018, this court interdicted the planned provincial conference, which was then rescheduled. While the provincial structures prepared for this July 2018 provincial elective conference, another last-minute attempted interdict to still halt the conference failed, the judge ruling lack of urgency. The ruling was similar to that of the South Gauteng High Court in July 2018 that dismissed an urgent application from some Ekurhuleni branches to halt the about-to-start ANC Gauteng conference. The ANC's KwaZulu-Natal Provincial Task Team convenor, Mike Mabuyakhulu, confirmed that the Provincial Task Team was encouraging inclusive leadership and forging ANC unity, but that the issue was to be determined by the branch delegates. Approximate leadership unity was forged at this conference.[15] The Provincial Task Team coordinator, Sihle Zikalala, revealed that the team had been meeting disgruntled branches who had taken the ANC to court and agreed with them on an out-of-court settlement. Zikalala affirmed the new unity principle: 'While there may have been certain areas of different interpretation of certain events, which is normal for a living organism like the ANC, we are united as ANC cadres in building a strong and united organisation.'[16] As part of this process, the ANC's National Dispute Resolution Committee visited the province and dealt with appeals and grievances from the Lower South Coast, Moses Mabhida and Harry Gwala regions of the ANC. The province was focused increasingly on the ANC's next (2022 was the pre-Covid scheduling) elective conference, and tried to mobilise around unity candidates that would ensure KwaZulu-Natal of representation in the top six.

The new approach of unity-inclusivity, submission to the Dispute Resolution Committee and avoidance of court action prevailed at times, but neither the longevity of agreements nor cross-provincial application could be assumed. In North West an epic battle for factional control over the province started as Supra Mahumapelo was ousted as North West ANC chair and the Provincial Executive Committee was disbanded; later, Mahumapelo was included in the new Provincial Task Team. In 2019, the Gauteng High Court in Johannesburg ruled that the ANC decision of September 2018 to disband the North West Provincial Executive Committee be set aside and that the disbanded Committee be reinstated, plus that '[t]he ANC's failure to consult [its branches] before taking a decision to dissolve NW PEC [North West Provincial Executive Committee] was noncompliant to its own constitution.'[17] The ANC had argued that it was a ruse, not provided for in the party's constitution, and that the National Executive Committee had to consult before disbanding a structure. Two days after this judgment, the court issued an enforcement order. The ANC appealed. Soon thereafter, Ramaphosa stepped in to broker peace and 'unity'; the Provincial Executive Committee and Provincial Task Team were collapsed into one structure. With these steps, the ANC stepped away from the protective shield of legal recourse for political problems, for the time being. Preparations for waves of new ANC regional and provincial conferences were starting to fall into place. New rounds of legal recourse, used when politics became too robust for unity to persist, were likely.

COMMISSIONS OF INQUIRY AS INSTRUMENTS OF CO-GOVERNANCE

The era of Ramaphosa rule brought in a world of slowly unfolding – albeit continuously challenged with allegations (and some evidence) that Ramaphosa and his changing camp of associates were not that clean themselves – clean-up and anti-corruption action. Progress in cleaning up state and government was at best along a jagged forward-backward curve. The calculated and careful operations angered many for the precaution not to alienate any comrade. It brought others to the point of believing that Ramaphosa was the vacillating and procrastinating president, too tactically considered most of the time to lead from the front. He stepped up his leadership style occasionally to address the national crisis of Covid-19, and then relapsed behind the wall of ANC weaknesses and contests that spanned the remnants of Nasrec and the spectres of a next generation of leaders taking over.

As the complementary part of his repertoire, Ramaphosa deferred many of the big clean-up decisions to persons or institutions that could (largely) not be accused of bias or having axes to grind. Commissions, judges and the judicial system fulfilled this need, relatively immune from purge accusations (see Table 5.2). They could nevertheless not escape such claims altogether and were subject to delegitimation through criticisms of overreach. The story of the multiple commissions of inquiry during the Ramaphosa presidency is also therefore the tale of a weakened ANC in power; of the ANC government executive relying on judicial apparatuses to affirm the legality of its operations.

Mushrooming of commissions of inquiry

The number of commissions grew at the time of South Africa's Zuma–Ramaphosa transition – not exactly an avalanche, but more than previously. The Nugent and Mpati commissions assisted the Ramaphosa regime to clean up core state institutions; the Zondo Commission was a longer-term project, its reach broader and its effects visible through subsequent prosecutorial action; it helped shed light on the political underworld of networks of corruption involving politicians, state officials and accomplices. Matters of past commissions were drawn simultaneously into the

Table 5.2: Core commissions of inquiry, 2004–2019: Illustrations

Name and date	Led by	Objectives	Outcomes, findings, select recommendations
Commission of inquiry into higher education and training, 2016	Justice Jonathan Heher	Appointed to help get resolution of #FeesMustFall campaigns.	Recommends post-secondary education funding to be increased through a system of block funding; a cost-sharing model of government and commercial banks; National Student Financial Aid Scheme to be revised; December 2017 Zuma announces free higher education for the poor, discarding Heher's findings.
Commission of inquiry into allegations of impropriety regarding the Public Investment Corporation (PIC), 2015–2018	Justice Lex Mpati	Appointed to determine whether PIC staff have misused their positions for personal gain; investigate whether legislation or policies regarding protection of whistleblowers are complied with; whether discriminatory practices were followed in remuneration and performance awards of PIC employees.	Final report to president April 2019, released by Ramaphosa March 2020; commission finds against PIC senior management and board members (present and past); they failed to manage decision-making in honest, professional manner, did not abide by due processes and prescripts, worsened by malfunctioning PIC board; recommends action by criminal justice system, National Treasury, reconstituted PIC board; recommends on governance, structure of the PIC.

continued

Name and date	Led by	Objectives	Outcomes, findings, select recommendations
Commission of inquiry into fitness of NPA's advocates Nomgcobo Jiba and Lawrence Sithembiso Mrwebi to hold office, 2018	Judge Yvonne Mokgoro	Deputy national director of public prosecutions Jiba and special director of public prosecutions Mrwebi are investigated on allegations against the two officials from courts of law, which raised questions regarding their fitness to hold office; decision not to prosecute former crime intelligence head, Richard Mdluli, central part of the deliberations.	In October 2018, the president provisionally suspends Jiba and Mrwebi pending the completion of the inquiry; in April 2019, commission advises they be removed from their positions and president follows through; commission report makes crucial findings on the independence of the NPA and its relationship to politicians.
Commission of inquiry into tax administration and governance by SARS, 2018	Judge Robert Nugent	Finds no evidence that so-called rogue unit established in SARS in 2007 when Gordhan was commissioner was unlawful; report says commission became aware it had been sought to be drawn into an onslaught upon those who managed SARS before commissioner Tom Moyane arrived (Zuma appointed him as head of SARS, 2014). Moyane had contracted a suspect consulting company to overhaul the SARS structure and strategy.	Final report to president in December 2018; recommended that national director of public prosecutions considers criminal prosecution for Moyane's awarding of a contract to Bain & Co. for restructuring SARS (this pushed SARS to near-collapse); that National Treasury reviews procurement processes where multiple contracts were envisaged for a SARS project to thereby prevent abuse arising from 'loss leaders' early on; Ramaphosa ends Moyane's SARS employment, November 2018.
Commission of inquiry into allegations of state capture, corruption and fraud in the public sector including organs of state, 2018	Deputy chief justice Raymond Zondo	Signed into existence, 8 February 2018, by Zuma (31 March 2021 date for completion of work).	By 2020 around a thousand implicated people had been issued with notices to present their side of the story at the inquiry; oral evidence continued to be heard; Zondo engaged in battle to get Zuma to answer to allegations that emerged from evidence before expiry of the commission's term.

continued

Name and date	Led by	Objectives	Outcomes, findings, select recommendations
Cassim Inquiry into the national director of public prosecutions' fitness to hold office, 2015	Advocate Nazeer Cassim	Inquire into the fitness of Mxolisi Nxasana to hold office as national director of public prosecutions.	Investigation called off in May 2015; Cassim said he was contacted by the Presidency and 'instructed not to continue with the Commission'; Nxasana's appointment was from 1 October 2013, but reports emerged that he had not disclosed an acquittal of murder in 1985 and had not received his security clearance.
Marikana Commission of Inquiry, 2012	Judge Ian Farlam	Investigate matters of public, national, international concern arising out of the incidents at the Lonmin Mine in Marikana, North West, from 11 August to 16 August 2012 that led to the deaths of 44 people; report highlights poor South African Police Service leadership as the main causal factor in the killings.	Commission process revealed the complexity of interpreting what had happened, but few consequences followed; several police officers were criminally charged regarding a mineworker death, but up to 2020, police officers who oversaw the massacre or who lied to the commission had not been held to account.
Commission of inquiry into allegations of fraud, corruption, impropriety or irregularity in the Strategic Defence Procurement Packages/Arms Commission, 2011	Judge Willie Seriti	The commission found 'no evidence' of corruption in controversial multibillion-rand procurement package; in August 2019 North Gauteng High Court set aside the findings of the earlier Seriti inquiry on application from Corruption Watch and Right2Know.	Gauteng judge president Dunstan Mlambo criticised Seriti Commission as a whitewash; report set aside for its failure to admit, interrogate and pursue evidence on the 1999 deal; Mlambo found it inexplicable for the commission to have ignored essential information before finding there was no evidence of corruption, improper influence or fraud.

Source: Author's Turning Points Monitoring Project (The Changing Dynamics of South African Politics), 2005–2020

present, especially the Seriti Commission into the ANC government's arms deal of the late 1990s; and questions were raised about the Donen Commission ('Oilgate I'). The historically unresolved cases reminded South Africa that the ANC had long had controversial interfaces with money, business and international money flows.

This section explores a selection of cases where the commissions of inquiry helped the Ramaphosa order to gain traction. The inquiries helped to neutralise roots of the Zuma order such as Zuma himself, kingpin Tom Moyane at SARS, key prosecutorial staff Nomgcobo Jiba and Lawrence Mrwebi, and high-rankers in prosecutions who worked in an anti-Ramaphosa alliance. Zuma was featured in the deliberations of several of the commissions: directly and indirectly at the Zondo Commission and in the Nugent Commission. His protégés and associates featured on other commission fronts. The more notable among these commissions, however, took time to deliver results, and by the time they did, new tranches of Ramaphosa-era corruption were eclipsing historical transgressions.

Nugent Commission: Edging into a post-Zuma order

Heeding the calls of the Nugent Commission of Inquiry, Ramaphosa suspended and then, in late 2018, fired the SARS commissioner, Tom Moyane (appointed by Zuma in 2014). Under Moyane, SARS had moved from being hailed as world-class to being characterised as corrupted and mismanaged. Moyane's legacy of failure and corruption turned the tax institution 'on its head', said the Nugent Commission. Ramaphosa described the sacking of Moyane as a step to 'forestall any further deterioration of our tax administration system'. Nugent recommended the national director of public prosecutions consider charging anyone involved in the awarding of the SARS management contract to the international advisory firm Bain & Co. What followed was Moyane's version of the Stalingrad strategy. In one of his challenges to the Nugent report, the North Gauteng High Court upheld Moyane's dismissal, ruling that a permanent SARS commissioner could be appointed in his place, and giving the go-ahead for the release of the final Nugent report. Moyane appealed his dismissal to the Constitutional Court, which concluded that the application should be dismissed and a new SARS commissioner then be appointed.[18] Moyane lost every case he and his lawyers instituted against his suspension and dismissal.

Moyane was emblematic of the Zuma order and became a symbol of the then changing political order. He had helped Zuma to dodge tax, and assisted Zuma associates in their state-aided business operations.[19] Zuma had supported Moyane in his Concourt application, arguing that his dismissal amounted to the overstepping of mandates. The objections were in vain. Cabinet endorsed the Nugent inquiry findings, further tipping the balance of power in the direction of the Ramaphosa order.

SARS at the time of Tom Moyane had also advanced the idea that a 'rogue unit', at the height of the state capture years (instituted when Pravin Gordhan was SARS commissioner), was illegally conducting espionage on high-level politicians. Gordhan had become the prime enemy of the Zuma-ists and the EFF. Public protector Mkhwebane used the Radebe Report of 2014 by the then inspector general of intelligence, Faith Radebe, to build the rogue unit case. She recommended far-reaching disciplinary (remedial) action against Gordhan, who was being deployed to a senior Cabinet position.

In a legal detour with implications for both Gordhan and the rogue unit case, subsequent to the 2016 Nkandla judgment the courts clarified that remedial action contained in public protector reports was binding unless challenged in court. A derivative question became: what happens when the report is challenged in court? The public protector and EFF argued that only in extraordinary circumstances would the protector's recommended remedial action not prevail. In June 2020 the Constitutional Court ruled otherwise, bringing victory to Ramaphosa and Gordhan.

As for the rogue saga, inspector general of intelligence Radebe had based the findings of her classified report overwhelmingly on evidence from state security operatives such as Thulani Silence Dlomo, known as Jacob Zuma's spy. Former SARS executive Johann van Loggerenberg, whose own evidence had been ignored, had turned to the courts in late 2019 after Mkhwebane had made it public that she had secured a redacted version of the report. In mid-2020 the North Gauteng High Court set aside the report, probably ringing in the end of the rogue unit saga and its calculated action to harm SARS, Gordhan and Ramaphosa.

Mpati Commission: Stabs at an opaque morass

The Mpati Commission under Justice Lex Mpati inquired into matters of how the Public Investment Corporation (PIC) conducted its work.[20] The commission started in late 2018 and began formal hearings in early 2019. Ramaphosa instituted the investigation pursuing the veracity of alleged improprieties and to restore confidence in this monolithic state-owned asset manager, the PIC, which at the time managed close to R2 trillion in assets, more than 98 per cent of which belonged to the government or its employees. By 2019–2020 it was seen increasingly as a potential saviour of the South African economy and state-owned enterprises, amid disputes about channelling PIC resources into, for example, the insecure Eskom.

The evidence revealed the depths of state corruption. Among the 80-odd witnesses were businesspeople, former board members such as former chairperson Mondli Gungubele, and axed CEO Dan Matjila, who appeared at the commission 12 times. The VBS Mutual Bank scandal[21] featured (the PIC had a 27 per cent shareholding in VBS). When majority shareholder Vele Investments[22] stepped in, the PIC's dreams for VBS evaporated. In mid-2020, two non-executive directors of VBS and nominees of the PIC were among those charged and appearing in court. The PIC's AYO investment was contentious. AYO, linked to the Sekunjalo Group, was linked then to Zuma-ists and a sustained anti-Ramaphosa campaign. Several witnesses at the hearings indicated that AYO had been vastly overvalued. The AYO Technology Solutions chief investment officer resigned in 2018, arguing that instead of the PIC's valuation of R14.8 billion, R700 million to R1 billion was closer to the actual value. The PIC litigated for repayment. Other PIC investments, such as Steinhoff,[23] had also ended in failure. Mpati's report stressed the deficient decision-making at the PIC as the root of its problems.

Mokgoro Commission: Dealing with the storm troopers of the previous order

Judge Yvonne Mokgoro investigated the fitness of two senior National Prosecuting Authority (NPA) employees and anchors of the Zuma order, advocates Nomgcobo Jiba, the deputy national director of public prosecutions, and Lawrence Mrwebi, the special director of public prosecutions, to hold office. The two had acted unquestioningly to protect Zuma's interests and those of his family members and associated politicians and businesspeople. Ramaphosa had suspended Jiba and Mrwebi provisionally in 2018. The Mokgoro Commission advised that the two be removed from their positions; Ramaphosa gave effect in April 2019. In Stalingrad mode, Jiba started litigating for reinstatement. The Western Cape High Court ruled against her application pending her review application against the Mokgoro findings. Next, she turned to Parliament for reinstatement, but gave up her fight in late 2019.[24]

The decision by Mrwebi, some years before, not to prosecute the former head of crime intelligence, lieutenant-general Richard Mdluli, on charges related to the death of the partner of a former Mdluli lover, was central to the findings against him.[25] Mokgoro found that Mrwebi's decision not to prosecute was unlawful and irrational.[26] The commission pronounced negatively, too, on compromised political independence at the NPA at the time. Later, the Zondo Commission heard that in 2012, when Mrwebi was appointed to the specialised commercial crimes unit, Mdluli had requested him to review charges of fraud and corruption that he (Mdluli) was facing.[27]

Mokgoro was scathing of Jiba's lack of professionalism. Jiba's involvement in the spy tapes saga (the alleged attempt to prevent Zuma from acceding into the presidency) added impetus to Mokgoro's finding that Jiba was unfit to hold her job. Mokgoro found that Jiba had been biased, had jeopardised the case and had failed to assist the courts in handling the matter. Zuma had suspiciously granted Jiba's husband a presidential pardon, roughly at the time the spy tapes matter was being heard. The NPA, with its copy of the spy tapes to which it denied access, was a co-respondent in the case. The Supreme Court of Appeal found that the NPA, and thus Jiba, had lacked interest to assist the courts.[28]

The Mokgoro inquiry also pronounced on Jiba's having 'allowed, and in fact enabled, the independence of the NPA to be compromised'. The NPA had prosecuted the retired KwaZulu-Natal Hawks head, Johan Booysen, for racketeering relating to the so-called Cato Manor 'death squad', after a series of articles in the *Sunday Times*[29] about the alleged extrajudicial killings by the Durban organised crime unit. The investigative journalist Jacques Pauw exposed the newspaper's stories as part of a plot engineered in the 'dirty tricks chambers' of the State Security Agency to get rid of the top executive of SARS who was conducting tax investigations into Zuma's associates and had to be stopped. Booysen was charged because he was investigating allegations of corruption by Thoshan Panday, a silent business partner of Zuma's son Edward. Booysen successfully challenged the racketeering charge authorised by Jiba; the High Court deemed it 'irrational'. Another manufactured piece of journalism 'exposed' the Hawks commander, lieutenant-general Anwa Dramat, and the Gauteng Hawks head, major-general Shadrack Sibiya, for conducting illegal 'renditions' of Zimbabweans. Pauw argued (and it was repeated at the Zondo Commission in 2020) that Zuma's keepers had wanted to get rid of Dramat and Sibiya because these two had ordered that Mdluli be investigated for murder, kidnapping, assault, fraud and corruption.[30] Mokgoro concluded that the 'inconsistencies in the reasons [Jiba] gave for establishing a national prosecuting team indicates that she acted with favour and with prejudice to the NPA'.[31]

Zondo Commission: Rot and discord deeper than imagined

The Zondo Commission became a type of truth and reconciliation commission on the Zuma era of governance. It was a bottomless pit of exposés. Investigative agency findings were affirmed, along with the #GuptaLeaks revelations. Much, nevertheless, remained obscured. As the commission received its final extension its investigations were curtailed to the original Madonsela terms of reference, enhancing the prospects of delivering findings in reasonable time. Ramaphosa also amended Zondo Commission regulations to give law enforcement agencies access to the information and evidence obtained by the Zondo investigators.[32] It was envisaged to help speed up prosecutions of corrupt members of the Zuma administration at precisely the time of rising evidence of Covid corruption in the Ramaphosa administration.

Zuma at Zondo

Zuma's appearances at the Zondo Commission confirmed that he was determined to play the game of innocence-ignorance-insubstantiality, combined with political plot persecution, commission unfairness, unconstitutionality, and, in the final instance, the collapse of the commission.[33] It also showed the limits of what even the judicial process could add to bring justice and help to correct government. Zuma twisted the fact that the Zondo Commission was created to investigate him, citing the report by the former public protector, Thuli Madonsela, as evidence of victimisation, injustice and the vengeance of 'former apartheid spies' (Madonsela had directed in *State of Capture* that Zuma's acts of proven and likely corruption and capture be investigated).[34]

By the time Zuma first appeared, several witnesses had implicated him, including ministers and former ministers Pravin Gordhan, Fikile Mbalula, Barbara Hogan and Ngoako Ramatlhodi; high-level civil servants Themba Maseko and Phumla Williams; and former Bosasa employee Angelo Agrizzi (who implicated Zuma and multiple associates for taking generous handouts or bribes). Zuma termed senior ANC members Ramatlhodi, Siphiwe Nyanda (former head of the South African National Defence Force) and Cyril Raymond as spies for the apartheid state who had been bent on 'character assassination' due to Zuma's having 'information' on spies within the ANC. Earlier, Ramatlhodi had said that the Guptas held immense influence over Zuma.

In Bell Pottinger style, Zuma alleged further that foreign and local agencies had infiltrated the ANC leadership and were nurturing their spies to smear him. Such spies were all around, according to Zuma – even the panel that investigated the State Security Agency contained 'two well-known apartheid spies'.[35]

Zuma's Zondo strategy was also in the realm of the counter-factual. To circumvent legal-judicial criteria, he pleaded lapses of memory, on multiple contentious issues claiming 'no recollection'. He could not recall having made a phone call in 2011 to instruct that former Government Communication and Information System (GCIS) head Themba Maseko be fired for not cooperating with the Guptas when they sought access to GCIS's R600 million advertising budget. Maseko's testimony, rather than Zuma's, was upheld in Cabinet and by employee performance records.[36] Zuma also reckoned that the arms deal corruption charges he was facing in the Pietermaritzburg High Court were part of a smear campaign.[37] He denied all guilt in the long-running arms deal 'debacle' and maintained that because he had not been in national government at the time he could not have influenced a national government deal. He remained silent about having been powerful in the ANC at the time.

At the Zondo Commission, Zuma furthermore projected himself as a 'procedural victim'. Zuma's first day at the commission saw him and his legal counsel contesting for control over the narrative. Zuma opened with a rambling monologue about being a target and political victim while his legal counsel objected to the evidence leader's questioning. Zondo ruled that Zuma would submit statements to the commission, based on specific allegations. Zuma's next step to escape Zondo's scrutiny was withdrawal. Zondo then secured commitment to continue working with the commission: its legal team would indicate to Zuma's lawyers the areas of interest in each witness's statement or affidavit on which the commission wanted the former president to testify and Zuma would provide statements that indicated his responses. When these rules no longer worked for Zuma, he pleaded ill-health, trying to thwart his November 2019 reappearance.[38] The saga of Zuma at the Zondo Commission continued as Zuma and his legal team tried to collapse the commission through insisting on Zondo's withdrawal due to 'bias' against Zuma.

ANC at Zondo

The ANC itself was embroiled in the Zondo Commission proceedings. The former ANC president's manipulation and abuse of government processes were much of the reason for the existence of the commission, but the ANC was not the focus per se. It was still under Zuma's leadership at the time of the incident under investigation. The vignette sheds light on how the ANC regarded the leader's interests and wishes as 'law'.

The Financial Intelligence Centre in 2016, dating back to 2012, had identified 72 suspicious transactions totalling R6.8 billion in some Gupta dealings.[39] To comply with banking laws and regulations, the big four banks cut ties with the Gupta family. The Gupta-associated company Oakbay appealed to the ANC, asking it to intervene 'for the sake of preventing job losses'.[40] The ANC summoned the banks. The National Working Committee – spearheading and protecting state capture and leadership corruption, and ignoring the legal requirements imposed on banks – said the bank action 'smack[ed] of collusion', was a 'threat' of abuse of power, job losses at Oakbay had to be 'raised sharply' and, contradictorily, there needed to be better understanding of how legislation related to politically exposed persons. The banks testified that they experienced this as ANC pressure to reopen the accounts. At the Zondo Commission, the ANC input was largely technical, focusing on what the ANC had explained to the banks and taking care not to reveal confidential client information. There was no recognition at the commission that the ANC had been acting in the interest of state capture – and would not be taking a stand to condemn its own actions.

Lingering shadows of commissions past

The history of commissions of inquiry in South Africa shows how they tended to define futility unless there was distance between the politicians commissioning or receiving the investigation and those being investigated. Depending on the commission chair, there would be a lack of courage to uncover or declare the truth, as was evident in the commissions that marked the regime change from Zuma to Ramaphosa. The fate of the Seriti Commission also demonstrated that it took a new judge, in a new era, to get the inconvenient truths to be asserted.

The phalanx of commissions of inquiry that marked the start of the Ramaphosa regime helped to confirm that the old order was closing, albeit in the vacillating style of two steps forward and one back. There was a fightback against the judiciary's determinations, combined with the knowledge that antecedent commissions did not (and those of the Ramaphosa era might not) bring closure. The political flickering of some prior commissions hovered.

Most prominently, the Seriti Commission into the arms deal was nullified in 2019.[41] The non-governmental organisations Corruption Watch and Right2Know approached the courts to review the 2016 findings of judge Willie Seriti's Arms Procurement Commission of Inquiry – the North Gauteng High Court had set aside its findings for ignoring essential information before concluding that there was no evidence of corruption, improper influence or fraud in the arms deal of up to R60 billion in the late 1990s. The Gauteng judge president, Dunstan Mlambo, said the omissions were inexplicable and asserted that the court was not concerned with the legality of the Strategic Defence Procurement Package or the veracity of allegations made against those implicated in corruption. This judgment eroded Zuma's attempts to win a permanent stay of prosecution: the Supreme Court of Appeal rejected his application and Zuma's Pietermaritzburg High Court appearance proceeded. He could no longer rely on Seriti's findings to argue victimhood, plots and persecution proceeded, even if serially postponed.[42]

The Donen Commission's (Oilgate I) inconclusive findings returned repeatedly to haunt contemporary politics.[43] The findings involved persons previously in high positions at the ANC head office, and the business deals that had been signed off out of ANC headquarters. Prominent politicians were involved in business deals around state resources, and there were unceasing allegations of ANC and/or connected individuals benefiting in the kickback industry over the UN Iraq Oil-for-Food Programme. The Donen report pretended to have unravelled the scandal, finding only innocent ANC politicians – but investigative journalists, by contrast, raised disquieting questions.[44] Oilgate II followed roughly a decade later, in December 2015, with the selling off of South Africa's strategic oil reserves.[45] Drawn-out investigations, court cases, settlements and counter-claims followed. In 2019 the Central Energy Fund investigated how the Strategic Fuel Fund (SFF) – with either the approval of, or lack of supervision by former energy minister, Tina Joemat-Pettersson – signed away state ownership. In late 2020 in the Western Cape High Court, details of the SFF transactions revealed that former acting SFF chief executive Sibusiso Gamede had facilitated the deals, and benefited personally. Glencore agreed to return its three million barrels, while other companies contested. The deal had stripped South Africa of its strategic oil reserves, at a fraction of their value. Pettersson might have thought she was signing off an oil rotation, rather than a sale, but the full truth was still to be revealed.[46]

The Marikana Commission of Inquiry also revealed the inadequacy of using commissions to bring resolution.[47] Rather, they helped uncomfortable political situations to pass. Judge Ian Farlam's findings were inconclusive in many respects, and action against perpetrators was largely absent. The two-year Moerane Commission inquiry into political killings in KwaZulu-Natal presented its report in late 2018. Findings pointed to the lethal prospects associated with being a local government councillor, especially for the ANC.[48] Councillorships were opportunities to access resources through tenders: 'This led to corruption, crass materialism and conspicuous consumption ... contestation for entry into politics, particularly at local level, is fierce and could easily become violent.'[49] Years later, the councillors were still falling.

The Heher Commission into fee-free higher education, established at the height of the #FeesMustFall protests of 2016, was a reminder of how commissions can fulfil their tasks yet be overruled by executive political decree, as happened in late 2017. Zuma's personal-interest intervention nevertheless favoured the ANC by defusing hostile student mobilisation and winning favour for the party.

The Hefer Commission of 2004 in some respects resembled the Zondo Commission, with witnesses manufacturing accusations of 'apartheid spies' in the ranks of senior politicians. Zuma had been unhappy with how Bulelani Ngcuka, national director of public prosecutions and head of the Scorpions, dealt with an investigation into Zuma's involvement in the arms deal.[50] ANC state security head Moe Shaik, and ANC veteran Mac Maharaj fuelled the allegations, for which the Hefer

Commission found no substantiation.[51] Vusi Pikoli was another national director of public prosecutions subjected to investigation by commission – through the Ginwala enquiry,[52] which recommended in November 2008 that Pikoli should remain in the position as there was insufficient evidence of irretrievable breakdown in his relationship with the minister.

These failed and inconclusive commissions and inquiries hint at traps for the commissions marking the Ramaphosa period. Many past commissions brought 'answers', including superficial and untruthful ones, on vexed issues. They bought time and helped to evade uncomfortable realities. The Ramaphosa commissions helped forge transitions out of conditions of capture and fightback, and played political roles where the Ramaphosa politicians dared not tread. Their findings could also be marginalised.

RAMAPHOSA PRESIDENCY VS PUBLIC PROTECTOR

One of Ramaphosa's early 'appearances' at the Zondo Commission was in name rather than person. Bosasa had had damning exposure at the Zondo Commission. It was an ANC donor and had paid bribes to many high-ranking ANC politicians, including Zuma and his associates (former minister Nomvula Mokonyane would point out that this was how the ANC operated normally).[53] Bosasa had also donated to the CR17 campaign, and in Parliament the DA questioned the gift. First, Ramaphosa gave a factually wrong answer; a few days later he self-corrected.

Opposition parties became interested and the public protector entered to try to bring Ramaphosa down. He recognised the attack in a 2019 affidavit: 'The role of the public protector is to strengthen our democracy – not to undermine confidence in the president by raising false alarms.'[54] Politicians could only partly resolve these issues; the onus concerning Ramaphosa and his presidential future was handed over to the judiciary.

The political-judicial events of the unfolding campaign against the Ramaphosa presidency – pivoting around the public protector, possibly cooperating with state intelligence agencies[55] – went to the heart of South Africa's precarious democracy. The dramatis personae included a president expected to stamp out corruption but accused himself for links to big capital and donors; a public protector acting against the president while she had already accumulated multiple adverse Constitutional Court and High Court findings for dishonesty, lack of integrity and incompetence;[56] and a Parliament that was still traumatised by its Jacob Zuma experience and now had to make rules to impeach a public protector. The following periodisation reveals how this interface between the executive and judiciary in the Ramaphosa era shaped government, governance and ANC political power.

Initial questions and answers in commissions and Parliament

In early November 2018, then DA leader Mmusi Maimane presents a signed affidavit by a former Bosasa auditor which reveals that a R500 000 payment was made in October 2017 to an attorney's trust account named 'EFG2', designating a law firm (Edelstein Farber Grobler) associated with CR17 finances. Ramaphosa responds in the National Assembly, stating that his son Andile was in business with Bosasa and the amount was payment on a contract.[57] Ramaphosa junior denies that such a payment ever reached him. In a letter to the speaker of Parliament, Ramaphosa admits to inadvertently having supplied the wrong information.[58] He concedes that the money was a donation by the Bosasa CEO, Gavin Watson, to his CR17 campaign. Maimane asks the public protector to probe suspicions of money-laundering.

Public protector stretching the mandate and issuing her report

In mid-2019 the public protector extends the ambit of investigating CR17 donations, citing a case in which the Supreme Court of Appeal had ruled that the public protector 'should not be bound or limited by the issues raised for consideration and determination by the parties but should investigate further and discover the truth and also inspire confidence that the truth has been discovered'.[59] A month later she releases her report into CR17 funding and Ramaphosa's obligations to declare. She finds merit in allegations of money-laundering, noting that the donation went through several intermediaries before appearing in the CR17 fund. The report argues that Ramaphosa may have been captured by his private donors. The protector also identifies campaign donations totalling close to R200 million, including three large amounts from one donor, and says that Ramaphosa has breached the Executive Ethics Code in failing to declare the CR17 donations to Parliament. Mkhwebane gives the speaker 30 days to refer her finding that Ramaphosa had violated the Code to Parliament's Joint Committee on Ethics and Members' Interests and to demand that Ramaphosa disclose all the donations to the CR17 campaign. The DA calls for an ad hoc committee to probe the public protector's findings against Ramaphosa.

Ramaphosa strikes in defence, launches a court review, approaches High Court

In July 2019, Ramaphosa launches a court review of the protector's Bosasa donation report. He approaches the High Court to set aside the report and, in the interim, to interdict the implementation of some of the remedial action directed by the protector. He argues that she was not empowered to unilaterally expand the scope of an investigation under the Executive Ethics Act – the DA and EFF complaints that gave rise to Mkhwebane's investigation were limited to the R500 000 donation and she was to investigate only what was in the complaints. It was a fundamental misreading of the Code to aver that he was obligated to disclose donations received by the campaign, he argued. Prior to the release of the final report, Ramaphosa had sent Mkhwebane a response in terms of section 7(9) of the Public Protector Act, which entitles someone implicated to respond to preliminary findings. In it, he identifies a number of instances where he says she had the facts wrong.[60]

Email leaks, approach to Gauteng High Court, accumulating parties to the case

In August 2019, the media receive and publish leaked emails[61] that had been circulating on social media and among Ramaphosa's opponents. They reveal the names of some of the Ramaphosa donors and undermine the defence that Ramaphosa was kept at arm's length in dealing with funders. The president's spokesperson notes that the protector had improperly broadened her investigation into what are considered to be private entities not subject to her purview.[62] Ramaphosa's campaign managers reckon their communications had been intercepted illegally, or revealed by a disgruntled former information technology adviser and that the protector's report relies on these emails to argue Ramaphosa's involvement in the campaign's fundraising.

Ramaphosa approaches the Gauteng High Court to have details of bank statements in the report sealed. He flags four such accounts: his own foundation's account, the EFG2 account, Linked Environmental Services and Ria Tenda Trust. The Gauteng High Court in Pretoria grants Ramaphosa an interdict, unopposed by Mkhwebane, to stay the remedial action stemming from her investigation into the Bosasa donation. The information regulator, Pansy Tlakula, asks to join as a friend of the court, noting Ramaphosa's concerns about how Mkhwebane had obtained CR17's financial information and that it may have been in breach of the Protection of Personal Information Act. Mkhwebane refuses to consent, arguing that Ramaphosa's concerns are 'academic' because the Financial Intelligence Centre had confirmed that the bank statements were lawfully received by the protector. In a supplementary affidavit, Ramaphosa reiterates matters concerning gaining access to private emails, breaches of the Protection of Personal Information Act, the rule 53 record, the Financial Intelligence Centre not having been the source and, generally, the emails having been obtained unlawfully. He 'strongly suggests that the bank account information was included … for improper or gratuitous purposes'. He surmises that the protector's 'eagerness to have bank account statements, and other personal or private information that the public protector obtained from the FIC [Financial Intelligence Centre] form part of the record, is motivated by an ulterior purpose'.[63] Next, the speaker joins the case as applicant instead of respondent. Then the Financial Intelligence Centre follows, arguing that there is no conclusive indication of money-laundering in the financial documents that the Financial Intelligence Centre provided to the protector. The amaBhungane Centre for Investigative Journalism follows, arguing that Ramaphosa's lawyers are correct about the Executive Ethics Code not requiring politicians to declare internal party campaign funding, and linking the Ramaphosa case to a precedent set when Maimane was absolved of violating the code of conduct for members of Parliament when he had failed to declare who had funded his campaign for DA leadership.[64]

From the High Court, Gauteng, to appealing to the Constitutional Court

Following Ramaphosa's review application regarding the public protector's having misapplied the law in her investigations, in March 2020 a full bench of the High Court in Pretoria finds that the protector had failed properly to analyse facts before this Section 9 institution and had demonstrated a lack of basic knowledge of the law and its application. There are fundamental difficulties with her finding that Ramaphosa had deliberately misled Parliament. The ruling describes her findings against Ramaphosa as irrational, reckless and informed by misdirected conflation and confusion and that she did not have the jurisdiction to investigate the conduct of the CR17 campaign as it did not constitute public or state affairs. The ruling finds furthermore that Ramaphosa has not derived personal benefit from the donations. The court sets aside the public protector's remedial actions against Ramaphosa as contained in her 2019 report on Bosasa. The public protector, with the EFF and the amaBhungane Centre for Investigative Journalism, receive leave to appeal the findings to the Constitutional Court, and the case is heard in late 2020.[65]

The judiciary and the executive, as two arms of the South African government, are interrelated and complementary. In the course of frequent disputes among politicians, or politicians and high-level bureaucrats, however, the courts rose in profile and assumed roles in mediating the precarious political power of ANC, government and state. The focus on the first few years of Ramaphosa's 2019–2024 term revealed the extent to which the judiciary shared power with the politicians, becoming de facto the kingmaker to the powers on the throne.

FIGHTBACK AND DELEGITIMATION OF THE JUDICIARY

Commissions and courts assisted the ANC and Ramaphosa in the period from 2017 onwards to consolidate power and clean up remnants of the ancien régime, and they helped to stabilise the Ramaphosa presidency. The courts and commissions of inquiry had become political actors – and they became fair game as well. The fightback against the Ramaphosa-judiciary 'alliance' came in the main from a range of Zuma-ists, in their ranks public protector Mkhwebane, and associated with these ranks the EFF's Julius Malema.

Historically there were cases of the commissions and court cases being appropriated to subvert otherwise sound, legitimate proceedings. The Nicholson obiter of 2008, which favoured Zuma's ascendency, was a classical instance of how a ruling that was wrong in jurisprudence created a fleeting political reprieve that Zuma-ists seized to push Mbeki out of the presidency. A unanimous Supreme Court of Appeal bench overturned the Nicholson ruling, which had asserted that the corruption charges against Zuma had been unlawful, with judge Louis Harms, deputy president of the Supreme Court of Appeal at the time, condemning the Nicholson ruling as 'failure to confine the judgment to the issues before the court', 'failing to distinguish between allegation, fact and suspicion' and 'transgressing the proper boundaries between judicial, executive and legislative functions'.[66]

The Mkhwebane strategy to bring down or sabotage the Ramaphosa regime converged on occasion with that of Julius Malema. At such moments, they constituted a powerful fightback frontline. Mkhwebane's approach followed the legal, investigative, prosecutorial route that this chapter has highlighted, whereas Malema and social media troops, including bots, pursued a project of discrediting the judiciary and judges, in addition to Ramaphosa and his circle,[67] manufacturing counter-narratives. When the legal and tax coils tightened around Julius Malema he became increasingly scathing in narratives to discredit 'the judges'. When public protector Mkhwebane wanted to further the project to get rid of Pravin Gordhan, she constructed a case based on the SARS 'rogue unit', irrespective of the fact that this would be a tenth probe into allegations surrounding the unit and contradictory, inconclusive and contested findings on the matter had spanned the best part of a decade, until in 2020 the national director of public prosecutions withdrew all criminal charges against the alleged perpetrators. The protector attempted to apply her binding powers to subvert the Ramaphosa presidency, delivering findings and instructing remedial action that could only be countered through matching courts of law action. In 2016, in the case of the *Economic Freedom Fighters v Speaker of the National Assembly and Others; Democratic*

Alliance v Speaker of the National Assembly and Others, it was confirmed that the recommendations of the public protector were binding, but the problem was that the contemporaneous context of the Concourt's earlier endorsement of the previous public protector's binding remedial powers did not fit well with a next protector who then abused those emphatic powers,[68] and who had several of her reports challenged in court.

The public protector-Malema campaign came in the wake of judgments handed down against the protector and the EFF leader. In mid-2019, in response to charges brought against Malema, deputy judge president Aubrey Ledwaba said the Riotous Assemblies Act No. 17 of 1956, which prohibits the incitement of violence, was in line with the Constitution. Malema had been charged for encouraging supporters to occupy land. He argued that the charge of incitement criminalises free expression.[69] The courts had also found against Malema for contravening the electoral code (for Twitter incitement of action against a journalist); Malema lost a defamation case that the former finance minister, Trevor Manuel, brought against him for a Twitter claim that Manuel had a corrupt relationship with the head of SARS, Edward Kieswetter. Malema's relationship with the judiciary also included occasional counter-evidence.

The public protector-Malema campaign aimed to make the judiciary – a final line of defence against malfeasance in South Africa – appear as if it had collapsed, and that it was targeting Malema and his associates, including the protector, while serving Ramaphosa and Gordhan.[70] Malema described judges as 'traumatised and old' and asserted that some were 'incompetent and threatened by politicians that appear before them'.[71] 'If judges judge according to who appears before them, they must know we will be left with no options but to take up arms, because there is no neutrality in South Africa ... A biased judiciary will force us into the bush.'[72] Social media campaigners circulated a list of names of judges who they claimed had committed wrongdoing and had been captured; Chief Justice Mogoeng Mogoeng urged anyone with credible, specific evidence on judges' capture to report the matter. The social media post had alleged that the judges in question, plus the national director of public prosecutions, had received payments from the CR17 fund. The list included the judges who had found against the EFF. Mogoeng responded: 'Only a sworn enemy of our democracy would make allegations so grave against the judiciary without evidence to back it up.'[73] He said his office had asked the national police commissioner to 'uncover the real forces behind the masks who are making apparently gratuitous allegations of corruption or capture against the judiciary'.[74]

CONCLUSION: JUDICIAL AUTHORITY AS ANALOGOUS GOVERNMENT

The ANC experienced precarious power on many fronts. Courts and commissions of inquiry stepped into roles of giving direction, practising judicial activism where ANC factions and their associates were bogged down in disputes. At stake was control over many of the most strategic, powerful and well-resourced institutions of the state. When the Ramaphosa ANC was unable to move for risk of attacks, commissions of inquiry – flaws and all – formed bulwarks of reason and action. When factions overstepped the mark and acted unprocedurally, or with prejudice, in trying to outmanoeuvre their intra-ANC opponents, judges of the High Court, Supreme Court of Appeal and apex court, the Constitutional Court of South Africa, frequently had to become uber-politicians and help the ANC return to reason and rule of law.

The political factors that fed into this condition included the post-Nasrec Zuma faction refusing to let go of power, or to let investigative and prosecutorial agencies explore the practices that were the trademarks of their era of governance, or to prepare the ground for new assaults on potential future ANC 'princes'. The judicial authorities themselves were targeted with accusations of judicial overreach, and being captured, compromised and biased. Yet, the role of the Constitutional Court as protector of the Constitution was in the final instance still accepted as authoritative.

The occurrences analysed in this chapter were still in the historically safe zone of the earlier parts of the Ramaphosa presidency. The transgressions of the Zuma era were so blatant that it appeared easy for the law and courts frequently to pronounce on the pre-Ramaphosa era. As this piece of writing concluded, there were growing signs of corruption in the ranks of Ramaphosa-ists operating in a grey zone where the compulsion for blatant money-making met entitlement in party and government to do business with the state, and met knowledge of how to play state procurement processes to stay technically on the right side of the law.

NOTES

1   Hugh Corder, 'Judiciary under attack', *The Citizen*, 23 August 2019.
2   The Constitutional Court plays a central role in politics and governance in South Africa; see https://www.concourt.org.za/index.php/about-us/role, accessed 26 September 2019.
3   The then minister of health had been critical of the courts stepping in to ensure that government policy matched constitutional requirements; see *News24*, 5 July 2002, 'State accepts Aids ruling', https://www.news24.com/SouthAfrica/AidsFocus/State-accepts-Aids-ruling-20020705, accessed 6 July 2019.

4   Constitutional Court judgment, 13 August 2018, Case CCT 48/17, www.saflii.org, accessed 6 October 2020.

5   The EFF appealed. As in several other cases, the EFF at the time aligned with the public protector. In an unrelated case, also involving SARS (at this time the new SARS under Ramaphosa), the EFF opposed the protector regarding her revealing SARS records pertaining to Zuma's taxes.

6   The emails indicated that Ramaphosa was aware of the funding of his campaign despite persistent denials that he had any direct knowledge of financial issues; roughly a week after publication, the head of the Presidential Protection Unit, Wally Rhoode, wrote to the head of the Hawks, General Godfrey Lebeya, asking for a probe into the possible hacking of Ramaphosa and his advisors' email accounts.

7   Denoting mostly Zuma's strategy to prolong and roll over legal charges and court appearances and thereby never be held accountable. It often amounted to using technicalities to avoid or delay the possible reinstatement of the charges of fraud, corruption, money-laundering and racketeering. It climaxed in 2019 in Zuma actually appearing in court on specific charges, and then applying for a permanent stay of prosecution.

8   See Pierre de Vos, 'Between judicial activism and judicial restraint', *Constitutionally Speaking*, 20 January 2009, https://constitutionallyspeaking.co.za/between-judicial-activism-and-judicial-restraint/, accessed 1 April 2016.

9   See Susan Booysen, 2011, 'Countered and cowered Congress of the People', in *The ANC and the Regeneration of Political Power*, Johannesburg: Wits University Press, pp. 325–355. The PAC post-1994 has always been small, but the internecine squabbles that frequently ended up in court made it decline even further; see *News24*, 4 November 2019, 'IEC awaits court outcome before deciding on PAC's rightful leadership', https://www.news24.com/news24/southafrica/news/iec-awaits-court-outcome-before-deciding-on-pacs-rightful-leadership-20191104, accessed 2 April 2020. Patricia de Lille was one of the members who took the DA to court; see *The South African*, 24 April 2019, 'I was not fired, I resigned', https://www.thesouthafrican.com/news/patricia-de-lille-da-court-not-fired-resigned/, accessed 29 April 2019.

10   See Applicant's Founding Affidavit, December 2012, regarding the Free State ANC provincial conference held in Parys, Free State, 21–24 June 2012. See also Susan Booysen, 2013, *The ANC's Battle of Mangaung*, Cape Town: Tafelberg, in the Shorts e-Book Series.

11   Kebby Maphatsoe (NEC member and Zuma-ist) accused the courts of interfering in internal ANC matters: 'Why is [sic] the courts making these judgments on the eve of conference. Why didn't they make these judgments last week?'; Qaanitah Hunter, 'ANC calls urgent NEC meeting on three critical court judgments', *Timeslive*, 15 December 2017, https://www.timeslive.co.za/politics/2017-12-15-anc-calls-urgent-nec-meeting-on-three-critical-court-judgments/, accessed 15 December 2017.

12   According to an attorney for the complainants, 32 per cent of the Free State branches had raised disputes.

13   North West judge president Monica Leeuw declared the regional ANC elections invalid: 'All branch meetings inclusive of its decisions, resolutions and elections held during October–November 2017 for the purpose of electing delegates to the national conference are irregular, invalid and unconstitutional and therefore set aside.'

14   Judge Rishi Seegobin presided; his judgment was delivered as delegates started arriving at Nasrec. As the Provincial Executive Committee scrambled to appeal, the original applicants applied for an enforcement order.

15   Sihle Zikalala was elected as provincial chairperson (unopposed); deputy provincial chairperson, Mike Mabuyakhulu; provincial secretary, Mdumiseni Ntuli; provincial treasurer, Nomusa Dube-Ncube (unopposed); and deputy, Sipho Hlomuka.

16   Zikalala, KwaZulu-Natal ANC leader, 2018, as cited in Mxolisi Mngadi, 'ANC KZN provincial conference delegates must decide on whether they want unity leadership – PTT', *News24*, 17 July 2018, https://www.news24.com/SouthAfrica/News/anc-kzn-provincial-conference-delegates-must-decide-on-whether-they-want-unity-leadership-ptt-20180717, accessed 20 August 2020.

17   The case of North West also showed how the approach of 'follow the judge' paid off. Judge Fayeeza Kathree-Setiloane, from a well-known North West political family, acted in South Gauteng at the time. See also Setumo Stone, 'Gloves off in wild ANC North West', *City Press*, 1 March 2020.

18   Cabinet statement, as cited in Carin Smith, 'Cabinet notes "massive failure" of governance, integrity at SARS under Moyane', *Fin24*, 29 March 2019, https://www.fin24.com/Economy/cabinet-notes-massive-failure-of-governance-integrity-at-sars-under-moyane-20190329, accessed 20 March 2020.

19   See Jacques Pauw, 2017, *The President's Keepers: Those Keeping Zuma in Power and out of Prison*, Cape Town: NB Publishers/Tafelberg.

20   Mpati was assisted by former Reserve Bank governor, Gill Marcus, and stockbroker, Emmanuel Lediga.

21   See Advocate Terry Motau, 'How VBS was looted: The full report', *PoliticsWeb*, 10 October 2018, https://www.politicsweb.co.za/documents/how-vbs-was-looted-the-full-report, accessed 1 March 2019. In August 2020 the Pretoria High Court set aside parts of the report. Judge Vivian Tlhapi found it was unconstitutional and unlawful that Motau failed to hear the implicated former Limpopo ANC treasurer Daniel Msiza's side of the story prior to releasing the report. Motau and the Reserve Bank appealed.

22   Peter Ramothwala, 'Suspended Vele Investments chairman Maanda Manyatshe hints at fraud', *Sowetan Live*, 20 June 2018, https://www.sowetanlive.co.za/business/2018-06-20-suspended-vele-investments-chairman-maanda-manyatshe-hints-at-fraud/, accessed 25 September 2020, gives details on Vele arguing that they themselves had been hoodwinked.

23   For an overview, see Jackie Cameron, 'The Steinhoff scandal unpacked: Five-part series in one place', *BizNews*, 6 July 2018, https://www.biznews.com/sa-investing/2018/07/06/steinhoff-scandal-unpacked-must-read-five-part-series, accessed 9 July 2019.

24   Earlier, the Supreme Court of Appeal in a majority judgment had found no grounds to deem Jiba and Mrwebi unfit to hold office in an application by the General Council of the Bar. The Concourt upheld this judgment.

25   Mdluli was found guilty on charges of kidnapping and assault (murder charges had been withdrawn, and he was cleared on lesser charges of intimidation after a Concourt ruling declared a section of the Intimidation Act unconstitutional).

26   Mokgoro Commission, Enquiry in terms of Section 12(6) of the National Prosecuting Authority Act 32 of 1998, Abridged version, 1 April 2019, https://mg.co.za/article/2019-04-26-read-it-in-full-unabridged-mokgoro-report, accessed 4 April 2019.

27   Hawks investigator, Kobus Roelofse, in oral evidence to the Zondo Commission of Inquiry, 19 September 2019, Parktown, Johannesburg.

28   To clarify the Supreme Court of Appeal's reasoning, see https://www.news24.com/Video/SouthAfrica/News/watch-live-sca-to-rule-on-zuma-spy-tapes-saga-20171013, accessed 25 September 2020, for its judgment in the appeal by Zuma and the NPA in the spy tapes saga, 13 October 2017.

29   See Jacques Pauw, 'Exposing the puppet masters behind the *Sunday Times* scandal', *News24*, 16 October 2018, https://www.news24.com/Columnists/GuestColumn/exposing-the-puppet-masters-behind-the-sunday-times-scandal-20181016, accessed 1 May 2019; Greg Nicolson, '*Sunday Times* Cato Manor "death squad" charges dropped', *Daily Maverick*, 17 July 2019, https://www.dailymaverick.co.za/article/2019-07-17-cato-manor-death-squad-charges-dropped/, accessed 2 May 2019.

30   Marianne Thamm, 'Nathi Nhleko's world: Tree of origin trumps democratic law – and whose laws are these anyway?' *Daily Maverick*, 28 July 2020, https://www.dailymaverick.co.za/article/2020-07-28-nathi-nhlekos-world-tree-of-origin-trumps-democratic-law-and-whose-laws-are-these-anyway/, accessed 29 July 2020.

31   Mokgoro Inquiry: These are the key findings against Jiba and Mrwebi, 25 April 2019, https://headtopics.com/za/mokgoro-inquiry-these-are-the-key-findings-against-jiba-and-mrwebi-5506353, accessed 6 October 2020.

32   Claudi Mailovich and Carol Paton, 'Ramaphosa boosts prosecutors' efforts in state-capture cases', *Business Day*, 28 July 2020, https://www.businesslive.co.za/bd/national/2020-07-28-ramaphosa-boosts-prosecutors-efforts-in-state-capture-cases, accessed 31 July 2020.

33   Pierre de Vos, 'Legal game plan: The lengths Jacob Zuma will go to evade the Zondo Commission of Inquiry', *Daily Maverick*, 7 September 2020, https://www.dailymaverick.co.za/article/2020-09-07-legal-game-plan-the-lengths-jacob-zuma-will-go-to-evade-the-zondo-commission-of-inquiry/, accessed 10 September 2020, spells out the legal and constitutional implications.

34   *State of Capture – A Report of the Public Protector*, 13 October 2016, https://www.sahistory.org.za/archive/state-capture-report-public-protector-14-october-2016, accessed 15 October 2016.

35   Jacob Zuma, message on Twitter, 10 March 2019, handle @PresJGZuma.

36   See Amil Umraw, 'Zuma's testimony to state capture commission "untrue"', *Sowetan*, 7 November 2019.

37   There were 18 charges against Zuma, concerning 783 payments that totalled just over R4 million. Zuma received the payments from his financial advisor at the time, Schabir Shaik, and his Nkobi group of companies (between 1996 and 2005). Zuma is accused of using his political influence to protect the company from investigations into the arms deal. Another charge is for trying to solicit a bribe of R500 000 from the company.

38   *IOL*, 8 November 2019, 'Jacob Zuma hospitalised for "unknown ailment"', https://www.iol.co.za/news/politics/jacob-zuma-hospitalised-for-unknown-ailment-36886348, accessed 8 November 2019. In late 2020 Zondo instructed commission staff to lay criminal charges against Zuma for apparent contempt, after Zuma had walked out on his refusal of Zuma's request that Zondo recuse himself.

39   The banking controls were linked to heightened awareness in the post-Panama period. The investigation dealt with corrupt money deals by politically exposed persons; see Bastian Obermayer and Frederik Obermaier, 2016, *The Panama Papers: Breaking the Story of How the Rich and Powerful Hide Their Money*, London: Oneworld.

40   Naledi Shange, 'Oakbay writes to Presidency, ministers about possibility of job losses', *News24*, 9 April 2016, https://www.news24.com/news24/southafrica/news/oakbay-writes-to-presidency-ministers-about-possibility-of-job-losses-20160409, accessed 1 June 2020.

41   Andrew Feinstein, Paul Holden and Hennie van Vuuren, 'Decision to set aside Seriti Commission findings will have a profound impact', *Daily Maverick*, 21 August 2019,

https://www.dailymaverick.co.za/article/2019-08-21-decision-to-set-aside-seriti-com-mission-findings-will-have-a-profound-impact/, accessed 17 September 2019.

42　A full bench of the High Court in Pietermaritzburg, comprising judges Bhekisisa Mnguni, Thoba Poyo-Dlwati and Esther Steyn, heard argument on the matter in May 2019 and handed down judgment on 11 October 2019. Zuma had applied for leave to appeal the ruling against a permanent stay; the Supreme Court of Appeal rejected the application in March 2020.

43　Michael Donen, 17 June 2006, *Commission of Inquiry into the Oil-for-Food Programme in Iraq, Commission Report.*

44　Sam Sole, 'Donen report: ANC bosses are not off the hook', *Mail & Guardian*, 9 December 2011, https://mg.co.za/article/2011-12-09-donen-did-not-clear-anc-men, accessed 2 September 2019. This contrasted with Michael Donen's defence of his report, 28 August 2009, 'Comment on certain misconceptions that have been created by certain media reports ...', facsimile transmission to the director-general of the Presidency, Vusi Mavimbela.

45　Crude oil stocks (10 million barrels) were sold at 28 US dollars a barrel at a time when the market was in contango. Joemat-Pettersson and the Strategic Fuel Fund chief executive at the time, Sibusiso Gamede, signed off on the sale of the country's stock oil reserves. It was sold without following a procurement process or approaching Treasury. The sale was to three companies: Taleveras, Vitol and Glencore.

46　Sabelo Skiti and Athandiwe Saba, 'Hawks investigate crude oil bribes', *Mail & Guardian*, 15 March 2019, https://mg.co.za/article/2019-03-15-00-hawks-investigate-crude-oil-bribes, accessed 17 March 2020.

47　Farlam Commission, 31 March 2015, Marikana Commission of Inquiry: Report on Matters of Public, National and International Concern Arising out of the Tragic Incidents at the Lonmin Mine in Marikana, in the North West Province, https://www.sahrc.org.za/home/21/files/marikana-report-1.pdf, accessed 26 September 2020.

48　This culture of ANC killings is recorded in Norimitsu Onishi and Selam Gebrekidan, 'Hit men and power: South Africa's leaders are killing one another', *The New York Times*, 30 September 2018, https://www.nytimes.com/2018/09/30/world/africa/south-africa-anc-killings.html, accessed 8 March 2020. The violence continued – see, for example, Rapula Moatshe, 'ANCYL: Accused up for murder', *The Star*, 19 November 2019.

49　Moerane Commission, 20 September 2018, Tabling of the Report of the Moerane Commission of Enquiry into the Underlying Causes of the Murder of Politicians in KZN, Pietermaritzburg, http://www.kznonline.gov.za/images/Downloads/Speeches/premier/2018/Tabling_of_the_Moerane_Commission_Report.pdf, accessed 8 October 2020. See also Right2Know, 20 August 2018, 'R2K files official request for Moerane Commission transcripts and report: 30 days to respond!' https://www.r2k.org.za/2018/08/20/r2k-files-official-request-for-moerane-commission-transcripts-and-report-30-days-to-respond/, accessed 4 October 2020.

50　The Hefer Commission of Inquiry Report, 7 January 2004, https://www.gov.za/documents/hefer-commission-inquiry-report-0, accessed 26 September 2020, pp. 23, 58–59.

51　Eastern Cape anti-apartheid activists, especially Janet Cherry, had pieced together information that showed, as Hefer confirms, that Agent RS452 was, in fact, human rights lawyer Vanessa Brereton, and not Bulelani Ngcuka. See Jonathan Ancer, 2019, *Betrayal: The Secret Lives of Apartheid Spies*, Cape Town: Tafelberg, Chapter 13. Shaik, Maharaj and journalist Ranjeni Munusamy had said that it was Ngcuka.

52　Ginwala Enquiry, Report of the enquiry into the fitness of advocate VP Pikoli to hold the office of national director of public prosecutions, 4 November 2008.

53 The money was in the main to secure substantial state contracts and through gratuitous payments to politicians, to secure favourable pro-deal political contexts.

54 As reported on *News24wire*, 19 September 2019, 'Ramaphosa: FIC gave Mkhwebane far more CR17 information than what she requested', https://www.polity.org.za/article/ramaphosa-fic-gave-mkhwebane-far-more-cr17-information-than-what-she-requested-2019-09-19, accessed 2 October 2019.

55 See also Juniour Khumalo and Mandisa Nyati, 'Busisiwe Mkhwebane hits back', *City Press*, 10 November 2011; *Sunday Times*, 10 November 2011, 'PP official accuses Mkhwebane of bias'.

56 The public protector also had a series of losses in court, especially in some highly politicised cases involving the minister of public enterprises, Pravin Gordhan, but also in her campaign of fighting Ramaphosa (as in early 2020).

57 Ramaphosa's words in his first response to Parliament were: 'My son has a financial consultancy business, and he consults for a number of companies. One of those companies is Bosasa. I asked him at close range whether this money was obtained illegally or unlawfully … He is running a clean business … if it turns out there was any irregularity or corruption I will be the first, I assure you Mr Maimane, I will be the first to make sure he becomes accountable. I will take him to the police station myself.'

58 14 November 2018; on this occasion his words were: 'I have been subsequently informed that the payment referred to … does not relate to that contract … I have been told that the payment to which the leader of the opposition referred was made on behalf of Mr Gavin Watson into a trust account that was used to raise funds for a campaign established to support my candidature for the presidency of the African National Congress.'

59 See Kaunda Selisho, 'Public protector shares Maimane's original letter in Ramaphosa investigation', *The Citizen*, 24 June 2019, https://citizen.co.za/news/south-africa/politics/2146391/public-protector-shares-maimanes-original-letter-in-ramaphosa-investigation/, accessed 7 October 2020.

60 See Franny Rabkin, 'Ramaphosa launches court review of public protector's Bosasa report', *Mail & Guardian*, 31 July 2019, https://mg.co.za/article/2019-07-31-ramaphosa-launches-court-review-of-public-protectors-bosasa-report, accessed 20 September 2019.

61 Details included, according to *News24*, that: (a) public enterprises minister, Pravin Gordhan, was central in raising funds for Ramaphosa; (b) the president was consulted by the managers of his campaign about plans to approach several donors, including a Greek shipping tycoon with links to the arms deal and a politically connected 'socialite' previously suspected of smuggling millions of rands of gold out of the country; and (c) despite efforts by the CR17 campaign to keep its communications secure, the emails were seemingly obtained through clandestine methods. Two emails from Ramaphosa's long-time assistant and CR17 campaign manager Donné Nicol to Ramaphosa and an email from Nicol's personal assistant to another manager of the CR17 campaign, Marion Sparg, are included in the leak. A typed note by Ramaphosa himself, to what is believed to be his banker, instructs the transfer of R20 million from a Money Market account (believed to be Ramaphosa's) to an account belonging to the Ria Tenda Trust, a trust used as part of the campaign's financial machinery. See Kyle Cowan and Lizeka Tandwa, 'Leaked emails reveal who Ramaphosa's CR17 campaign asked for money', *News24*, 3 August 2019, https://www.news24.com/SouthAfrica/News/exclusive-leaked-emails-reveal-who-ramaphosas-cr17-campaign-asked-for-money-20190803, accessed 2 September 2019.

62 Khusela Diko, then presidential spokesperson, statement, 9 August 2019. They argued that confidentiality was required in terms of the public protector's own rules and the Protection of Private Information Act.

63 In a letter to the FIC, Ramaphosa's lawyers said that the FIC acted unlawfully in obtaining additional information from the relevant banks and handing it over to the public protector. The Directorate for Priority Crime Investigation (DPCI, or the Hawks) and South African Police Service crime intelligence were seeking to establish the origin of the leak; see Kyle Cowan, 'Inside the CR17 leaks and the conflict between Cyril's men', *News24*, 13 September 2019, https://www.dailysun.co.za/News/inside-the-cr17-leaks-and-the-conflict-between-cyrils-men-20190913, accessed 2 June 2019.

64 In August 2017, Parliament's Committee on Ethics and Members' Interests had examined the same issue with respect to Maimane. It found the committee could not make a finding because the parliamentary code was not clear enough on the issue of internal party campaign donations. See Sam Sole, 'The public projectile', amaBhungane, 26 July 2019, https://amabhungane.org/stories/analysis-the-public-projectile/, accessed 30 August 2019. Believing that the code should force politicians to declare funding for internal party campaigns, amaBhungane wished to have the code declared unconstitutional because it did not. This did not sway a ruling by the Supreme Court of Appeal in early 2020.

65 This meant that at the earliest the matter would be resolved in 2021.

66 Supreme Court of Appeal, 12 January 2009, as summarised in Legalbrief Today, '"Lynched" lawyers should be commended...', 17 April 2020, Issue 4919, https://legalbrief.co.za/story/lynched-lawyers-should-be-commended/, accessed 5 October 2020.

67 See Ferial Haffajee, 'Merchants of disinformation (Part 2): How the EFF dominates the disinformation market', *Daily Maverick*, 12 December 2018, https://www.dailymaverick.co.za/article/2018-12-12-how-the-eff-dominates-the-disinformation-market/, accessed 20 December 2018; 'Quantifying the spread of EFF & RET disinformation', 13 December 2018, http://www.superlinear.co.za/quantifying-the-spread-of-eff-ret-disinformation/, accessed 1 May 2019.

68 Michelle le Roux and Dennis Davis, 2019, *Lawfare: Judging Politics in South Africa*, Johannesburg: Jonathan Ball, p. 287.

69 The Constitutional Court reserved judgment.

70 Yonela Diko, 'Judges should have no fear', *City Press*, 29 September 2019.

71 Malema, at a Women's Day commemoration, 9 August 2019.

72 Mandisa Nyathi, 'South Africa's judiciary is independent: Mogoeng', *City Press*, 14 August 2019, https://www.news24.com/citypress/news/south-africas-judiciary-is-independent-mogoeng-20190814, accessed 31 August 2020.

73 As cited in Earl Coetzee, 'Chief justice calls out accusers', *The Citizen*, 14 September 2019.

74 Legal Practice Council, 30 September 2019, '"Give our judiciary the respect it deserves" – Legal Practice Council', https://www.polity.org.za/article/give-our-judiciary-the-respect-it-deserves-legal-practice-council-2019-09-30, accessed 4 October 2019.

6

Reconstituting the Limping State

DEVASTATION AND ATTEMPTED REDEMPTION

In the Ramaphosa epoch the state was fragile and continuously incapacitated, even if argued to be on track to better functionality, integrity and efficiency. The state in the heydays of ANC party political dominance had been plundered and institutionally disfigured. The damage had been inflicted largely, but far from exclusively, in the so-called 'wasted' decade of 2007 to 2017. This chapter considers the actions of trying to redeem the state from systemic corruption and extensive capture committed by entrenched forces of the previous ANC factional regime – and to do so while a continuously predator class of political elites remained in charge.

Parts of government had come almost to a standstill from the point when an ANC faction campaigned for Jacob Zuma to become ANC president. Mbeki-ists had resisted in vain as Zuma-ists occupied strategically important and resource-rich parts of the state. The ANC and its key organisational and government organs, such as the National Executive Committee, Cabinet and parliamentary caucuses, stood by Zuma far beyond the point of clarity about the damage unleashed. Cyril Ramaphosa was complicit in first accepting the ANC deputy presidency under Zuma and subsequently maintaining a prolonged silence while corruption flourished.[1] He then reconsidered and, through his candidacy for the ANC presidency, volunteered for the task of undoing the damage. He had to work with an ANC whose problems had accumulated and worsened in many respects.

Most state institutions had continued working – in the ways of South African public sector culture of paper-pushing and contracting procurement from the new national bourgeoisie. Much public sector delivery continued to unfold, amid devastation wrought by corruption, capture and tolerance of incapacity among civil servants and politicians in public office.[2] There was the unquantified knowledge that the amount and quality of delivery would have been better had the politicians and their associated public servants not been preoccupied so frequently with politics or with schemes to draw personal benefits from their public sector work. Many had been diverting public funds into paper contracts that saw transfers that benefited them alone, or vast amounts of facilitation fees being paid for no work, and contracts going to the tendering party that paid the best bribe to officials and politicians or retainer to the ANC.[3] The ANC, in its 54th conference policy resolutions, recognised this state of public affairs, noting that '[w]hether we call this state capture or simply corruption, this has undermined the integrity of our institutions, cost our economy hundreds of billions of rands and contributed to the further impoverishment of our people'.[4]

President Cyril Ramaphosa's team started its work, but the state coffers were bare and resources continued to decline. Deficits and bailouts accumulated, and the cost of borrowing to keep the state afloat outstripped the funds available to fulfil core state functions. The last of the ratings agencies had bequeathed junk investment status, South Africa was in recession, and then Covid-19 struck and shrank employment to previously unimagined lows. Investments had been trickling in, recognising the Ramaphosa clean-up pledges, but the state continued to leak funds, especially through the state-owned enterprises, and entertained unrelenting demands for public sector salary increases and inflated state contracting. Civil servants' wage costs consumed more than a third of the pre-Covid national budget.

This chapter explores the trials of the Ramaphosa state. Deep state capture in the Zuma era had brought the bequest of shadow state operations that could in many instances only be countered through the use of new-order parallel structures. The chapter assesses the extent to which the state had metamorphosed to an out-of-control aberration. It incorporates case studies of a cross-section of state institutions. It considers the early Ramaphosa-era state-institutional clean-outs that were effected, and the fightbacks that resulted in the name of the ostensible 'revolution' and 'radical economic transformation'. The focus is on the attempts at corrective measures, and the setbacks suffered due to the care that had to be taken not to alienate internal ANC opponents.

STATE AS CORRUPTION PLAYGROUND OF PRESIDENTS AND RULING ELITES

The ANC ruled while the state was being emasculated by greed and looting or abandoned by administrative arrogance. In many cases, state functions had been diluted while the senior capture-oriented elites organised state business for the personal benefit that they or their associates would be deriving. The state was operating, but limping. It invoked images of a failed state, yet without all of the features of a failed state. Parts of the state operated and delivered, albeit suboptimally.

Most of the strategically oriented institutions in powerful functions had once been taken over by the Zuma-ists (sometimes in response to prior occupation by Mbeki-ists). The switches followed seamlessly after Zuma had won his Polokwane war and assumed the South African presidency in 2009. His promise was to reassert the ANC over the state, to counter the Mbeki days when the president used his state deployees to control the ANC.

Mbeki had instituted a resourceful state apparatus boasting a highly organised and systematic state administration. He failed, however, to take the ANC with him on this path. Those in the ANC who were excluded from the Mbeki administration and executive structures were hungry for their turn at the state trough. Intra-ANC populist mobilisation generated the Polokwane momentum and ousted Mbeki. Next, the Zuma-ists were deployed extensively – from the moment of 2009 ANC electoral candidate lists to Zuma's last-ditch Cabinet reshuffle of October 2017. The ANC parliamentary caucus, the Cabinet in multiple iterations, commanders of the state-owned enterprises, tax authorities, security and intelligence operations and – above all – the investigative and prosecutorial state apparatuses, were prized deployment positions, first under Zuma and then – in corrective mode – Ramaphosa. Core state departments, such as the National Treasury, Public Enterprises, and Minerals and Energy were prized deployment platforms. A near impenetrable circle had been drawn around powerful Zuma-occupied state institutions – and the Ramaphosa administration targeted and conquered these institutions in piecemeal fashion. Cabinet reshuffles and commissions of inquiry were two of his instruments.

The rampant abuse of state resources fed off tendencies present in the ANC since at least 2000.[5] Attributes such as corrupted, compromised, captured, incapable and unaccountable extended across all levels of the state.[6] Patronage networks extended into the provincial and local state, and private sector agents prompted willing ANC politicians and officials with benefits that would accrue to both the persons and the party. As noted by former president Kgalema Motlanthe, 'This rot is across the board. It's not confined to any level or any area of the country. Almost every project is conceived because it offers opportunities for certain people to make money. A great deal of the ANC's problems are occasioned by this.'[7]

State-owned enterprises were frequently hollowed out, using projects and contracts. Extended networks of capture ensured that there would be high-level cover-ups, while the investigative and prosecutorial arms of the state were incapacitated. The Ramaphosa era came to be about reconstituting this state and rehabilitating pillars of capture. The task unfolded amid delegitimation of personalities, of Ramaphosa and his inner circle, and of core state institutions. Anti-Ramaphosa-ism stood in the context of citizens increasingly distrusting public institutions.[8] Ramaphosa did not have an unambiguous ANC licence to proceed with a clean-up project. When he assumed presidential power, citizens were asked to suspend their disbelief that the state could govern with integrity, progressively and in ways that would lessen socio-economic injustice. Ramaphosa's antagonists found fertile ground to foster this through nurturing suspicion against the president – he was the billionaire with friends who donate many millions to his campaigns, the president with links into white monopoly capital, the embodiment of post-apartheid black capital. An evolving counter-campaign pitched Ramaphosa as just another captured president. The counter-Ramaphosa project in the early phases was an unfolding wave of Bell Pottinger-ism arguing that the Ramaphosa turnover would not be in the interest of the masses.[9] Ramaphosa was compromised by capital and lacked integrity, they contended.

Zuma attempted to exploit this suspicion in his letter of August 2020, which tried to drive a wedge between Ramaphosa and ANC members. Zuma argued that his successor pleaded guilty on behalf of many innocent ANC members, thereby discrediting the movement.[10] Ramaphosa had said that the ANC stands 'as Accused No. 1'. These later phases of questioning Ramaphosa built on evidence that even seemingly clean Ramaphosa-ists had feet of corruption, lured by lucrative state contracts. The Ramaphosa ANC used standard repertoires of trying to own criticism of the ANC through self-criticism, using claims that those committing corruption were not the real ANC, and continuously issuing statements, activating processes and designing guidelines for better organisational behaviour that held out the vision of a future and better ANC. When this continuously 'new' ANC was confirmed not to be the antidote to corruption, levels of cynicism accumulated in both the ANC and the state.

After the compromised, 'wasted' Zuma years, triggered by the shortcomings of and alienation caused by the Mbeki years, Ramaphosa had to work with a state that was built on a complex grid of past problems blending with the present.[11] In this configuration, multiple parallel, shadow, supplementary and even rogue state institutions[12] intersected with the constitutionally delineated state framework.

ANATOMY OF THE RAMAPHOSA STATE

The fundamental anatomy that Ramaphosa was tasked to convert into a capable and viable operation was one of frequently dysfunctional, at best partially effective, operations, in a vast state configuration of well-remunerated civil servants operating in a politicised context. The Zuma years had witnessed the construction of a compliant state, ruled by Zuma at the top, a circle of hand-picked high-level deployees and their business kingpins – including the brothers Gupta, Gavin Watson, Roy Moodley and a host of others.[13] The networks shared the spoils, splitting up project-tender incomes between the public and the private interests.[14] The brazen proliferation that came to corrupt state operations was only possible under the hand of a patron-president like Zuma. The corruption and state looting problem had roots in pre-Zuma times – and it was diffuse and entrenched in the Ramaphosa present.

One of Ramaphosa's prime tasks was to unravel and neutralise the strategically premeditated takeover that Zuma had effected in his close to a decade in state power. Through strategic appointments, such as the national director of public prosecutions, the South African Revenue Service (SARS) commissioner, and heads of strategic state-owned enterprises, Zuma ensured control. Compliance and silence by the National Executive Committee and Cabinet were Zuma's protective barrier. Until its reversal, the Seriti Commission findings had helped to subdue his (and the ANC's) arms deal problems. When the state was overwhelmingly Zuma-compliant, credible investigative journalists and issue-specific civil society organisations kept exposés going, while complicit journalists helped foster the web of deception that helped the Zuma network to flourish.[15]

The anatomy of the Ramaphosa state was determined further by the evasion of accountability that Zuma had inculcated. Ramaphosa's predecessor had not hesitated to abuse the ANC culture of democratic centralism and its belief that its elected leaders were wise. The unravelling had started with Zuma's Nkandla mistake. Nkandla, of modest monetary value in the overall state corruption scheme of things, nevertheless painted Zuma as a rogue president. The Constitutional Court's 2016 judgment was a turning point, joining civil society and popular mobilisation to leverage power away from the Zuma dispensation – and it started dawning on the ANC that the Zuma order of things would cost it outright victory in Election 2019.[16] Zuma exited formal power and Ramaphosa inherited the degraded state apparatuses.

Zuma-ists did not all leave with Zuma; together with often comparably corrupt deployees of the Ramaphosa era they remained in many corners of the state, across spheres and levels. They were entrenched and in control of multiple key state institutions: the National Prosecuting Authority (NPA) remained occupied by Zuma loyalists; SARS continued as a bulwark for state looting; the State Security Agency (SSA) manipulated events to defeat the new political dispensation; the public protector wanted to reincarnate the Zuma order. The list is extensive. This chapter sketches the damage and the reversals that were required.

A malfunctioning state

At national level, multiple state departments and state-owned enterprises were captured and close to wholly corrupted when the Ramaphosa era started. The Ramaphosa state became characterised by its forced compromise: some rehabilitation of the state over time, but the core problems were not going to dissipate and were even reinforced. Zuma-ists were frequently those who were entrenched in the state structures that needed correction and the Ramaphosa regime had to go about its clean-up with circumspection; they were accused, generally, of purging the Zuma-ists.

Corruption was not the only ill that afflicted state institutions. Political wars took centre stage frequently, and governance suffered. Widespread malaise was due to lack of capacity and poor management of state operations. At national level, multiple departments and units were malfunctioning under the control of Zuma-ists and, later, Ramaphosa-ists. Provincial governments were performing poorly; several had had periods under administration. The education and healthcare systems epitomised these problems.[17] The health minister interpreted health as a system 'under stress but ... not collapsing'.[18] In local governments, basic services like water and sanitation were frequently not delivered or were interrupted for long periods. The auditor-general's annual reports, spanning the Zuma and Ramaphosa states, testified to perpetual gross levels of poor management, ill-advised spending, lack of accountability, and disregard of advice to become accountable.[19]

Parallel state orders defined

Much of Ramaphosa's early time in the Presidency was taken up with endeavours to untangle discredited, captured and often emasculated networks of state institutions. Parallel state operations were a distinct problem. The constitutionally mandated institutions were shadowed by processes that served Zuma and other masters in veiled operations which were revealed incrementally while the old guard fought to retain vestiges of the antecedent order that had given them ongoing access to patronage and privilege.

When Ramaphosa became president, the mandated institutions were ready for action, but the parallel ones, in many instances, were not ready to cease operating. The state security and intelligence apparatuses had fought factional political battles to build Zuma-ism and prevent or contain Ramaphosa's power.[20] The actions included the Special Operations operatives in the SSA influencing media, monitoring non-governmental organisations critical of Zuma and placing undercover agents as bodyguards to Zuma and allies such as Dudu Myeni. In mining, energy and Eskom, parallel operations ensured preferential business deals and state operations that served private interests.

Parallel actions went beyond direct factional battles and included infiltration of the #FeesMustFall movement and formation of a trade union, the Workers Association Union, to destabilise the Association of Mineworkers and Construction Union. Several of the names are clarified when the SSA report of 2019 is read in conjunction with the inspector-general's intelligence report of 2014. In opaque parallel structures the public protector cooperated closely with rogue SSA officials, constituting parallel and special-purpose operations. Across several government departments, Zuma-ist ministers offered departmental spaces to advisers who assumed the work of the director-general.

Zuma's parallel state operations

The scope of Ramaphosa's presumed state turnaround was illuminated through evidence at the Zondo Commission, and investigative reports and leaks, including #GuptaLeaks.[21] Many of the schemes through which state funds had become privately appropriated came to the surface.[22] Voices at the Zondo Commission of Inquiry sketched details of the anatomy of South Africa's parallel state. While particulars of Zuma's role in the Gupta political-business dynasty often remained opaque, it was undisputed that the ANC, organisationally and as government, allowed or was part of many capture projects.

Zuma's attorney argued that the statements at the Zondo Commission prior to Zuma's first appearance in person in mid-2019 had failed to prove his client had violated the law. Zuma himself did not cooperate at the commission, but other evidence flagged him as the kingpin, captured and compromised to the point of dancing to the strings of his Gupta puppet-masters. Zuma had ceded substantial executive power to the Gupta brothers Ajay, Atul and Rajesh. As the Guptas themselves claimed, speaking about Zuma and their parallel power arrangements: 'You must understand that we are in control of everything – the NPA, the Hawks, the National Intelligence Agency and the old man will do anything we tell him to do.'[23]

Zuma and his scouts had recruited those with crass ambition and skeletons in their cupboards to head important state institutions and operations; such persons became manipulable, compliant deployees in the capture project.[24] The aim was to recruit into strategic state positions, at ministerial and at board levels in departments and state-owned enterprises, persons who would facilitate looting-by-tender in procurement-friendly state-owned enterprises and in strategic departments concerned with public works, mining, minerals, energy, nuclear energy and state finances generally. Communication, the media and security apparatuses such as

Special Operations in the SSA had to deliver the positive media for the captors and the legitimation of the capture project in the terms of the Bell Pottinger blueprint. The Guptas had the power to threaten consequences for non-compliance. In a public protector report by Thuli Madonsela, the former Government Communication Information System head Themba Maseko referred to Ajay Gupta as having threatened to have him 'sorted out' for lack of cooperation.

In witness statements at the Zondo Commission, specific, legally incriminating words on Zuma's role were hard to come by. His limited and vague (if not denied or evaded for lack of recollection) interactions with witnesses suggested that he had been alert throughout his sojourn in state power not to incriminate himself. Maseko testified that Zuma, in a brief exchange, asked him simply to 'help' the Gupta family. Zuma's son Duduzane's evidence confirmed how he acted as the 'de facto Zuma', thereby absolving his father. Zuma junior on one occasion commandeered the then deputy finance minister, Mcebisi Jonas, into a meeting where the Guptas offered him a ministership in exchange for substantial monetary benefits.

Similarly, project state capture ensured that the compromised, compliant ministers and executives of state-owned enterprises (Eskom, Denel, South African Airways, Transnet, the National Energy Regulator of South Africa, for example) would execute dirty work on behalf of the principals (and gain financially themselves). The executives, in turn, had advisers and other underlings to take high-level strategic decisions on their behalf.[25] Only some of Zuma's top-executive-level sidekicks were named publicly; they included former ministers Faith Muthambi, Malusi Gigaba, Nomvula Mokonyane, Tina Joemat-Pettersson, Lynne Brown and David Mahlobo. In her Zondo evidence, the government communicator Phumla Williams described Muthambi's actions in words with wider resonance: 'I had to accept this was not a minister,' this was 'the enemy. She was not interested in serving the people of South Africa' but 'working against the state'.[26]

State institutions were hollowed out and rendered dysfunctional – not just as a consequence of capture, but as a calculated proactive strategy to *enable* capture. Zuma executed the strategies, which belonged to him and the Guptas; it was only with a president like Zuma in control that the Guptas and other captors were enabled to gain power. Other spokes in the capture wheel, as per Zondo Commission testimonies, included:

- Take over procurement and finance, with specific attention to opportunities in the supply chain; create the conditions in which procurement processes may be flouted – this basic operating rule applied widely.
- Push out reluctant employees – fire them, coerce them into retirement or resignation, demote them and render positions redundant; simply ignore and

override them through ministerial advisers; parachute in co-opted, compromised new functionaries.

- Control the media – *The New Age* breakfast show, of Gupta fame, scored double-points in the capture stakes; hundreds of millions of public money was funnelled into the Gupta purse while the Zuma-legitimating narrative of 'radical economic transformation' was disseminated. Otherwise, get Special Operations in the SSA to influence the media through co-opted journalists.

State of capture in the South African state: A typology

Capture was executed through well-placed, hand-picked senior politicians, possibly with vulnerabilities in terms of unsavoury histories[27] or simply individuals with the compulsion to please high-level politicians like the president or one of his designated proxies, in the name of serving the movement, or respecting the ANC's anointed one. The typology is a rough guide to the forms and levels of capture and corruption that defined the state that Ramaphosa inherited:

- A core ingredient of the Zuma regime was capture-control over state entities such as the NPA, SARS and the National Treasury. Capture by the Guptas, in association with Zuma, was at the pinnacle. Zuma created parallel, shadow state features through these entities.
- A tier of more individualised national-level sectoral interests linked to specific ministers and their national departments followed. The departments of Energy (nuclear deals, coal procurement, independent power production), Mineral Resources (preferential mining licences, and no enforcement of post-mining clean-up), Social Development (massive cash payment systems to preferential parties), and state-owned enterprises, such as Eskom and Denel (coal supplies for Eskom power generation, media influence, selling off intellectual property of defence equipment), Transnet (unusable locomotive supplies), and many more instances came to light. Clearing up the problems was a shifting target and the complications spilled over into the Ramaphosa era.
- A subset of this capture was capture of state business by the ANC as an organisation – for example, through its investment arm, Chancellor Holdings and Chancellor House,[28] which had major holdings in the company that provided the boilers for Kusile and Medupi power stations. These boilers and the fact that they were overheating due to design faults (and required major, costly adaptations after their installation) were a major cause for the lack of functionality of power generation, especially in the period of the sixth administration when Ramaphosa was responsible for state functionality.

- The chain of capture extended into provincial and local government, with some of the provinces delivering more evidence than others. The Free State, under former provincial leader and then secretary-general of the ANC, Ace Magashule, stood out. The Vrede-Estina dairy project, largely used for money-laundering favouring the Guptas, was an example. In Limpopo province, at the time that Economic Freedom Fighters (EFF) leader Julius Malema was in the ANC and ANC Youth League specifically, he underdelivered on contracts with multiple municipalities.[29] The metropolitan coalition governments failed serially to deliver cleaned-up government, and Ramaphosa faced the prospect of acknowledging his inability to find a resolution.
- There were favours to individual politicians and/or the ANC as a subcategory to capture activities – this was confirmed in the Zondo Commission in relation to the Bosasa-Watson capture. Multiple politicians and associates of politicians in government and the ANC were plied with gifts and cash to help secure lucrative contracts. Alternatively, once individuals had been compromised through acceptance of gifts, they were, in essence, compelled to favour the givers and keepers in subsequent tender processes. This direct personal angle was the platform for much of the capture and systemic corruption cases. Even more, in evidence Nomvula Mokonyane presented the normal way of the ANC's doing politics-business: contracts to favoured companies would include direct monetary benefit or in-kind business exchanges with the ANC.
- 'Normal' business deals also entailed well-connected ANC figures being alerted to opportunities for tendering, or hand-picked to submit predetermined-as-successful bids in areas of business specialisation, or where ability to leverage procurement of goods or services was the only requirement. Delivery ranged from perfect with acceptable profit margins, to excessive and inflated and combined with compromised quantity or quality, to no delivery. This was one of the most frequent forms and was widespread, evident from council contracts at the lower end up to top provincial and national levels – and reaching crisis point in the looting of Covid-19 relief funds.

Corruption and capture occurred at all levels of state operations, but at the same time not all of the state was captured or corrupted. There were always significant exclusions that coexisted with captured operations.[30] Nor was the Zuma-Ramaphosa transition the corruption-capture termination point. The bulk of the service aspect of government – national, provincial or local – was through procurement contracts with consultant companies or individuals (often in the existing or a budding ANC circle). Licensing of operations, applicants for project grants, certification of operations and a multitude of other functions lent themselves to corruption – and compromised, suboptimal government services and projects. The risk of corruption in the time of Ramaphosa's presidency receded marginally, at best.

RAMAPHOSA'S HALTING RISE INTO STATE POWER

Ramaphosa's election as president of South Africa and his occupation of the Presidency amounted to an arrangement of 'power-sharing' with the antecedent Zuma order. Zuma's departure was muddled.[31] His network of drinkers from the trough in and beyond government, in formal and parallel state operations, meant that Ramaphosa's becoming president was merely a starting point to gaining power. The residue of power had to be secured incrementally, largely through salvos of factional confrontations.

Ramaphosa's actions to dislodge Zuma-ists were incremental and entailed both clean-up and tolerance. There were three main, halting phases in Ramaphosa's advancing his state power base in the earlier parts of his presidency.

ANC power as starting block for cleaning up the state

Ramaphosa's starting block was of necessity to ensure that the ANC's National Executive Committee (NEC) would be backing him sufficiently, following the tenuous Nasrec victory. Without the party power, his state power would be impossible but there were variable indications of the factional balance of power in the NEC. In 2018, after an NEC meeting, Ramaphosa made a late-night live television appearance to tell the nation that he supported expropriation without compensation.[32] He was applauded in the NEC upon declaring his willingness to do so. In contrast, in September 2019, the NEC endorsed the Tito Mboweni economic plan, which was anchored in several antecedent ANC economic plans[33] but was not of the radical economic transformation genre. Ramaphosa used the 2019 State of the Nation address to emphasise the structural adjustment of the state, to save operational costs, but simultaneously to create a platform to clean out the worst of the corrupt ones; the 2020 State of the Nation address was more tentative and subject to the dearth of economic hope. Ramaphosa's standing in the ANC was strengthening modestly as more consensus developed about the ANC's policy positions, as the bigger economic and fiscal problems and the state-owned enterprise drains on the fiscus brought home bigger realities, and the national and global impact of Covid-19 sank in.

Ramaphosa's position in the ANC was also only consolidating in that he carried provincial support as well, with particular progress in KwaZulu-Natal and Eastern Cape. He had to tread with care in both the 2019 pre-election (when he was still working towards consolidating his provincial standings) and post-election periods (when he found that the base required ongoing work). In KwaZulu-Natal, Ramaphosa gained the working allegiance of Sihle Zikalala, whose rise into the provincial leadership and premier positions helped to seal the deal. At ANC provincial level in KwaZulu-Natal, zebra-style factional alternation was the province's stepping stone into the Ramaphosa order.

Follow-through: Routine state changes coming with presidential ascension

Post-Election 2019, Ramaphosa executed a calculated strategy to consolidate a hold on the executive and the top-level state bureaucracies. It involved the Cabinet and the Presidency. Ramaphosa reduced the 35-member Cabinet modestly, shedding another few of the remaining Zuma-ists, but also re-employing some who had been excluded from his 2018 Cabinet to more innocuous portfolios. The strategy was to employ senior, influential Zuma-ists (like David Mahlobo and Mosebenzi Zwane) but on Ramaphosa's terms. Others were discarded from Cabinet – and Ramaphosa made sure that he would also exclude some of his own high-profile followers, for example Jeff Radebe, who subsequently became a special envoy to Ramaphosa. Other omitted ones included the strongly pro-Zuma Bathabile Dlamini (of the ANC Women's League, subsequently controversially appointed by minister Lindiwe Sisulu as interim board chairperson of the Social Housing Regulatory Authority), Nomvula Mokonyane, Michael Masutha and Siyabonga Cwele. Easier exclusions were the underperformers Gugile Nkwinti, Susan Shabangu, Senzeni Zokwana, Nomaindia Mfeketo and Thokozile Xasa.[34] The execution of Cabinet clean-up was ongoing, in calculated manoeuvres.

The Presidency had to be reinvented, along with the rest of the executive. In routine steps, new ministerial and presidential advisers and support staff were recruited, and new consultative councils appointed. Ramaphosa brought in key players, some of whom had served him in the deputy presidency. Others were remnants from Nkosazana Dlamini-Zuma's 2018–2019 sojourn as minister in the Presidency for the National Planning Commission for Policy and Evaluation, and those who were permanently employed bureaucrats and fragments from the Zuma era.

Ramaphosa built a new centre through the introduction of the Policy Analysis and Research Services Unit. The statistics on Presidency staff turnover rates, comparing the 2016/2017 and 2018/2019 financial years, show the growing exodus of

Zuma staff.[35] The number of posts in the Presidency decreased minimally; 16 out of the previous 632 positions were rationalised.

High stakes in consolidating Ramaphosa state power: Departments, state-owned enterprises, watchdogs

In a third phase of claiming and asserting power, Ramaphosa contested case by case to get control of strategic government institutions and positions – in the main, the National Treasury, NPA, SSA, SARS, Public Investment Corporation and public protector. Progress was made by stealth and was unfolding continuously. To minimise or forestall potential fightback, the interventions had to proceed in as factionally neutral a way as possible. Action took the form of commissions of inquiry, followed by legal steps against perpetrators, or the president's firing of some key figures, following recommendations by the commissions.

Ramaphosa and his associates, inclusive of public enterprises minister Pravin Gordhan, had to unlock a matrix of compromised state institutions and then restore some credibility, while retaining the pretence of one unified organisation in power. The full Ramaphosa inner circle was operational. Besides Gordhan, finance minister Tito Mboweni was on board. Deputy president David Mabuza was pulled in on many occasions to help get compliance. International relations minister Naledi Pandor, minister of agriculture, land reform and rural development Thoko Didiza and minister in the Presidency, Jackson Mthembu, were trusted ones from the cabinet circle. Other inner-circle ones were from the ANC stalwart ranks, the CR17 core campaigners and Ramaphosa's circle of special envoys.

Consolidating presidential power was an ongoing project and was not unidirectional. The case of the public protector showed how the law and the watchdog rules could be inverted and turned on the president; how the president's or his staff's mistakes in the games of campaign money and contracts that involve conflict of interest could threaten the state clean-up project and public trust. Ramaphosa's consolidation of power was eased by the unravelling of the Zuma coalition and political hibernation accompanying the Covid period. The case studies that follow reveal the intricacies of this third phase.

STRAIGHTENING OUT THE PARALLEL STATE: CASE STUDIES

The specific accounts of reclaiming institutions of the South African state case by case, away from the Zuma network, are the tale of how Cyril Ramaphosa simultaneously constructed his presidency and command. The cases hold lessons for con-figuring the practical interface between president, government and state in times of unstable or acrimonious presidential transitions.

Base zero was Zuma's second-term administration, characterised by 'even more aggressive and reckless interventions by the Gupta-captured network, which often conducted itself as a shadowy, parallel state outside of collective cabinet discipline and above answerability to Parliament or the ANC'.[36] Recklessness was due to ongoing incumbency not being assured for the Zuma-ists beyond 2019. There was some desperation among those around whom scandals were accumulating.

Amid many intra-ANC constraints, Ramaphosa acted to reduce parallel and shadow operations – and then found the need to construct some of his own. At times, and especially when the Covid-related National Coronavirus Command Council took shape, Ramaphosa was suspected of building his own shadow state. It was not a factional construct, but had the effect initially of circumventing potentially time-consuming consultation and inter-party deliberation. In addition, through his multiple supplementary advisory bodies and special envoys, Ramaphosa was also obviously dabbling in parallel state structures. His main actions notwithstanding were to bring alignment between the constitutionally and legally mandated and parallel (also paralegal) structures dating from the Zuma era.

He focused on the appointment of two new cabinets and reconstructing the Office of the President of South Africa; the clean-up of leadership of the high-level, high-risk state institutions like SARS, the Public Investment Corporation and the NPA, and on following through with the state-owned enterprises.

Cabinet

The fulcrum of capture was in cabinet appointments. This is where Ramaphosa first worked to reconstitute the state. While cabinet reshuffle was the primary instrument available to counter capture, many political factors defined the possible and permissible.

A capturist milestone had been reached under Zuma when he fired the then minister of finance, Nhlanhla Nene, from Cabinet in December 2015. In evidence to the Zondo Commission, Nene revealed that he was axed because he had refused to sign off on South Africa's Russian nuclear deal. As a 'four-day minister', Des van Rooyen, holder of multiple degrees (Zuma liked to argue) but manifestly unqualified, stepped into Nene's shoes. Economic indicators plunged, and Zuma was forced to replace Van Rooyen with Pravin Gordhan. Roughly a year later, Zuma fired Gordhan and appointed Malusi Gigaba, reinstating the capture project. Gupta-ist

Gigaba lasted into the early Ramaphosa period but fell on his sword for inter alia having lied to Parliament about an aviation deal with the Oppenheimer family (he had tried to rescind on the deal to favour the Guptas). Gigaba had also used both his ministerial deployments, home affairs and public enterprises, to advance the Gupta network.

The cases of former ministers Lynne Brown and Mosebenzi Zwane also demonstrated the capture havoc which had to be reversed to reconstitute the wobbling state. Brown was assumed to be clean, until reports about Gupta gifts and trips piled up. Mere months into her ministerial term in public enterprises, the Zondo Commission heard, she installed a new Denel board and chairperson (lawyer Daniel Mantsha, subsequently representing Zuma in some court battles); helped to engineer a joint venture between Denel and VR Laser Asia disregarding Treasury requirements and internal opinion; and handed over Denel's intellectual property to a minor Gupta-linked offshore company.[37] The former mineral resources minister Mosebenzi Zwane acted as a direct agent for Gupta interests, in both mining and in banking, as also confirmed in evidence at the Zondo Commission. He was instrumental in the Guptas' acquisition of Optimum Coal Mine; he accompanied a Gupta delegation to Switzerland where the family negotiated the sale of the mine, owned by Glencore, to the Guptas' Tegeta Resources. He also tried to coerce major banks into not closing Gupta accounts, appropriating powers and issuing a 'Cabinet statement' against the banks (from both of which the ANC distanced itself).[38] In the internal workings of the Department of Mineral Resources, Zwane was a willing, silent bystander while three Gupta-linked advisers (Kuben Moodley, Malcolm Mabaso and Zarina Kellerman) took charge. These advisors were the mediators when department director-general, Thibedi Ramontja, needed inputs from the minister. They issued orders to the inspector of mines regarding which mines had to be visited for inspection,[39] according to Ramontja at the Zondo Commission.

This governance arrangement mirrored that of former finance minister Van Rooyen. He installed two special advisers (Mohamed Bobat and Ian Whitley, who were not known to him at the time) to run the department briefly. In this time, they issued instructions to the director-general and forwarded confidential Treasury documents to the Gupta-linked company Trillian, and its CEO Eric Wood. Upon arrival at the department, with Van Rooyen, they had a work plan and were ready to assume some departmental functions. Their sojourn was brief but an invaluable opening for capture. The Guptas had been urging Zuma to assert his control over the Treasury, a state institution that had been obstructing key family deals.[40]

The case of David Mahlobo, former minister of state security, illustrates another iteration on the theme of capture. The High Level Review Panel into the SSA reported in late 2018 that when Mahlobo had presided over it, the agency showed 'an almost complete disregard for the Constitution, policy, legislation and other prescripts ... turning our civilian intelligence community into a private resource to serve the political and personal interests of particular individuals'.[41] Zuma enlisted Mahlobo in the State Security Ministry at the start of his second administration. Mahlobo served both the president and the Guptas loyally, and was redeployed in the last-ditch Cabinet reshuffle in October 2017 when Zuma needed to rescue his Russian nuclear deal, before possibly being sidelined at Nasrec. Mahlobo's predecessors were Tina Joemat-Pettersson (redeployed probably because she had become too controversial in the context of Oilgate II) and Mmamoloko Kubayi-Ngubane (whom Zuma had expected to be more compliant).[42] Legal, procedural and civil society mobilisation factors prevented Mahlobo from realising the Zuma-Gupta nuclear dream. In 2010, the Guptas had acquired the mine envisaged to supply the nuclear plants' uranium needs. Shiva Uranium, bought with the assistance of a R250 million loan from the Industrial Development Corporation, continued facing an uncertain future.

These cases of executive-level capture represented the tip of the iceberg. There were many more instances of Gupta-ist and other capture: the former communications minister, Faith Muthambi, as evidenced in the #GuptaLeaks investigation by amaBhungane, transgressed and shared government policy plans with the Guptas. The South African Broadcasting Corporation's Hlaudi Motsoeneng was captured in projects with Zuma, where personal-presidential interests ruled instead of the national interest. Former minister Nomvula Mokonyane was indicated as a recipient of major Bosasa patronage. Former social development minister Bathabile Dlamini extended protection to Net1/Cash Paymaster Services, responsible for payment of social grants.

State-owned enterprises

Under the presidency of Cyril Ramaphosa, state-owned enterprises became a core focus of the attack on the president as the indirect, actual target, and on the minister of public enterprises, Pravin Gordhan. Ramaphosa had Gordhan positioned as his right-hand aide to drive the clean-up and rationalisation of faltering state-owned enterprises.[43] In this war, the prevailing narrative of 'radical economic transformation' and resistance against 'white monopoly capital' was elaborated to include 'stop political interference in the state-owned enterprises' and 'end the destruction of state assets' (both sensitive and emotive, politically charged). This delegitimation narrative reached a peak as the state-owned enterprises' financial drain on the economy became fiscally unbearable and rationalisation ensued. Clean-ups of corrupt and unqualified boards and executives suffered setbacks, and intra-ANC opponents worked to consolidate attacks on Ramaphosa, given new rounds of succession contests that were taking shape. The struggles of the state-owned enterprises personified the political wars of the Ramaphosa state.

In the pre-Ramaphosa era the state-owned enterprises had been repurposed widely to allow complexes of politically connected vulture capital, multinational auditing and consulting companies and banks to reorganise and loot them. The Zondo Commission shed light on this capture phenomenon: unprecedented amounts of state resources had been diverted illegally and in multiple cases cabinet members had prepared the ground for lucrative tenders to go, for example, to the Guptas. Elaborate networks of collusion transpired.

Among the state's interventions to reclaim the state-owned enterprises after the prime-time of capture were the appointment of Gordhan, former minister of finance with close knowledge of the heydays of post-1994 looting as minister of public enterprises, of new boards and executives, turnaround strategies (focusing on mandates such as market development, strengthening of corporate governance structures and stabilising finances), plans for restructuring, and ongoing negotiations for bailouts from the government. There were improvements in the Ramaphosa era, yet there were fears that the ravaged state-owned enterprises could still wreck the entire national economy (Table 6.1).[44]

Ramaphosa and his cabinet changed managements and boards, for example at Eskom. The changes were *relatively depoliticised* because they happened in a context of continuously faltering state-owned enterprises and ongoing adjustments to board composition, but this changed once the altered appointments were recognised as ammunition against the Ramaphosa state and presidency. Most of the big and problematic enterprises[45] – Eskom, SAA, Denel, Transnet, Prasa, the National Energy Regulator of South Africa and the South African Nuclear Energy Corporation – had suffered deep structural and finance issues; new boards and executives were not a panacea. Proposals for restructuring or salvaging followed, in some cases business rescue or liquidation. Several proclamations were signed, instructing the Special Investigating Unit to investigate allegations of wrongdoing, supplementing the work of the Zondo Commission.

South African Airways was a prime example. A 90-day action plan was implemented and several new boards were inaugurated in the course of the Zuma years (Zuma cronies served in prominent roles) and beyond. Non-submission of financial

Table 6.1: South Africa's incurable state-owned enterprises: Select cases, 2018–2020

State-owned enterprise (SOE)	Core clean-up actions under-taken	Timing	Ongoing problems
Eskom	Ramaphosa announces a new board and directs it to appoint a permanent CEO and chief financial officer (CFO). Former CEO Matshela Koko is removed. New CEO resigns mid-2019, reportedly re political interference; Eskom chair becomes acting CEO. Eskom pursues appointment of a chief restructuring officer (CRO) – appointment aligns with proposed restructuring of Eskom into business units of generation, transmission and distribution, outlined in 'Roadmap for Eskom' (released late 2019). Ramaphosa gives assurance Eskom will not be privatised. André de Ruyter appointed as new CEO. Deloitte repays Eskom large amount in out-of-court settlement. Corruption and victimisation charges brought against chief operating officer (COO).	Early 2018 \n\nMid-2019 \n\nLate 2019–2020 \n\n2020	Financial position deteriorates continuously. New board appointed. Government grants first R60bn and the R59bn to ensure that Eskom continues to operate as a going concern. Moody's warn on Eskom investment risk. CRO appointment is a condition of the additional financial support to Eskom. Tripartite Alliance opposes restructuring. \nFurther bailouts, unbundling into three entities face labour headwinds. Transition into next Integrated Resource Plan (IRP) requires repositioning. Leadership through the IRP 2019, roadmap for Eskom and medium-term budget falls short; Fitch downgrades Eskom to junk, Eskom contributed to poor ratings for SA generally. Corona crisis brings worsening, e.g. sharp drop in Eskom revenue on lower usage. Worsening state liquidity affects SOEs. \nEstimated in 2020 that Eskom would need R226 billion in bailouts until 2026.

continued

State-owned enterprise (SOE)	Core clean-up actions undertaken	Timing	Ongoing problems
SAA	New SAA executive chairperson appointed; ongoing erosion of skills at the airline and leadership disruptions undermine turnaround implementation. Earlier in 2019 the CEO resigns over uncertainty about future funding for turnaround. SAA to undergo far-reaching restructuring. Workers and organised labour fight the looming job losses. Crisis of viability of routes exacerbated by Covid-19 collapse of air travel; speculated that the crisis might lead to end of SAA. Business rescue plan approved in July 2020. Retrenchment notice served on SAA employees. Business rescue plan requires R10.5 billion in funding in 2020.	October 2017–2019

September–December 2019

2020 | Operational problems and financial woes. A R5.5bn capital injection approved by Treasury for the 2019/2020 financial year (as part of agreed SAA turnaround strategy). SAA in ongoing struggle to service debt. Executive director tells parliamentary committee that shutting down the entity would come at a staggering cost. Financial instability claims tolls – strikes and collapse of confidence that SAA can recover. SAA placed in business rescue. Most SAA domestic routes cancelled and international rationalised. Covid brings the final nail. Funding for SAA's rescue plan problematic. Several companies enter talks with government, offering support to SAA to fly again after a period of dormancy. |
| Prasa | New board appointed; its term later extended until late 2019. New human capital management, new group chief procurement officer. At least eight senior officials and executives have serious probity allegations against them. Prasa suspends some, others on special leave while investigations unfold. New procurement chief appointed; first permanent chief financial officer in five years. Zondo Commission unearths massive corruption, capture in Zuma times. | 2018
October 2019
September 2019

March 2019

Late 2019

2020 | 2016/2017 annual report to Parliament – almost 12 months behind schedule; failing to deliver on its core mandate, which the agency blames on governance and leadership instability; Prasa records rising and huge losses.

Auditor-general gives Prasa a disclaimer of opinion in its annual report (management failed to account properly for assets). Swifambo (subsequently liquidated) provided wrong-size trains and supplied only 13 of the 70 envisaged trains. Owner claims to have channelled money to the ANC. Several senior officials remain under investigation. |

continued

State-owned enterprise (SOE)	Core clean-up actions undertaken	Timing	Ongoing problems
Denel	Three new board members approved. Daniel du Toit appointed as the group chief executive (resigns in July 2020); board chairperson has to defend it against union's allegations of discrimination. Appoints a new group CFO. Denel's turnaround strategy aims to include plans to diversify and end loss-making operations.	March 2018 January 2019 Late 2019 2020	For 2017/2018 financial year, auditor-general flags huge irregular expenditure and issues disclaimer audit opinion. Suffers severe liquidity problems. Delays, uncertainty in paying salaries. Cannot deliver on contract because no longer owns intellectual property. Annual report shows Denel losses grew by two-thirds in 2018/2019 financial year. Received R1.8bn bailout to 'restabilise' and improve solvency in 2019/2020. Implements accounting reforms, works to limit job losses as it exits from manufacture of aircraft parts. Bailouts realised were insufficient; Denel in court for non-payment of salaries.

Source: Author's monitoring project of South African politics, 1994–2000, based on media reportage and interviews.

Note: The state-owned enterprises suffered generally from lack of permanent CEOs.

statements continued and there were continuous applications for massive bailouts (also the case among other state-owned enterprises, notably Eskom). Previous turnaround strategies had often not found traction; strikes followed and contested business rescue ensued.[46] This process meandered between labour disputes, additional state bailouts sought after close to a decade of financial losses, a restructuring plan, and commitment to let a new national carrier rise out of SAA's ashes.

Eskom had concluded major capture contracts on coal provision which favoured the Gupta network of companies. On occasion, the parastatal was called the 'main theatre where corruption and state capture was taking place'.[47] While the ANC's investment arm did well through contracts for boiler infrastructure to two coal-fired power stations, much of the country's energy generation problems linked back to these deals. Overstaffing was problematic. Eskom's employment spree may have helped with unemployment but it drained finances for roughly a decade – estimates were that it was up to 66 per cent overstaffed. Possible staff rationalisation became a major point for trade union mobilisation and extended the anti-Ramaphosa-Gordhan axis. Staffing costs and debt servicing (of R450 billion) were Eskom's main expenditure items. Its condition deteriorated further as Covid-19 struck: even fewer people and businesses could pay for electricity, and the number of defaulting municipalities rose. Restructuring Eskom was contested and the selling off of problematic assets was seen as national betrayal.[48]

The problems at other strategically important state-owned enterprises were of a lesser scale, yet still with massive fiscal implications. Eskom, Transnet, the South African National Roads Agency Limited, SAA and the SABC required serial bailouts.[49]

Security operations

Parallel state configurations were rife in the state security or intelligence community, in both institutional form and operations executed.[50] They went beyond the mandate of security and became extensions of factional party politics – a prime example of Zuma-ist capture. The High Level Review Panel Report affirmed:

> It is clear from ... information available to the Panel that [Special Operations] had largely become a parallel intelligence structure serving a faction of the ruling party and, in particular, the personal political interests of the sitting president [Zuma] of the party and country. This is in direct breach of the Constitution, the White Paper, the relevant legislation and plain good government intelligence functioning.[51]

The unit had become politicised, and the then minister[52] had involved himself fully in the operation of the unit. The main person responsible for this politicisation, according to the report, was deployed directly by the then president.[53] Therefore, the Special Operations Unit, the panel surmised, was 'a law unto itself and directly served the political interests of the Executive'.[54] Among the unit's unconstitutional and illegal functions were intelligence operations; the training of undercover agents in VIP protection and assigning some of them to provide protection to the then president and others (VIP protection is a police mandate); infiltrating and influencing the media to counter bad publicity, especially for the president; establishment of the Workers' Association Union to 'neutralise worker instability' on the platinum belt; and putting trade unions critical of Zuma under surveillance. There was interference in the #FeesMustFall protests 'to influence the direction of the student movement which was justified as supporting "young bright minds" to be patriotic …'.[55]

The repurposing of the Special Operations Unit to serve ANC factional and general political purposes was evident from the High Level Review Panel Report's references to 'successes' (in the view of the unit) of three operations to promote Zuma and counter Ramaphosa. The special operations included that it had impeded the distribution of CR17 regalia, and disrupted the transportation that would have been used to take Ramaphosa-supportive 'dissident groups' from Gauteng to an ANC meeting in Rustenburg. During the 2016 State of the Nation Address, the unit infiltrated the leadership structure of the pro-Ramaphosa–anti-Zuma movement, used disinformation and minimised the numbers that marched on Parliament. During the ANC's 2016 local government manifesto launch in Port Elizabeth, the unit 'initiated a media campaign to provide positive media feedback through the placement of youths of various ethnic groups in photographic vision [sic] of media personnel, thereby promoting social cohesion'.[56] The Special Operations Unit took pride in having monitored the non-governmental organisations – South Africa First, Right2Know, Save South Africa, Council for the Advancement of the South African Constitution and Greenpeace – which had taken part in anti-Zuma mobilisation. President Zuma and the minister also made sure that they deployed 'their people' into the SSA.

Zuma was in control of many of the intelligence functions in the government, and this influence persisted into the Ramaphosa state and helped to divide it. Ramaphosa only re-established the National Security Council in 2020, after having publicly envisaged the step of reconstituting a professional national intelligence capability since 2019. The Council was to be responsible for approving the National Security Strategy, the National Intelligence Estimate and National Intelligence

Priorities, and coordinating the work of security services, law enforcement agencies and relevant organs of state.[57]

Public protector Mkhwebane's calculated parallelism

Several of public protector Busisiwe Mkhwebane's reports were struck down by higher courts and the Constitutional Court from 2019 to 2020. It was a subject of debate whether the dubious report content was due to ignorance of the law and serious flaws in interpretation of the law (as several court indictments found), or poor legal advice to her office (or from SSA advisers, as frequently suggested), or whether it was a calculated political campaign (irrespective of legal soundness) to bolster anti-Ramaphosa, pro-Zuma public narratives and damage the Ramaphosa presidency.[58] In substance, these public protector actions amounted to a parallel operation under the veil of being the watchdog.

The public protector also acted on the SARS 'rogue unit', which she and her EFF associates had been arguing was established unlawfully. Pravin Gordhan was the major target[59] – and she released the report (regarding dated events, which had been investigated several times before) on the eve of Ramaphosa's cabinet announcement of May 2019. This fostered doubt as to whether Gordhan could be eligible for appointment to Cabinet, given that Mkhwebane had ordered remedial action. Only in February 2020 did the national director of public prosecutions, Shamila Batohi, drop the charges against three former SARS officials who had been framed as rogue operators. The Gauteng High Court in Pretoria formally withdrew the charges. In late 2020 further action followed: the same court nullified Mkhwebane's rogue unit report.

Mkhwebane had drawn on a report by inspector-general of intelligence Faith Radebe, who had switched her investigative brief from a focus on the SSA to SARS, a step reckoned to have been under the influence of spy operatives in double-agent roles. Radebe argued that 'it would be remiss of this office not to report the alleged unlawful activities in a state institution, especially as it may involve intelligence and security activities'.[60] In the interim, the *Sunday Times* had retracted and apologised for the falsehood of its reportage on the rogue unit. Gene Ravele, SARS head of enforcement, testified at the Nugent Commission that the SARS High Risk Investigations Unit (aka the rogue unit) had 'hurt' people who were politically connected and that was the reason for its being targeted.[61] In an earlier SARS decision that aborted charges, Ravele had been accused of 'sanctioning or approving the conducting of unlawful covert and/or clandestine intelligence gathering activity in SARS'.[62] As the *Daily Maverick* observed about the Radebe report, 'a number of discredited SSA witnesses interviewed may have crafted a tailor-made narrative that an illegal unit existed in SARS'.[63]

The public protector's cases against Ramaphosa hinted at operations from within a parallel semi-state. While there was a need to establish whether Ramaphosa had misled Parliament about his CR17 campaign donation and had contravened the Ethics Code, the protector moved beyond her brief and accessed confidential CR17 campaign emails which had little bearing on the donation. The Pretoria High Court set aside the protector's remedial actions against Ramaphosa and also ruled that Ramaphosa had not deliberately misled Parliament. Later, the Concourt ruled that the protector's remedial orders would be suspended in case of appeals against them. The protector, however, was embedded in a parallel world. She would not let go voluntarily.

National Prosecuting Authority

The NPA had been a key spoke in the capture wheel, spanning presidential eras from Mbeki onwards. The institution was used not only for prosecutorial functions, but also for politics. Evidence abounded of the political roles of the institution, its national director of public prosecutions and its provincial functionaries. The focus here is on the political roles the NPA assumed (Table 6.2), the extent of its having been captured and its role in the Ramaphosa state. The historical roles simultaneously illuminate the complexities surrounding the Ramaphosa-era NPA.

An earlier variant of NPA capture emerged under President Thabo Mbeki. The national director of public prosecutions Vusi Pikoli came under pressure when former ANC exile comrade and then police commissioner, Jackie Selebi, was exposed after NPA action for the corrupt receipt of gifts from the Brett Kebble empire – while criminals and later murderers (related to other parts of the Kebble business) were walking away on plea bargains. Succumbing to political pressure, Pikoli resigned before the end of his term.

Cross-cutting political influence and control were flagrant in the transition from Mbeki to Zuma, and throughout the Zuma period. The national directors of public prosecutions were in the crossfire for decisions on whether to institute corruption charges against Zuma for his actions in the arms deal of the late 1990s.[64] There were legal grounds to charge him for arms deal corruption around the time of Polokwane 2007, but Zuma had insurance in the political volatility of the moment – high levels of populist mobilisation restrained prosecution and helped Zuma into power when the NPA postponed lodging the charges against him until after Polokwane. Zuma's second layer of insurance was to charge that Mbeki was orchestrating political collusion and conspiracy. Since this time, the 'Zuma issue' has undergirded the turnover of several national directors of public prosecutions.

Table 6.2:   Succession of national directors of public prosecution

Period	NDPP	Reason for change	Political–Zuma context
1998–2004	Bulelani Ngcuka	Resigned after political fallout with minister and Mbeki	August 2003 Ngcuka announces will charge Schabir Shaik (convicted 2005).
2005–2007	Vusi Pikoli	Dismissed, challenged in court, out-of-court settlement	June 2005 Pikoli indicates charges against Zuma; to trial July 2006 but NPA not ready; Mbeki suspended Pikoli due to prosecution of police commissioner Jackie Selebi.
2007–2009	Mokotedi Mpshe	Acting	December 2007 Mpshe decides to indict Zuma on 18 counts (same subject matter as Shaik trial); September 2008 Nicholson rules in Zuma's favour (Supreme Court of Appeal overturns it in January 2009); Mpshe withdraws charges but Democratic Alliance brings steps to review decision.
2009–2012	Menzi Simelane	Concourt found appointment irrational	Democratic Alliance challenged Zuma's hiring of Simelane; in December 2011 the Supreme Court of Appeal invalidates the appointment for Zuma's failure to adhere to proper appointment procedures.
2012–2013	Nomgcobo Jiba	Acting	Continuously embroiled in legal proceedings following adverse findings against her re unlawful authorisation charges against KwaZulu-Natal Hawks head, Johan Booysen.
2013–2015	Mxolisi Nxasana	Resigns with golden handshake under pressure from Zuma	Removed by Zuma who was taken aback by Nxasana's independence.
2015–2018	Shaun Abrahams	Resigns, after Concourt rules appointment was irregular	April 2016 Pretoria High Court sets aside Mpshe decision; Abrahams avoids prosecution against corrupt ones.
2018–2019	Silas Ramaite	Acting (from position of deputy NDPP)	Routine stand-in by deputy; applied and was short-listed; had been deputy for 15 years.
2019, ongoing	Shamila Batohi	Ongoing	Appointed after rigorous, transparent process. Finds multiple obstacles to improving NPA office.

Source: Author's monitoring of state institutional change

The suppression of Zuma's corruption charges specifically, and the creation of a tolerant environment for the misdeeds of the era of state capture (in the form especially of looting of state resources by party functionaries) were key factors in the NPA's paralysis in the decade that followed. Much of the immobilisation was 'by design' to undermine NPA capacity, while at least two of the national directors of public prosecutions changeovers were irregular.

For Ramaphosa's assumption of power to make a difference, on the assumption that he wanted to be true to the clean-up mandate, the NPA had to be professionalised away from failed, withdrawn and inadequately prepared prosecutions of key state capture cases.[65] The appointment procedure for advocate Shamila Batohi was by all accounts rigorous and professional, and not subject to the preferences of the president. The NPA's work was cut out for it: eliminate parallelism by pursuing one-track judicial-prosecutorial rigour and political will to take decisions with political implications. Ramaphosa appointed advocate Hermione Cronjé to head the NPA's investigative directorate.[66] He created the directorate to focus on corruption and fraud, specifically in cases emanating from the Zondo Commission. The unit was boosted when in 2020 Ramaphosa amended regulations that had previously prohibited agencies such as the Zondo Commission and the NPA from sharing information. The NPA would in future also be allowed to recruit much-needed specialist investigators from the ranks of the commission.

State prosecutorial functions generally were also being cleaned up under Ramaphosa. The Hawks acquired a new head, Godfrey Lebeya, who had left the South African Police Service after falling out with the Zuma-appointed former commissioner of police, Riah Phiyega. The position of commissioner of police went to lieutenant-general Khehla Sitole.[67] The disgraced head of South African Police Service crime intelligence, Richard Mdluli, was fired.

The scene was set therefore for charges to be laid, and actual high-level, significant prosecutions to unfold – yet progress was slow. This would undermine Ramaphosa's credibility, unless if, in the bigger scheme of things, there was to be relentless roll-out instead of hasty and reversible actions.

Special Investigating Unit

The Special Investigating Unit[68] was another strategically important state institution that had to be repurposed, back to its original intent. The president gave it extra powers and renewed its leadership. It was given its own dedicated court, with the status of a special tribunal. Previously, it had been limited to making recommendations to the NPA on individuals or companies linked to government or government officials to be prosecuted for involvement in irregularities. It also had the powers to sue on behalf of the state or its entities, and to retrieve money from irregular payments. The special tribunal was to contribute to the speedier resolution of cases.

The release of large amounts of public funds to counter the coronavirus outbreak, and escalating evidence of misuse of resources, prompted Ramaphosa to establish a government coordinating centre that brought together nine state institutions, including the Special Investigating Unit, Hawks, NPA, Independent Police Investigative Directorate, Financial Intelligence Centre, SARS and the SSA. They were to investigate cases of suspected misuse of Covid-19 resources. This new mechanism came with heightened awareness of the future political implications for the ANC, should it be seen amid the misery of Covid-19 to be abusing resources intended to care for the sick and the poor.

The need for the speedier handling of cases was illustrated through the report regarding alleged Bosasa tender rigging that the Special Investigating Unit had handed to the NPA a decade earlier. The tender rigging concerned Bosasa directors and CEO Gavin Watson paying bribes valued at approximately R1.5 billion to the Department of Correctional Services to secure tenders in the period 2004 to 2007, details that would re-emerge at the Zondo Commission and in court. Other cases that illustrated prosecutorial progress included the Special Investigating Unit suing Giyani water contractors for R2.2 billion; investigating theft of R139 billion from Eskom's Medupi and Kusile power stations[69] (the investigation started in June 2018 and also involved the NPA's Asset Forfeiture Unit and the Hawks); maladministration at the National Health Laboratory Service; a vehicle tender issued by the City of Johannesburg (R86 million, awarded in 2014 by the ANC and cancelled by the Democratic Alliance); and the R255 million 2014 contract between the Free State Department of Human Settlements and Blackhead Consulting and Diamond Hill Trading 71 for an audit and assessment of asbestos roofs in the province.[70] The line-up included politically contentious cases.

Provincial and local government

Steps to deal with corruption in provincial and local government increased in frequency when Ramaphosa assumed power – although the cases that required clean-up far outstripped the state's capacity to deal with them, and new cases emerged continually. In addition, political deployment and associated sensitivities about acting against comrades, even more so if they were in the right faction, continued detracting from stated political will. Ramaphosa authorised the Special Investigating Unit to probe multiple provincial government departments (and municipalities) regarding irregularities in procurement, unlawful appropriation and improper conduct by employees. Entities included provincial treasury departments, the KwaZulu-Natal departments of public works and transport, and several Eastern Cape institutions, such as the metros of Buffalo City and Nelson Mandela Bay. Other proclamations followed.

The situation hardly improved subsequently – and national government had not been leading by example. The auditor-general reported overall deteriorations in the audit results of national and provincial government departments and their entities, year after year.[71] For example, across the financial years of 2017/2018, 2018/2019 and 2019/2020, irregular expenditure by national and provincial departments had risen.[72] The auditor-general's reports commonly observed that at local level irregular expenditure remained high, few municipalities were achieving clean audits, audit outcomes declined continuously, and the auditing environment had become hostile. There was increased contestation of audit findings and pushbacks whereby audit processes and the motives of audit teams were questioned. There was a municipal culture of no fear and no consequences for non-compliance.

A kind of lawlessness ruled in the municipalities, fostered by politicians who operated as if they were above the law. Beyond the auditor-general's reports, this culture was evident in the Venda Building Society (VBS) 'bank heist'. It was a case of gross financial misconduct at the local level, siphoning off public funds that municipalities had invested in the VBS. The proceeds swelled the pockets of political elites associated, for example, with the EFF, the ANC and the Venda king, Toni Mphephu-Ramabulana. The VBS was the bank that had granted Zuma a bond (in a bogus deal) to pay his Nkandla residence debts to the state. The king facilitated the VBS deal for Zuma in exchange for formal recognition as king. The Hawks reported that 19 municipalities between them deposited in excess of R1.8 billion, violating the Municipal Finance Management Act and National Treasury regulations.[73] The ANC had removed 11 mayors linked to VBS transactions from municipalities in Limpopo and North West provinces. President Ramaphosa assented to the Public Audit Amendment Act, which gave the auditor-general new powers to act against irregular state spending. The changes, however, took a long time to come into effect.

Then auditor-general, Tembekile Kimi Makwetu, blamed the Zuma years for the culture of looting with impunity. The escalation that prevailed in the time of Zuma's reign, Makwetu argued, was because appointees had the confidence that there was a lack of accountability and no consequences.[74] The Ramaphosa state was confronted by serious doubts as to whether there could be sufficient political will and administrative and prosecutorial strength to make the difference that had been promised. The alternative was the endless spinning out of small markers as major achievements, augmented with assurances that all was 'on track'.

CONCLUSION: STATE OF PARALLELISM AND LAWLESSNESS

Investigation and clean-up of state capture, corruption and incapacity was the name of the state's reincarnation game that Cyril Ramaphosa took on when he stepped into the presidency of South Africa. The task was of such magnitude that it could probably not be concluded in his or any successor's term of office, with the best political will and even if there had been evidence that the Ramaphosa-ists had the appropriate moral standing and clean records. The best that could be forthcoming was a continuous flow of new findings and gradual steps that could reclaim the state bit by bit, if new evidence and new cases did not overwhelm the process.

The case studies in this chapter demonstrated, case by case, the half-measure nature of the state that Ramaphosa inherited. For Ramaphosa to deliver a definitively refocused state operation – a prerequisite to fulfilling his popular mandate – many nearly impossible changes would need to be made, given the political culture of the organisation and the state – apart from deficient financial resources. The case studies cited here illustrated the limitations and the culture. The constraints included ceasing diversionary attacks on political opponents (including the president), ceasing parallel state 'security' operations, and releasing all human and financial resources necessary to effect rapid and thorough prosecutorial operations, and fostering a facilitative culture in the ANC which would be transferred to the state. The magnitude of his task – based on the Ramaphosa promise to clean up the state and to bring in ethical politics – was probably going to defeat achieving the goal.

A host of the interventions that Ramaphosa effected, including reshuffling Cabinet and changes to the management and strategic focus of the state-owned enterprises, had a bearing on ending state capture and corruption. Ramaphosa argued that 'it was not until the details of the so-called Gupta leaks were published from June 2017 onwards that one became aware of the extent, depth and methodology of state capture'.[75] In late 2019, Ramaphosa gave the undertaking that '[w]e have stemmed the bleeding, we are ready to open a new chapter. Those responsible will be brought to book … We will chart a new course of clean governance and avoid corrupt tendencies'.[76] Commensurate action, to match these words step by step, was still to build up.

The state of the South African state, in the first few years of Ramaphosa's reign, was light years away from the world of Jacob Zuma. The task of state clean-up, however, was immense and the price for its pursuit was high – and it was not clear whether the political will to see it through was present. The ANC was an ambiguous driver of the project; the fightback was coming largely from within ANC ranks and there were limits at high political level as to what degree of clean-up of institutions and politicians would be tolerated.

While this incomplete transition to a reinvented ANC state order was unfolding, and remained uncertain in terms of final outcome, two parallel state orders persisted. This etched the precarity of ANC power. The ANC also gained from fusion between party and state. Yet, this state anchor of ANC power was torn and tainted.

NOTES

1   In one of multiple explicit references to the Ramaphosa silence amid overwhelming evidence of high-level ANC corruption and Zuma's facilitative role, former Passenger Rail Agency of South Africa (Prasa) board director and one-time ANC premier of the North West, Popo Molefe, testified (Zondo Commission, 13 March 2020) that he had briefed the ANC top six, including Zuma and Ramaphosa, on the corruption at Prasa.

2   The definition by Michelle le Roux and Dennis Davis, 2019, *Lawfare: Judging Politics in South Africa*, Johannesburg: Jonathan Ball, p. 267, pinpoints the essence of state capture as manifested in South Africa: '[t]he construction of a parallel state utilising existing organs of state, state-owned enterprises and constitutionally mandated institutions for corrupt objectives, primarily by deploying leaders to those organisations that display a firm commitment to subverting accountability or diverting them from their lawful mandates and a resolute determination to ignore the consequences of their conduct for the people they serve'.

3   Nomvula Mokonyane, 20 July 2020, testimony to the Zondo Commission, Day 235, https://sastatecapture.org.za/site/hearings/date/2020/7/20, accessed 25 July 2020; ANC, 16 December 2017, Organisational report delivered to the 54th national conference, Nasrec, Gauteng, by the ANC secretary general Gwede Mantashe.

4   ANC 54th National Conference Report and Resolutions, December 2017, p. 82.

5   Discussion at the first ANC National General Council meeting, July 2000, Port Elizabeth.

6   A Public Service Commission report of May 2018 urged government to charge officials accused of misconduct within three months; see Public Service Commission, 2018, *The Pulse of the Public Service*.

7   Kgalema Motlanthe, 19 January 2007, as quoted in Gareth van Onselen, 'Prince's letter a manifestation of the ANC's creed', *Business Day*, 1 February 2016.

8   The World Values Survey South Africa 1982–2013, 2015, reveals declining levels of trust in public institutions, as public knowledge of corruption accumulates; see https://www.datafirst.uct.ac.za/dataportal/index.php/catalog/471/study-description, accessed 5 December 2016.

9   For details on the Bell Pottinger project, and the white monopoly capital narrative, see Jackie Cameron, 'News "prostitute" Bell Pottinger's Victoria Geoghegan has "sold her soul": Mailbox – #GuptaLeaks', *BizNews*, 8 June 2017, https://www.biznews.com/guptaleaks/2017/06/08/bell-pottinger-victoria-geoghegan, accessed 8 June 2017.

10   Cyril Ramaphosa, 23 August 2020, Letter by President Cyril Ramaphosa to ANC membership, 'Let this be a turning point in our fight against corruption'; Jacob Zuma, 28 August 2020, Letter to Cyril Ramaphosa; letters received by direct broadcast.

11   At the World Economic Forum in Davos, January 2019, Ramaphosa referred to this, and later moderated his standpoint; see Juniour Khumalo, 'Ramaphosa backtracks on "nine wasted years" under Zuma', *City Press*, 2 February 2019, https://city-press.news24.com/News/ramaphosa-backtracks-on-nine-wasted-years-under-zuma-20190202, accessed 1 March 2019. Zuma offered counter-evidence; see 'What South Africa lost in the "9 wasted years" under Zuma', *BusinessTech*, 9 February 2019, https://businesstech.co.za/news/government/298278/what-south-africa-lost-in-the-9-wasted-years-under-zuma/, accessed 1 June 2019.

12   See Office of the Inspector General of Intelligence, 31 October 2014, Report on an investigation into media allegations against the Special Operations Unit and/or other branches of the SSA, https://effonline.org/wp-content/uploads/2019/09/ANNEX-URE-FS2.pdf, accessed 3 October 2019, for the details of how the term 'rogue' came to be associated with the SARS data collection unit.

13   Prince Mashele suggested the Gumede dynasty should be investigated; see Prince Mashele, 'ANC needs to institute an inquiry into capture within its ranks', *Sowetan*, 4 March 2019, https://www.sowetanlive.co.za/opinion/columnists/2019-03-04-anc-needs-to-institute-an-inquiry-into-capture-within-its-ranks/, accessed 1 April 2019; many other families and business dynasties would be able to offer valuable insights too.

14   Heribert Adam, Frederik Van Zyl Slabbert and Kogila Moodley, 1998, *Comrades in Business: Post-Liberation Politics in South Africa*, Cape Town: Tafelberg. See also Dale McKinley, 2017, *South Africa's Corporatised Liberation: A Critical Analysis of the ANC in Power*, Johannesburg: Jacana.

15   The case of the *Sunday Times* journalists who were sucked into the web of manufactured evidence around the SARS 'rogue unit' and General Johan Booysen's 'police murder squad' stand out. Some of these journalists went on to join the Independent group at the time that it became a leading force in trying to discredit the Ramaphosa order.

16   Susan Booysen, 2018, 'The African National Congress and its transfer of power from Zuma to Ramaphosa: The intraparty-multiparty nexus', *Transformation*, 98, 1–26.

17   Education in public schools was often low standard: problems included poorly qualified, often absent teachers, and learners being out of control. Schools were not coping with the weight of demands. In health, there was a deluge of information on operating theatres that did not work or were not equipped, nursing staff that failed to perform, and beds and medicines being unavailable. Such problems were rife in Gauteng and North West, for example.

18   Minister Aaron Motsoaledi, 6 June 2018, media briefing, Johannesburg.

19   Auditor-general, 26 June 2019, 'Auditor-general flags lack of accountability as the major cause of poor local government audit results', media release; Auditor-general, 1 July 2020, 'Not much to go around, yet not the right hands at the till', media release.

20   High Level Review Panel Report of the State Security Agency, December 2018, redacted version released by the president of South Africa, 9 March 2019, http://www.thepres-idency.gov.za/download/file/fid/1518, accessed 12 September 2019; see also Qaanitah Hunter, 'Zuma "spooked" Cyril's campaign' and '"Lawless" spies threaten Cyril's state clean-up', *Sunday Times*, 10 March 2019, pp. 1–2; Ngwako Modjadji, 'Zuma is to blame for intelligence mess', *City Press*, 10 March 2019, p. 14.

21 Emails leaked to journalists at amaBhungane and the *Daily Maverick's* Scorpio. The bank of correspondence has been dubbed #GuptaLeaks. If there was any doubt, many of the details have been corroborated in evidence to the Zondo Commission of Inquiry.

22 See for example investigations by amaBhungane, *Daily Maverick's* Scorpio, and the details in #GuptaLeaks. See also Ivor Chipkin and Mark Swilling, 2018, *Shadow State: The Politics of State Capture*, Johannesburg: Wits University Press.

23 Mcebisi Jonas, as reported in Karyn Maughan, 'Gupta brother told me "we are in control of everything"', *Timeslive*, 24 August 2018, https://www.timeslive.co.za/news/south-africa/2018-08-24-mcebisi-jonas-gupta-brother-told-me-we-are-in-control-of-everything/, accessed 25 August 2018.

24 Interview with former ministerial adviser, 24 September 2019, Cape Town, granted on condition of anonymity.

25 Dudu Miyeni, chair of the South African Airways (SAA) board until 2017, for example, got her adviser to execute high-level decisions on acquiring aircraft. See Luyolo Mkentane, 'Adviser to Myeni "ran the show at SAA"', *Business Day*, 16 June 2019, p. 2. Her status as Zuma confidante also leveraged her influence over the operations of other state-owned enterprises, including Eskom.

26 Interview with former ministerial adviser, 24 September 2019, op. cit.

27 Interview with former ministerial adviser, 24 September 2019, op. cit.

28 AmaBhungane reporters, 'Hitachi's Chancellor House dodging', *Mail & Guardian*, 23 April 2010, https://mg.co.za/article/2010-04-23-hitachis-chancellor-house-dodging, accessed 30 May 2018.

29 See Susan Booysen, 2015, *Dominance and Decline: The ANC in the Time of Zuma*, Johannesburg: Wits University Press, Chapter 7, relating that the public protector's reports on the Malema contracts speak to lapses in state procurement, accounting for projects and funding, and the Malema-centred elite benefiting from multiple projects in Limpopo province. What Malema did was similar to thousands of transactions that unfolded across the bulk of municipalities and provinces.

30 See SACP Central Committee, 2017, Our strategic tasks – now and over the next 10 years, https://www.politicsweb.co.za/documents/our-strategic-tasks--now-and-over-the-next-10-year, accessed 6 October 2020.

31 In terms of the parliamentary system of government, the president of South Africa is elected indirectly by the members of Parliament.

32 See Natasha Marrian, 'Late night shock – ANC will amend Constitution on land – President Cyril Ramaphosa announces the decision taken at the ANC's National Executive Committee lekgotla', *BusinessLive*, 21 July 2019, https://www.businesslive.co.za/bd/national/2018-07-31-breaking-news-anc-to-change-constitution-to-expropriate-land/, accessed 20 August 2019.

33 ANC NEC statement, 1 October 2019, on the policy document for discussion, Economic Transformation, Inclusive Growth, and Competitiveness: Towards an Economic Strategy for South Africa.

34 For full details of the Cabinet, see https://www.parliament.gov.za/ministers; some of the discarded ministers were made ambassadors, subject to getting security clearances from the SSA. Siyabonga Cwele and Dipuo Letsatsi-Duba, both former intelligence ministers, were not cleared.

35 The Presidency, *Annual Report 2017/2018*, https://www.google.com/url?sa=t&rct=j&q=&esrc=s&source=web&cd=18&ved=2ahUKEwigna2etMflAhXoVRUIHRYhDxYQFjAR-egQICBAE&url=https%3A%2F%2Fwww.gov.za%2Fsites%2Fdefault%2Ffiles%2Fgcis_doc-

ument%2F201810%2Fpresidency-annual-report.pdf&usg=AOvVaw25nLiOdLi58FHg5nA-Jdkad, accessed 1 May 2018.

36   Hlengiwe Nhlabathi, 'Nzimande laments "smash and grabs"', *City Press*, 18 December 2016, https://www.pressreader.com/south-africa/citypress/20161217/281621009981322, accessed 6 October 2020.

37   Deputy director-general, Kgathatso Tlhakudi, in evidence to the Zondo Commission, as reviewed by Jessica Bezuidenhout, 'Lynne Brown told us, "You're captured", senior official tells commission', *Daily Maverick*, 19 March 2019, https://www.dailymaverick.co.za/article/2019-03-19-lynne-brown-told-us-youre-captured-denel-senior-staff-tell-commission/, accessed 1 May 2019.

38   Zwane insisted that the September 2016 statement about a possible investigation against banks that broke ties with the Guptas was not sent out by him alone. He related the statement to the work of Cabinet's inter-ministerial committee that was established to consider allegations that some banks and other financial institutions had colluded in closing bank accounts and terminating contractual relationships with Oakbay Investments.

39   Such inspections, ordered by the department during Zwane's tenure, were used as weapons against some mining companies. This tightly centred operation became the platform for the purchase of the Optimum colliery by the Guptas' Tegeta Resources company. Zwane worked with Eskom executive Matshela Koko to expedite the transfer of mining rights to Tegeta and arranged that the department would approach the Competition Commission to process the transaction urgently. This enabled Tegeta to raise capital to fund the R2.1 billion purchase of Optimum and secure Eskom approval of the deal. Royal Bafokeng Platinum, for example, underwent a series of safety stoppages after it stopped the services of JIC, a mining contract linked to the Guptas. See Allan Seccombe, 'Zwane, Koko "planned Optimum's takeover"', *Business Day*, 15 March 2019, pp. 1–2.

40   See Ferial Haffajee, 'How Gupta-linked adviser went over Van Rooyen's head – ex-Treasury DG', *News24*, 22 November 2018, https://www.news24.com/SouthAfrica/News/how-gupta-linked-adviser-went-over-van-rooyens-head-ex-treasury-dg-20181122, accessed 2 December 2018.

41   High Level Review Panel Report of the State Security Agency, December 2018, op. cit.

42   Kubayi-Ngubane was appointed as minister of energy in March 2017 and redeployed in the reshuffle in October the same year.

43   Referred to in a government document as consolidation and rationalisation, which included 'repurposing for economic growth'; see Natasha Marrian and Genevieve Quintal, 'A marked man', *Financial Mail*, 13 February 2020, pp. 20–25.

44   State-owned enterprise debt contributed significantly to South Africa's national debt. In 2019, the Treasury imposed strict conditions for future bailouts, and required reportage in line with outlines of a restructured Eskom. Eskom pleaded that it was expected to subsidise consumers, while the permitted electricity price did not match production costs – and while large proportions of consumers and their municipalities were not paying; see, for example, Lameez Omarjee, 'Mboweni claps back: If you want services, pay up', *fin24*, 2 October 2019, https://www.fin24.com/Economy/mboweni-claps-back-if-you-want-services-pay-up-20191002, accessed 2 October 2019.

45   There are over 700 state-owned enterprises at national, provincial and local levels of government. The majority are unproblematic. The Department of Public Enterprises has oversight of Alexkor (diamonds), Denel (military equipment), Eskom (electricity

generation), Transnet (railway transport and pipelines), South African Express Airways, South African Forestry Company (Safcol), and the South African Broadcasting Corporation (SABC).

46 Auditor-general, 8 October 2019, report on state-owned enterprises presented to Parliament, http://www.sabcnews.com/sabcnews/auditor-general-presents-startling-report-on-soes/, accessed 8 October 2019.

47 As reported in Canny Maphanga, 'Eskom was the "main theatre where corruption and state capture was taking place" – Mabuza', *News24*, 22 February 2019, https://www.news24.com/SouthAfrica/News/eskom-was-the-main-theatre-where-corruption-and-state-capture-was-taking-place-mabuza-20190222, accessed 2 April 2019.

48 SACP general secretary, Blade Nzimande, SABC3 interview, 21:00 news, 6 October 2019.

49 See *Timeslive*, 20 May 2019, 'Salim Essa: The state-capture mastermind in the shadows', https://www.timeslive.co.za/politics/2019-05-20-salim-essa-the-state-capture-mastermind-in-the-shadows/, accessed 20 May 2019.

50 High Level Review Panel Report of the State Security Agency, December 2018, op. cit., p. 64.

51 High Level Review Panel Report of the State Security Agency, December 2018, op. cit., p. 65.

52 State Security had little ministerial stability, either in the Zuma or Ramaphosa terms. In Zuma's first term, it was Siyabonga Cwele (controversial inter alia because his wife was convicted of drug dealing), and the second term saw some rapid succession from David Mahlobo (2014–2017) to Bongani Bongo (2017–2018), and then under Ramaphosa to Dipuo Letsatsi-Duba (2018–2019) and Ayanda Dlodlo (2019). In November 2019 Moe Shaik gave evidence to the Zondo Commission, highlighting how Cwele enforced Zuma's wish that the Guptas should not be investigated by intelligence.

53 Not available in the redacted report that was made public, but opposition parties and several media reports identified this person as Thulani Dlomo. At an 18 July 2019 media briefing, the Department of State Security's acting director-general, Loyiso Jafta, said Dlomo 'remains a member of the SSA'; see also Jacques Pauw, 'Top-spioen agter "komplot" teen Ramaphosa verdwyn spoorloos', *Vrye Weekblad*, 19 April 2019, https://www.vryeweekblad.com/nuus-en-politiek/2019-04-19-top-spioen-agter-komplot-teen-ramaphosa-verdwyn-spoorloos/, accessed 9 October 2019. Dlomo was suspected of being behind a scheme to undermine Zuma post-Election 2019; in 2014 he was said to have been behind a project to cull the SARS top management and enable Zuma to appoint Tom Moyane to the top SARS position.

54 High Level Review Panel Report of the State Security Agency, December 2018, op. cit., p. 65. Several staffing changes were made as part of the immediate post-Zuma clean-up, and these were unfolding: the director-general of the SSA, Arthur Fraser, was moved to Correctional Services, and Loyiso Jafta became the SSA acting director.

55 High Level Review Panel Report of the State Security Agency, December 2018, op. cit., p. 65. It had been known all along that the ANC had met with and influenced a faction of the student movement; Susan Booysen, 2016, 'Two weeks in October: Changing governance in South Africa', in Susan Booysen (ed.), *FeesMustFall: Student Revolt, Decolonisation and Governance in South Africa*, Johannesburg: Wits University Press. In the fallist period, and despite the ANC efforts, the ANC-associated South African National Students Congress had often lost out to the EFF Youth Command and the Pan Africanist Student Movement of Azania.

56 High Level Review Panel Report of the State Security Agency, December 2018, op. cit., p. 66.

57 See Loyiso Sidimba, 'President Cyril Ramaphosa re-establishes security body', *IOL*, 11 March 2020, https://www.iol.co.za/news/politics/president-cyril-ramaphosa-re-establishes-security-body-44593887, accessed 11 March 2020.

58 The narratives reflected tenets of Zuma-ism and hooked into 'white monopoly capital' and 'radical economic transformation'.

59 Another public protector finding against Gordhan was his 2010 decision on former acting SARS commissioner, Ivan Pillay. Former NPA head, Shaun Abrahams, had already had to withdraw a proposed prosecution. Gordhan's representations showed that he had drawn on six opinions from lawyers and experts on the public service. They had endorsed his granting of early retirement to Pillay.

60 Office of the Inspector-General of Intelligence, 31 October 2014, Report on an investigation into media allegations against the Special Operations Unit and/or other branches of the SSA, https://effonline.org/wp-content/uploads/2019/09/ANNEXURE-FS2.pdf, accessed 3 October 2019.

61 Kyle Cowan, 'Rogue unit allegations hogwash, former SARS enforcement head tells inquiry', *News24*, 28 June 2018, https://www.fin24.com/Economy/rogue-unit-allegations-hogwash-former-sars-enforcement-head-tells-inquiry-20180628, accessed 4 October 2019.

62 See Angelique Serrao, 'EXCLUSIVE: Former SARS executive cleared of criminal charges', *News24*, 1 September 2017, https://www.news24.com/SouthAfrica/News/exclusive-former-sars-executive-cleared-of-criminal-charges-20170901, accessed 1 June 2018; *Noseweek*, March 2019, 'Two-faced Ravele on short-list for SARS commissioner', pp. 8–11.

63 Marianne Thamm, '2014 Radebe report into "rogue unit" based on discredited witnesses, sheds light on genesis of attack on SARS', *Daily Maverick*, 2 October 2019, https://www.dailymaverick.co.za/article/2019-10-02-2014-radebe-report-into-rogue-unit-based-on-discredited-witnesses-sheds-light-on-genesis-of-attack-on-sars/, accessed 2 April 2020.

64 Africa Criminal Justice Forum, October 2018, 'The appointment and dismissal of the NDPP: Instability since 1998', factsheet, Dullah Omar Institute.

65 Raymond Suttner, 3 June 2019, 'New cabinet and constructive support for the "new dawn"', https://www.polity.org.za/page/raymond-suttner/page:2, accessed 6 October 2020.

66 In March 2019, Ramaphosa proclaimed the establishment of the Investigating Directorate in the Office of the National Director of Public Prosecutions. It was done in terms of section 7(1) of the National Prosecuting Authority Act No. 32 of 1998.

67 Lebeya beat Robert McBride (former head of the Independent Police Investigating Directorate), former Gauteng Hawks head, Shadrack Sibiya, and then acting Hawks head, Yolisa Matakata.

68 Established in terms of the Special Investigating Units and Special Tribunal Act No. 74 of 1996, with the core mandate to investigate 'serious malpractices or maladministration in connection with the administration of state institutions, state assets and public money as well as any conduct which may seriously harm the interests of the public'.

69 Graeme Hosken, 'Eskom: R139bn theft probed – Rampant looting at new power plants pushes state capture costs to R500bn', *Timeslive*, 24 February 2019, https://www.timeslive.co.za/sunday-times/news/2019-02-24-eskom-r139bn-theft-probed/, accessed 2 October 2019.

70 Proclamation R 39 of 2019, approved by Ramaphosa, allows the Special Investigating Unit to probe allegations of unlawful or improper conduct regarding the R255 million contract. It could have consequences for the ANC's secretary-general, Ace Magashule.

71   Auditor-general, 10 October 2018, Audit Outcome 2017/18: Briefing to the Public Accounts (SCOPA) committee of Parliament, https://pmg.org.za/committee-meeting/27176/, accessed 2 January 2019.

72   Kimi Makwetu, auditor-general, 13 November 2019, as reported by Linda Ensor, 'Auditor-general bemoans national and provincial audit outcomes', *Timeslive*, 20 November 2019, https://www.timeslive.co.za/news/south-africa/2019-11-20-auditor-general-bemoans-national-and-provincial-audit-outcomes/, accessed 2 September 2020.

73   Terry Motau, 'How VBS was looted: The full report', *PoliticsWeb*, 10 October 2018, https://www.politicsweb.co.za/documents/how-vbs-was-looted-the-full-report, accessed 1 March 2019.

74   Kimi Makwetu, in an interview with Msindisi Fengu, 'Why it's getting worse', *City Press*, 27 May 2018.

75   Bekezela Phakathi, 'State capture, fight goes on, says Ramaphosa', *Business Day*, 3 July 2018, https://www.pressreader.com/south-africa/business-day/20180703/281505046965525, accessed 4 July 2019.

76   *News24wire*, 14 October 2019, 'Ramaphosa says state capture cost SA more than R500bn, criminals will be brought to book', https://www.polity.org.za/article/ramaphosa-says-state-capture-cost-sa-more-than-r500bn-overseas-criminals-will-be-brought-to-book-2019-10-14, accessed 15 October 2019.

7

Parallelism, Populism and Proxy as Tools in Policy Wars

POLICY IDEAS AND IDEALS AS ANC TOOLS OF WAR

The need for more radical, far-reaching transformation and redistribution was evident, all around, in this time of precarious ANC power. The unbearable inequalities and socio-economic need existing before Covid-19 were magnified harshly when the coronavirus epoch unfolded. There was no hiding from re-exposed racialised poverty and inequality, from government mismanagement or self-congratulatory policy arrogance.

The times of the coronavirus reasserted the imperative to correct the incongruence between statement and realisation in policy-making – to show compelling evidence of the successful implementation of the policies that had been proclaimed. The new times showed the effect graphically of decades of using the adoption of policies – and the creation of state bodies – as evidence that problems were being addressed.

The ANC's existential need to be left, ideologically, had been central to its policy narratives since at least the 1950s.[1] As the post-1994 policy and transformational deficits towered, 25 years plus, into politically liberated South Africa, it became even more important for the ANC to prove that it had not given up on the ideals of radical economic justice, and its main way of dealing with frustrated expectations was to present policy-making and delivery as a work in progress on the trajectory of economic transformation, every measure presented as a step towards the ANC's revolution. Throughout, the ANC, owing to the lags in its policies bringing evidence of more definitive deracialisation and post-apartheid class realignment, had a compulsion to show that its policy work was on the appropriate path, the left path, on which ultimate delivery and transformation were destined to happen. There had been an elaboration of *phases* towards the completed revolution, with the ANC toiling to show that its policies were left-revolutionary and that their full revolutionary character would be revealed in time, irrespective of twists and turns and attempted 'counter-revolutions'.[2]

Post-1994, in the world of governance and exercising power, much of the ANC revolutionary-speak metamorphosed into mainstream-speak. The Mbeki presidency, anchored in his tenure as deputy president under Nelson Mandela, pursued neoliberalism and new managerialism alongside public spending on social reconstruction. At the launch of the ANC's 1996 Growth, Employment and Redistribution (Gear) policy, Mbeki declared, 'Just call me a Thatcherite'.[3] He paid the price when Jacob Zuma played the ANC Alliance partners and intra-ANC discontent with Mbeki to build his ascent into power. Zuma entered on a pseudo-populist mandate, pledging to reintroduce the radical into the ANC. The ANC had grappled with finding its exact revolutionary platform, conceptualising the 'second transition' associated with Kgalema Motlanthe's fleeting challenge for power in 2012 and correcting the formulation to refer to the 'second phase of the transition to a democratic society'. 'Radical' hardly featured in the Zuma times that followed – until it belatedly became the vehicle to create a legacy for Zuma, and to differentiate his faction from that of his successor, Ramaphosa.

Cyril Ramaphosa entered the presidency on the blended mandate of his pre-Nasrec 'New Deal' and a contested set of radical ANC policy resolutions.[4] The conference policy outcomes were bi-factional compromises to accommodate the two major ANC groupings at the time. The carefully worded resolutions from the ANC's 54th national conference would be 'policy laws' for the sixth administration – except that time was necessary to bring in constitutional changes, some policy resolutions would be practically near-impossible to effect, and the post-Covid conditions dictated many new policy priorities.

The policy of expropriation of land without compensation epitomised the struggle for the left in the ANC as much as it was a weapon in internal factional wars. Radical economic transformation, white monopoly capital and expropriation without compensation were the triumvirate of weapons used mostly against Ramaphosa, as opponents tried to fault him for non-compliance with ANC policy positions. Expropriation without compensation as narrative served as proxy for the inter-leadership, inter-factional contests for position in the ANC. It had been confirmed at previous ANC conferences, but earned new weight at the 54th national conference. The conference resolution agreed on expropriation without compensation as one of the mechanisms for land reform available to government. This was not new: the 53rd conference resolution had already affirmed expropriation without compensation on land that had been acquired unlawfully and urged the promulgation of new, matching legislation.[5]

On this base of ANC inner politics, the rest of this chapter explores how the public world of state policies evolved, analysing the political evolution of 'radical economic transformation' and the organisational demand for heightened radicalism, and how this contributed to the ANC's condition of precarious power. It offers case studies of public policy-making that reflect shaky balances of power. The cases reveal presidential authoritarianism, popular revolt, people's policy-making by stealth, reticent government policy-making in the time of Covid-19, and politicians walking policy tightropes. The policies of nuclear power and energy, land reform, fee-free post-secondary education and e-tolls shed light on precarious ANC policy-making and on the extent to which the ANC, in the world of government, was often an accidental 'radicalist'.

RADICALISM, SELF-HELP POPULISM AND THE VISION OF FURTHER LEFT SHIFTS[6]

For the ANC government, policy populism by citizens came largely as a boost to – rather than detracting from – its power. Unlike in some international situations when populism undermined institutional politics or when citizens felt they had to choose between populism and institutional-democratic politics,[7] institutional engagement in South Africa coexisted with populist forms of involvement. Dissent and anger often took the populist, non-institutional route, still leaving space for discontented votes to go to the ANC and its government.

Populism in this study therefore entails both procedural (direct action, in competition with institutional and electoral participation) and substantive policy dimensions (citizens claim or take the basic services and amenities that will help correct their conditions of poverty and relative disadvantage, to whichever extent possible). In useful expositions, Roger Eatwell and Matthew Goodwin point out that national populism as challenge to mainstream liberal politics in the West is not necessarily anti-democratic,[8] and this was the case in South Africa as well. While South Africa had been experiencing de-alignment from party politics, citizens in general did not necessarily abandon party identification or voting when they chose populism as means of action. Many also retained an allegiance to the ANC – party and government – despite embracing populism.

ANC national conferences and their policy resolutions tell the story of the ANC's longstanding, repeatedly repackaged and rejuvenated pursuit of radicalism in order to satisfy more of the groundswell of popular need for help from the 'father' state (who brings home the food).[9] Its policy practices had already been steering left-wards, judging by the network of the social wage (as found in the 19 million recipients of social grants, and Covid-19 additional grants and top-ups), the provision of an extensive albeit flawed range of social services, and the state's wilful 'decision' to allow leeway for self-help policy populism to citizens who feel aggrieved or are truly socially disadvantaged (to help themselves to what the Constitution promises but cannot guarantee in practice owing to government incapacity). The fiscus, already under stress before the onset of the Covid-19 pandemic, then declined into distress; South Africa was accumulating debt, debt escalated to try to counter Covid demand, and repayments started constituting impossible burdens.[10]

South African citizens often brought in their own populist policy-making which had the effect of self-help to services to fill in remaining and emerging delivery gaps, supplementing the world of formal, proclaimed policies and laws. It was a populist policy practice that included land grabs, especially in urban areas, and which was condemned officially[11] although the ANC government tolerated widespread boycotts of payments for water and electricity consumed over and above the free basic allowances. Occasionally, government campaigned to enforce payments, but the culture was not reversed. People blamed government (often, although not always, rightly so) for the fact that they, the citizens, were breaking the law. When citizens looted shops and trucks, which often belonged to foreigners or were operated by them, they asked, 'What are we expected to do if government does not create jobs?' When they took electricity without paying, they asked, 'How are we supposed to pay if we do not have jobs?' The same question often followed when people were asked to pay municipal rates. Invasion and occupation of land followed the same line of argument – and government was reluctant to act, because it knew there had been intolerable shortfalls in economic transformation and delivery.[12] The ANC in government hoped to protect its electoral majorities by not alienating citizens when the government shared culpability. It allowed citizens to make de facto policy.

The government's sympathetic treatment of defaulting and legally defiant citizens complemented its recognition that many in its own ranks were law-breakers. The argument that government was not comprehensively to blame for its own failings, given that apartheid and colonialism had caused much of the structural inequalities,[13] helped in exempting government from responsibility and justifying not acting harshly against defaulting citizens. The ANC also recognised that its policies had failed to keep track with community needs and harsh grassroots realities.

The ANC had steered leftward in its policy practice generally, and the populism was not entirely for lack of delivery and transformation. Even if the Reconstruction and Development Programme of 1994 and many other policy initiatives (the Gear strategy 1996, the Accelerated and Shared Growth Initiative for South Africa 2005, the National Growth Path framework 2010, and the National Development Plan 2012) had not delivered as promised, elements of social democracy and public service caring for citizens had been realised. Social grants and social services, housing provision, free education for the poor, school feeding schemes and an anticipated free national health service for the poor (besides the inadequate but free healthcare for indigent citizens already provided since the 1990s) posited elements of a social democratic order. The restitution of land had been unfolding, slowly and subject to delays and frustration caused by policy indecision, corruption and economic crises. These and many other policies qualify as left, but not as left as anticipated. South Africa remained highly unequal,[14] dependent on the private sector, with the state unable to assume more responsibility. As increasing numbers came to depend on the state, questions accumulated about the sustainability of a social welfare system.[15]

OWNING (RADICAL) ECONOMIC TRANSFORMATION: PRESIDENTIAL ROOTS

According to the Polokwane narratives, Jacob Zuma rose to power in the ANC to realise a more radical orientation and ensure that the ANC would connect better to its base and deliver better to those who had been left behind economically. Before Zuma, it had been expected that Thabo Mbeki, after the conciliatory Mandela rainbow period, would govern to effect economic justice for black South Africans. Many changes came and delivery targets were ticked,[16] to the extent that many of the Mbeki-era achievements at the celebratory points of 21 and 25 years of South African democracy were those achieved under Mbeki's watch.[17] Mbeki had overseen a pre-global-recessions period in which more delivery targets were ticked than in the other presidential eras. Yet, the shortfalls remained sufficiently large for Zuma to argue that *his* era would be the definitively transformative one.

Polokwane 2007 propagated that the developmental state would be the vehicle for closing the policy delivery gaps on the ground. 'Economic transformation', at that stage still without the addition of 'radical', was the core phrase. By the time of Mangaung 2012, the hints about *intensifying* the ANC efforts started gathering momentum. A range of resolutions stressed that *this* would be the character of Zuma's second term. Zuma-ists used the so-called second-term Lula moment to 'prove' by analogy that Zuma needed a second term (to start at Mangaung, 2012) to realise the radical, far-reaching policy and governance changes he had promised at Polokwane.[18] He never convincingly explained his failure to make better first-term progress – the 2008 global recession played a role, but the legion of reasons related to capture and corruption were underplayed.

The Mangaung conference resolutions, in contrast to Lula-moment expectations, boasted of meek and vague promises such as '[m]ore radical projects will have to be implemented aimed at total emancipation of the people of South Africa' and 'we need to intensify our programme of economic transformation'. There would be 'decisive action to effect economic transformation'.[19] Despite the sentiments, little happened to cast Zuma's two terms as portrayals of radicalisation or intensification of delivery and transformation. Zuma's own listing of top government achievements under his rule were the provision of HIV treatment, adoption of the National Development Plan, increasing access to social grants, establishing two universities and (announcing, upon his departure) fee-free higher education for the poor.[20]

Populist rhetoric in Zuma's time was a tool to mobilise against Ramaphosa when the 2017 transition loomed; it remained in place in the aftermath of Ramaphosa's win and became a tool for the discrediting of Ramaphosa. The Zuma-ists needed retrospectively to construct a legacy after his December 2017 and February 2018 exits. Radical economic transformation and white monopoly capital articulated with the narratives of the Economic Freedom Fighters (EFF) and some Zuma–ANC proxy persons and parties. Radical economic transformation became the new catchphrase, although there had been antecedents in ANC policy statements, previous iterations including references to the attainment of new phases of the transition to economic delivery and economic justice. It was promised in the Mangaung resolutions that the second phase of the transition to the national democratic society would be characterised by more radical policies. Come Nasrec, the narrative was elevated to say that the ANC would be pursuing, with stronger determination, a radical path for the second transition, along with, as they emphasised, 'the *need* to enter into a more radical second phase of the national democratic revolution'.[21] There was no difference, however, between this last phrase and that of Mangaung, when the ANC said the second phase of the transition to a national democratic society would be characterised by more radical policies.

The policy contradictions, often paralysis, of Ramaphosa's early period related to his narrow Nasrec victory and his interpretation of his ANC 'unity mandate'. Consequently, whenever he proposed action or initiated policy that did not pay obvious homage to radical economic transformation, his Nasrec detractors accused him of deviating from the Nasrec mandate. Ramaphosa had to adhere to the policy resolutions adopted under the radical economic transformation banner.[22]

'White monopoly capital' was the Bell Pottinger-Gupta-associated symbol of the 'Zuma left'. The Zuma-ists had not invented these concepts,[23] but appropriated them to get traction to entrench Zuma in power. They zoomed in on racial tensions and anger about ongoing economic exclusion. The Nasrec policy resolutions were infused with this purported new radicalism (to be differentiated from a real societal need for radical policies for economic justice), although careful wording countered some of the thrust. Zuma-ists also tried to inject more racial profiling into the conference outcomes. The resolutions, however, lacked reference to white monopoly capital, or to monopoly capital. The ANC's 2019 election manifesto followed suit, referring to 'the need to deal with excessive economic concentration and abuse by large corporations'.[24] It was one part of the ANC – not necessarily ideologically to the left of the other – that used the 'radical economic transformation' idiom to pressurise the opposing faction. The purported 'left' faction failed to explain why its own resolutions of five (Mangaung) or ten (Polokwane) years before had not been implemented.

Following Nasrec, there was a tentative softening of the factional policy divisions. Ramaphosa, for the time being, brought about a consensual centre in the deliberations emerging from the National Executive Committee: there was debate and contest, and a modestly left-moving base, evidenced in agreement to amend the Constitution to allow for expropriation without compensation in certain conditions. The opportunistically constituted ANC 'left faction', irrespective of credibility and motivation of this particular Zuma-ist iteration, pushed the ANC out of the comfort zone of yet another round of routine, ineffectual policy resolutions.

FINDING POLICY CERTAINTY AMID DEAD-ENDS AND ULTIMATUMS

Policy uncertainty followed the ANC as it routed through leadership and organisational contests in which Zuma-ists aspired to embarrass the Ramaphosa-ists by revealing insufficient radicalism. There were many different interpretations of what exactly the ANC's policy was – for example, on the South African Reserve Bank, and whether the Constitution needed to be changed in order to help a 'radical' acceleration of land reform to the symbolic point of taking back through expropriation without compensation.

There were even diverging interpretations of what had gone wrong in preceding policies. The blame was located generically in 'just the implementation' that had gone wrong, while 'good policies' had been in place. Another obvious argument was that the preceding policies had not been radical enough. The Ramaphosa-ist regime stressed that state capture and corrupted governance went far in explaining why resources had not reached their targets, preventing policies from being realised. Much of the available public funds had been siphoned off; politicians were often preoccupied with scoring their own enrichment-by-state-tender deals, and many had little time or desire to serve the national interest, or even just the interests of those who had voted for them. The series of global and South African recessions, 2008 and 2020–2021, exacerbated further by the Covid-19 meltdown, destabilised many good intentions. The structural deficits anchored in the ravages of apartheid-colonialism, combined with neglect by successive post-1994 governments, and policy-makers being distracted by policy as proxy for intra-ANC wars, rendered policy-making and policy implementation a fraught, uncertain terrain.

South African Reserve Bank at the radical economic transformation epicentre

The policy-making of the South African Reserve Bank demonstrates how closely policy uncertainty connected with intra-ANC contest, and what the disruptive effects were. The ANC's public spat on the mandate of the Reserve Bank unfolded from 2017 to 2020. ANC factions were gambling with public perceptions of policy, while the ANC in government was working to raise investor confidence. Because of internal divisions, however, it was too weak to lead assertively. The Nasrec ANC conference resolution was to nationalise the central bank, a decision that was interpreted as a concession to Zuma-ists. The ANC's Enoch Godongwana explained that the intention had been to improve coordination between fiscal and monetary policies. In essence, there were two issues: of the Reserve Bank's mandate, and of nationalisation and the role of private shareholders. The resolution illuminates the contest: 'It is, however, a historical anomaly that there are private shareholders of the Reserve Bank. Conference resolves that the Reserve Bank should be 100% owned by the state. Government must develop a proposal to ensure full public ownership in a manner that does not benefit private shareholder speculators.'[25]

In uncoordinated policy action, the ANC's 2019 election manifesto pursued a broader interpretation of the Reserve Bank mandate, arguing that the Reserve Bank 'must pursue a flexible monetary policy regime, aligned with the objectives of the second phase of transition. Without sacrificing price stability, monetary policy must take into account other objectives such as employment creation and economic growth.'[26]

A change in the Reserve Bank mandate would require that the Constitution be changed. The governor of the bank argued that its mandate already included a focus on 'balanced and sustainable growth', as enshrined in the Constitution: 'what we do is in the interests of balanced and sustainable growth ... The fathers and mothers of our Constitution took the view that, for you to have balanced and sustainable growth, you need price stability.'[27]

The Reserve Bank policy contest persisted. In briefing the media on ANC annual lekgotla outcomes, secretary-general Magashule announced a statement that manipulated what had actually been said to seemingly include expanding the Reserve Bank mandate beyond price stability, to include growth and employment.[28] The additional emphasis was on the National Executive Committee's having confirmed that all Nasrec decisions *must be implemented* – disregarding the past reality of conference resolutions having frequently been buried or remaining work in progress. Godongwana, as head of ANC policy, corrected Magashule on the ANC's stance, denying that the ANC had decided to expand the Reserve Bank's mandate (to go beyond price stability and include growth and employment). In his June 2019 State of the Nation address, Ramaphosa reiterated the existing mandate: 'Today we reaffirm this constitutional mandate, which the Reserve Bank must pursue independently, without fear, favour or prejudice.'[29] The pressures to amend the mandate continued.

Some denouement followed when in Covid times the Reserve Bank effected significant measures to help stabilise the economy. The Reserve Bank governor, Lesetja Kganyago, in explaining the bank's asset (government bond) purchases, observed that 'if we just told people our asset purchases were QE [quantitative easing], they might stop complaining that "the SARB is conservative" ... despite ... how much the SARB has already done'.[30]

Radicalism and opportunistic policy bots surfing 'radical economic transformation'

Economic policy and economic transformation – amid South Africa's crises of recession, Covid-19, leaping joblessness, flagging investor confidence, declining assessments by ratings agencies, and threatened retrenchments from the state-owned enterprises and the amply staffed public sector – were among the tasks handed to Ramaphosa. Whereas in Covid time the explicit focus on radical economic transformation became subdued, the thread was picked up again and the Ramaphosa government's post-Covid peak actions needed even more evidence of definite intervention for the poor.

The notion of radical turns in ANC policy might have been used largely oppor-tunistically by Ramaphosa's opponents, but it was also the original ANC intent, which had been diluted over the first 25 years of ANC rule. The challenge to be more radical, upon Ramaphosa's assumption of power, came at a vexed time. More radical policy was required on land reform and fee-free post-secondary education. A radicalised youth generation was taking shape, having experienced deprivation under ANC rule. Without the youth's trust and allegiance, ANC power would be threatened – the youth's needs had become more pronounced amid lack of oppor-tunities and dismal life prospects, even before, with the onset of Covid, prospects declined further. Citizens had urbanised, and socio-economic expectations were concentrated in employment, land, shelter and basic services. This grassroots need for more tangible economic and socio-economic change was positioned vis-à-vis the radical economic transformation narrative.

Part of the narrative concerning the need for drastic and further-reaching eco-nomic transformation was real. Much of it, however, was manufactured through Black First Land First botwebs. The African Network of Centres for Investigative Reporting pointed out that this manufactured part of the populist rhetoric 'taps into the latent fears and prejudices that are common to all humans and harnesses those emotions for its own ends'. The investigative network explained the 'white monopoly capital' narrative as

> ... a populist message that taps into the very real discontent felt by many
> South Africans. It provides a convenient scapegoat for the poverty and lack
> of material progress that so many South Africans feel. It also mixes together
> the right amount of facts in order to create a message that resonates with
> many [South Africans'] lived experiences, fears and prejudices by bringing
> a concept that was only used within a small corner of South African politics
> into the mainstream.[31]

Leadership demands and Ramaphosa's approach to national policy crises

The ANC's problems of policy uncertainty were due in part to the capture of a range of strategic state institutions, or enclaves within them. Ramaphosa legiti-mately wanted to protect his presidential position from factional threats that might censure him for non-implementation of ANC resolutions, such as that about the Reserve Bank. He treaded cautiously therefore, intent on not antagonising his intra-ANC opponents. The need for pacification and compromise triggered images of leadership weakness – problematic, when Ramaphosa had to lead the country into big policy decisions.

Ramaphosa had to lead on major policy items, including economic resurrection pre- and post-Covid, bringing dignity and sustenance to millions of newly unemployed amid Covid aftershocks, and resolving all policy problems that had preceded Covid. Assisted generally by his re-established National Security Council and Presidential Economic Advisory Council, he first had to lead the country away from a threatening International Monetary Fund (IMF) rescue in light of state-owned enterprises, especially Eskom and South African Airways, failing and draining the national fiscus.[32] His next task, when Covid struck, was contradictorily to obtain favourable terms for South Africa in the subsequent inevitable borrowing from the IMF.[33] On the rest of the economic front, the presidential investment envoys and investment conferences supplemented the work of the presidential councils to mobilise capital. The Small and Medium Enterprises Fund worked on investment in small and medium-sized enterprises; the South African Revenue Service was attending to the banking licence application for the Postbank; the national minimum wage was adopted; the new Mining Charter took shape; and the Youth Employment Service was elaborated. New infrastructure projects were being assessed and activated as Covid landed. The crisis motivated a renewed focus on infrastructure, which Ramaphosa announced would be placed at the centre of post-pandemic stimulus efforts to help recovery from the growth- and job-destroying crisis.[34]

Ramaphosa had to lead nationally when xenophobic-criminal violence engulfed major cities; gender activists staged protests about femicide and the judicial system regularly failed to bring perpetrators to account (one, in Cape Town, outside the venue where Ramaphosa was hosting the World Economic Forum for Africa); and smaller (hampered by lockdown conditions) Black Lives Matter protests unfolded after the security force-related death of Collins Khoza in Alexandra.[35] Crime statistics profiled South Africa as a country with an intimate-partner murder rate five times the international average[36] and Ramaphosa suffered when his and his predecessor's promises failed repeatedly.

The president had to step up to lead the country out of the pandemic crisis when old policies no longer sufficed. He assumed the role, controversially, alongside the National Coronavirus Command Council, after National Executive Committee and Cabinet resolutions.[37] With a range of new medical, economic and statistical projection bodies, Ramaphosa first veered into a world of crisis decision-making in terms of the Disaster Management Act, marked by lack of transparency and allowing decisions by bodies not constitutionally mandated. Court action and the threat thereof brought wake-up calls, and Ramaphosa and his teams reverted to Cabinet and Parliament as the final authorities. Ramaphosa addressed the nation intermittently to announce new measures. His addresses were reassuring up to a point, and then lost credibility and impact for being contradicted by Cabinet colleagues, vacillating and often lacking logic, with a dubious scientific base. Ramaphosa came across as muddling through, rather than being in command and speaking authoritatively. He acknowledged as much: 'So we are crossing the river by feeling our way on the stones, and sometimes we put our feet on slippery stones or rocks, and sometimes on firm ones.'[38]

Attention at the time had moved away from ANC factionalism. But the game of factions was being played in the Covid policy and governance arena and re-emerged from the time of the August 2020 National Executive Committee meeting.

Corrective policy surges in the early Ramaphosa period

The period of policy rebuilding after the transition from Zuma to Ramaphosa holds illustrations for how the next delivery of policy renewal might be handled. In some respects, Ramaphosa's policy operations were held back in this earlier phase by the campaign of factional delegitimation. Otherwise, there was an upwelling of policy renewal and change, concerning both substantive policy-making, denoting the contents, ideas and actions that policy contained, and procedural policy-making with reference to the way in which – and the institutions and public policy actors by which – the policies were being made.[39]

There was systematic action on major policy fronts, even if sustainability was uncertain.[40] Fee-free higher education and training for the poor was phased in after Ramaphosa accepted the curveball that Zuma had discharged in December 2017. There was progress on land reform. Nasrec 2017 moved government out of a slumber of gradualism in land reform and tolerance of much systemic corruption, although permitting land injustices to continue. After its Land Summit of May 2018, the ANC said it would test the Constitution on whether expropriation without compensation was permitted already. The Panel on Land Reform added clarity on categories of land to be subject to expropriation without compensation.[41] The parliamentary committee on land expropriation proceeded with the bill to amend the Constitution so that compensation could be nil where land and the improvements on it are expropriated for land reform.

Other crucial public policy that could help the ANC to demonstrate grassroots connection, compassion and transformation included the National Health Insurance initiative, which gained momentum but remained beset with issues of practicability – and would be tested severely by the Covid pandemic. On the energy policy front there was a jagged curve on which vested interests of politically con-nected business on both sides of the lobby regularly impeded movement to a just, green future. The nuclear component faded but then rose again, and dubious cycles of politician interests came to the fore. The government's work was to ensure that corruption would not be tolerated and would carry consequences,[42] but the evi-dence of success remained patchy.

After Ramaphosa's takeover, business confidence rose to the highest level in a decade, fell back subsequently, but remained resilient at first as business and inves-tors looked beyond the ANC squabbles. South Africa was slipping into full invest-ment 'junk' status when economies around the world cascaded downward with the impact of the pandemic. Before that there had been reality checks in Rand Merchant Bank and the Stellenbosch University Bureau for Economic Research Business Confidence Index, which had fallen to its lowest level since the 1998–1999 emerg-ing-market debt crisis, just before the 2020 crises struck.[43] Simultaneously, even before South Africa's February–March 2020 coronavirus onset, the South African Chamber of Commerce and Industry's confidence index had fallen to its lowest level since April 1985 when the UN Security Council called on members to intro-duce more sanctions against apartheid South Africa.

WIND TUNNEL OF CHANGE: FOUR POLICY CASE STUDIES

Policy power in the Ramaphosa phase of South African and ANC politics had to be reconstructed, in a precarious process. There was policy action and progress, yet every ingredient of some core policies was affected by challenges from intra-ANC opponents, by legitimate critiques from affected citizens and experts, and by national and international economic conditions and domestic public finance prob-lems. Ramaphosa and his camp embraced the conference resolutions, persuading business that these policies were essential for the creation of a stable future. Rama-phosa had to walk the policy tightrope, leveraging his links to big business and capital while defending himself against radical economic transformation–white monopoly capital interest groups, and moving the ANC to a position of building popular credibility with new generations of voters.[44]

The case studies of land reform, nuclear and energy policy, fee-free post-sec-ondary education, and Gauteng e-tolls reveal the need for correction – of content, process or both. The cases illuminate the role of populism and demands for more radical or further-reaching policy, versus elite manipulation and corruption of pol-icy processes. The cross-factional policy mandate from the ANC 2017 conference was to effect faster and more profound transformation, and to bring in clean government to manage the policy and match it with scarce resources.

Parallel streams of land policy

Land reform post-Nasrec was a faction-defining issue, which also rippled out to bring urgency to longstanding stalling policy.[45] Expropriation without compensation, as a sub-issue to land reform, became the new shorthand for radical economic transformation and economic justice. Land policy debate in the ANC illustrates how a longstanding item on the ANC's policy agenda became factionalised and elevated. The ANC needed to fend off the radicalisation of a youth constituency, and land was an incisive symbol of change. The ANC also wanted policy that could offer the radical-land constituency a home in the ANC rather than in the EFF.

Soon after the conference resolution, the ANC affirmed in Parliament its belief in expropriation without compensation, and echoed the EFF on this. The ANC had found a new window of opportunity for land activism. Communities latched onto ANC and government land policy statements of early 2018 with fervour – even if the actual process of expropriating significant tracts of land was going to be long and complex. In urban areas, while Parliament was debating constitutional change, people forged new land claims and occupied portions of state (but also centrally located private) land. The approach was one of occupation and retreat. Authorities often gave up trying to block occupations, or scrambled to deliver land at the exact or nearby sites to quell aggressive community protests. Policy was made ground level up – the spaces for policy change were claimed. New land policy gained substance and was pushed beyond the boundaries set by high-level statements and central government initiatives. In dealing with land in a focused and targeted manner, the ANC was catching up with the people[46] – legalising and constitutionalising de facto, already-taking-shape land policy, especially in the urban areas.

Such policy had been asserted frequently by urbanising citizens when need for residence and livelihood had dictated action in the form of invasion or illegal occupation of undesignated public and private land. It had been happening for much of the time of democratic South Africa and it defined land hunger where it most met the need for land to live on, close to opportunities and livelihoods. These settlement imperatives combined with those of 'land entrepreneurs', business agents (on occasion with political connections) who initiated occupations and then sold portions or erected informal structures and rented them out.[47]

The ANC was no newcomer to promises on the deepening of action on socioeconomic transformation, including land (Table 7.1). Its undertakings were routine offerings at policy and elective conferences. It had remained content with not being overtly self-critical of progress, until Nasrec, when ANC factionalism and its contest for leadership ensured that this time around more action and accountability would be demanded. ANC government policies[48] that had been in place pre-Nasrec were comprehensive and provided, in terms of section 25 of the Constitution, for expropriation in certain circumstances. The Department of Land Affairs had implemented the policy,[49] but with little urgency. Numerous reports of corruption testified to this, including the diversion of land reform budgets to elites[50] and, frequently, simply a lack of efficiency. In a 2018 judgment, the Constitutional Court said about the Department of Land Affairs:

> ... [the] Department's failure to practically manage and expedite land reform measures in accordance with constitutional and statutory promises has profoundly exacerbated the intensity and bitterness of our national debate about land reform. It is not the Constitution, nor the courts, nor the laws of the country that are at fault in this. It is the institutional incapacity of the Department to do what the statute and the Constitution require of it that lies at the heart of this colossal crisis.[51]

The inefficiency of government officials and the political leaders' deficient political will to implement existing policy and legislation were recognised by ANC politicians. Minister Jackson Mthembu noted that '[b]laming the Constitution for the embarrassingly slow pace of land reform is both disingenuous and scapegoating'.[52] The same thrust came from the 2017 High Level Report on Fundamental Change:

> ... government has not used the powers it already has to expropriate land for land reform purposes effectively, nor used the provisions in the Constitution that allow compensation to be below market value in particular circumstances ... government should use its expropriation powers more boldly, in ways that test the meaning of the compensation provisions in Section 25(3), particularly in relation to land that is unutilised or under-utilised.[53]

After the 54th national conference, Parliament worked on amending the Constitution and bringing that elusive urgency of action to those who had been dispossessed and had suffered because of past and continuous land injustice. The ANC convened a summit in early 2018, and mobilised its parliamentary caucus to support the EFF's parliamentary resolution. On 27 February 2018, the National Assembly adopted the motion for constitutional review with a view to introducing an amendment for expropriation without compensation, and conducted national hearings. With these frameworks fleshed out, government and the governing party seemed formally to be directing land-focused socio-economic change again[54] – apart from the popular community-driven processes that followed their own dynamic in the slipstream of the official initiatives.

Other parliamentary and cabinet steps included that the parliamentary ad hoc committee was reactivated post-Election 2019. The report of the Expert Advisory Panel on Land Reform and Agriculture was handed to Ramaphosa and the Cabinet in mid-2019, and at cabinet level there was a push to identify and release state-owned land for restitution and human settlement developments.[55] The committee fleshed out the thrust of the constitutional position in preparation for the 18th Constitution Amendment Bill, with a view to amending section 25. It aimed at addressing the historical wrongs caused by land dispossession and to 'ensure equitable access to land that would empower the majority of South Africans'.[56] The committee built on public hearings from across the country.[57]

These parliamentary processes halted at the onset of Covid, until in mid-2020 Parliament voted in a virtual sitting to re-establish the ad hoc committee (whose term had ended in May 2020) and to finish work by year-end. ANC government initiatives hoped to achieve a single stream of policy action, rather than work with parallel streams. There remained much scope, however, for bottom-up land reform policy. The tardiness of official processes meant that in the time of Covid-19 there were tenacious land occupations which government and its auxiliary eviction forces could not rebuff, including in Cape Town's Khayelitsha and Kraaifontein, and in south-western parts of Gauteng. New ground-up policy-making rules were consolidating. De facto rules included: if one community benefits from invasion and protest and gets results, others will follow (across lines of 'racial group' and occasionally class); settle on uninhabitable land and become eligible for resettlement; and become a backyarder, then mobilise, claim justice, and delivery can be forged.[58] Lockdown regulations also limited local municipalities' eviction options. The parallel policy practices had already been established and were then consolidated once land activists realised they had a licence from above to assert land policy.

The case of the Marikana informal settlement in Philippi, Cape Town, illustrated the dynamic of ingrained ground-up action followed by government catching up to legalise it. 'Marikana' (covering 28 hectares and home to 60 000, to be differentiated from Marikana in Zwelihle) was a big urban land grab. The Western Cape High Court ruled that the City of Cape Town had to buy the land, had to get financial help from national and provincial government and had to consider expropriation should the preceding steps fail. Next, the Supreme Court of Appeal directed the

Table 7.1: Landmarks in post-Nasrec land policy: ANC directives

Date and occasion	Statement
ANC, December 2017, Nasrec resolution	'Expropriation of land without compensation should be among the key mechanisms available to the government to give effect to land reform and redistribution. In determining the mechanisms of implementation, we must ensure that we do not undermine future investment in the economy, or damage agricultural production and food security. Furthermore, our interventions must not cause harm to other sectors of the economy ...' 'Concrete interventions are required to improve the functioning of all three elements of land reform. These interventions should focus on government-owned land and should also be guided by the ANC's Ready to Govern policy document which prioritised the redistribution of vacant, unused and under-utilised state land, as well as land held for speculation and hopelessly indebted land ...'
President Cyril Ramaphosa, State of the Nation address 2018	'... accelerate our land redistribution programme not only to redress a grave historical injustice, but also to bring more producers into the agricultural sector and to make more land available for cultivation. We will pursue a comprehensive approach that makes effective use of all the mechanisms at our disposal ... Guided by the resolutions of the 54th national conference of the governing party, this approach will include expropriation of land without compensation.'
EFF proposal to Parliament, 27 February 2018 (carried by 241 to 83)	Amendments to section 25 of the Constitution to make it legal for the state to expropriate land in the public interest without compensation. The EFF also proposed the establishment of an ad hoc committee to process the intended amendment for Parliament to conduct public hearings to get the views of ordinary South Africans. The ANC supported the motion, but proposed that it should be the work of Parliament's Constitutional Review Committee to review section 25.
Former minister of land affairs, Gugile Nkwinti, in debate on the EFF motion, February 2018	'The ANC unequivocally supports the principle of land expropriation without compensation as moved by the EFF. We may disagree on the modalities but we agree on the principle ... In the thirties already, the first president of the ANC, Dr John Langalibalele Dube, said the following: "... In asking for more land I do not think we are asking for charity..." The resolution of the ANC's 54th national conference ... speaks to this historical injustice, and as the ANC we are committed to correcting it.'
Mcebisi Skwatsha, ANC MP in Parliament, February 2018	'Land was taken by force. Anything you steal is when people do not notice it is being done. Our ancestors were murdered and enslaved on their own land.'

Date and occasion	Statement
President Cyril Ramaphosa in late-night address post-ANC lekgotla, 31 July 2018	'We thought it was important for the president of the ANC to clearly and unambiguously articulate the position of the organisation on two matters critically important to the economy of the country and the well-being of its people.' 'It has become patently clear that our people want the Constitution to be more explicit about expropriation of land without compensation, as demonstrated in the public hearings.' 'The ANC Lekgotla reaffirmed its position that a comprehensive land reform programme that enables equitable access to land will unlock economic growth by bringing more land in South Africa to full use and enable the productive participation of millions more South Africans in the economy.'
ANC 2019 election manifesto	'We will carry out a sustainable land reform programme that expands participation in, and ownership of, agricultural production, advances food security and helps reverse the apartheid spatial separation of our cities and towns. This will be done through a range of measures, including expropriation without compensation.'
Cabinet member Jackson Mthembu, 12 February 2019	'We are fast-tracking land reform by implementing our resolution on the expropriation of land without compensation. Parliament is already in the process of crafting a constitutional amendment to amend section 25 of the Constitution to make it explicit that our Constitution allows expropriation of land without compensation ... We are also awaiting a redistribution bill from our government and we will be passing the Restitution of Land Rights Amendment Bill that is currently before the National Assembly during this term of Parliament.'
Cyril Ramaphosa questions and answers in Parliament, 22 August 2019	'Through providing poor South Africans with land on which to farm, to live and to run businesses, we will be able to break the cycle of poverty in which many people are trapped.' 'The IMC is making progress in the development of the National Spatial Development Framework, which will guide our efforts to ensure land use and planning is developmental and transforms people's lives. The Department of Public Works and Infrastructure has released 100 parcels of land for land restitution purposes. For the remaining parcels of land, land-use studies are being finalised, which include land identified for human settlements. Progress is being made in the development of an integrated model for farmer support. The model entails the provision of financial and non-financial support through the value chain.'

continued

Date and occasion	Statement
Former president Kgalema Motlanthe, 19 October 2019	'... parliamentarians in their wisdom decided that actually, this Section 25 is not explicit enough. So they want to amend it to make it explicitly clear that there shall be expropriation without compensation. That's not going to happen in a hundred years' time, I can assure you that.' 'We even crafted a draft law of general application. We called it indicative law. We said you must pass this law and it looks as follows, but the report was submitted. Very few people read it in Parliament. It wasn't read at all.'
Cyril Ramaphosa questions and answers in Parliament, 31 October 2019	'The [Advisory] Panel has called on government to immediately identify well-located and unused or under-utilised land and buildings for the purposes of urban settlement and to prioritise poor tenants for upgrading their rights. In line with this recommendation, Cabinet has already taken decisions on the release of land for human settlements.' 'Cabinet is therefore determined to shortly finalise its consideration of the recommendations so that the land reform process can proceed at a faster rate and have a greater impact. This is necessary not only to address the plight of the landless, but to boost the economy, create jobs and reduce poverty, particularly in rural areas.' 'In the end, we need to make sure that the land is returned to the people of South Africa.'
President Cyril Ramaphosa, State of the Nation address 2020	'Government stands ready – following the completion of the parliamentary process to amend section 25 of the Constitution – to table an expropriation bill that outlines the circumstances under which expropriation of land without compensation would be possible. To date, we have released 44 000 hectares of state land for the settlement of land restitution claims, and will this year release around 700 000 hectares of state land for agricultural production.'
Parliament in virtual sitting, 30 June 2020	Parliament votes to re-establish the parliamentary ad hoc committee to finish the work on section 25 with a view to finishing the report by the end of November 2020. The previous committee's term had ended in May 2020 and had been interrupted by Covid-19 and Parliament going into lockdown operational mode.

Source: Author's monitoring project through observation and media monitoring

parties to abandon their appeal. A negotiated agreement followed and it was made an order of the court: the City of Cape Town was to purchase the properties at a price to be determined by arbitration.[59] The size of the community, the fact that they settled on the land out of desperation (largely upon migration into the Cape Town area), having nowhere else to go, motivated the earlier judgments. Owners had appealed, because occupation had reduced the value they had come to attach to the land. The authority of the courts to act on issues of human rights and justice for poor and desperate people meant that it was reducing the difference between the parallel policy thrusts.

Crossed lines of nuclear and energy policy

Nuclear energy policy became a major battleground of parallel policy-making for the Ramaphosa regime. It had been a reason for former president Zuma's clinging to power through proxies and associates. The approximate move away from nuclear under Ramaphosa's ANC, associated with the growing embrace of independent and green power production (with an emphasis also on gas), battled to consolidate the supposed move away from nuclear power as old and new lines of political power crossed. While nuclear was discredited through both Zuma-era corruption and the global retreat from it, Ramaphosa struggled to firmly establish alternatives. His political opponents, old and new, lined up for battle in this new field of lucrative procurement.[60]

The ANC under Ramaphosa had to overcome an epoch of nuclear policy-making that had been dictated by Zuma, whose attempted nuclear deal with Russia's Vladimir Putin and nuclear agency Rosatom revealed his parallel system of decision-making. He had superimposed his own decisions on the formal mandated processes and institutions – and his decisions diverged from the required and expected content, and from the expected probity in policy-making. Civil society organisations, public opinion, the courts and, in the end, the ANC at Nasrec thwarted Zuma's nuclear plans. His nuclear expansion agenda had originated soon after he had taken power in 2008, following an energy crisis. In June 2008, Cabinet had adopted the National Nuclear Energy Policy. It confirmed expansion ambitions and the country's so-called 'Nuclear Renaissance', in the words of the then Department of Minerals and Energy. The extent to which state capture – in this instance by Zuma and 'the Russians' (Putin) – went against the national interest shows in South Africa's embrace of nuclear amid an international turn against it. The Fukushima Daiichi nuclear disaster of 2011 prompted reconsideration of new nuclear power, whereas the Russians had still hoped to use South Africa as the base for nuclear expansion into Africa.

The ANC government managed to avoid the nuclear trap despite the former president having manoeuvred himself into a kingpin parallel policy-making position. The National Nuclear Energy Executive Coordination Committee (NNEECC), a Cabinet subcommittee that was proposed in the National Nuclear Energy Policy of 2011 to oversee the nuclear energy policy, would have been in charge of the procurement process and new build programmes. In 2014, Zuma transformed the

NNEECC into the Energy Security Cabinet Subcommittee (ESCS), still a Cabinet subcommittee, but now under the direct leadership of the president (Zuma). The ESCS included some of NNEECC members plus the ministers of state security, of defence and veteran affairs, and of international relations and cooperation, revealing the emphasis on energy security and internationalisation. In terms of the Minimum Information Security Standard Act, its proceedings and documents are classified as top secret.

The ANC under Zuma pursued multiple Cabinet reshuffles to get a minister compliant enough to execute the Russian nuclear deal. The succession of ministers of energy, 2009 to 2018,[61] confirmed Zuma's determination to capture and seal nuclear policy-making (he shed ministers each time their nuclear policy performance did not live up to his requirements): Dipuo Peters (11 May 2009–10 July 2013), Ben Martins (10 July 2013–25 May 2014), Tina Joemat-Pettersson (25 May 2014–31 March 2017), Mmamoloko Kubayi (31 March 2017–17 October 2017) and David Mahlobo (17 October 2017–26 February 2018).

Joemat-Pettersson played a substantial role in executing Zuma's nuclear wishes. At the Zondo Commission, the former minister of finance, Nhlanhla Nene, testified that Zuma had fired him when he refused to sign a letter to the Russian authorities which Joemat-Pettersson had pushed him to endorse. The letter would have constituted a binding commitment to the Russian government on the nuclear programme if the Russians were to finance it.

As Zuma's time as ANC and possibly South African president was running out, he deployed David Mahlobo, a former state security minister with experience of working with Russian intelligence, into the portfolio.[62] With the ANC's Nasrec conference pending, Mahlobo tried to force through Zuma's nuclear plans, rushing the review of the Integrated Resource Plan into action four months ahead of schedule. By November 2017, the Integrated Resource Plan was finalised and it was approved by Cabinet in December 2017. In February 2018, days into the Ramaphosa regime, the new president assured the Portfolio Committee on Energy that no major projects on nuclear energy had been forged clandestinely. This followed shortly after he had declared to the World Economic Forum that South Africa could not afford to build any new nuclear power stations.

These turns of event at government executive level shadowed changes in Parliament.[63] In 2014–2015 the ANC majority in the parliamentary energy committee had wanted to 'reconfirm nuclear as its supply-side solution to meet environmental and macroeconomic development objectives'[64] while the Democratic Alliance (DA) stressed that the government's 20-year energy master-plan (at the time the Integrated Resource Plan) stated the opposite. Nuclear had not been part of the agreed energy mix, and no funding mechanisms or frameworks for financing and economic controls were in place. There were fears in this world of parallel ANC policy-making that the deal with the Russians had been sealed, but it had not.[65]

In May 2018, the new deputy president, D.D. Mabuza, was dispatched to Russia[66] to congratulate Putin on his re-election as president – as the cover for the Ramaphosa regime to explain to Putin that the deal was off (although doubts were cast when Mabuza subsequently showed pro-nuclear colours himself). The unaffordable mega-level nuclear deal was abandoned. In integrating the parallel with the formal policy process, the Ramaphosa government confirmed that South Africa would acquire nuclear at the price, pace and scale that the country could afford. Nuclear power would remain a modest part of the energy mix.

Ramaphosa's ANC brought an end to the epoch of nuclear mega-deals that had entered through parallel processes of policy-making. Yet, in smaller measure nuclear persisted. The Ramaphosa regime's energy power players lined up in new configurations – energy minister Mantashe balanced his coal-mining past ambiguously with championing a new independent power producer order, and D.D. Mabuza headed government's energy war room. Core Ramaphosa government figures were swayed by nuclear lobbies, inter alia from young nuclear professionals and black business empowerment camps that mobilised against the whiteness of the independent power producer industry.[67]

The budgetary reprioritisation that came with Covid-19 had implications for the country's scaled-down nuclear ambitions. Around mid-2020, confusion reigned about the nuclear policy directive. At first there would have been an immediate start with procuring 2 500 MW of nuclear power by 2024. The minister of energy withdrew and replaced the statement with one that said planning should commence, and that procurement would proceed at a pace and scale that the country could afford.[68]

Fee-free post-secondary education for the poor, illustrating dual-track policy-making

Policy-making for fee-free higher education for the poor and working class was a feat of populist action, and student activists were prepared to accept the victory in whatever form it was achieved: 'we must take our victories where we can find them,' remarked a student leader.[69] Zuma had gone against the cautious national-budget-conscious advice of the ANC government's own commission of inquiry, the Heher Commission, and against the wishes of the National Treasury, to proclaim a policy which was proposed by an 'adviser' close to the Zuma family. He announced the policy hours before the ANC's Nasrec elective conference. It came with flavours of capture and parallelism, implemented through a process that ran in opposition to the formal and public government process.

Zuma had hijacked policy-making for higher education in ways he could not achieve for nuclear. In the process he aligned himself with student populism and found ready-made legitimacy for the fee-free policy. #FeesMustFall students entrusted policy change to the ANC government under Zuma and the Heher Commission of Inquiry.[70] They moderated their protests from late 2015 on the expectation that government would deliver on Zuma's late 2015 promise at the Union Buildings of no fee increases for 2016 and attention to the matters of free education, institutional autonomy and racism. Zuma's policy adviser on student affairs, Mukovhe Morris Masutha, also a one-time state security agent, brought Zuma the December 2017 policy concept.[71] Zuma pushed the new policy into the hands of a compliant minister of higher education, Hlengiwe Mkhize, defying both the National Treasury and the Heher Commission – he had received the report but did not release its fiscally cautious recommendations.[72]

Zuma's policy announcement was a populist, anti-Ramaphosa intervention. The Banking Association of South Africa remarked that Zuma announced 'unaffordable populist policies in the name of the poor without the ability or even the political will to deliver'. The DA highlighted the uncosted nature of the announcement, including the likely doubling of the National Student Financial Aid Scheme (NSFAS, the delivery vehicle) budget to R22 billion: the statement was 'a combination of populist politicking, deceptive language, uncosted proposals'.[73] The increase of university subsidies from 0.68 to 1 per cent of GDP in the following five years was equally uncosted, as was the promise of 'no fee increase' in 2018 for students whose families earned under R350 000 a year.

Given the new socio-political postcolonial culture at the time, the policy had moral legitimacy. Possible university disruption and protracted student struggles would be a high price to pay for the ANC at crucial times – and in the run-up to Election 2019 – in which the youth vote was to be pivotal. The policy was there to stay, even if it exacerbated the problems of balancing the national budget (an issue that assumed further immense proportions in the wake of Covid-19).

Budgetary issues notwithstanding, the ANC, two years earlier and following a full decade of policy neglect, had passed a resolution to support free post-secondary education. Zuma himself had not assumed responsibility, except through his last-minute policy announcement that emanated from parallel processes (protest, followed by Zuma's legacy and revenge on Ramaphosa motives). Finding the money for implementation, and for sustaining the associated programmes of funding living costs, transport and accommodation for growing numbers of students (including large numbers of cases of historical debt and funding despite unsuccessful studies) became a Ramaphosa problem.

E-toll activism ... Alliance of popular parallel power[74]

A different type of parallelism emerged in the case of policy-making on e-tolls in the economic heartland of Gauteng province – a de facto and parallel system of freeway usage without paying imposed on government through a populist rebellion. With the aid of well-operating civil society organisations, citizens established the policy of extensive non-payment. Part of their argument was that they were paying already in the form of general citizen taxes and fuel levies – payments that continued rising throughout the period of this policy action. The Gauteng Freeway Improvement Project (GFIP) consequently required large bailouts – while the ANC government stumbled from one offer of moderated user payment to the next, all serially rejected by citizens and their partners in non-governmental organisations.

The citizens had power over government as their payments were required to pay for the road structure that had been improved in 2010. The government attempted sanctioning the road users through pursuing them for payments, select prosecutions and threats to their vehicle licensing. All failed. Prolonged delaying power through court action had been part of the process, but legal options ran out. Electoral power also weighed heavily. The ANC was on the verge of losing its outright majority in Gauteng and the party's stance on e-tolling was a strong contributing factor. The ANC itself skilfully used the division between the ANC provincial (anti e-tolls) and ANC and government nationally (pro e-tolls), to gain electoral benefit without scrapping the tolls.

The anti-e-tolling alliance was the first widespread tax revolt in democratic South Africa apart from specific-locality revolts (such as the Sannieshof local council) where municipal rates and taxes were channelled to private service providers, and the large-scale township cross-class non-payment for electricity. The e-toll revolt was similarly cross-class. The sustained rejection, and establishment of their parallel policy, was associated with the work of the Opposition to Urban Tolling Alliance, later renamed the Organisation Undoing Tax Abuse (Outa), plus a broad anti-tolling network. Civil society support organisations were, inter alia, the Automobile Association, the Justice Project South Africa and the Congress of South African Trade Unions (also having a financial stake in the operation, through its investment arm). Network actors were the courts and political parties. The DA, for example, through the party's funding of R1 million for Outa to continue its anti-e-toll legal challenges, and the South African Communist Party, which urged Cabinet to abandon the South African National Roads Agency (Sanral) project. The EFF at one stage threatened to physically remove the toll gantries. Church bodies, including the South African Council of Churches, arguing the impact of e-tolling on the poor, swelled the ranks of the anti e-tolling alliance. The Road Freight Association and the National Taxi Alliance were occasional participants, the latter because many of its taxis had not been issued with operating licences, making them liable for billing. Taxis generally had secured exemption in the pre-election time of early 2014, as millions of financially burdened working-class citizens used taxi transport daily in Gauteng (and the ANC feared that their voting allegiance might shift away from the party).

The government tried to lure the freeway users into compliance, using both stick and carrot. In May 2015, it offered a compromise position: unpaid fees would be attached to the renewal of motor vehicle licences, but fees would be lowered and new discounts applied. In late 2015, government initiated legislation that would make it a points-demerit penalty-bearing traffic offence not to pay e-tolls; in 2019, the Administrative Adjudication of Road Traffic Offences (AARTO) Act was signed into law, but after outcries at the e-toll connection there were reassurances that e-tolls fell under the GFIP system and not the Road Traffic Infringement Agency .

Although it was illegal not to pay, Sanral at first, and up to March 2016, refrained from pushing legal action against offenders. Outa activated legal support for anyone being charged formally, initiating a collective 'defence umbrella'. Sanral won default cases but the e-toll GFIP test cases aimed at individuals and companies remained tentative. Outa challenged the e-tolls in a renewed Constitutional Court bid. Come Election 2019, Sanral suspended summonses and default judgments against those who were not paying e-tolls.[75] Government handed Sanral further bailouts while it tried to close legal loopholes and enforce payment – despite anticipated policy change. E-toll debt to Sanral escalated to many billions. Under pressure to make budgets balance, the minister of finance described the possible amendment of the official policy as 'careless' in the middle of a 'very difficult' financial situation. He countered Sanral's recognition of citizen power to bring down an unpopular policy.

The ANC played a vacillating role in and out of the anti-e-tolling network. The Gauteng ANC rose in mild opposition to e-tolls, but succumbed to the dictates of central government and top ANC structures. In 2016–2017, the government, through Sanral, had come to the point of closing the legal loophole to strangle the network and force citizens to pay; in 2018 it was back to promising to abandon the tolls. Come the time of the Ramaphosa regime, the president instructed the minister of transport to find a solution. The Gauteng premier told the Gauteng legislature that it was 'loud and clear' that e-tolls had not worked. Covid-19 and its associated reduction in road traffic pushed Sanral into even deeper financial troubles.[76] The stalemate was unabated and the defeat of e-tolls inevitable. Indirect payments – such as ring-fencing a part of the fuel levy – appeared to be the only type of solution.

The e-toll rebellion, an illustration of parallel and populist power, showed how popular and organisationally supported resistance, even if not backed by the courts, can win against national government – and can achieve this on the basis of popular legitimacy, irrespective of the law and political pressure.

CONCLUSION: DISCORD OF PARALLEL POLICY

This series of case studies illustrates multiple forms of capture and parallelism in policy practice, and the broad and belated radical thrust in public policy in the ANC government. A large component of precarious ANC power on the policy front was that there was a multiplicity of poorly performing and dismal policy areas which could, at almost any time, become explosive – and become bases for widespread popular mobilisation. Health and education were examples. The minister of education said about this portfolio that '[w]e allow mediocrity to spread like cancer to the highest echelons of the basic education system, thereby threatening the very foundation of the system'.[77] The system of National Health Insurance was unfolding tentatively, amid many doubts as to the ability of the public health sector to support the public component, and the fiscal drain it would place on government. Covid-19 and government's management confirmed the fault-lines: good intentions and the mobilisation of massive resources unlocked the doors to the parallel world of procurement-related corruption. Land policy was unfolding although there were concerns as to whether the land affairs department would be able to carry out its mandate any better than it had done before more radical land policy arrived.

Electricity provision was ripe for recognition of parallel systems in an order of non-payment, in some respects reminiscent of the anti-e-tolling policy system. Local areas and municipalities, Soweto for example, owed substantial sums (towards R20 billion, by 2020) to Eskom,[78] and systems to extract payments from communities amounted to small stabs at big mountains, while a parallel system of electricity dissemination-payment had become ingrained.

Parallel policy systems had taken root on migration and the inflow of other African citizens, and several other nationalities. Frequently defective border controls meant people could enter undocumented, or on tourist visas, and stay. This had a knock-on effect on perceived competition for social services, and resulted in selective Afro-xenophobia. Government ambiguity was highlighted when members of the ANC's MKMVA marched with truckers against foreigners employed in the trucking industry in eThekwini in late 2020. The parallel policy system on crime, frequently linked to capture and corruption at the community level, was harmful. Corruption in the South African Police Service was rife and the policy was that corruption could buy 'tolerance' of criminal deeds or that there would be no consequences. It helped to subvert the formal criminal justice policy and unleashed a parallel policy of lawlessness.

Amid this cacophony, this chapter and its four main case studies have shown up the prevalence of parallel policy-making practices, bottom-up and top-down. On land, it took the factionalisation of a core policy issue before the ANC rose above drifting policy-making processes to prioritise action. In the struggle for fee-free post-secondary education, students asserted their needs through a populist policy-directed campaign, whereas former president Zuma subverted the formal policy process to assert his own. The policy had popular traction and benefited the ANC, keeping a young constituency relatively appeased. In nuclear energy, though, an extreme case of parallel policy-making had Zuma as the intended beneficiary – the rise of Ramaphosa-ists returned the policy to established tracks, but attempts to ensure the return to nuclear were unrelenting. The e-toll saga was a case of populist politics eclipsing the government and popular mobilisation defeating official authority.

The case study trends demonstrate the extent to which populism in South Africa ruled on the public policy front. While policy-makers played factional politics and competed for an ideological upper hand, the grassroots identified openings and opportunities and asserted their own de facto policies, covering the fields of crime, xenophobia, land appropriation, electricity usage and post-secondary education. Many of these policy-making actions arrived through the vehicle of protest.

NOTES

1   As evidenced in the Freedom Charter's 'economic clause', introduced by late ANC intellectual Ben Turok.

2   See Jeremy Cronin, 'Why a second radical phase of the NDR is an imperative – Jeremy Cronin', *African Communist*, 1 July 2015, https://www.politicsweb.co.za/opinion/why-a-second-radical-phase-of-the-ndr-is-an-impera, accessed 15 March 2020. Gwede Mantashe, ANC national chairperson, argued that Zuma's letter of attack on Ramaphosa, 28 August 2020, was part of a counter-revolution; see SABC-SAFM news, 11 September 2020.

3   See Sipho Kings, 'South Africa shaped by Thatcherism', *Mail & Guardian*, 12 April 2013, https://mg.co.za/article/2013-04-12-south-africa-shaped-by-thatcherism/, accessed 14 March 2020.

4   Cyril Ramaphosa, 'My New Deal for SA – and 10-point action plan for jobs, growth, transformation', *Biznews*, 14 November 2017, https://www.biznews.com/thought-leaders/2017/11/14/ramaphosa-new-deal-for-sa, accessed 15 March 2020.

5   The expropriation clause in the ANC's 52nd conference resolutions was nondescript and was stated in terms of the expropriation of property in the public interest to get equity, redress and social justice.

6   The section is based on the author's comparative content analysis, for purposes of this chapter, of the three sets of ANC conference resolutions of the Polokwane, Mangaung and Nasrec ANC national elective conferences.

7   This was explored in an Afrobarometer survey, in which 62 per cent of respondents (South African citizens) chose 'delivery' over 'democracy'; see http://www.afrobarometer.org/, accessed 22 March 2020.

8   See Roger Eatwell and Matthew Goodwin, 2018, *National Populism: The Revolt against Liberal Democracy*, London: Pelican, pp. xi–xii, 226–266. The book explores national populism's challenge in the early twenty-first century to mainstream liberal politics in the West.

9   Susan Booysen, 2013, *Twenty Years of South African Democracy: Citizen Views of Human Rights, Governance and the Political System*, Washington, DC and Johannesburg: Freedom House.

10 As outlined in the 2020 national budget speech, Tito Mboweni, 26 February 2020, '2020 Budget speech – minister of finance', https://www.gov.za/BudgetSpeech2020, accessed 26 February 2020. See also Carol Paton, 'Treasury pledges to pursue debt ceiling', *Business Day*, 29 July 2020.

11 For example, by deputy president David Mabuza in the National Council of Provinces, 3 March 2020, http://www.thepresidency.gov.za/speeches/oral-replies-deputy-president-david-mabuza-national-council-provinces%2C-parliament%2C-cape-0, accessed 20 March 2020.

12 The inequality report from StatsSA, 2019, gives a comprehensive statistical overview of inequality attesting to policy failure; see http://www.statssa.gov.za/?page_id=1854&PPN=Report-03-10-19&SCH=7680, accessed 22 November 2019.

13 Chief justice Mogoeng Mogoeng articulated the idea of extensive albeit not sole liability to apartheid and colonialism in the Annual Nelson Mandela Lecture, 23 June 2019, Soweto.

14 World Bank data confirmed South Africa as the most unequal country in the world; see http://povertydata.worldbank.org/poverty/country/ZAF, accessed 20 November 2019.

15 See Lynley Donnelly, 'IMF flags public finances', *Business Day*, 20 January 2020. As Covid relief programmes unfolded, social welfare minister Lindiwe Zulu repeated on several occasions in 2020 that the additional Covid-related payments were not sustainable.

16 See Presidency of South Africa, 2019, *Towards a 25 Year Review*; StatsSA, 2019, *Inequality Trends in South Africa*, Pretoria.

17 For some of the details, see Alan Hirsch, 2007, *Season of Hope: Economic Reform under Mandela and Mbeki*, Pietermaritzburg: UKZN Press.

18 The Lula moment is in reference to former president of Brazil, Luiz Inácio Lula da Silva, first elected in 2002 and re-elected for a second term in 2006.

19 All quoted phrases in this paragraph from the ANC conference resolutions of the 52nd and 53rd national elective conferences, respectively at Polokwane and Mangaung.

20 Jacob Zuma, 'These were not nine wasted years', Twitter, 29 January 2019, https://www.politicsweb.co.za/documents/these-were-not-nine-wasted-years--jacob-zuma, accessed 2 March 2019.

21 These words are as extracted by the author from conference discussions and media briefings, 16–20 December 2020, Nasrec, Johannesburg and documents, ANC 54th National Conference Report and Resolutions, December 2017.

22 See ANC 54th National Conference Report and Resolutions, December 2017, http://www.anc.org.za/54th-national-conference-reports, accessed 2 May 2018.

23 See also the debates on the National Democratic Revolution (NDR), as captured in Joel Netshitenzhe, 2014, 'The "two delinks" and the poverty of radicalism', *African Communist*, Issue 187, Fourth quarter, pp. 41–51; Jeremy Cronin, 'Why a second radical phase of the NDR is an imperative – Jeremy Cronin', *African Communist*, 1 July 2015, https://www.politicsweb.co.za/opinion/why-a-second-radical-phase-of-the-ndr-is-an-impera, accessed 15 March 2020.

24 ANC, 2019, *Let's grow South Africa together: 2019 election manifesto summary*, p. 31.

25 ANC 54th National Conference and Resolutions, op. cit., p. 32.

26 ANC, 2019, *Let's grow South Africa together: 2019 election manifesto summary*, op.cit., p. 35.

27 Lesetja Kganyago, as reported in Lynley Donnelly, 'Kganyago calls out ANC manifesto on the Reserve Bank', *Mail & Guardian*, 18 January 2019, https://mg.co.za/article/2019-01-18-00-kganyago-calls-out-anc-manifesto-on-the-reserve-bank, accessed 2 February 2019.

28 The pertinent section of the statement that Magashule presented read (4 June 2019, Luthuli House, Johannesburg): 'It was agreed that all deployees will ensure that resolutions of the 54th National Conference will be fully implemented in this regard the ANC NEC Lekgotla agreed to expand the mandate of the South African Reserve Bank beyond price stability to include growth and employment. It also directed the ANC government to consider constituting a task team to explore quantity [sic] easing measures to address intergovernmental debts to make funds available for developmental purposes. These measures should consider inflationary impact on the currency and the poor and all must be done to cushion them. This is consistent practice by developed countries to save their economies. This will go a long way in dealing decisively with the triple challenges of unemployment, poverty and inequality.'

29 To add to the discordance, deputy finance minister, David Masondo, appeared to back an expanded mandate while talking to the fact that other central banks were generally nationalised; see David Montalto, https://outlook.office.com/mail/deeplink?version=2019052703.06, accessed 4 June 2019.

30 Phillip de Wet, 'The Reserve Bank has now bought R20.9 billion in govt debt – but promises it isn't guiding prices', *Business Insider SA*, 30 June 2020, https://www.businessinsider.co.za/sarb-purchases-of-government-bonds-on-the-secondary-market-now-worth-r209-billion-2020-6, accessed 2 August 2020.

31 See the African Network of Centres for Investigative Reporting, 2017, 'Manufacturing divides: The Gupta-linked Radical Economic Transformation (RET) media network', p. 6, https://s3-eu-west-1.amazonaws.com/s3.sourceafrica.net/documents/118115/Manufacturing-Divides.pdf, accessed 11 November 2019.

32 See, for example, Thanduxolo Jika, Sabelo Skiti and M&G Data Desk, 'The high price of coal connections', *Mail & Guardian*, 11 October 2019.

33 Economists like Duma Gqubule argue that such borrowing was a mistake: 'Duma Gqubule reacts to IMF's 70 billion Covid 19 emergency loan', SABC-SAFM, Update@Noon, 29 July 2020, https://iono.fm/e/899616, accessed 1 August 2020.

34 Terence Creamer, 23 June 2020, 'Ramaphosa says infrastructure to be placed at heart of South Africa's postpandemic stimulus', https://www.polity.org.za/article/ramaphosa-says-infrastructure-to-be-placed-at-heart-of-south-africas-postpandemic-stimulus-2020-06-23, accessed 3 August 2010.

35 The Black Lives Matter protests unfolded in early June 2020 in Johannesburg, Cape Town and Pretoria. The protests resonated with both the many international iterations and the #RhodesMustFall student movement that started in 2015.

36 SABC Radio Sonder Grense, analysis by experts, 12 September 2019, of mid-September 2019 national crime statistics; SA Police, 31 July 2020, crime statistics, media statement.

37 See Cyril Ramaphosa, 'President Ramaphosa on South Africa's answer to Covid-19', *DispatchLive*, 15 March 2020, https://www.dispatchlive.co.za/news/2020-03-15-full-speach-president-ramaphosa-on-covid-19/, accessed 15 March 2020.

38 ANA, 'Ramaphosa: National Command Council will consider whether schools should remain open', *IOL*, 15 July 2020, https://www.iol.co.za/news/politics/ramaphosa-national-command-council-will-consider-whether-schools-should-remain-open-51025258, accessed 16 July 2020.

39 To get progress on public policy, action is required on both fronts. It happens that laudable policy is adopted but non-implementation or ineffective or corrupt diversions on the implementation process halt progress. It includes the types of occurrence where corrupt political principals, and many layers of politicians, bureaucrats and business, and crosses between politician-bureaucrats and business, hijack policies and rape all possible good effects.

40 See also Ferial Haffajee, 'Judging the "Cyril effect" after 100 days', *Business Times*, 27 May 2018; Stuart Lowman, 'Ramaphoria brings stability: S&P affirms "stable" outlook, junk status – analysis', *Biznews*, 25 May 2018, https://www.biznews.com/sa-investing/2018/05/25/ramaphoria-sp-stable-outlook-junk-statusanalysis/?acid=-bLlv7TzsmoYzlOOOYw3skQ%3D%3D&adid=jO%2FuSoZaphAQ9pc0JfeO-sA%3D%3D&date=2018-05-28, accessed 26 May 2018.

41 Presidential Advisory Panel on Land Reform and Agriculture, 4 May 2019, Final Report of the Presidential Advisory Panel on Land Reform and Agriculture, https://www.google.com/url?sa=t&rct=j&q=&esrc=s&source=web&cd=2&ved=2ahUKEwiqsIDNt-J7lAhVSeMAKHQYqDSsQFjABegQIAhAE&url=https%3A%2F%2Fwww.gov.za%2F-sites%2Fdefault%2Ffiles%2Fgcis_document%2F201907%2Fpanelreportlandreform_0.pdf&usg=AOvVaw1rmEQeJjdyAdPdW6_I6FAI, accessed 2 July 2019.

42 As evident in the people's hearings conducted by the Civil Society Working Group on State Capture, Johannesburg, 12 October 2019; see also Azarrah Karrim, '"They are stealing our future": How state capture affects its faceless victims', *News24*, 12 October 2019, https://www.news24.com/SouthAfrica/News/they-are-stealing-our-future-how-state-capture-affects-its-faceless-victims-20191012, accessed 15 October 2019.

43 As one illustration, it dropped to 21 index points in the third quarter of 2019, from 28 in the previous quarter. The Business Confidence Index fell to 89.1 index points in August 2019 as business confidence reached its lowest point in more than 20 years. The Covid-19 outbreak added additional and extensive global decline.

44 Cyril Ramaphosa, 'My New Deal for SA – and 10-point action plan for jobs, growth, transformation', *BizNews*, 14 November 2017, https://www.biznews.com/thought-leaders/2017/11/14/ramaphosa-new-deal-for-sa, accessed 15 November 2017.

45 Presidency of South Africa, 2019, *Towards a 25 Year Review*; StatsSA, 2019, *Inequality Trends in South Africa*, Pretoria.

46   Susan Booysen, 'Constitutionalise, legalise, catch the shifting land target', *Daily Maverick*, 23 May 2018, https://www.dailymaverick.co.za/opinionista/2018-05-23-constitutionalise-legalise-catch-the-shifting-land-target/, accessed 24 May 2018.

47   In one early instance, in 2001, the Bredell land occupation in Gauteng drew attention especially because the Pan Africanist Congress was said to be organising the action.

48   High Level Panel on Fundamental Change, November 2017, *Report of the High Level Panel on the Assessment of Key Legislations and the Acceleration of Fundamental Change*, panel led by former president Kgalema Motlanthe.

49   For an overview of the deficits in prevailing land policy in South Africa, see Ben Cousins, 'South Africa's land debate is clouded by misrepresentation and lack of data', *The Conversation*, 8 March 2018, https://theconversation.com/south-africas-land-debate-is-clouded-by-misrepresentation-and-lack-of-data-93078, accessed 10 March 2018.

50   See, for example, High Level Panel on Fundamental Change, 2017, op. cit., p. 300; *Noseweek*, December 2019, 'Hartebeesthoek hustle: Over-valued land raises eyebrows', p. 9.

51   It was a majority judgment upholding an order by the Land Claims Court that a special master be appointed to assist the Department of Rural Development and Land Reforms (DRDLR) to process land claims. See Constitutional Court of South Africa, 20 August 2019, Case CCT 232/18, *Mwelase and Others v Director-General for the Department of Rural Development and Land Reform and Another* [2019] ZACC 30, Saflii data base.

52   Jackson Mthembu, 3 March 2017, commemoration event in the National Assembly to mark the twentieth anniversary of the Constitution, Cape Town.

53   High Level Panel, 2017, op. cit., p. 300.

54   This was conditional on the national land budget being increased from the pre-2018 0.4 per cent of the national budget at the time, and corruption of mismanagement being contained.

55   See Siviwe Feketa, 'De Lille urgently pushing ahead with land restitution', *Business Day*, 24 February 2020.

56   Parliament of South Africa, Ad hoc committee on the amendment of Section 25 of the Constitution of the Republic of South Africa, 1996, Constitution Eighteenth Amendment Bill, 6 December 2019.

57   For further details, see Marianne Merten, 'Land expropriation, the final push: Constitutional amendment drafting committee set up, Cabinet approves draft Expropriation Bill', *Daily Maverick*, 7 December 2018, https://www.dailymaverick.co.za/article/2018-12-07-land-expropriation-the-final-push-constitutional-amendment-drafting-committee-set-up-cabinet-approves-draft-expropriation-bill/, accessed 8 December 2018.

58   The author's case study (unpublished), 2019, of land invasion, protest and policy delivery, 2018–2019, in the Greater Hermanus Municipality demonstrates these patterns; see also Chapter 8.

59   Tania Broughton, 'Marikana occupiers reach landmark agreement with property owners', *GroundUp*, 6 March 2020, https://www.groundup.org.za/article/marikana-occupiers-reach-landmark-agreement-property-owners/, accessed 17 March 2020.

60   Ferial Haffajee, 'Stage 4 load shedding hits as Cabinet divide on energy deepens', Energy update, *Daily Maverick*, 11 March 2020, https://www.dailymaverick.co.za/article/2020-03-11-stage-4-load-shedding-hits-as-cabinet-divide-on-energy-deepens/, accessed 12 March 2020; see also *Business Day*, 13 March 2020, 'Energy supply wheels moving – but slowly', editorial.

61   Ramaphosa became president of South Africa on 16 February 2018 and appointed Jeff Radebe on 26 February 2018. After the 2019 elections in Ramaphosa's second Cabinet, Gwede Mantashe became the minister of mineral resources and energy.

62   Setumo Stone, 'Mahlobo rushes nuclear deal', *City Press*, 5 November 2017, https://www.news24.com/SouthAfrica/News/mahlobo-rushes-nuclear-deal-20171105-2, accessed 30 September 2020.

63   See, for example, The Presidency of South Africa, 3 October 2014, 'President Zuma works with Cabinet on nuclear matters', http://govza.dev.gcis.gov.za/president-zuma-works-cabinet-nuclear-matters, accessed 4 November 2015.

64   Paul Vecchiatto, 'MPs accused of rewriting nuclear policy', *Business Day*, 29 October 2014.

65   Also see Sibongakonke Shoba, 'Outwit. Outlast. Outfawn. The bizarre survival of Teflon Tina', *Sunday Times*, 7 December 2014; Jeff Radebe, quoted in Paul Vecchiatto, 'Cabinet still not briefed over nuclear agreements – Radebe', *Business Day*, 7 November 2014. There were denials of the conclusiveness of the agreement with Russia, but no documents were released.

66   See Matuma Letsoalo and Govan Whittles, 'DD must tell Putin the deal is off', *Mail & Guardian*, 18 May 2018.

67   Haffajee, 11 March 2020, op. cit., and Martin Creamer, 'Coal miner Exxaro driving rigorous renewable energy strategy', *Engineering News*, 12 March 2020, https://m.engineeringnews.co.za/article/coal-miner-exxaro-driving-rigorous-renewable-energy-strategy-2020-03-12, accessed 21 March 2020, shed light on the emerging centres of power in the energy sector, in which Zuma-ists again featured. Christina MacPherson, 16 March 2020, 'Politics, secrets, lies and civil liberties', https://nuclear-news.net/category/africa/south-africa/, accessed 2 August 2020, sketches this world of power play.

68   See, for example, Kevin Mileham, 'ANC government is determined to pursue nuclear at any cost', *BusinessLive*, 12 May 2020, https://www.businesslive.co.za/bd/opinion/2020-05-12-anc-government-is-determined-to-pursue-nuclear-at-any-cost/, accessed 1 August 2020.

69   Richard Poplak, 'How the ANC managed to birth the Ramabuza monstrosity', *Daily Maverick*, 19 December 2017, https://www.dailymaverick.co.za/article/2017-12-19-trainspotter-how-the-anc-managed-to-birth-the-ramabuza-monstrosity/#.WxRZmdfB2, accessed 21 December 2017.

70   Report of Commission of Inquiry into the Feasibility of making High Education and Training Fee-free in South Africa, August 2017; submitted to President Zuma 30 August 2017, released by President Zuma 13 November 2017; http://www.thepresidency.gov.za/press-statements/release-report-commission-inquiry-feasibility-making-high-education-and-training, accessed 15 November 2017.

71   Ranjeni Munusamy, Qaanitah Hunter and Sabelo Skiti, 'Zuma's free tertiary education shocker – controversial plan devised by president's 28-year-old future son-in-law', *Sunday Times*, 7 November 2017, https://www.timeslive.co.za/politics/2017-11-07-exclusive-zumas-free-tertiary-education-shocker/, accessed 14 October 2019; Angelique Serrao, 'Zuma's free education adviser was a spy', *News24*, 13 November 2017, https://www.news24.com/SouthAfrica/News/exclusive-zumas-free-education-adviser-was-a-spy-20171113, accessed 14 October 2019.

72   See *Timeslive*, 16 December 2017, 'President Jacob Zuma's final speech as ANC president', https://www.timeslive.co.za/politics/2017-12-16-in-full--president-jacob-zumas-final-speech-as-anc-president/, and *News24*, 16 December 2017, 'Zuma announces

free higher education for poor and working class students', https://www.news24.com/SouthAfrica/News/zuma-announces-free-higher-education-for-poor-and-working-class-students-20171216, accessed 17 December 2017.

73 Citations of the DA's Belinda Bozzoli, as reported by *Timeslive*, 16 December 2017, 'Free university education for poor: Breakthrough or hollow promise?' https://www.timeslive.co.za/news/south-africa/2017-12-16-university-free-for-poor-is-it-a-breakthrough-or-hollow-promise/, accessed 2 March 2018.

74 Parts of this section draw on Susan Booysen, 2019, 'Public policy-making through adversarial network governance in South Africa', in David Everatt (ed.), *Governance and the Postcolony: Views from Africa*, Johannesburg: Wits University Press, Chapter 7.

75 In September 2018, for example, summonses issued for e-toll non-payments had increased nearly 20-fold over the preceding three years, yet collections were down, according to data supplied by the minister of transport to members of Parliament. The minister gave details on the number of summonses issued by Sanral since 2015, in a written reply to a question from the DA. The reply showed that the number had ballooned from 331 in 2015/2016 to 6 626 in the 2017/2018 financial year.

76 See Mia Lindeque, EWN, 7 September 2020, interview with Sanral CEO Skhumbuzo Macozoma, https://ewn.co.za/2020/09/07/sanral-lost-over-r640m-in-revenue-during-hard-lockdown-ceo-macozoma-reveals, accessed 12 September 2020.

77 Angie Motshekga, 24 January 2016, https://www.politicsweb.co.za/opinion/the-anc-in-its-own-words-50-quotes, accessed 2 March 2019.

78 See Andile Sicetsha, 'Soweto racks up more than R1-billion Eskom debt since January', *The South African*, 24 June 2019, https://www.thesouthafrican.com/news/soweto-r1-billion-eskom-debt-january-2019, accessed 25 June 2019.

Protest as Parallel Policy-Making and Governance

PROTEST IN POST-HEGEMONIC SOUTH AFRICA: CITIZENS EXTRACTING POLICY, DOING GOVERNANCE

The time had passed for citizens to queue patiently for government to deliver better services and more economic transformation. Protest in the 'lost decade' in which the ANC had condoned and endorsed (and finally opposed) Jacob Zuma took over much of political life. Citizen trust in the ANC, also as government, had declined markedly.[1] While politicians were fighting over ownership of the ANC, and whether to let the ANC go into 'self-correct', citizens generally (and including many ANC supporters) were adopting alternative and supplementary ways to get their demands across to government. Alternatively, they took government into their own hands. It was little wonder that in Election 2019 participation had dropped significantly, in addition to the further decline the ANC had suffered in national-level support percentages. Protest was not the sole or all-round dominant mode of political action, but it had become a significant, widely used part of citizens either doing government and policy-making for themselves or pushing government into doing more, faster, for specific communities or constituencies.

This newly institutionalised era of citizens making and implementing their desired policies for the immediate conditions of their lives built on existing cultures of challenging and subverting official policy. It was informed by conditions of constructive lawlessness. E-tolls, services such as water and electricity, and fees for post-secondary studies, were examples of how protest worked by making de facto policy or forced government decisions where government had been failing.

Conventional community (or 'service delivery') protests persisted. Election 2019 offered evidence of multiple repertoires of protest and voting, beyond the simple dual repertoire of 'protest *and* vote'. The smooth coexistence of protest and pro-ANC voting was under threat – still used, but complemented by the actions of 'self-service' policy-making and governance – and, to a lesser extent, by angry abstention and vote-switching. The only barrier to deep disruption of prevailing ANC majorities, with protest superseding pro-ANC voting, was the formerly wide buffer of ANC electoral majority, but Election 2019 showed that these majorities were approaching points of depletion, as in the case of Zwelihle in Hermanus. Simultaneously, conventional protests became more disruptive, with major transport arterials and infrastructure under threat and under siege.

Citizens were learning and relearning the political uses of protests within the ANC to help select political leadership as well as drive demands on policy and governance. The successes they had recorded included helping the ANC to realise the dangers of retaining Zuma – mass protests helped to drive the message home. In North West province, street protests helped to create the opening for the Ramaphosa ANC to start lifting the former premier, Supra Mahumapelo, from his premiership power. Protest *within the ANC against the ANC* often took the form of legal challenges against factional manipulation. In Alexandra township, ANC-inspired protest against the DA-coalition-led metro council on the eve of Election 2019 helped the ANC electorally. Protest had become ingrained as part of the citizen interface with the dominant party.

The policy and governance use of protest in the years of Ramaphosa's ANC government were, however, the main focuses. The cases of fee-free higher education and e-toll policy-making had shown how policy was changed through citizen protest. Citizens had stepped in and claimed the position of government when, in Afro-xenophobic protests, they set down policy on migration – moderated by government, but with popular directives as to what the policy would be. Truck protests, looting and burning trucks driven by foreigner-drivers (or drivers presumed to be foreigners) accentuated the 'policy' further, and it metamorphosed into highway looting, by protesting communities, of any truck. Bottom-up public policy-making on land had been progressing by means of protest in the form of invasion and settlement, mostly in urban centres. This repertoire escalated when under Covid-19 regulations occupations increased while evictions became more difficult. Self-help of service delivery – especially electricity protest by means of non-payment, tapping illegally into delivery networks and resisting Eskom counter-action by force – set new de facto policy that competed effectively against government's 'user pays' model.

This chapter first considers the changing nature of protest action, then, with a series of investigations of voting trends in protest communities in Election 2019, explores the state of evidence on the protest-voting dual repertoire. The analysis follows through with case studies of major protests that occurred in the period 2015–2020 and how these made policy – and concludes by setting out an emerging continuum, circa 2020, of political protest in the time of the Ramaphosa government.

EVOLUTION OF THE BALLOT AND THE BRICK: SELF-HELP POLICY AND ALTERNATIVE GOVERNANCE

Protest had been ingrained in the repertoires of political action since at least 2005, and particularly from 2007. The Zuma takeover of government encouraged citizen action; there were popular expectations of a president who would be reconnecting with people, who would better understand their needs and fill the 1994 gaps. Multiple communities across the country acted to ensure that government would be reminded of their demands and needs. Protest and burning tyres became the 'smoke that beckons'.[2] Burning tyres attracted some attention, while burning infrastructure assured meetings with people from government, and burning trucks on major routes brought dedicated attention to demands.

Citizens used protest, except when prohibited under conditions like strict Covid-19 lockdown, to ensure that their grievances reached the government at whichever level. Protest became an institutionalised supplementary mechanism – although it was still not guaranteed to bring delivery.[3] It was used frequently in the years that followed Zuma's installation, applied as a stream of action to remind politicians of their substantive responsibilities and also of the need for accountability. It was used by communities to extract more out of their elected representatives. Even if protest was vehement (most of the time), the protesters continued voting for their ANC when elections arrived. The ballot and the brick became a well-known phenomenon in South African politics.[4]

The repertoires of political protest as modus operandi, and the substantive purposes to which they were applied, were elaborated in the Zuma and Ramaphosa years. The Zuma government had set the example of living by parallel rules and shadowy state structures. The laws of the country and constitutionally mandated institutions through which to govern were merely a part of the terrain in which government operated. Government was often distracted from the task of serving citizen interests above all and in the view of protest-prone citizens, government could not be trusted to govern as required. The time of Zuma's reign reinforced such perceptions, and the Ramaphosa incumbency saw initial high hopes crushed when Covid looting via procurement contracts reminded citizens to be vigilant against government avarice.

Government often rebuffed the actions, but the protests persisted. Citizens knew how to play the guilt of the ANC government for not having brought a better quality of life to more of its citizens – at least not consistently over the major fronts of socio-economic life. Increasingly, some in protest ranks would ask: 'If government does not provide us with jobs, how can they expect us to find money to pay for electricity?'[5]

Protesting citizens established new and alternative policies over a wide front. The ANC government's policies did not always stay abreast of citizens' needs; it could have done better, despite the country's severe economic crisis, and alternative people's policies found fertile soil, often established because of the ineffectiveness (in places to the point of near-collapse) of the policing, investigative, prosecutorial and judicial functions of the state. These compromised operations added to government and politicians often not playing by constitutional, legal or ethical rules. It was a time of lawlessness.

REDISTRIBUTIVE POLICY THROUGH PROTEST: MODUS OPERANDI ON URBAN LAND, AFROPHOBIA

Protests over quality of life and access to resources – redistribution, in effect – had been ongoing for years, reaching substantial numbers in the early years of the Ramaphosa era, assuming the character of a bottom-up establishment of an alternative, populist order, which was simultaneously *in a strong symbiotic relationship with the ANC government*. Protesters operated under an umbrella of legitimation created by government's aspirational policy statements, constitutional ideals, ANC feelings of guilt for not having done more, and ANC determination not to alienate much-needed voters. Protester action articulated with the top-down alternative order of lawless government, one where capture and corruption ruled, despite a set of formal processes and power that was to be positioned in constitutionally mandated institutions.

The alternative policies included the invasion of unused urban and metropolitan land, especially when it was owned publicly. Municipalities, police and private security forces reversed the settlement in many but not all instances. The authorities' reactions also depended on the ownership of the land – whether it was state, commercial, or private.[6] The rules of this 'policy' of land acquisition included that once there was a peg in the ground and an informal structure attached to it, the settlement initiative afforded starter rights. Then it became an issue for negotiation and finding mutually acceptable solutions. The land settlers had also learned to use legal rights and the courts. Once a settlement root was established, through invasion of virgin land or by becoming a backyarder attached to an existing structure, new and aspiring residents had a bulwark.[7]

In the wake of the ANC's resolutions at conference and in Parliament for land expropriation without compensation, urban-area activism for access to land escalated.[8] Citizens who had fathomed the dynamics figured that an umbrella of legitimacy would henceforth cover land activism. The actions unfolded in traditionally white and business-oriented areas, and in township areas. Municipal servitude areas were among the targeted prime, vacant urban land.

Many variants of supplementary 'housing structure policy' accompanied alternative land provision policy. Over many years, housing waiting-list politics had played out prominently. Places on the waiting list could be bought from corrupt officials – and such injustices triggered many protests. Those aspiring to urban land found land adjacent to established suburban or township areas, and in many cases, new class-race dynamics unfolded when owners of formal and relatively middle-class homes (also in established township areas) protested against invasion by new settler-squatters. In Gauteng, for example, middle-class or relatively middle-class areas became the sites of these new struggles; Ivory Park, Protea Glen, Kliptown, Ennerdale and Lenasia South were examples. The Protea Glen class protests materialised amid rapid urbanisation and the strains that such migration placed on urban infrastructure.[9] In an extreme instance in Lenasia South (as in many other areas over time), temporarily unoccupied homes were invaded or looted. Zama-zamas also took over entire areas, such as those around the abandoned Roodepoort City Deep mine.[10] Existing residents protested that their safety and the value of their properties were deteriorating.

Policy was being asserted bottom-up on foreigners in the living spaces of often poor and unemployed South Africans[11] – policy against fellow Africans, Afrophobia. It was not universally against illegal Africans – in all the communities that this study covers there were exceptions, depending on the individuals and their relations with the community. The alternative policy being established was that foreigners *could be targets for protest and looting*, and indeed, that they were often (again, not necessarily) in South Africa illegally made them particularly susceptible to being targeted. The asserted policy, despite government denials, was Afrophobia (which also included Pakistanis) against those who were trading in the community spaces, who had outsider identities, and who had goods that were not available relatively freely to South Africans sharing the same geographic space. Greed and opportunism were present too, besides need. Afrophobic looting attacks included the pillaging of shop fridges and non-essential items, while police members sometimes took part.[12]

Looting from highway trucks after accidents, and truck arson in campaigning against cut-rate employment of foreigner truck drivers were related phenomena. The campaign against foreign truck drivers became prominent at the time of the 2018 Mooi River truck blockade, which came with arson and looting.

The government and law enforcement agencies were relatively powerless, alternatively haplessly sympathetic with communities that were striking out.[13] Besides, these citizens often targeted trucks that were transporting food. Government's responses were muted in the face of the alternative policy and 'law' being asserted. The practice was so extensive, and corruption and incapacity in the South African Police Service (SAPS) (and some metropolitan police services) so pervasive, that options to counter the attacks were limited. The political restraints on government, largely ANC government, were even bigger. Government faced alienating citizens – and potential pro-ANC voters – should the law have been applied strictly (even if it had been possible) to masses that were going hungry. SAPS responses against protesters and looters were likely to appear in the form of how many people were arrested on the day, followed by how many appeared in court. Communities mobilised frequently when protest leaders were arrested, threatening to mount further protests and perhaps use tyre-burnings and road blockades to obtain the release of leaders and get the charges dropped. Pro-release second-wave protests were used also to get ordinary protesters released.

It became so uncommon for protests to have legal consequences that there was outrage when a #FeesMustFall protester, Kanya Cekeshe,[14] was denied both leave to appeal and bail by the Johannesburg Magistrates Court. Almost without exception, #FeesMustFall protesters had been granted pardons by their universities as well. This was in the face of infrastructure damage on campuses around the country (estimated to have been in the region of R786 million) from 2015 to 2018.[15] There was empathy for the just nature of the students' struggle, and because goodwill was essential for the ongoing operation of universities – for the ANC government it was important not to alienate the youth constituency. Cekeshe eventually benefited from a general presidential remission of prison sentences and was paroled in late 2019.

Further illustrations abounded of asserting policy through active and passive actions anchored in poverty and lack of resources (or, on occasion, simply justified through the *use* of these arguments). Variations on the theme of poaching (illegal mining and the pilfering of natural resources) demonstrated the case – Gauteng informal gold miners, frequently from neighbouring countries, argued that they were simply taking what was supposed to have been 'due to their South African brothers', who had been exploited by the mining company when the mine was shut down.[16]

RISING PROTEST, SHRINKING VOTING

Protest was the rule rather than the exception in repertoires of political action (Figure 8.1; Table 8.1).[17] The details show the extent to which the province of Gauteng, the main site of in-migration and new formal and informal urban settlements, was the hotbed of protest. Gauteng was also the province (in the ranks of the eight provinces governed by the ANC) where the ANC had the slimmest of majorities (Chapter 3). The Western Cape in the pre-election year of 2018 had also become a protest magnet. This could have been a process of citizens protesting to draw attention to demands for better living conditions, or a process instigated by non-governing parties, and the ANC in particular, to destabilise opposition strongholds, highlight issues of poor governance and accumulate support. There were reports, for example, that the ANC encouraged the multiple 2018 protests in the Overberg area (where the municipalities were Democratic Alliance [DA] controlled) from Bot River and Kleinmond in the west, to Stanford and Gansbaai in the east. This was echoed in Gauteng (with its DA-coalition-led metropolitan governments, at the time) where the ANC was inferred to have been central to unleashing the Alex shutdown protests on the eve of Election 2019.

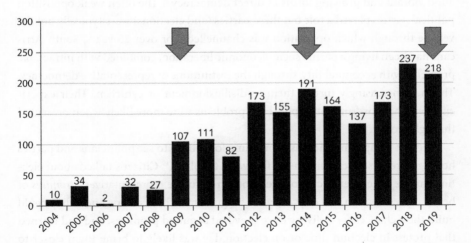

Figure 8.1: Community protest at and around election times in South Africa, 2009, 2014 and 2019

Source: Municipal IQ, image provided by Municipal IQ, 5 August 2020

Table 8.1: Protest tracking, trends summary, 2004–2018

Province	2004–2017 number of cases	2004–2017 % of total	2018 number of cases	Total number of cases
Eastern Cape	245	13.51	43	288
Free State	94	5.18	21	115
Gauteng	479	26.42	23	502
KwaZulu-Natal	216	11.91	30	246
Limpopo	144	7.94	5	149
Mpumalanga	142	7.83	4	146
Northern Cape	61	3.36	30	91
North West	205	11.30	10	215
Western Cape	227	12.52	41	268
Total	1 813	100	207	2 020

Source: Based on Ronesh Dhawraj for the SABC Research, Monitoring project, 2019

Parallel democracy through the ballot and the brick

The ANC was in government continuously beyond Election 2019, but it governed amid vibrant and growing forms of direct democracy.[18] The often weak opposition political parties played a role but these parties (and elections) were typically not the vehicle through which opposition was channelled. For over 25 years, South Africans had been living a partial socio-economic liberation, combined with intractable problems with accountability, through the institutions of representative democracy. This had increasingly turned them to disillusionment or cynicism. Their experience was that government responses to problems were more likely when presented through protest.

Election campaign time was prime time for getting to see politicians and parties hoping to represent citizens in the five years to follow.[19] Citizens talked about elections as the time to extract promises from their future representatives. *Promises of* better representation and delivery were no guarantee, but citizens knew they could build their chances for delivery once they had acquired promises, and had learned that protest in election time or on election day was likely to bring them closer to actually getting attention for their grievances.[20]

Ever since 2005, research has shown,[21] many of the exact communities that had engaged in protest action had not only also participated in the subsequent election, but had often also come out in strong electoral affirmation of the ANC, the party in government against whose services and policies the protest had been directed. In 2019 pre-election public opinion polling, Ipsos South Africa provided evidence of the ongoing dual repertoire, identifying equal endorsements of elections and protest to advance community interests. Forty-two per cent of respondents agreed to the statement '[i]t is quite acceptable to turn to protest such as strikes and marches if you are dissatisfied with the standard of services in your community', whereas only 37 per cent disagreed.[22] The same research found that 42 per cent disagreed and 40 per cent agreed to the statement that '[v]iolent protest is the only way to get service delivery'. The responses demonstrated citizens' penchant for supplementing electoral behaviour – and doubling up on repertoires of action to get better representation and governance.

This relationship persisted, but weakened over time. The edge by which the protesting communities were still endorsing the ANC was shrinking, even though the ANC was still emerging as the party of choice.[23] The ANC's buffer of support over other parties had been substantial enough to absorb the shrinkage in the party's support base and helped the ANC to postpone ceding outright majorities to the opposition. The extension of the repertoire of action, of bringing protest into elections, is explored through a set of case studies across several provinces in the rest of this section, assessing the extent of damage to the ANC's support in communities that had engaged in protest action on the eve and on the day of Election 2019.[24]

Extending the ballot and brick repertoire: Case studies

From 2019 onwards, citizens and voters *extended* their actions – from simply using the brick in between elections, to incorporating it *into* elections. Previously, the tendency had been to protest, and then to tolerate the election day rituals without interrupting them.[25] The use of the brick within the ballot process became an added tool. On election day 2019, violent protest disrupted elections altogether in multiple communities. Not all, by far, of the communities that had threatened disruptive electoral protest before the election actually delivered protest, some because they had merely been threatening, others – as in Nelson Mandela Bay's Asinavalo and Nomakanjani areas – because electricity was delivered after the threat to disrupt voting with protest.

Government knew that the community service protests were from areas of lower socio-economic status where conditions of deprivation were rife – communities from which much of the ANC's electoral support came, and that, in the language of the SAPS, 'unrest' was a threat to Election 2019.[26]

The chapter now zooms in on select communities that had protested in the weeks leading up to Election 2019, and a few that protested into the May 2019 election. The analysis[27] captures ongoing protests and those protests launched on the eve of the election, and covers Alexandra, Ivory Park, Kraaipan, Ganyesa and Vuwani.[28]

Alexandra, Gauteng: Community protest as tool of the politicians

In April 2019, residents from Alexandra protested about ailing infrastructure, lack of development, crime, land and informal structures erected by incoming migrants. Alex was part of the Johannesburg metropolitan municipality, led by a DA coalition, whereas the community itself was strongly pro-ANC. The Economic Freedom Fighters (EFF) and the Inkatha Freedom Party (IFP) had pockets of Alex support. Residents marched to the regional municipal offices and demanded that the Johannesburg DA mayor, Herman Mashaba, accept their memorandum. Contradictorily, they resolved that they would only speak to President Ramaphosa or to the Gauteng premier, David Makhura.

The protest became a political contest between the DA and ANC; the latter had been in power in Johannesburg until 2016 and was responsible for much of the problem in Alex, but such nuance was not relevant at the time. Possible corruption in the Alexandra Renewal Project was the core focus (the Human Rights Commission stepped in too, to conduct hearings). The ANC emerged from Election 2019 with high proportions of the vote (from percentages in the late 60s into the mid-70s) from the Alex protest communities. In two voting districts the ANC failed to get outright majorities, but these had traditionally been strong IFP bases, and the IFP did substantially better in 2019 than in 2014 (improving by 9 and 13 percentage points in the two voting districts). The outcomes showed that the EFF had not gained substantially in the protest voting districts; in one instance it registered small gains of between one and six percentage points. In all of the Alexandra voting districts assessed, the DA declined by two percentage points. Voter turnout in Alexandra's wards 105 and 106 brought evidence of the coexistence of protest and voting, although ANC mobilisation against the DA made the protest-voting relationship more complex.

Ivory Park, Gauteng: Middle-class rebellion, ANC vote

In mid-January 2019, informal settlement residents of the otherwise middle-class Ivory Park and the adjacent Ebony Park in Midrand embarked on protests that brought a total shutdown of the municipal housing department offices. Residents demanded land, water and sanitation, and wanted to 'hear the voice of President Cyril Ramaphosa' as a condition for them to go and vote. They complained that they had been living in an informal settlement since 1993 and government had been promising them housing all along. The dispute dragged on. By April, residents of nearby Rabie Ridge tried to stop the 'land grabbers', as the formal residents called them, hurling stones to prevent them from occupying a new piece of vacant land. The protest showed similarities (also in class character) to those in Protea Glen, Soweto (2018), Lenasia South (ongoing) and Ennerdale and Kliptown (ongoing).

Despite these protests, the voting districts in question gave the ANC large (generally 70 per cent plus) majorities. Turnout was down modestly, compared with 2014. The EFF result across the associated voting districts was generally stable. Where the EFF gained, it was by around three to four percentage points (with one exception of seven); in two of the voting districts it declined marginally. The DA result, too, remained pegged roughly at its 2014 levels, hovering between three and five per cent. The Ivory-Ebony Park results reflected the consolidation of the vote in the hands of the ANC, EFF and DA as main parties. Post-election, the feud escalated, when informal settlers tapped illegally into the formal residents' electricity transformers. The power supplier, Eskom, would not enter the area without police protection[29] – but the ANC had secured its victory.

Kraaipan, North West: Extreme service deficit, no challenger rising

Kraaipan village in Ngaka Modiri Molema district municipality suffered disintegrated services that had led to the municipality being placed under administration eight months before Election 2019.[30] Years-long on-off protest about services and mining jobs at the Kalgold mine turned into the torching of the Tlhakajeng Primary School five days before the election (the school would have been a voting station). Residents were also angry that renovations to the old, dilapidated and unsafe school had been promised since 2014, yet were still not done. This rural village also lacked access to domestic water; 10 000 people in one local area were estimated to be using one community tap and household water came in by containers on wheelbarrows, from a source two kilometres away.

Kraaipan's 2019 turnout rates across three of the four voting districts were about ten percentage points lower than in the 2014 election. The fourth of the voting districts, where the school was located, had an effective boycott (turnout rate 6 per cent). Besides the lower electoral participation, ANC results declined in most of the relevant voting districts. The ANC won, but its electoral endorsements dropped by about ten percentage points, substantially more therefore than the national average of 4.7 percentage points. In the voting district at the heart of the boycott, the ANC had the smallest decline – a result suggesting that those most discontented with ANC government in the area chose to boycott. The EFF emerged as the most likely party to take up the slack left by the ANC, but also gained some of the support residues from the erstwhile Bophuthatswana bantustan-associated United Christian Democratic Party and the Congress of the People. In September 2019, a tender bid was published for improved waterworks in Kraaipan.

Ganyesa, North West: Poll boycott, inflated ANC majority

In Ganyesa, in the community of Madinonyane in the Ruth Segomotsi Mompati district municipality, election preparations were disrupted by community protest right in the electoral space. Angry community members set alight the car of the Electoral Commission's presiding officer, on-site for special voting two days before polling day. On election day, residents barricaded the roads leading into the village and the point where voting was set to take place. Their grievances included that government had allocated R264 million to build a 55 kilometre road between Ganyesa and Madinonyane in 2015, but the road had not been completed. Protesters patrolled roads on election day to maximise community compliance with the boycott.

Voter turnout in Ganyesa dropped substantially from 2014 to 2019. Turnout in two of the four voting districts was 20 per cent or just above – compared with turnout of over 70 per cent previously. The ANC received high proportions of the votes cast, despite the boycott. In all cases at the heart of the protest the ANC proportions were still 70 per cent and above – well above the national average, though the contribution to the ANC's overall tally was minimal. The EFF picked up support that the ANC shed and which was not affected by the boycott. After Election 2019, protest subsided and the road remained incomplete. The dismissed Zuma-ist premier, Supra Mahumapelo, argued it was because he had been axed that he was unable to see the road through to completion.

Vuwani, Limpopo: Scorched earth, ANC king

Protracted protest in the Vuwani area (comprising about 30 villages) in far-north Limpopo province commenced in 2016 after the relocation of the area from the Makhado municipality to the Collins Chabane municipality. In the ensuing protest, more than 28 schools were burned down or damaged. The ongoing resistance was led by the pro-Makhado task team, which argued that municipal services had worsened because of the relocation, and that there had been no consultation. Service-related grievances concerned lack of water, sewage spills, no refuse removal and lack of medication at clinics. In election time 2019, residents threatened violence and abstention.[31] In an effort to quell the protests, a task team leader was arrested on the eve of the election.

The eight Vuwani voting districts at the centre of the protest delivered low turn-out rates. Apart from one, of 63 per cent, they ranged from 32 to 46 per cent. Large numbers chose to let abstention be their political message. Although Vuwani's demarcation and municipal placement issues divided the ANC in the area, the party results at voting district level showed that those who chose to continue voting supported the ANC overwhelmingly. In all of the most-affected and boycotting vot-ing districts, the ANC emerged with close to or over 90 per cent of the vote (mostly improvements on ANC performances of 2014). Even the EFF, which had gained support in Limpopo generally, either did not feature or declined in the Vuwani results. The stalemate continued post-election, with no immediate resurgence of the protests – at least, not until the next round of elections.

Collectively, these case studies show how the ANC as previously the predomi-nant party in the protest communities either shed support in Election 2019 or sus-tained proportionate support but on a foundation of lowered turnout. In most of these communities, voter turnout was lower than the national average, sometimes substantially lower, but discontent with the ANC was not channelled into replacing it with another political party. Where protests became boycotts, higher proportions (or consistently high proportions) of electoral support for the ANC followed; in the case of Vuwani the ANC emerged with impressive majorities. However, low num-bers of voters were sustaining the majorities: at the surface level, the ANC majori-ties appeared more substantial than they were after low turnout, as the base of the victory was included in the equation. Ongoing voting district majorities did not deliver voter numbers, something crucial in a proportional representation electoral system at the composite level. The case studies show that the weak-in-government ANC was losing support, but that no opposition party was rising to the occasion. Protest wreaked havoc in many places, yet the ANC remained in power.

SOUTH AFRICA'S EVOLVING PROTEST CULTURE: FOUR CASES OF ASSERTING GOVERNANCE AND POLICY

Many of South Africa's community and shared-interest protests were not in the domain of electoral bargaining. Rather, they were about demanding changes in for-mal or de facto government policy and asserting governance, the latter often in contexts of governance voids. A series of civil society protests in the Zuma-Ramaphosa transitional period 2017–2018, and then the Ramaphosa governance period, illustrated the evolving roles of protest politics, depicting in particular the contemporary relationships between people and the party closest to most of them – the ANC. The protests in North West in April–May 2018, the Mooi River truck-torching protests of April 2018, the 2018–2020 Hermanus land occupation protests, the 2016–2017 #ZumaMustFall protests, and the hybrid collection of Covid-19 protests helped to unpack these configurations of bottom-up and protest-driven policy and governance assertion.

Mobilisation and protest to exorcise Zuma: #ZumaMustFall

Popular mobilisation to give traction to demands for former president Zuma to be removed focused on the role that popular resentment played to end his reign of capture. Over time, the protests became inclusive of race and class, segments of the ANC, of the main opposition parties, of some state institutions and of a broad base of public opinion/voter sentiment.[32]

The ANC was in crisis mode, torn between tolerating Zuma and pushing him out. Many in the ANC were wary of institutionalising the removal of ANC state presidents once their ANC presidential terms had expired, as had been the case with Thabo Mbeki – and yet in March 2016 the Constitutional Court had pronounced on Zuma and the stream of corruption-capture allegations and investigative exposés had accumulated.[33] The ANC realised that it would not retain outright electoral dominance should the party remain associated with Zuma.[34] Public opinion polls showed that opposition parties were rising as the ANC dithered about a president whose popular ratings were lower than those of the party.[35]

Some of the most unifying moments post-1994 were found in civil society mobilisation to help remove Zuma from the presidency.[36] The protests were about distancing change from the Zuma order and, in effect, helped the ANC to again 'self-correct'. The protests helped to end the prolonged silences of those high up in the ANC who knew about the transgressions by Zuma and others but believed ANC culture dictated loyal silences.

The chain of #ZumaMustFall protests illustrates how these events accumulated and embodied the spirit of changing governance of the time:

- 16 December 2015: Protests in Johannesburg, Cape Town and Durban organised by the pop-up protest movement 'Unite Against' were supported by a coalition of interfaith and civil society organisations. The protests followed immediately after Zuma's crude capture cabinet reshuffle.

- 27 April 2016: #ZumaMustFall pickets unfolded countrywide, with Johannesburg, Cape Town and Durban again as the epicentres.[37] Reports followed that the City of Johannesburg had prevented the assembly from meeting outside the provincial legislature. Protesters said their assemblies were to defend the Constitution, after the Concourt had ruled against Zuma.
- 30 March 2017: Protests took place in Pretoria to support Pravin Gordhan and Mcebisi Jonas (among others) after Zuma had dismissed them.
- 4–7 April 2017: The Pretoria People's March, on the eve of Parliament's vote of no confidence in Zuma (which would choose to retain Zuma), saw between 25 000 and 40 000 converging on the Union Buildings; Save SA and the Organisation Undoing Tax Abuse were among the organisers; Save SA members occupied Church Square, calling the camp Vukani Mzansi. The march was supported by the EFF and the DA, trade unionist Zwelinzima Vavi and public intellectual Sipho Pityana. Protesters converged on the Gupta compound in Saxonwold. Also in Johannesburg, protesters from churches, political parties and trade unions marched from the Westgate Transport Hub to Mary Fitzgerald Square. Congress of South African Trade Unions (Cosatu) workers wore their union paraphernalia to work. In Cape Town, Voices to Save SA, We are South Africans, and #ZumaMustFall organised a human chain from Muizenberg to the city centre.
- 6 April 2017: In Cape Town, at a memorial service in honour of Ahmed Kathrada (vocal in opposing Zuma) at St George's Cathedral, former finance minister Gordhan and Archbishop Thabo Makgoba were speakers.
- 12 April 2017: Zuma's small birthday party contrasted with a Day of National Action, and protest in Durban and Pretoria, with Save SA taking a central role.
- In the intermediary months, protests made place for a focus on the ANC as it went into its Nasrec policy conference and through the rituals of electing delegates to the December 2017 elective conference.
- 11 February 2018: Three days before Zuma resigned as president of South Africa, the #ZumaExitMarch took place, said to include ANC and South African Communist Party (SACP) members marching to the Union Buildings and threatening a national shutdown if Zuma did not resign by 18 February 2018.

In the final instance, the #ZumaMustFall protests helped ANC branches and the Nasrec conference delegates, along with parliamentary players, realise that popular and electoral endorsements would dissipate should the ANC not reposition itself. Besides the anti-Zuma protests, the 2018 Mahikeng protests helped to draw the ANC's attention to the potential of popular revolt forging government change, the ANC becoming an onlooker. Citizens, forever ready for service delivery, housing and jobs protests, and suffering extensively under inefficient local governments, slipped seamlessly into political revolt. A thin line separated the socio-economic from the political.

Popular revolt changing the Mahumapelo-Mahikeng political order

Before the Mahikeng-Mahumapelo protests of April 2018, community protest (often equated with 'service delivery protest') had not translated into the generalised uprisings that unseat governments, even when they targeted municipal councillors. In the anti-Zuma protests, the actions were geographically diffused. As more and more North West communities joined, it seemed possible that this wave of protests against Supra Mahumapelo's provincial leadership could become the first to unseat a (provincial) government. The revolt could have been quelled with the use of force, but given the political context of inter-factional ANC tensions, and accusations that Ramaphosa was executing a purge of a Premier League member, a more restrained set of events unfolded. Ramaphosa was hamstrung by the edict of party unity.

In the main, it was the towns of Mahikeng, Vryburg, Taung, Christiana and Delareyville that erupted. The targets were largely 'soft' and identical to the targets of most community protests: foreigner shop owners, a few bigger shopping centre tenants, burning street barricades, the burning of an evacuated bus and of large trucks that transported lootable goods, and municipal infrastructure (besides threats to burn the houses of the premier and the mayor of Mahikeng). Beyond Mahikeng and its surrounds, the protests resembled standard local-level protests. The North West protests, however, were a landmark – community protests were meshing across municipal boundaries to constitute a generalised uprising that forced change in political incumbency.

Citizens who had been living under the Mahumapelo provincial regime had seen dubious government projects unfold and had heard about a litany of enrichment schemes. Their priority demand was for political change; they *expected to see* the Nasrec Ramaphosa victory replicated at the provincial level – and the municipal level where North West municipalities were the worst performing among the provinces. The protesting citizens were influenced by anti-Mahumapelo leaders, but most were reacting against maladministration locally and provincially.

This highlighted Ramaphosa's dilemma. In the mere two months since Zuma's Valentine's Day 2018 resignation and the formal end of Zuma power, Ramaphosa oversaw the start of legal processes against suspected corruption perpetrators. With the start of investigations into Mahumapelo and his associates, Mahumapelo's ANC praise singers lauded their patron's governance and ANC provincial regions and branches defended their 'Black Jesus' (Mahumapelo).[38] Mahumapelo alleged that the calls for action against him were factional, harming ANC unity. He ignored the popular thrust and focused his fightback on provincial ANC and government structures that were loaded in his favour. The Mahumapelo camp hid behind the mantra of 'innocent until proven guilty' and argued that it is dangerous to set a precedent by bowing to the protest pressures.

Instead of triggering the outright fall of the provincial premier, the North West protests of April 2018 introduced a chain of prevarication – getting and not getting change in provincial government. This political response to the protest string included (roughly sequentially):

- Ramaphosa deployed an inter-ministerial committee to investigate North West governance. The committee reported in May 2018, and Ramaphosa placed the province under administration.
- Mahumapelo tendered his resignation in early May, and withdrew it because 'he had not consulted about it with his provincial ANC party structures';[39] he took special leave instead and appointed the finance MEC, Wendy Nelson, as interim premier.
- Sporadic protests resurfaced in Mahikeng the day after the withdrawal of Mahumapelo's resignation; in late May 2018 Mahumapelo opted for early retirement.
- The ANC National Executive Committee disbanded the North West ANC Provincial Executive Committee in September 2018, and Job Mokgoro, appointed acting premier, became ANC provincial task team convener.
- In February 2019, Mahumapelo won two cases[40] for reinstatement as North West ANC chairperson (Judge Fayeeza Kathree-Setiloane presided), but the ANC appealed.
- ANC North West's Provincial Executive Committee and provincial task team agreed to work as a single unit following the political intervention of the ANC's National Executive Committee, senior government member Obed Bapela leading the new provincial task team.
- Mahumapelo, still provincial leader, became an MP and committee chairperson in Parliament following Election 2019. Job Mokgoro became the new premier.

Thus, the protest was a trigger for provincial government change, but political leadership negotiated compromise governance and leadership. Despite the agitation for change, a new order in the province was slow to arrive. The protest dissipated, away from the interlocking broad front evident in April 2018, returned sporadically and in specific communities and towns, and in the run-up to the 2021 NGC accumulated factional momentum, with renewed threats of street action. The ANC's mantra of unity superseded the demand for far-reaching change.

Mooi River truck-torching protests: Escalating repertoires[41]

The Mooi River, KwaZulu-Natal, truck-torching protests of April 2018 demonstrated how protests increasingly moved beyond actions about community services and into more general issues of employment and poverty. Angry, hungry or even just relatively deprived, citizens were the actors. The truck protest (and several repeats, throughout 2020) was significant on three fronts: it involved major destruction and looting – a type of redistribution of movable and consumable goods, a bottom-up policy assertion on 'foreigners in South Africa taking local jobs' and a major case in the repertoire of occupying national roads to push socio-economic grievances to the top of the public agenda.

Road occupations ensured high visibility, by major disruption, of grievances, and the occupation of major arterial roads such as the N3 at the Mooi River Plaza became one of the expanding weapons of choice for angry citizens. As a bonus it put food and goods on the table. The issue in truck protests (the employment of unregistered foreign nationals instead of more expensive South Africans)[42] was predominantly a national-level concern, but also had a local community job creation character.

Since Mooi River's large-scale truck protest there have been multiple other comparable cases. The type of protest was escalating, and was duplicated in late 2020 across major arterials when 40-plus trucks were torched in acts said to be carried out with military precision.[43] A 2020 Human Rights Commission inquiry heard that between March 2018 and early 2020 violent attacks on long-distance trucks had killed more than 213 people, cost the economy in excess of R1.2 billion, threatened the freight industry, and damaged and destroyed more than 860 vehicles.[44] The Road Freight Association recorded nearly 600 incidents for this period. The N3 was a particular target in the areas around Mooi River, Estcourt and Pietermaritzburg in KwaZulu-Natal; the N1 in the Western Cape near Touws River, De Doorns and Beaufort West; in Gauteng the major secondary roads like the R550 near Eikenhof, R101 near Hammanskraal, R59 between Sasolburg and Meyerton; and in the Eastern Cape the N2 between East London and Kokstad.

The major case of Mooi River, 2018, saw the torching and looting of 23 trucks, plus damage and looting to a further ten. It was an amplified replay of the events of the preceding Easter Monday at the same spot, a repeat playout of an alliance of grievances and actions between poverty-stricken communities alongside the N3 and truck drivers who objected to long-haul transport companies hiring foreigner drivers. Direct, violent action substituted for advocacy and negotiation.

The sequences of events revealed the texture of this type of protest. In the Easter 2018 highway revolt, the local truck-driver community appeared to lead the revolt against foreign truck drivers on the road. The police minister, Bheki Cele, told of how two lorries carrying drivers arrived from the nearby town of Estcourt and started to torch; the looting followed. In the variant of 29 April, the local community was part of the action from the start. There were some aggrieved unemployed truck drivers in the local community, but the community actors knew the repertoires by then and were ready to play their roles. The 'Mooi River type' of protest was epitomised therefore by the convergence of three protest strains. First, aggrieved truck drivers stood up for improved employment prospects and labour rights, even if their actions were xenophobic.[45] Second, there were the angry and hungry or more generally poverty-stricken communities that lived alongside the N3 at Mooi River or along the other targeted routes. Like comparable communities along this multitude of other arterial roads, these protesters were like fish in the water of local communities – the chances were that their looting would remain undetected or without repercussions, even if they had been arrested on the day. Third, looting flowed into lawlessness and opportunism. The operations elicited questions of whether political destabilisation might be a motive. Poverty, unemployment and hunger dissipated respect for the property of others. The communities knew by then, too, that the chance of arrest and prosecution was small and that of conviction minimal. After the local police conducted house-to-house searches to find looted goods, 54 Mooi River community members were arrested. A week later, six local residents appeared in court in relation to the looting of the trucks (the rest of the charges were withdrawn for insufficient evidence).[46] Then reports of the justice process dried up. Overall, the National Prosecuting Authority lamented its lack of capacity, and put much of the blame for follow-through on foreign drivers who avoided pursuing charges because of their illegal status in the country.

From the majority of past experiences, and possibly with good reason, it is clear that little came of arrests and court appearances when community protesters tried to extract, from government, socio-economic rights such as food on the table and municipal or provincial service delivery. It was a guilt-ridden government; one that knew it shared responsibility for failing its people and entered elections on the grace of the forgiveness of the continuously disadvantaged. Popular sentiment saw it as a case of 'if you cannot provide, you tolerate or turn a blind eye to relatively harmless self-help'. There was more concerted police action when 53 high-end television sets were looted from a truck near De Doorns in the Western Cape.

The couplet of Mooi River revolts signified a new and severe form of public protest, more systematically planned and executed, and magnified in spectacle, than the protests that had gone before, moving beyond conventional service delivery protests and arterial route occupations – with more impact than taxi blockades of Gauteng's N1 and the erstwhile 'poo protesters' Cape Town blockades of the N2 freeway. The Mooi River protest operators also blocked alternative Midlands routes, the R103 and R33. The substantial damage to private property and public road infrastructure exceeded the routine damage of burnt tyres and mutilated road signs, or torched municipal buildings. At the same time as the truck action, Mooi River police thwarted an attempted spillover looting of a local supermarket.

The Mooi River protests, plus all those that followed, albeit on a smaller scale, served as reminders of South Africa's vulnerability to arterial-occupation protests generally. In addition to the road occupations already noted, there were – as early as 2007 and into 2020 – anti-removal (from the Joe Slovo and other settlements) N2 occupations in Cape Town; repeated service delivery and local government leadership protests on the N2 near Grabouw; on Gauteng's Golden Highway as it meanders through poverty-stricken settlements with housing and unemployment problems; and the N12 in North West where race protests spilled onto the road.

The Mooi River revolts came at a time when a different political culture had emerged – one of a government that balanced itself precariously on the edge of ongoing outright electoral majorities. It was a government that could not afford to be seen to be acting against poor people – and in the context of unemployment and poverty the boundaries of criminality could be vague. The ANC was between a rock and a hard place. The hesitant tones of a statement by the KwaZulu-Natal MEC for transport, community safety and liaison were relevant beyond the specific community of reference on the day: 'People must understand that we are still a country with laws so we can't break them and expect that nothing will be done. We are calling on the community to make sure that we calm the situation …'[47]

Hermanus land wars: From Schulphoek to Marikana and Dubai

'The veracity of allegations of unlawful sale and corruption aside, the current conflict has revealed complex dynamics which resonate with a broader South African conversation around access to urban land and housing in the post-apartheid period' was a comment on one of South Africa's more tangible and unfolding urban land protests.[48] The battle in Hermanus for access to favourably located land, adjacent to current living areas, in a land-constrained and still overwhelmingly racially geographically divided area, offers an example of how street battles for land have emerged in the period since early 2018. At this time the ANC had endorsed the EFF's motion in Parliament for expropriation without compensation. That motion set the context. The direct trigger for the 2018 Hermanus land invasions was the daily community struggle of backyarder women from the township of Zwelihle, on the edge of the Hermanus town centre, who had been protesting to the municipality.[49] A complex set of protest actions unfolded: from advocating for more land allocation for informal urban settlement to direct action through land invasions and occupations; to court action to protect the invasion gains; to the Land Party's contest with the ANC; to contests among historically dispossessed groups about rights to land released for settlement; and to intra-Zwelihle battles between newcomers and longer-term dispossessed inhabitants. Chronologically, the major points in this multifaceted amalgam of the 2018 and ongoing protests were:

- March 2018: A small group of backyarder-tenant women from Zwelihle marched to the Overstrand municipal office, hoping to get relief from deprivation of services due to landlords not paying the municipality (an estimated 7 500 backyarders lived in the Zwelihle area).
- April–June 2018: The protest grew, the Schulphoek (area between Zwelihle and the Atlantic Ocean) invasion started; street protests unfolded (participation was obligatory, dictated by the community leaders); large numbers were arrested as a police vehicle and municipal infrastructure were torched (a satellite police station and a library, along with an income and job-generating private waste recycling plant). The protests spread to surrounding communities, from Gansbaai and Stanford to Hawston and Bot River. The R43, the only major road connecting Hermanus with the outside world, was under siege.
- Mid-2018: The Overstrand municipality made available the area of a former municipal dump for temporary emergency informal settlement, hence Marikana arose.
- July 2018: Police minister Bheki Cele helped to broker peace (acting on grievances about the police using rubber bullets), while the community agitated for its arrested Zwelihle Renewal leader, Gcobani Ndzongana, to be released from detention.
- September 2018: Red Ants returned to repel the siege of Schulphoek, no longer to deny occupation but to clear the land as a condition to its being sold back to the government. The municipality released emergency land for temporary settlement.[50]
- May 2019: The Land Party, formed out of Zwelihle Renewal, contested elections. It failed narrowly to win a parliamentary seat but won one Zwelihle voting district and did well in others (Figure 8.2).
- June 2019: Schulphoek protesters were in the Cape High Court to oppose eviction; that application was granted was due to the pending repurchasing

of the land for release to the settlers; Ndzongana appeared in court in Stellen-bosch on the 2018 public violence charges.

- July 2019: Zwelihle Renewal embarked on new campaigns against the dispro-portionate employment of foreigners, and racism in town.
- August 2019–2020: Power struggles unfolded between Zwelihle Renewal and the new Zwelihle Community Forum, part of the Greater Hermanus Stake-holders Forum, to represent residents in interactions with the municipality and community security.
- 2020: A new battle ensued between local-provincial government to imple-ment the multi-housing-type Better Living project, which entailed formal structures, and Zwelihle Renewal campaigning for serviced sites on which informal structures could be erected.[51]

The initial March 2018 protest escalated, resonating with experiences of land need: the Schulphoek land was on the Zwelihle doorstep, albeit privately owned at the time. The Overstrand municipality had sold it to a private developer in 2010 but the development plans had yet to materialise. After year-long sporadic protests, and negotiations with the council and the Western Cape province to buy the land back, it was confirmed that Schulphoek was again municipal property, for development to accommodate the Zwelihle protesters.[52]

Given competing community claims to land in the area, resolution was complex and it worsened as the protests unfolded.[53] One of the conditions of resale of the land back to government was that it had to be unoccupied. It was a losing battle: thousands of aspiring residents had started pegging down plots, including in envi-ronmentally sensitive conservation areas. Court action helped to protect residents against Red Ant-led eviction orders. In mid-2019, a community lawyer was repre-senting over 2 000 individuals and close to 3 000 had been living on the land (by early 2020, the number had risen to more than 5 000). Pre-emptive occupation of 'Dubai' (the Schulphoek area) was proceeding.

The municipality's Better Living development plan, formal housing with recrea-tional, medical and shopping facilities, was increasingly eclipsed as it would require the removal of the 2019 Dubai settlers.[54] Municipal housing waiting lists were con-structed in consultative meetings arranged by the Overstrand municipality. Zwe-lihle Renewal resisted by collapsing the meetings. Inter-community tensions also arose between the coloured community of Mount Pleasant, who historically had used Schulphoek as a recreational area, and the new African settlers. These inva-sions of state and private/state land unfolded, therefore, on a landscape of cross-cut-ting political and cultural identities.

Table 8.2: Voter turnout for Zwelihle, Western Cape: Wards 12, 6 and 5

Voting district*	Election								
	2009			2014			2019		
	Regis-tered	Turnout	%	Regis-tered	Turnout	%	Regis-tered	Turnout	%
97960089	3 339	2 890	86.55	2 958	2 138	72.28	3 828	2 888	75.44
97960078	1 421	1 389	97.75	1 414	1 109	78.43	2 058	1 657	80.52
97960146	–	–	–	1 544	1 290	83.55	2 427	1 927	79.40
97960135	–	–	–	1 349	1 322	98.00	1 640	1 289	78.60
97960034	3 015	2 051	68.03	4 064	2 805	69.02	3 264	1 769	54.20

Note: * Legend to voting district numbers: 97960089 – Zwelihle Primary School, 97960078 – Lukhanyo Primary School, 97960146 – Zwelihle Community Hall, 97960135 – Hou Moed Centre, and 97960034 – Qhayiya Secondary School.

Sources: IEC, various windows, www.elections.org.za/ieconline/Reports/National-and-Provincial-reports, http://elections2014.sabc.co.za/elections2014/RaceForVotes.aspx, accessed 20 June 2019

Zwelihle Renewal participated in Election 2019. The Land Party pipped the ANC to the post (Figure 8.2) in the Zwelihle voting district that operated out of Lukhanyo Primary School (54 per cent to the Land Party, compared with the ANC's 40 per cent). In two other Zwelihle voting districts the ANC won narrowly over the Land Party (by 49 versus 46 per cent). Post-election violence between the two parties followed.[55] The ANC's performance over the three elections from 2009 to 2019 in the Zwelihle area was particularly damning: it declined in the five voting districts from 82 to 49, 82 to 40, 91 to 49, 87 to 55, and 84 to 64 per cent (Figure 8.2).

The Hermanus land protests, along with multiple other bottom-up land actions around the country, brought evidence of citizens taking action themselves to get or to take the implemented policy they wanted – land for urban settlement in this instance. This differed from protests where participants relied simply on government stepping in to provide roads, houses, sanitation and electricity. It converged into these protests, nevertheless, in that self-help ensued. Instead of waiting for government housing waiting lists to deliver, and on the basis of land being available in the direct proximity, people took the land and built informal structures. The land protests could be placed on a continuum, therefore, that encapsulated frustration with government inaction or inability to act, and the availability of the type of service or provision – and specifically whether it lent itself to being grabbed or looted.

Figure 8.2: Zwelihle: Party results in five voting districts, Elections 2009–2019

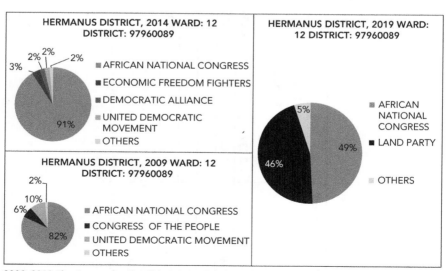

2009–2019 Election results, Zwelihle Primary School, Zwelihle

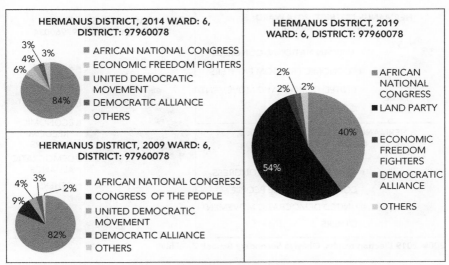

2009–2019 Election results, Lukhanyo Primary School, Zwelihle

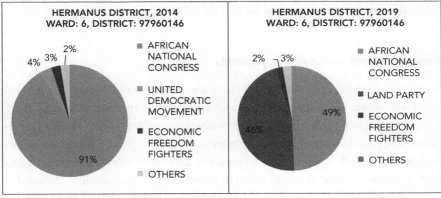

2014–2019 Election results, Zwelihle Community Hall, Zwelihle

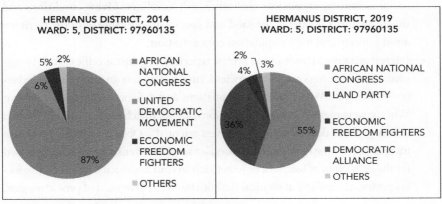

2014–2019 Election results, Hou Moed Centre, Zwelihle

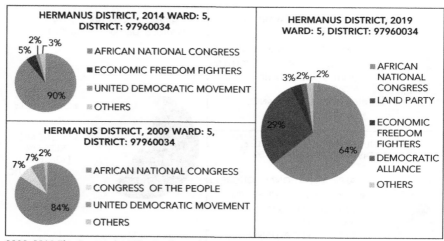

HERMANUS DISTRICT, 2014 WARD: 5, DISTRICT: 97960034
- AFRICAN NATIONAL CONGRESS
- ECONOMIC FREEDOM FIGHTERS
- UNITED DEMOCRATIC MOVEMENT
- OTHERS

HERMANUS DISTRICT, 2009 WARD: 5, DISTRICT: 97960034
- AFRICAN NATIONAL CONGRESS
- CONGRESS OF THE PEOPLE
- UNITED DEMOCRATIC MOVEMENT
- OTHERS

HERMANUS DISTRICT, 2019 WARD: 5, DISTRICT: 97960034
- AFRICAN NATIONAL CONGRESS
- LAND PARTY
- ECONOMIC FREEDOM FIGHTERS
- DEMOCRATIC ALLIANCE
- OTHERS

2009–2019 Election results, Qhayiya Secondary School, Zwelihle

Source: IEC, various windows, www.elections.org.za/ieconline/reports, accessed 20 June 2019
Note: Zwelihle is a growth area; therefore some of the voting districts were only demarcated after the 2009 election. In a December 2020 by-election, the Land Party won Ward 12 with a 56 per cent majority.

Covidpreneurs to Covid-19 protests

Anti-government protest turned full circle when citizens reacted against government incompetence, ineffectiveness and corruption[56] in combating Covid-19. They revolted, too, against raging cadre profiteering and looting of Covid-19 emergency relief funds. Protest and anger mirrored the ravages of poverty, inequality and hunger – while opportunism, criminality and forms of political racketeering and government abuse of power featured prominently. Manifestations included:

- Communities often practised passive resistance against lockdown and the social distancing regulations that came with lockdown. Living conditions and the necessity of queueing for food and special grants came with the territory amid poverty and high population concentration.

- Interest groups and trade union protest repertoires against specific Covid-19 regulations saw teachers and churches, and, later, restaurants and the tourism industry, lobbying the ANC, or using negotiations and defiance to get their own way. When government's Covid-19 regulations did not match the demands of the taxi industry, it was defiant until government relented.[57] Objectives of the protesters included obtaining concessions to conduct services, to ensure that schools closed for the protection of teachers, or to get taxis to load to capacity. Healthcare workers protested regularly at medical facilities for better provision of protective gear, which was also the main focus of irregular procurement contracts. The tobacco and liquor industries protested against illogical and unscientific bans on retailing, using all means from street protests to high-level court action.

- Civil society organisations mobilised proactively for wearing masks, for government to act more effectively against hunger and job losses, and also protested against government looting and mismanagement. The C-19 Coalition combined forces with the Simunye Workers Organisation, the Community Organising Working Group with the campaign Asivikelane (with the calls of 'we must protect each other' and 'we are hungry') and the Casual Workers Advice Office. Protests were dispersed across the country and converged on social media platforms.

- Community protests were subdued in the period of lockdown, given the restrictions on gatherings and community fear of security force violence. There were food protests, such as in Mitchells Plain and Tafelsig in Cape Town, and many land invasion protests, such as in Lawley in the south of Johannesburg and Khayelitsha in Cape Town. Truck protests and looting of the trucks formed part of community efforts to survive in conditions of deprivation.

- Protest came in the form of passive resistance against or monitoring of government for abuse of power. Outcries followed the death of some ten civilians through the security enforcement of lockdown. The actions were triggered by the National Coronavirus Command Council, and the president and Cabinet ceding power to an institution that was not constitutionally mandated. The protest worked through threatened and real court challenges, and the Covid-19 regulations generally. Power was returned (formally at least) to the legitimate bodies.

- There was a revolt across class and community against the ANC-linked political elite benefiting corruptly (or at best inappropriately) through contracting against scarce funds intended to combat the Covid-19 outbreak. The R50 billion emergency health procurement budget was at stake.[58] Protests were realised in some banner-bearing demonstrations, but mostly through public outcries and anger and disillusionment aimed at the ANC.

If there had still been a lingering belief in the authenticity of the Ramaphosa new dawn, Covid corruption ended it. The job losses and re-exposed poverty and hunger flooded the country in what came to be seen as the second pandemic. The ANC would have enjoyed far more credibility had its deployees and high officials, or their families and associates, not been seen as depriving fellow citizens in need of life-sustaining resources.[59] The Covid gravy train threatened to engulf the ANC and become one of the major instances of scandal in the life of the ANC in power.

Government and the ANC suffered lasting injury, despite Ramaphosa's rushing in to counter it with measures such as renewed ANC National Executive Committee commitments to definitive action against corruption, the creation of a hub for investigative and prosecutorial functions, and the Ramaphosa ANC owning up and warning that corrupt conduct contributes

> ... to a perception and a culture of nepotism, favouritism and abuse. And it undermines public confidence in the integrity of our institutions and processes ... Those found to have broken the law to enrich themselves through this crisis will not get to enjoy their spoils, regardless of who they are or with whom they may be connected.[60]

CONTINUUM OF PROTEST ACTION

Community or citizen protest is deeply anchored in the socio-economics of poverty and deprivation and the politics of getting a dominant and entrenched party to deliver better. The socio-economic roots of protest metamorphosed. Deprived, angry and frustrated citizens did not merely express anger and ask by protesting – when it was within their reach, they also appropriated the services (such as urban land) or turned to judicial institutions over the head of their government. Through their actions, they established the policies that they believed ought to be in place. Between the continuum end-points of 'ask-agitate for' and 'make-take', there were many possible combinations and degrees of expression and action.

Much of public policy was being made through protest. Protests about service delivery were examples of the 'take', which usually followed after years of asking and peacefully protesting for the services to be delivered, and hoping for jobs that would enable them to pay for the services. In the absence of affordable delivery, growing networks of citizens pirated services, tapping into electricity connections or redirecting water.[61] Rates payments were comparable; e-toll protests were in the same category. Land, as in the case study, was a 'take-make' policy – without drastic community action, there would have been a long-enduring cycle of probably fruitless negotiations with the local council.

The truck protests (symbolised by but not confined to the Mooi River case) asserted policy in the wake of government inaction in a contested, sensitive area of Afrophobia and jobs. Associations of truck drivers operated to enforce change. Communities organising and attacking (looting) foreign-owned shops was another variant of de facto policy-making. Citizens were hoping for government to change policy and proscribe foreign economic involvement, and government acted in small and mostly subtle ways, trying to foster social tolerance and issuing statements about South Africans not being xenophobic.

Looting objectives were manifest in many of the variants of socio-economic-political protest. They never surfaced as the primary objective, but the bulk of the protests unfolded in disadvantaged and poor communities, where much reason and rationalisation existed for feeling and showing anger about historical and ongoing injustice. It would be exceedingly difficult for government to condemn and punish such de facto laws of restitution.

Community self-asserted policy-making came against the backdrop of government not having done more to correct problems, and government had to tolerate much of the self-help and supplementary action, for without empathy and tolerance many more would become alienated from the ANC.

Government had to receive 'help' (be corrected in acting against community interests and favouring commercial exploitation) from communities involved in the preservation of their right to live on the sites of natural resources. The protest victories of the Xolobeni[62] community in the Eastern Cape and the ongoing struggles of Empembeni in KwaZulu-Natal[63] spoke to protest equating with the fight for livelihood. It took widespread organised protest and court action to halt fracking for gas extraction in the ecologically sensitive Karoo. The Treasure Karoo Action Group was a key player in bringing the Supreme Court of Appeal to rule that the ministers of mineral resources and environmental affairs did not have the authority to implement the regulations for petroleum exploration and production, including shale gas exploration.[64] These protests were not for services, for a promised school to be delivered,[65] or for access to land – the communities were pitched against their own government, and often against the Department of Mineral Resources, which had been siding with mining and commercial operations against the local interest in the name of 'development'.

Protest against government acting against community interest by plan (rather than by neglect, such as in basic services) emerged when workers protested against actual or anticipated job losses, even before the Covid jobs bloodbath. Cosatu, the National Education, Health and Allied Workers' Union and other unions protested against the unbundling and/or privatisation of Eskom and South African Airways, which came with job losses.[66] The action was complicated because of state-owned enterprise institutional failures and prospects of the whole institution collapsing and shedding all jobs. The times of Covid-19 also asserted new rules for government which was increasingly being forced into reconsidering its interface with citizens and exercising its duties with improved accountability.

CONCLUSION: INSTITUTIONALISATION OF POPULISM

Politics became the theatre of both direct action and non-electoral protest against the governing party. There was no assumption that electing a political party into power and gaining representatives in the public institutions would lead to interests being served and promises fulfilled within specified periods of time. Politics had become far more layered and continuously bartered. Citizens often had to work for such representation of interests to happen. Protest became institutionalised, as in the supplementary-to-elections action to ensure that representatives and their appointed officials prioritised the specific needs of the particular community. It happened at both national and local levels – and ranged from passive placard demonstrations to arson and force. The protests were not necessarily antagonistic to the ANC government, although many of them were violent and destructive.

It was part of a new order of things. This form of populism was the order of the day, but not to the exclusion of mainstream, institutional and representative electoral politics. It became the way to help achieve representation, the means to help push through policy rapidly or to get authorities to fast-track policy-making and, especially, implementation. This repertoire was so effective, and *seen to be effective*, that it became 'institutionalised' in its own right.

Such populism was part of democracy as it existed in South Africa a quarter of a century past the moment of political liberation. The Constitution endorsed electoral democracy, participatory democracy and the right to protest – but protest also supplanted these formal aspects of political participation and governance. With high levels of ongoing legitimation of the former liberation movement, and continuous delegitimation of opposition parties, citizens often preferred the supplementary instrument of protest which allowed them to assert opposition and rebellion without removing a liberation icon from power. The result was precarious power.

NOTES

1   The ANC's NGC 2021 discussion documents conceded this point. See Umrabulo Special Edition, NGC 2020, Discussion Documents, p. 139: '...our people no longer belief [sic] we have *"good plans to create jobs and change the economy"*'.
2   The pointed phrase emerged in the study by K. von Holdt, M. Langa, S. Molapo, N. Mogapi, K. Ngubeni, J. Dlamini and A. Kirsten, 2011, *The Smoke that Calls: Insurgent Citizenship, Collective Violence and the Struggle for a Place in the New South Africa*, Johannesburg: Centre for the Study of Violence and Reconciliation, Social Work Development Institute.

3   In the Nelson Mandela Bay twin communities of Asinavalo and Nomakanjani, protests did work – and both communities received their electricity; see Nosipiwo Manona, 'A protest pays off', *City Press*, 28 April 2019.

4   Susan Booysen, 2007, 'With the ballot and the brick … The politics of service delivery in South Africa', *Progress in Development Studies*, 7 (1), 21–22; Susan Booysen, 2009, 'Power through the ballot and the brick', in The *ANC and the Regeneration of Political Power*, Johannesburg: Wits University Press, pp. 126–173, and Susan Booysen, 2015, 'ANC in the cauldron of protest', in *Dominance and Decline: The ANC in the Time of Zuma*, Johannesburg: Wits University Press, pp. 261–291, which first conceptualised this dual repertoire.

5   Quote from unnamed woman in a community protest, shown in SABC-TV3 news broadcast 3 September 2019. Yethu Dlamini and Asanda Mathlare, 5 July 2019, 'Soweto residents take to the streets', *Business Day*, 5 July 2019. These sketch the unfolding sequences in these protests.

6   About 80 per cent of urban land belongs to companies (e.g. mining companies) or is held in trust by government on behalf of black communities. See, for example, South African Cities Network, 2015, The Urban Land Paper Series, Volume 1, https://www.google.com/search?sxsrf=ACYBGNS_mFdj9khlQA6ftpsaTcKP32LfEw%3A1571730888085&-source, accessed 1 July 2018; Kevin Mwanza, Thomson Reuters Foundation, 4 July 2018, 'South Africa's "dispossessed" urban poor call for land reform', https://www.moneyweb.co.za/news-fast-news/south-africas-dispossessed-urban-poor-call-for-land-reform/, accessed 8 July 2018.

7   These urban settlement practices played out against the background that roughly two-thirds of the South African population was urbanised. See David Gardner, April 2018, *South African Urbanisation Review: Analysis of the Human Settlement Programme and Subsidy Instruments*, National Treasury. Data projections indicate that by 2050 urbanisation will be approximately 80 per cent.

8   Musa Gwebani (Social Justice Coalition): 'The declaration that there will be expropriation without compensation fuelled a hunger for land and brought to the fore the levels of desperation of the dispossessed black majority'; see *BusinessLive*, 5 July 2018, 'SA's slum dwellers losing patience: Rising protests and land invasions signal people have had enough', https://www.businesslive.co.za/bd/national/2018-07-05-sas-slum-dwellers-losing-patience/, accessed 7 October 2020.

9   Ian Palmer, Susan Parnell and Nishendra Moodley, 2017, *Building a Capable State: Service Delivery in Post-Apartheid South Africa*, London: Zed Books, illustrates these processes.

10 Zama-zamas are illegal artisanal miners.

11 Statistics vary as to the exact scope of foreigner presence: StatsSA in its 2011 census set the figure at 2.2 million; the 2016 StatsSA Community Survey estimated 1.5 million; UN figures for 2017 said 4 million.

12 The phenomenon is illustrated in *City Press*, 18 August 2018, 'Police behave badly as looters invade'.

13 The Human Rights Commission conducted an inquiry on attacks of foreign nationals in the truck-driving industry, 10 to 12 March 2020, and confirmed the large scope.

14 Cekeshe, a University of the Witwatersrand student, had been in prison since December 2017. He had been convicted and sentenced to eight years (three suspended) for public violence and malicious damage to property concerning setting a police vehicle alight during a #FeesMustFall protest in 2016.

15 Minister Naledi Pandor, 8 August 2018, in answer to written questions, Parliament of South Africa, Cape Town.

16 See Don Makatile, 'Where zama-zamas rule', *Sunday Independent*, 11 August 2019.

17 Peter Alexander, Carin Runciman, Trevor Ngwane, Boikanyo Moloto, Kgothatso Mokgele and Nicole van Staden, 2018, 'Frequency and turmoil – South Africa's community protests 2005–2017', *SA Crime Quarterly*, 63, 27–42, analyse details of these trends.

18 Susan Booysen, 'Zebra stripes, leopard spots and the troubled king of the political jungle – the ANC of 2019', *Daily Maverick*, 24 July 2018, https://www.dailymaverick.co.za/opinionista/2018-07-24-zebra-stripes-leopard-spots-and-the-troubled-king-of-the-political-jungle-the-anc-of-2019/, accessed 25 July 2018, highlights the variations on this theme.

19 The focus group study by Susan Booysen, 2013, *Twenty Years of South African Democracy: Citizen Views of Human Rights, Governance and the Political System*, Washington, DC and Johannesburg: Freedom House, unpacks the citizen narratives on this theme. See also Jane Duncan, 2016, *Protest Nation: The Right to Protest in South Africa*, Pietermaritzburg: UKZN Press; and Julian Brown, 2015, *South Africa's Insurgent Citizens: On Dissent and the Possibility of Politics*, London: Zed Books.

20 This observation was confirmed in research by the HSRC; interview with principal researcher, 4 February 2019.

21 See Susan Booysen, 2007, op. cit.

22 Marí Harris, April 2019, *The People's Agenda*, presentation, Ipsos South Africa, Johannesburg.

23 Susan Booysen, 2011, *The ANC and the Regeneration of Political Power*, Johannesburg: Wits University Press; 2015, op. cit.

24 Other cases in the Mapungubwe Institute for Strategic Reflection (Mistra) study, beyond the scope of the current report, assess cases of longer-term and ongoing protests along with their associated patterns of voting. See Susan Booysen (ed.), 2019, *Voting Trends 25 Years into Democracy: Analysis of South Africa's 2019 Election*, Special report, Mapungubwe Institute for Strategic Reflection, Johannesburg. The author expresses her thanks to Nkoe Montja for his help in extracting the statistics.

25 Author's observation while working with SABC television teams, crossing in elections of 2014 and 2016 to multiple protest hotspots. On these, election day turnout would be moderated, but elections would proceed without interruption. Voters were not obstructed when they wished to cast their ballots.

26 Major-general Zeph Mkhwanazi, as quoted in *The Citizen*, 20 March 2019, 'Unrest can mar polls'.

27 Parts of this section draw on the Mistra publication edited by Susan Booysen, 2019, op. cit.

28 Each of the case studies starts with a brief outline of the nature of the protest, followed by the 2019 results on turnout and party support in voting districts at the heart of and in the immediate environment of the protests. The Alexandra analysis is based on the details of two wards, containing ten voting districts; Kraaipan on one ward and four voting districts; Ganyesa on two wards and five voting districts; Ivory Park on two wards and eight voting districts; and Vuwani on two wards and eight voting districts. These voting district selections were performed recognising that protests often cross the boundaries of specific wards and voting districts, both in terms of issues and participants. The selections took into account the locations of the protests, and the communities that were most directly affected. See also Booysen, 2019, op. cit.

29 Ntwaagae Seleka, 'Feud in Ivory Park over illegal electricity, residents threaten to blow up substation', *News24*, 1 August 2019, https://www.news24.com/SouthAfrica/News/

feud-in-ivory-park-over-illegal-electricity-residents-threaten-to-blow-up-substation-20190801, accessed 1 June 2019.

30   The Ngaka Modiri Molema district municipality, along with Kagisano-Molopo, Ramotshere Moiloa, Ditsobotla, Kgetlengrivier, Maquassi Hills, Naledi and Mahikeng local municipalities were placed under administration under section 139(1)(b) of the Constitution, and section 137 of the Municipal Finance Management Act soon after Supra Mahumapelo's 2018 removal as premier of North West.

31   See, for example, Ngwako Modjadji, 'Makhado task team demands cash for elections', *City Press*, 7 April 2019.

32   In the early mobilisation period, starting in late 2015, the big city protests against Zuma's dismissal of finance minister Pravin Gordhan were overwhelmingly white and with high DA presences. This changed over time.

33   See, for example, the definitive details in Amabhungane Centre for Investigative Journalism, 2017, #GuptaLeaks, digital=amabhungane.org@mail13.atl11.rsgsv.net, http://amabhungane.co.za/article/2016-09-23-two-to-tango-the-story-of-zuma-and-the-guptas, accessed 24 September 2016.

34   See Susan Booysen, 2018, 'The African National Congress and its transfer of power from Zuma to Ramaphosa: The intraparty-multiparty nexus', *Transformation*, 98, 1–26.

35   Susan Booysen, 2018, 'Hegemonic struggles of the African National Congress: From cacophony of morbid symptoms to strained renewal', *Africa Spectrum*, 2/2018, 1–31.

36   Among the many participants were church organisations, reminiscent of mobilisation in the 1980s. See, for example, South African Council of Churches (SACC), 18 May 2017, SACC Report to the Church Public on the Unburdening Panel Process, Regina Mundi Church, Soweto, http://sacc.org.za/news/sacc-report-church-public-unburdening-panel-process-regina-mundi-church-soweto-may-18-2017/, accessed 21 May 2017.

37   An earlier march, of February 2016, had been countered and minimised by the State Security Agency – as evidenced in the High Level Panel on Fundamental Change, November 2017, *Report of the High Level Panel on the Assessment of Key Legislations and the Acceleration of Fundamental Change*, p. 66: 'During the February 2016 State of the Nation Address the unit was "able to infiltrate and penetrate the leadership structure" of the movement against the then president. Indications were that more than 5,000 people would march on Parliament, but with efficient and effective countering actions, and the dissemination of "disinformation" to supporters, only approximately 50 anti-president supporters attended the march.'

38   Susan Booysen, 2015, *Dominance and Decline: The ANC in the Time of Zuma*, Johannesburg: Wits University Press, gives the context of this designation.

39   See South Gauteng High Court, Johannesburg, *Motswana and Others v African National Congress and Others* (35398/18) [2019] ZAGPJHC 4 (6 February 2019), Saflii database, http://www.saflii.org/za/cases/ZAGPJHC/2019/4.html, accessed 7 October 2020.

40   Mahumapelo and his supporters argued that the ANC National Executive Committee had disregarded a report by ANC deployee Obed Bapela: he warned against disbanding the provincial leadership. They further argued that the ANC had not consulted its leadership and members in North West and had failed to give reasons for disbanding the Provincial Executive Committee.

41   Extended and updated from Susan Booysen, 'The Mooi River truck protests – rewired citizen revolt', *Daily Maverick*, 2 May 2018, https://www.dailymaverick.co.za/opinionista/2018-05-02-the-mooi-river-truck-protests-rewired-citizen-revolt/, accessed 2 May 2018.

42   The All Truck Drivers Forum reported that foreign nationals accept R8 000 net salary per month, while South African drivers expect employers to pay R20 000, which includes a meal allowance, sleep-out and overtime.

43   See Poloko Tau, 'Riding the killer highway', *City Press*, 18 June 2019.

44   Jan Bornman, 'Trucking violence blamed on high unemployment', *New Frame*, 11 March 2020, https://www.newframe.com/trucking-violence-blamed-on-high-unemployment/, accessed 14 March 2020.

45   Truck operators/owners explained that the non-English-speaking country origins of loads that go to the Durban port often rely on the drivers' ability to speak French or Portuguese.

46   Fanele Mhlongo, '54 people to appear in court for torching of trucks', *SABC News*, 2 May 2018, http://www.sabcnews.com/sabcnews/54-people-appear-court-torching-trucks/; and 'Six Mooi River suspects to appear in court for looting', *SABC News*, 7 May 2018, http://www.sabcnews.com/sabcnews/six-mooi-river-suspects-to-appear-in-court-for-looting/, accessed 3 May 2018.

47   *SABC News*, 30 April 2018, 'Nzimande slams Mooi River Toll Plaza violence', http://www.sabcnews.com/sabcnews/l-nzimande-slams-mooi-river-toll-plaza-violence/, quoting then MEC Mxolisi Kaunda, accessed 3 May 2018.

48   Daniel Hartford, 2018, 'Who belongs? Understanding urban land and violence in Hermanus', in Malose Langa and Daniel Hartford (eds), *Urban Land and the Genesis of Violence*, Cape Town: Centre for the Study of Violence and Reconciliation, p. 19.

49   On 22 March 2018, about 15 women from Kwasa Kwasa, Zwelihle, marched on the nearby Overstrand municipal offices. They had been paying high rentals on small backyard dwellings attached to Reconstruction and Development Programme homes, and were frustrated at the lack of services when their landlords failed to pay rates and electricity. They demanded serviced land to build their own homes. They were turned away – and the next day a large group of peaceful protesters returned to the municipality.

50   This refers to the Red Ant security company that focuses on 'Relocation & Eviction Services'; see https://red-ants.co.za/, accessed 18 March 2020.

51   Raphael da Silva, 25 February 2020, 'Schulphoek housing progress delayed', https://the-villagenews.co.za/schulphoek-housing-progress-delayed/, accessed 19 March 2020.

52   By law, the municipality was not permitted to buy back the land directly; hence it was bought back from Rabcav (a joint venture of Cape Theme Parks and Cavcor) by the Western Cape provincial government, at a price of roughly R34 million (in a complex deal, of which many of the developmental details of the original sales contract remained disputed). See also 'Schulphoek deal was above board', *Property 360*, 30 September 2010, http://www.iolproperty.co.za/roller/news/entry/schulphoek_deal_was_above_board, accessed 2 October 2019. An investigation by the Western Cape government found that no laws had been broken, despite the fact that the property was sold to Rabcav for R5.3 million (effective price out of a total purchase amount of roughly R24 million), while the municipal value was set at R29 million and the market value estimated at R200 million.

53   Unless otherwise referenced, this section is based on the author's monitoring study of land reform in the Greater Hermanus and Overstrand areas, 2017–2020, done through observation and interviews.

54   See Ndzongana, as quoted in Bianca du Plessis, 'Zwelihle power struggles', *Hermanus Times*, 26 September 2019.

55 These results were reminiscent of the December 2017 by-election developments in Metsimaholo in the northern Free State where the SACP contested on its own. The ANC percentage vote fell dramatically: in Ward 4 (Refengkgotso Phomolong) from 70 to 44 per cent; in Ward 1 (Zamdela Amelia) from 66 to 40 per cent; and in Ward 3 (Refengkgotso Deneysville) from 55 to 35 per cent. The SACP won a proportional representation seat.

56 For an overview, see Richard Poplak, 'Covid-19 brought us to the edge of the abyss; Ramaphosa's ANC goes a step further', *Daily Maverick*, 30 July 2020, https://www.dailymaverick.co.za/article/2020-07-30-covid-19-brought-us-to-the-edge-of-the-abyss-ramaphosas-anc-goes-a-step-further/, accessed 3 August 2020.

57 Taxis are powerful because they do 70 per cent of South Africa's commuter transport, and many of the operators enter into deals with the ANC, including transport of voters on election days. Only 60 per cent of taxis are formally registered.

58 Inflation of contract prices was a prominent form of the associated corruption at the higher end, and at the lower the acts included theft of food parcels and water from emergency water trucks.

59 State departments were allowed emergency procurement whereby they could deviate from normal legal processes although National Treasury guidelines were still to be followed. In amounts, the Covid contracts ranged from less than a million to hundreds of millions.

60 Cyril Ramaphosa, 3 August 2020, 'From the Desk of the President', http://www.thepresidency.gov.za/from-the-desk-of-the-president/desk-president%2C-monday%2C-03-august-2020, accessed 3 August 2020.

61 This is not to deny that many citizens could afford to pay but latched onto the for-free services.

62 Sam Sole, 'Xolobeni: The mine, the murder, the DG – and many unanswered questions', for amaBhungane, 30 June 2019, https://www.dailymaverick.co.za/article/2019-06-30-xolobeni-the-mine-the-murder-the-dg-and-many-unanswered-questions/, accessed 2 July 2019; Lucas Ledwaba, 'We will fight for this land', *City Press*, 7 April 2019.

63 See Sizwe Yende, 'KZN's killing fields', *City Press*, 10 February 2019; and 'eMpembeni killings spike after cops leave', *City Press*, 19 May 2019, https://city-press.news24.com/News/empembeni-killings-spike-after-cops-leave-20190518, accessed 26 October 2019.

64 The Department of Mineral Resources would then be required to go back and draft a set of appropriate regulations. In the interim, Shell, one of the companies that would have embarked on this type of hydraulic fracturing, pulled back from Karoo fracking when a study found that gas in the area had been dissipated by underground heat sources and had been reduced from the expected 485 trillion cubic feet (Tcf) to about 13Tcf; see Kevin Brandt, 'Ruling on Karoo fracking a victory for environment, says action group', *Eyewitness News*, 5 July 2019, https://ewn.co.za/2019/07/05/ruling-on-karoo-fracking-a-victory-for-environment-says-action-group, accessed 6 July 2019.

65 Parents at the Durban Deep Primary School in Roodepoort took hostages at the school after non-delivery on government promises to build a new school; see *Roodepoort Record*, 'School shut down', 22 February 2019.

66 Eskom was known to be hugely overstaffed, after a decade of disproportionate job growth; see Bloomberg, 'Eskom's massive workforce problem: Over-staffed and over-paid', *Business Tech*, 3 April 2018, https://businesstech.co.za/news/business/235299/eskoms-massive-workforce-problem-over-staffed-and-over-paid/, accessed 4 April 2018.

9

Parallel Power, Shedding Power and Staying in Power

DEMOCRACY IN TIMES OF TROUBLE AND DEEP ENTRENCHMENT

Democracy in South Africa in the time of my analysis was evolving, through parallelism to the supplementation and substitution of institutions and processes ordinarily associated with constitutional and participatory democracy. Simultaneously, seemingly contradictorily, constitutionally mandated institutions were affirmed by many. The country's multipartyism was celebrated, even if citizens also found it inadequate.[1] Participation in elections was down, but elections were endorsed as the best way to determine political leadership. ANC rule was being augmented, as if citizens and voters were trying to find reasons to keep the former liberation movement party, turned governing party, in power.

The coronavirus struck and the world and South Africa were affected, severely and adversely. Politics was going to be different. The ANC government would need immense credibility and popular trust to see the way through the economic fallout of the Covid-19 crisis – and yet 2020 onwards was a time in which the ANC's trust renewal through erstwhile Ramaphoria and new dawn-ism were crushed through the Covid looting crisis on top of state coffers that had been running dry. The presence of the new ANC elite greed was confirmed precisely when the state of poverty, and human suffering, were being re-exposed. Although the ANC promised serially to deliver the purified version of itself, popular cynicism mounted, with reason.

The combination of Covid-19 hardship and ANC cadre corruption evoked a colossal crisis in the ANC and its government. The question was whether the country's fundamentals, as I have outlined in this volume, would be sufficient to predict the road ahead. Or were the crisis and fallout of Covid-and-corruption (or even just Covid-19 on its own) so severe that known political life would also be a thing of the past? The reality falls in-between. The fundamentals of ANC tenacity and resilience would be affected, and the effects were likely to unfold along the lines mapped in this volume. The ANC would bleed further trust and support, partially redeemable by the time of the next set of national election campaigns. Opposition parties were unlikely to be embraced as alternatives. The ANC, organisationally and as government, was likely to remain in a volatile but symbiotic relationship with popular forces that extracted and bartered policy and delivery on their own terms. ANC perseverance would depend, more than in the past, on the actions of supplementary and parallel institutions that helped it to govern. This was a fragile stability, and it would last for as long as the ANC held the resources to afford such delivery and simultaneously keep content its vast public sector and its grant recipient constituency.

The quality of ANC power, overall and as outlined in this book, was precarious. In conditions of lower electoral participation, the ANC, with a clearly outright national majority, retained a critical and substantial edge over other political parties but the power was fragile because President Cyril Ramaphosa had bought time for the ANC, persuading the electorate that the 'new dawn ANC' was not a phantom party. As evidence started accumulating that the ANC had not fundamentally changed, Ramaphosa intervened by the spring of 2020, promising decisive action once again. The chances for his promises to be realised were questionable, which by summer 2020 had lost much of their credibility. But although ANC support was brittle, none of the existing or emerging opposition parties was strong enough to catch up.[2] Growing voter cynicism and criticism of the ANC were finding a footing in alternative and supplementary politics like protest and rebellious self-government, rather than in moving to the opposition. The ANC was being kept in power, but the texture and quality of the base was fundamentally different, and very precarious, compared with the times of relatively unquestioned ANC legitimacy and hegemony.

The ANC's hold on the state was contentious. Parallel processes regularly eclipsed core operations. Many of the core and strategic institutions were malfunctioning, through to corruption and capture that did not stop at the formal ending of the Zuma order. Many state institutions and state-owned enterprises were damaged through poor capacity and public officials who prioritised the private entrepreneurship applications of public funds over optimising service to the people. The state apparatuses had to be cleaned up and realigned to the envisaged Ramaphosa order. Yet clean-up progress was impeded by ANC organisational accusations that factionalism undergirded purges, evidence that corruption spanned the factions, and the indecisive character of ANC disciplinary procedures.

The ANC was catching up continuously in making policy to address popular needs. Citizens, through protest action, had acquired the skill of appropriating policy-making windows of opportunity and asserting de facto policies ground-up, while the ANC organisationally and as government was often otherwise preoccupied, caught up in ANC battles that had permeated the state. Policy hiatuses resulted when the ANC used policy as a proxy war for leadership contests and radical ideological narratives as bait to lure voters. The ANC was a precarious policy patron because it balanced needs for (radical) policy that would bring more change faster with procedurally conservative government processes and a fiscus on the brink of depletion, in conditions of a faltering economy and Covid-related crimes.

Above all, the ANC was organisationally in a precarious state because it depended on factional unity. The factions were a fusion of the two basic groups, with split-offs, defections and mutations filling the gaps. Such unity dictated considerable tolerance of transgressions and alleged misdeeds in dealing with public money and positions – but this contradicted the electoral mandate the ANC had received. The ANC gambled with that majority, straining its latitude to ask for future endorsements.

This book has explored the amalgam of contradictions that surrounded the phenomenon of a strong but fragile ANC. My objective was to unravel and synthesise the ANC's place and role in contemporary South African politics. To do this, my analysis looked beyond the constructs of post-liberation politics, the conventional lines of liberal democracy, ordinary multipartyism and possible party rotation, the state as simple instrument of political power, or popular protest as an alternative to mainstream political participation. It assessed, in essence, the dynamics of what was happening in South Africa in the politics of party and state, in the aftermath of guaranteed dominance, when the predominant party acted erratically but the people were not ready to replace it – at least, not with another political party.

PRECARIOUS POWER IN RUPTURE-PRONE, POST-HEGEMONIC TIMES

The chapters in *Precarious Power* have focused on the ANC, and the ANC in government, in the period since December 2015. The epoch started when former president Jacob Zuma overstepped a mark of political probity beyond the ample ANC toleration levels. The tide started turning until it ruptured, away from outright Zuma-ism, in 2017–2018. This volume is the third in a trilogy of analyses of the ANC in its time of declining hegemony.[3] The ANC had moved beyond the point where it could rely unambiguously on consent and the unquestioning loyalty of citizens and, specifically, its supporters. There was a decline in people's positive affirmation of the rightness of being ruled by this former liberation movement that had turned into governing party, sustaining itself in power for over a quarter of a century. Antonio Gramsci links hegemony to the ways in which a governing power wins consent to its rule from those it subjugates.[4] As Valeriano Ramos argues, grounded on the Gramscian base, in hegemonic predominance by consent a fundamental class exercises a political, intellectual and moral role of leadership which is held together by a common world view or organic ideology.[5] The details in this volume show that these were not the conditions in which ANC rule was unfolding at the time of writing.

This book has presented details of the configuration of Cyril Ramaphosa's conflicted dual presidency of the ANC and of the country. Contradictions and constraints abounded. There was cross-factional ideological delegitimation by the ANC's metamorphosing factions.[6] The ANC survived Election 2019 while multiple undercurrents were, nationally and provincially, eroding the foundations of the party-movement's majorities. State capture-related disorganisation in state administration, corruption (as a co-optive, patronage dispersing measure), and delegitimation of ANC clean-up operations undermined state authority. The ANC's political and government's fiscal sustainability depended on success with corruption clean-up, besides being at the mercy of national and global economic crises.

These were inverse correlates of ANC hegemonic power: the bases of ANC power were all fragile and challenged by, for example, parallel streams of organisational and state power. Yet the ANC retained a fairly firm hold on power. There was no opposition party that challenged it. Opposition parties were weakening, either in stature or in electoral support, as the ANC was reaching *its* weakest moment in its period of governance from 1994 onwards. With Ramaphosa's entrance, the ANC received popular endorsement to be a substantially more ethical ANC – which was soon ruptured by unrelenting old and new party elites who thrived amid irresolute party action.[7] In comparison, the removal from power of a discredited president of the party and the state, and the steps to clean up at least some of the corruption-infested and often dysfunctional state institutions, were among the acts of potential hegemonic renewal. The actions were challenged by forces within the ANC. There was nothing singular and simple in the relationship between counter-hegemonic and pro-hegemonic indicators: some of the actions to renew hegemony (such as cutting the co-optive corruption link) could in turn elicit fractious intra-organisational effects. The spawning of parallel power operations in politics was telling as to the character of the post-hegemonic ANC. Commissions of inquiry and courts, themselves not always beyond reproach, were helping to dissect the right from the wrong when the ANC itself was too paralysed, conflicted and compromised to extract itself from the morass of enforced 'indecision', policy uncertainty and factional warfare.

The ANC's descent from hegemonic status was marked neither by a straight line of decline, nor by consistent decline over all four fronts of power. *The ANC and the Regeneration of Political Power* had set the base of how the ANC operated to maintain itself in power. *Dominance and Decline: The ANC in the Time of Zuma* took stock of the ANC through many of the lows of disgrace that the party-movement suffered. The cut-off point of *Dominance and Decline*, late-2015, was the exact time of the ANC's starting to come to terms with political life beyond Zuma in the interest of 'self-correction'.[8] Its legitimacy would depend on rebuilding a base beyond patronage and rotational drinking from the trough.

Much had changed in the time the Zuma-ists were in power, including popular political culture, beliefs in and practice of democracy, and trust in political leaders and state institutions. Come the time of Ramaphosa's ANC it was in some respects a different world in which the ANC was operating, compared with a mere decade earlier. The strongest precondition, at this time of analysis, for the ANC remaining in power, was internal to the ANC: as long as it could maintain inter-factional unity, with a credible face of integration, supported by credible state-level governance, and evidence of ethics in governance, it could maintain itself in power. Below this level of power, however, there was a wealth of countering trends, parallel and populist politics that constituted subaltern or alternative worlds of power, where the ANC was defied and confronted. This political underworld, fathomed in this book, could override the above-surface dynamics. It could pull the ANC down. On the popular front non-institutional politics had become ingrained, suited to a political world where discontent with the ANC was expressed through protest rather than voting.

The ANC, in this post-hegemonic time, was declining in power on all four fronts[9] that defined its political prominence – organisationally, in relation to the people, in the state and in elections. Many hegemonic, consensual, affirmative elements persisted, yet there was no longer widespread popular trust that the ANC and the state institutions under its control were vestiges of goodwill and competence, or could reinvent themselves to achieve this status. The system was not necessarily condemned through explicit action and agitation, or by the choice of another political party. Rather, citizens went their own way increasingly, made de facto policies, as far as possible saw to their own governance, executed self-help of services and ignored many of the rules of the system, while depending, nevertheless, on a massive state social security system (that was linked to a stressed fiscus). They frequently created their own political worlds. A subaltern layer of politics and political action was fostered. In important respects it challenged and changed the ANC's predominant system of politics.

PARALLELISM AND DUALITY SOLIDIFYING AS SIDE EFFECT OF ANC PREDOMINANCE

Parallelism in multiple formations was an important part of the ANC's precarious power, especially from 2015 onwards. The factional contestation mutated and continued to predominate, constituting one of multiple layers of leadership, parallel governance and policy-making. Parallelism confirmed the decline of the ANC's predominance in society, while its electoral dominance remained, albeit in damaged and volatile form. As citizens and voters became discontented with the partial or compromised fruits of ANC rule and promised rehabilitation, they looked for alternatives and found their options in alternative layers of political action. Some withdrew and observed as the ANC, through its apparatuses of political influence, reminded them of the great deeds of its anti-apartheid struggles and of ongoing battles against the legacies of apartheid and colonialism. These big occurrences resonated in lived experiences, besides the narrative serving the ANC's project of regenerating power.

The people continued relating to the ANC and as a result rebellion was often not channelled into other political parties. The opposition parties assisted the ANC to retain its own base as they often lacked credibility and were not synchronised to demands for authenticity in terms of changing postcolonial and racially affirmative nationalism[10] (as in the case of the Democratic Alliance), or leaders (such as those of the Economic Freedom Fighters) showing themselves to be as corrupt and conflicted as their worst ANC opponents. *Internal ANC fallout* that led to splits – subsequent to the Congress of the People (Cope), which had registered resistance against the rise of Jacob Zuma – had lost traction. The Cope dissidents could not overcome the ANC counter-assault and in due course many returned to the ANC. In light of the ANC's edging closer to losing outright electoral majorities, splitting it again would spell minority electoral status. ANC factions preferred living together in acrimony to being in an ostensibly cold world beyond.

Parallelism in the ANC, *internally and organisationally*, followed. Although the Ramaphosa-ists had won at Nasrec they were tied into a unity accord with

269

their internal opponents. There were no guarantees that the Zuma-ists would not still try to subvert the Ramaphosa-ists, in whose name and reputation the 2019 electoral victory had been won. But around the mid-term point of 2020, factions were realigning and no other ANC leader was equalling Ramaphosa's popular ratings, even if those wavered. The formation of the co-governance (organisational and state) arrangements between the two predominant factions was giving rise to new power interests, for example, in the Gauteng and KwaZulu-Natal provinces. Where the National Executive Committee and Provincial Executive Committees were cooperating to counter corruption and capture, such as in the eThekwini municipality, previous ANC power blocs were rearranged and possibilities grew for fewer levels of internal parallel operations. Some in the Zuma faction felt free to experiment with factional realignment.[11] In the powerful KwaZulu-Natal province, new ANC unity arose with a view to ensuring the rise of a new-generation ANC top leader.

The futility of splitting was evident in the actions of the ANC's Tripartite Alliance members, the Congress of South African Trade Unions (Cosatu) and the South African Communist Party (SACP), which were loath to forfeit inside-track influence and powerful deployment prospects for opposing the ANC electorally. In 2015, in conditions of anti-Zuma fallout, Cosatu expelled the National Union of Metalworkers of South Africa (Numsa) and Numsa ventured into electoral politics through the United Front in the Eastern Cape 2016 local elections, and next via the 2019 elections nationally with the Socialist Revolutionary Workers Party (SRWP). By 2019 ANC–Cosatu relations had thawed, and the SRWP failed to win a parliamentary seat. The SACP's threat over time to 'go it alone' in elections – which had surfaced ritually since the late 1990s – did not deliver much.[12] There was only one case of the SACP actually entering elections, in late 2017, just before the Zuma-ists lost at Nasrec, when the SACP contested in general by-elections in the Metsimaholo municipality, Free State, and won a proportional representation seat.

These trends of parallelism were reflected in broader engagements in political society and in the ANC as ruling party in government. Rather than channel dissatisfaction into electoral and party politics, citizens reinforced demands for improvements in delivery and policy change in protest action, across class and culture, into self-help or self-make of services and policy. The actions did not supersede all formal government processes, but were used as complementary, at the community level. They were also domain-specific. Citizens anticipated and pre-empted government policy-making and implementation (on land reform, for example). In local-area service delivery and payment for services, or electronic e-toll payment in Gauteng, they asserted policy through self-help and non-payment. Lower and working classes often justified these 'policies' with reference to the ANC, the patrons of the 'parent state',[13] which had not been delivering the promised land of jobs and income.

Practitioners of such policy-making still accepted government authority and actions in many other areas of political life. The parallelism did not cover all important areas of politics but occurred as targeted action in specific domains. It was enough neverthe-less to indicate further cracks in ANC hegemony. On the ANC redemption side, other parties were not trusted sufficiently to take over, but the people corrected ANC policy for the governing party, and thus forged a transactional relationship, telling the ANC, in effect: allow this policy, work to give more; as a result there will be more pro-ANC votes, and protest will not be escalated to demand a change of government.

My analysis also dissects the parallelism in state operations, arguably the most disempowering of all ANC power holdings. Crucial, strategic parts of the state became potent shadow states within the state.[14] The capture network of the Gup-tas,[15] the Watsons,[16] and many others (still to be revealed in full[17]), constructed and operated networks of large-scale collusion between government and narrow private interests.[18] The parallel government structures worked especially through the influ-ence of former president Zuma to appoint Gupta apparatchiks as cabinet mem-bers. State-owned enterprises, in custody of abundant budgets at one stage, were major targets, along with government departments such as Energy and Mineral Resources. Auditing companies lubricated the process. The National Treasury and South African Revenue Service were captured for some time.

Parallel action was evident in additional overwhelmingly corrupt streams of government action that existed alongside formal, official and sometimes not cor-rupted operations. Corrupted governance dominated in much of the strategic gov-ernment processes, especially but not exclusively in the time of Zuma. Come the release of substantial funds to combat Covid-19, the worst of the looting tendencies of the antecedent order were metastasising into the Ramaphosa regime. Networks unfolded, subverting formal policy and government processes. The official gov-ernance streams could continue, although with circumscribed powers, while some areas of operation such as big, lucrative operations probably executed by tender were no-go territory. Much of the evidence at the Zondo Commission, the writing of Mcebisi Jonas,[19] and the team publication, the *Shadow State*,[20] confirmed graphic particulars of the inner workings of capture.

Some of the most pronounced parallel state operations were in state intelligence, in the national investigative and the prosecutorial agencies. Detailed evidence emerged, especially after 2018, of the State Security Agency and the extent to which it drove the factional pre-Ramaphosa ANC agenda. Long before, the SACP had regularly asserted how the security apparatuses had been targeting opponents. State agencies like the National Prosecuting Authority had been captured comprehensively. In state intelligence operations those who resisted Zupta capture went silent and left the institution.[21] Come Ramaphosa's ascendance, the space for capture shrank, but not all, by far, of those who had been practising high- or low-level corruption were touched by this transition. Some remained because the ANC's unity accord made them untouchable; others found amnesty in the vastness of parallel corrupt state operations.

THE PRECARIOUS FACES OF ANC POWER

The parallel, shadow, supplementary and even rogue state operations and structures, combined with citizens often choosing direct action and informal politics over formal engagement, rendered ANC power precarious but also helped to explain why the ANC's hold on political power was still significant. Because the discontent and distrust of the ANC was not being relayed proportionately into the electoral, inter-party-competitive domain, the pressures built up inside the ANC support base. Discontent, funnelled into protest or other forms of non-party political dissent, flowed into radical policy statements or self-help policy-making. Such policy-making was in many respects more radical than 'radical' statements of policy – which could still be diluted or redirected away from claimants. It was also handled electorally, where abstention was growing.

This section of the book builds on the highlighted parallelism, synthesising my main findings and arguments about precarity across the four pillars of ANC power. The bottom line was that the ANC was losing power but staying in power, and that its remaining power was marked increasingly by fragility and volatility.

The ANC in ambiguous electoral decline

The ANC's electoral majorities had started declining from their 2004 high, across all spheres of government. Nationally, Election 2019 saw a small but unsteady and conditional increase in the ANC's proportion. At times, and beyond this national result, in provinces and municipalities, the party clung to power by ultra-thin majorities or coalition government. Elsewhere, it slipped into opposition roles but was strong enough to be a destructive opposition that could undermine and collapse governing coalitions.[22] In many places in the local sphere it still won electoral majorities but this power was combined with direct action and disruptive-ranging-to-destructive community protests.

The ANC's power in the national and provincial elections of 2019 was also precarious because it had contested as 'the ANC', yet in essence two factions were contesting for the heart and soul of the party. The ANC was 'on message' of unity and anti-corruption in the script of the campaign, yet below the surface and beyond the campaign mixed messages abounded. Voters could not be certain which they were voting for, the Cyril Ramaphosa ANC, the Ace Magashule-Zuma-ist ANC, or some undetermined future amalgam of the factions.

The ANC's electoral power was volatile and was as much an indication of the state of the electoral system as of ongoing outright endorsement. The ANC, well ahead of any other political party, was supported by 57.5 per cent of the electorate and a far smaller proportion of the adult voting-eligible population (roughly 25–28 per cent[23]). The balance of the voters and citizens more generally did not endorse the ANC, but abstention was a mild endorsement in effect. This equation softened the turnout rate, which had declined from 73.5 to 66 per cent from Election 2014 to 2019 (a big drop for South Africa, even if acceptable by international comparison). The decline also hollowed out the ANC victory because much of the abstention was due to voters having ceased to believe that voting, and voting for the ANC, could make a difference.

Election 2019 again confirmed that protest can go hand in hand with endorsing the ANC electorally. In preceding elections, the edge of validity of the proposition showed some decline. Specific case studies shed further light on this relationship. Behind the facade of the ANC still winning voting districts in areas that experienced intense protests was the fact that its margins of victory had been shrinking. In the case studies of Zwelihle and the Land Party, land protest metamorphosed into the establishment of a specific-interest political party. The Land Party won a voting district off the ANC, and in other voting districts in the ward it pushed the ANC into the 40 per cent range, down by about 40 percentage points from electoral performances a decade earlier. This protest party also replaced the EFF in the community. The ANC had maintained face by still winning the voting districts (and other comparable ones in the rest of the country), but the precarity of its power was on display.

The ANC's support in many of the electoral domains dipped below levels that could be regarded as strong, even below outright-majoritarian levels, yet in the game of the strongest party, measured by the most votes, the ANC was sustaining itself at a higher level than the other parties for most of the time. The ANC was in power, but no longer hegemonically in power. It was a precarious, increasingly fragile power, even if sufficient for the time being to keep the ANC ensconced in government.

The ANC in precarious state and government power

The ANC, in government for more than 25 years, had in many respects fused organisationally with the state. Power became increasingly precarious when the factional divisions (in modest scope quite normal for a political party)[24] became superimposed on the state and had a regressive effect on the ANC's already compromised ability to manage the state and deliver sound policy and governance: incapacity and mismanagement were rife.[25] Deployment and retention in public office were overwhelmingly a political qualification, based on loyalty and reward plus an overall sense that the state belonged to the ANC. Consultants and consulting companies frequently did the work that the deployed civil servants had been hired to do. Small and often comradely businesses were created to gain contracts and do business with the state, on occasion ploughing parts of proceeds back into the ANC. Civil servants and municipal officials were the tender brokers, or both the brokers and the beneficiaries. The processes fostered vast networks of political investment.

Across all arms of the state this condition gave power to civil servants to dispense patronage, either for themselves, or on the instruction of their principals. The culture spanned the presidencies. In mobilisation for the 2007–2009 Zuma takeover there was much ANC cadre agitation for rotation in drinking from the trough. Corruption was implied, as was soft oversight. Zuma entered the presidency without being disqualified by his role in the arms deal scandal. As president for the next decade, he provided a shielding umbrella for the diffusion of corruption through state apparatuses. The annual reports of the auditor-general were but one small indication of ever-worsening audit outcomes across state institutions, well into the Ramaphosa era. Corruption was so widespread, the corrupt class so esteemed and numerous, and well-remunerated employment opportunities beyond the state and the adjunct tender-state so limited, that corruption itself came to be 'acceptable' behaviour.

The merging of corruption into party and state contributed nevertheless to the ANC's declining hegemony. There were silences, mostly when it came to the ANC as a business operation and how it benefited from its fusion with the state. Its investment arm remained largely veiled in secrecy. Beyond this, the outcome of the Oilgate II investigation remained inconclusive. The possibilities that the ANC itself, in addition to individuals, had been gaining through the arms deal, as well as other energy and mining operations, loomed large and helped to foster popular cynicism. The judiciary and commissions of inquiry – state institutions – were often called on to help the ANC resolve disputes concerning intra-party and intra-state fallout. At the time of this analysis, jurisprudence and commissions prevailed on the side of the Ramaphosa clean-up and restoration of the rule of law although there were projects associated with the status quo ante that worked to delegitimise the interventions. There were arguments that the judiciary itself was captured politically.[26]

The people, protest, policy and ANC precarity

The ANC was not entirely in control of the state, nor of its policy-making processes, even if it was in power. The people had had experience, over the years, of governance by the ANC – of policies being in place but not being taken to the point of effective implementation and visible effects on citizens' lives. In many cases, in fact, citizen protest helped the ANC to realise and act on policy implementation gaps.

Widespread capture and corruption in the state heightened citizen anger and cynicism – the grassroots became more aware that the ANC government was frequently better focused on enrichment deals and pleasing political principals than on serving its constituents and spending public funds prudently and in ways that would optimise development and transformation. This helped to crack the public image of state institutions, ranging from the Electoral Commission to the South African Police Service, Parliament and many others. These diminished institutions, in charge of core interfaces between government and the people, all suffered shrinking levels of public trust. Public protests zoomed in on the most immediate, local government that delivered substandard services or no services at all, or the trucks laden with desirable goods and driven by foreign nationals, and the tertiary institutions that the students exposed as alienating and untransformed. Government often capitulated, through law enforcement 'lite', allowing citizens the space to claim the deficits – which included claiming available urban land, dictating transformation in higher education institutions, or tapping for free into unaffordable basic services.

Through protests, citizens took up – in tangible, community-level formats – many of the big policy issues that government tried to solve through high-level speeches and aspirational laws. Citizens often took up community-level battles against racism and gender-based violence in their own communities, on occasion with the support of institutions such as the South African Human Rights Commission. From Sandbaai-Zwelihle in the Overstrand municipality to Saldanha-Langebaan on the Cape West Coast, citizens took action, inter alia against new concrete walls of racism that were being erected to restrict free movement between residential areas that were still racially defined. The Equality Court was functional in helping to assert policy on racism, yet it remained reactive and followed up on easily identifiable personal cases, often letting institutional racism slip by. The #FeesMustFall generation took over, raised awareness and increasingly targeted racism in institutional contexts. Elsewhere, gender-interest communities asserted new anti-femicide, anti-gender-violence policies, their actions a response to policies and constitutional endorsements being in place, existing, but ineffectual in prohibiting or even limiting femicide. In the cases of racism and femicide, government became stronger on action once civil society had mobilised and shown the way.

Within government, the ANC's power in policy-making positions was precarious because policy uncertainty thrived in crucial areas. Policy in fields of transformation, including land reform, became ammunition in the ANC's factional proxy battles. The ANC needed factional battles to spur on urgency in action, to fast-forward an issue even as important as land justice.

ANC organisationally self-regenerating, despite itself

The ANC organisationally, in this period, was still at a level of apparent self-regeneration, albeit with precarious uncertainties hovering. The most pressing were the medium- to long-term effects of Covid-related economic degeneration and ongoing waves of corruption revelations wiping out impressions of a reconstituted ANC. The positive condition existed, therefore, alongside considerable organisational disgrace: many malfunctioning state organisations; the poor command exercised over policy-making; and community protest establishing a world in which the ANC did not rule.

The ANC was in power and sustaining its power by forestalling other parties from catching up with it. It remained in charge of core state institutions, even if continuously metamorphosing factional contests for control meant that it was not always clear which ANC faction – or emerging mutation of an old faction – was in control of a particular institution. It made policies that helped to legitimate the organisation-party in power, ranging from social grants (and in particular elevated Covid grants) and public housing to National Health Insurance – even if the policies were stronger on promise than practical substance. In the final instance, the ANC could retain power and prevail over other parties because it continued holding an outright electoral majority nationally – and in most provinces and municipalities despite challenging and disruptive (protest-driven) populist governance happening in parallel streams.

The ANC continued on this perilous path. It was divided through multiple cross-cutting factions, and the strongest glue was that it could not afford to split, again. The two most precarious aspects were its inability to surmount factionalism and to shed corruption. Both could demolish the ongoing esteem and trust that the ANC still enjoyed – and yet factional wars were perpetrated as if such a day of

Figure 9.1: Four faces of ANC power: Interpretation of precarious trends

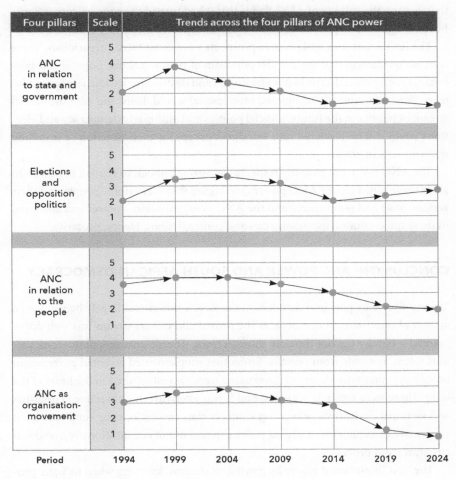

Source: Author's summative interpretation of trends identified in this book

reckoning by the voting public could never arrive, and corruption was committed as if it were the core principle of prescribed government practice. At the level of national politics, the day of reckoning appeared to be remote: the ANC slipped by 4.65 percentage points in national-to-national 2014 to 2019 comparisons, yet turned away from the precipitous decline curve it had entered in the trends across national and local elections from 2004 to 2016 (15.4 percentage points down, from 69.9 per cent in 2004 to 54.5 per cent in 2016, nationally calculated). The widespread (albeit not all-encompassing, by far) national hope for the ANC to continue self-correcting carried it into a renewed electoral commendation. The recovery was predicated therefore on the validity of ANC claims that it had turned the page on corruption – but post-Nasrec and post-election developments posted a contrary reality.

The ANC's victories and positive prospects were constituted precariously. There were no guarantees that the parallel populism of policy-making, popular self-governance, and political-criminal underworlds and destructive lawlessness (gang violence, femicide, worlds of drugs and mob justice) would daunt and dent the official stream of politics in the future. Official politics and multiparty democracy and elections could still be rendered into sideshows except for their function of installing governments in power.

The ANC was weak in many respects, yet strong enough to remain in power. In all of these four faces of ANC power (see Figure 9.1) – elections, people and their actions, state and government and the ANC as organisation – power was anchored in these uncertainties, inconsistencies and contradictions. Hence, precarity.

CONCLUSION: ANC POWER AND SOUTH AFRICAN DEMOCRACY

Twenty-five years plus into democracy, the ANC's power was largely by virtue of a system of multi-stream democracy. The formal and official stream was well documented – but, by far, not the only show in town. The alternating politics took various forms, not only from populist forces that supplemented essential government processes – alternative layers of governance were also established in the heart of the state. There were multiple varieties, and it was alternatively subversive (Zuma-ists and factional derivatives subverting strategic state institutions) or supplementary, supportive or facilitative. It played politics in and out of constitutionally mandated structures and processes.

The ANC maintained power by playing all streams, knowing when to 'fight' protests and when to let them develop and bring the fruits of alternative governance to communities, depending on their geography and interests. Organisationally, it gained in elections from the public's identifying Zuma with the ANC era of disgrace and the voting public then disproportionately rewarding Ramaphosa for bringing in the alternative ANC. The contrast with a Ramaphosa order was easy on the electoral mind – it helped to build a new ANC allegiance when it had been the ANC that had permitted individual presidents to rise, and had permitted post-1994 corruption and capture to flourish. The ANC stayed electorally in charge almost as a by-product of having created enemy leaders against whom the electorate needed to defend it. The removal of a fallen president helped to redeem the ANC. This strategy of self-renewal was evident in the cases of both Mbeki and Zuma, albeit with important variations on what comprised the 'evil'. When Ramaphosa had to deal with corruption and patronage under his own watch, he could not blame another president, but tried to apportion blame to another ANC, not his new dawn party, finding it difficult to understand the utter lack of conscience of the perpetrators. This ANC was the embodiment of precarious power.

Populism has risen and become ingrained as the alter ego of the ANC. South Africa's Constitution and system of government require consultation on policy decisions of note. The people have taken this process further. Unruliness, on occasion mayhem and anarchy, besides frequent lawlessness, form part of the repertoire of actions, which often unfold as bottom-up desperation and exasperation with the government. On several policy and leadership fronts, people have fostered lawlessness by doing what they deem good for their own socio-economic interests, and argue that if government does not serve them they will use their own agency to gain the advantage. Government frequently encourages populism by not implementing law and maintaining order – and also because it knows that the people, their voters, have reason for anger. ANC government knows that definitive enforcement of law and order is likely to alienate supporters and voters, and so a deep symbiotic relationship has been established between an underperforming government and people who 'take' policy that the ANC is not brave, willing or capacitated enough to make. People stretch the boundaries of the law and, in return, get protection in the form of a softened application of the law. All the while, South Africa's constitutional democracy, run by a well-designed and respected set of institutions, remains in operation. It is on this base that Covid-19 landed in South Africa in 2020. Already disadvantaged citizens (and many others) suffered hardships but also knew how to position, through protest and protestation vis-à-vis a disgraced political elite, to get their share of alleviation from government.

In this duality, populism is the ANC's alter ego; it is a populism that helps to support the ANC mainstream. There is no certainty as to the tipping point away from this type of ANC endorsement as symbiotic relationships are not always consensual, in mutual recognition or in good faith.[27] To date, suppression from above has not been executed in ways that suggest determination to end populism and policy self-help. From below, it has been about claiming spaces to get access to services and rights. The ANC has been assisted in remaining in power in the wake of incapacities and malgovernance – amid winning elections. The details speak to a complex system of governance that has enfolded South African politics. It has, in effect, and through the combinations of the complexities of top-down and ground-up politics, confounded opposition political parties. The ANC retains dominance *for now*, and possibly for some time to come, while subaltern processes accumulate.

NOTES

1 Dominique Dryding, 14 July 2020, 'Are South Africans giving up on democracy?' Afro-barometer Dispatch No. 372.

2 Herman Mashaba's The People's Dialogue was launched in late 2020 and Mmusi Maimane's One South Africa movement was waiting in the wings. There were few indications that either would capture major electoral followings.

3 See also my 2018 article 'Hegemonic struggles of the African National Congress: From cacophony of morbid symptoms to strained renewal', *Africa Spectrum*, 2/2018, 1–31. The article provides an in-depth account of the ANC and the state of its hegemony.

4 Antonio Gramsci, 1971, 'Wave of materialism, and crisis of authority', in Quintin Hoare and Geoffrey N. Smith (eds and trans.), *Selections from the Prison Notebooks*, London: Lawrence and Wishart, pp. 275–276.

5 Valeriano Ramos Jr, 1982, 'The concepts of ideology, hegemony, and organic intellectuals in Gramsci's Marxism', *Theoretical Review*, 27, March–April, https://www.marxists.org/history/erol/periodicals/theoretical-review/1982301.htm, accessed 20 September 2020.

6 Zuma-ists sowed the suspicion that Ramaphosa-ists are sell-outs to big capital; Rama-phosa-ists were subtle in their counter-campaign, instilling moderation and reverting in effect to preceding slow-implementation policy modes.

7 The ANC's pronouncement of more definitive action in the spring and summer of 2020 hinted at change, but the seeming determination was tainted by a continuously weak ANC Integrity Commission and the fact that new guidelines and ANC anti-corruption policies were yet to evolve. The matter became more urgent when Magashule had to explain himself to the Commission in late 2020, and the ANC top officials were specifically reminded of the task to 'pull together' the guidelines (Cyril Ramaphosa, Post-NEC briefing, 8 December 2020).

8 Raymond Suttner, 'ANC "self-correction", self-examination and rebuilding democracy', *Daily Maverick*, 7 December 2016, https://www.dailymaverick.co.za/article/2016-12-07-op-ed-anc-self-correction-self-examination-and-rebuilding-democracy/, accessed 17 September 2019; SACP, 8 January 2018, 'ANC needs era of decisive self-correction – SACP', statement on the occasion of the 107th founding anniversary of the ANC, https://www.politicsweb.co.za/archive/anc-needs-era-of-decisive-selfcorrection--sacp, accessed 19 March 2020.

9 Susan Booysen, 2011, *The ANC and the Regeneration of Political Power*, Johannesburg: Wits University Press. These four fronts are also termed the four faces or pillars of political power of the ANC.

10 See, for example, Francis B. Nyamnjoh, 2016, *#RhodesMustFall: Nibbling at Resilient Colonialism in South Africa*, Cameroon: Langaa RPCIG.

11 In the aftermath of the marginal Nasrec Ramaphosa victory, his faction, incrementally and by most indications, was consolidating its comparative standing, bolstered by the ANC conference resolutions on the elimination of corruption: the top six split 4–2 in favour of Ramaphosa; the National Executive Committee (estimated on the slate lists at Nasrec to have been roughly 42–38 at best in favour of Ramaphosa) started featuring stronger pro-Ramaphosa majorities; and subsequently, the National Working Committee that had an original slight balance in favour of Ramaphosa, carried pro-Ramaphosa resolutions routinely. These balances, nevertheless, were never carved in stone.

12   One of the most recent was in late 2019 when the SACP was again considering participating directly in the 2021 local government elections. See, for example, Zingisa Mvumvu, 'SACP mulls flying solo in local elections', *Sunday Times*, 20 September 2019.

13   My 2013 publication *Twenty Years of South African Democracy: Citizen Views of Human Rights, Governance and the Political System,* Washington, DC and Johannesburg: Freedom House, clarifies citizen views on the 'parent state'.

14   Ivor Chipkin and Mark Swilling, 2018, *Shadow State: The Politics of State Capture*, Johannesburg: Wits University Press, shed further light on the intricacies.

15   See Thuli Madonsela, 2016, *State of Capture: A Report of the Public Protector*, Tshwane.

16   James-Brent Styan and Paul Vecchiatto, 2019, *The Bosasa Billions: How the ANC Sold its Soul for Braaipacks, Booze and Bags of Cash*, Pretoria: LAPA Publishers.

17   Analyst Prince Mashele has suggested that prominent patriotic capital families like the Gumedes be investigated; see *Sowetan Live*, 4 March 2019, 'ANC needs to institute an inquiry into capture within its ranks', https://www.sowetanlive.co.za/opinion/columnists/2019-03-04-anc-needs-to-institute-an-inquiry-into-capture-within-its-ranks/; *Africa News*, 6 March 2019, 'Billionaire Gumede gives *Sowetan* columnist 24-hour ultimatum', https://www.africanews24-7.co.za/index.php/south-africa/billionaire-gumede-gives-sowetan-columnist-24-hour-ultimatum/, both accessed 1 August 2019.

18   Jacques Pauw, 2017, *The President's Keepers: Those Keeping Zuma in Power and out of Prison*, Cape Town: NB Publishers/Tafelberg, adds to these understandings. In some instances, the South African state turned into a gangster state, as explained by Pieter-Louis Myburgh, 2019, *Gangster State: Unravelling Ace Magashule's Web of Capture*, Cape Town: Penguin.

19   Mcebisi Jonas, 2019, *After Dawn: Hope after State Capture*, Johannesburg: Picador Africa. See also Judith February, 2019, *Turning and Turning: Exploring the Complexities of South Africa's Democracy*, Johannesburg: Picador Africa.

20   Chipkin and Swilling, 2018, op. cit.

21   Evidence at the Zondo Commission told the story of Moe Shaik, Gibson Njenje and Jeff Maqethuka; Moe Shaik, 2020, *The ANC Spy Bible: Surviving across Enemy Lines*, Cape Town: NB Publishers, gives his personal account of what had happened.

22   See my 2016 article 'Edging out the African National Congress in the City of Johannesburg: A case of collective punishment', *Journal of Public Administration*, 51 (3.1), 532–548. In late 2019 and 2020 the ANC reclaimed, in coalition arrangements, metropolitan municipalities it had earlier ceded to DA-led coalitions.

23   Depending on the base population statistics.

24   Francoise Boucek, 2009, 'Rethinking factionalism: Typologies, intra-party dynamics and three faces of factionalism', *Party Politics*, 15, 455–485, brings to the fore aspects of the normalcy of factionalism in party politics.

25   Auditor-general reports showed over several years that most of the modest number of municipalities that achieved clean audits were in DA-controlled areas. See, for example, Auditor-general, 25 June 2019, Media statement: 'Auditor-general flags lack of accountability as the major cause of poor local government audit results'.

26   The case of an attempted interference in Constitutional Court decision-making had, after many years, not been solved, and it was known that, for example, the North and South Gauteng divisions of the High Court were likely to reach politically different decisions.

27   Steven Levitsky and Daniel Ziblatt, 2018, *How Democracies Die*, London: Penguin Books, argue that democracies die suddenly, with a coup d'état, or slowly, in piecemeal fashion, when an authoritarian leader is elected, government power is abused and the complete repression of opposition happens.

SELECT REFERENCES

Adam, Heribert, Frederik Van Zyl Slabbert and Kogila Moodley. 1997. *Comrades in Business: Post-Liberation Politics in South Africa*. Cape Town: Tafelberg.

Ajam, Kashiefa, Kevin Ritchie, Lebogang Seale, Janet Smith and Thabiso Thakali. 2019. *The A–Z of South African Politics: People, Parties and Players*. Johannesburg: Jacana.

Ancer, Jonathan, 2019. *Betrayal: The Secret Lives of Apartheid Spies*. Cape Town: Tafelberg.

Basson, Adriaan. 2019. *Blessed by Bosasa: Inside Gavin Watson's Capture Cult*. Johannesburg: Jonathan Ball.

Basson, Adriaan and Pieter du Toit. 2017. *Enemy of the People: How Jacob Zuma Stole South Africa and How the People Fought Back*. Johannesburg: Jonathan Ball.

Booysen, Susan. 2005–2020. Turning Points Monitoring Project (The Changing Dynamics of South African Politics). Personal data base and trends analysis.

Booysen, Susan. 2011. *The ANC and the Regeneration of Political Power*. Johannesburg: Wits University Press.

Booysen, Susan. 2013. *The ANC's Battle of Mangaung*. Shorts e-Book series. Cape Town: Tafelberg.

Booysen, Susan. 2013. *Twenty Years of South African Democracy: Citizen Views of Human Rights, Governance and the Political System*. Washington, DC and Johannesburg: Freedom House.

Booysen, Susan. 2015. *Dominance and Decline: The ANC in the Time of Zuma*. Johannesburg: Wits University Press.

Booysen, Susan (ed.). 2016. *FeesMustFall: Student Revolt, Decolonisation and Governance in South Africa*. Johannesburg: Wits University Press.

Branch, Adam and Zacharian Mampilly. 2015. *Africa Uprising: Popular Protest and Political Change*. African Arguments series. London: Zed Books.

Brown, Julian. 2015. *South Africa's Insurgent Citizens: On Dissent and the Possibility of Politics*. London: Zed Books.

Butler, Anthony. 2019. *Cyril Ramaphosa: The Road to Presidential Power*. Johannesburg: Jacana.

Chipkin, Ivor and Mark Swilling with Haroon Bhorat, Mbongiseni Buthelezi, Sikhulekile Duma, Hannah Friedenstein, Lumkile Mondi, Camaren Peter Nicky Prins and Mzukisi Qobo. 2018. *Shadow State: The Politics of State Capture*. Johannesburg: Wits University Press.

Duncan, Jane. 2016. *Protest Nation: The Right to Protest in South Africa*. Pietermaritzburg: UKZN Press.

Eatwell, Roger and Matthew Goodwin. 2018. *National Populism: The Revolt against Liberal Democracy*. London: Pelican.

Everatt, David (ed.). 2019. *Governance and the Postcolony*. Johannesburg: Wits University Press.

February, Judith. 2019. *Turning and Turning: Exploring the Complexities of South Africa's Democracy*. Johannesburg: Picador Africa.

Gramsci, Antonio. 1971. 'Wave of Materialism, and Crisis of Authority'. In Quintin Hoare and Geoffrey N. Smith (eds and trans.), *Selections from the Prison Notebooks*. London: Lawrence and Wishart.

Hartley, Ray. 2017. *Ramaphosa: The Man Who Would Be King*. Johannesburg: Jonathan Ball.

Hirsch, Alan. 2007. *Season of Hope: Economic Reform under Mandela and Mbeki*. Pietermaritzburg: UKZN Press.

Hunter, Qaanitah. 2019. *Balance of Power: Ramaphosa and the Future of South Africa*. Cape Town: NB Publishers.

Jonas, Mcebisi. 2019. *After Dawn: Hope after State Capture*. Johannesburg: Picador Africa.

Lagoutte, Stéphanie, Thomas Gammeltoft-Hansen and John Cerone. 2016. *Tracing the Roles of Soft Law in Human Rights*. Oxford: Oxford University Press.

Langa, Malose and Daniel Hartford (eds). 2018. *Urban Land and the Genesis of Violence*. Cape Town: Centre for the Study of Violence and Reconciliation.

Le Roux, Michelle and Dennis Davis. 2019. *Lawfare: Judging Politics in South Africa*. Johannesburg: Jonathan Ball.

Levitsky, Steven and Daniel Ziblatt. 2018. *How Democracies Die*. London: Penguin Books.

Mashele, Prince and Mzukisi Qobo. 2016. *The Fall of the ANC: What Next?* Johannesburg: Picador Africa.

McKinley, Dale T. 2017. *South Africa's Corporatised Liberation: A Critical Analysis of the ANC in Power*. Johannesburg: Jacana.

Mistra. 2019. *Voting Trends 25 Years into Democracy: Analysis of South Africa's 2019 Election*. Susan Booysen (ed.). Johannesburg: Mistra.

Murray, Martin. 1994. *The Revolution Deferred*. London: Verso.

Myburgh, Pieter-Louis. 2019. *Gangster State: Unravelling Ace Magashule's Web of Capture*. Cape Town: Penguin.

Obermayer, Bastian and Frederik Obermaier. *The Panama Papers: Breaking the Story of How the Rich and Powerful Hide their Money*. London: Oneworld.

Olver, Crispian. 2017. *How to Steal a City: The Battle for Nelson Mandela Bay*. Johannesburg: Jonathan Ball.

Palmer, Ian, Susan Parnell and Nishendra Moodley. 2017. *Building a Capable State: Service Delivery in Post-Apartheid South Africa*. London: Zed Books.

Pauw, Jacques. 2017. *The President's Keepers: Those Keeping Zuma in Power and out of Prison*. Cape Town: NB Publishers/Tafelberg.

Ranchod, Rushil. 2013. *A Kind of Magic: The Political Marketing of the ANC*. Johannesburg: Jacana.

Rossouw, Rehana. 2020. *Predator Politics: Mabuza, Fred Daniel and the Great Land Scam*. Johannesburg: Jacana.

Schreiber, Leon. 2018. *Coalition Country: South Africa after the ANC*. Cape Town: Tafelberg.

Schulz-Herzenberg, Collette and Roger Southall (eds). 2019. *Election 2019: Change and Stability in South Africa's Democracy*. Johannesburg: Jacana.

Shaik, Moe. 2020. *The ANC Spy Bible: Surviving Across Enemy Lines*. Cape Town: NB Publishers.

Styan, James-Brent and Paul Veccchiato. 2019. *The Bosasa Billions: How the ANC Sold its Soul for Braaipacks, Booze and Bags of Cash*. Pretoria: LAPA Publishers.

Sundaram, Rajesh. 2018. *Indentured: Behind the Scenes at Gupta TV*. Johannesburg: Jacana.

Van Loggerenberg, Johann, with Adrian Lackey. 2017. *Rogue: The Inside Story of SARS's Elite Crime Busting Unit*. Johannesburg: Jonathan Ball.

Van Vuuren, Hennie. 2017. *Apartheid Guns and Money: A Tale of Profit*. Johannesburg: Jacana.

Wiener, Mandy. 2018. *Ministry of Crime: An Underworld Explored*. Cape Town: PanMacmillan.

Yende, Sizwe Sama. 2018. *Eerie Assignment: A Journalist's Nightmare in Mpumalanga*. Cape Town: Lesedi House Publishers.

Zegeye, Abebe and Julia Maxted. 2002. *Our Dream Deferred: The Poor in South Africa*. Pretoria: SAHO and Unisa Press.